# The Lines of Nazca

# The Lines of Nazca

**Anthony Aveni, Editor**

The American Philosophical Society
Independence Square   Philadelphia
1990

Memoirs of the

AMERICAN PHILOSOPHICAL SOCIETY
*Held at Philadelphia*
*For Promoting Useful Knowledge*
*Volume 183*


Copyright 1990 by the American Philosophical Society
for its *Memoirs* series, Volume 183



Library of Congress Catalog Card No: 89-84667 ⊗
International Standard Book No. 0-87169-183-3
US ISSN: 0065-9738

# *Preface*

Why have the Nazca lines become the most well-known remnant of South American antiquity? Their mammoth size and sheer number immediately attract our attention. And we are surprised by their widespread distribution—over a relatively inhospitable looking area—a lifeless place where it almost never rains. Why would people have invested the vast amount of time that presumably would have been required to construct these enormous figures, never to be able to see them from the ground? How could the construction on a grand scale of such perfectly proportioned figures actually have been accomplished? Was there a plan—a blueprint? Did the builders employ a measuring unit? Is not an advanced technology needed to undertake such a project?

These are some of the modern myths associated with the mystery on the desert, for in these questions, the ones most widely asked about the Nazca lines, reside many basic false assumptions that have been generated and nurtured by the ever-widening stream of uncritical popular literature that has flowed forth in the past few decades. The Nazca lines are treated as wonders of the ancient world. We read about them in tourist magazines and Sunday supplements. We see them on television productions and in the occult book stands. In the trade-book literature, they appear in side-show chapters as a reminder that, though we have progressed in our understanding of the past, we have not made rational common sense of all the actions of our predecessors.

Historian Jacquetta Hawkes once suggested that "Every age has the Stonehenge it deserves—or desires" (1967: 74). She was critical of the scientists who rushed headlong into one of Britain's most ancient monuments with computers in hand to decode the mystery without ever appealing to archaeological or other cultural evidence. And, in an age of technological achievement and dependence, the public fascination with the more grandiose artifacts of ancient man has teased out some rather narrow-minded explanations for the Nazca lines. States one author: "Incredible technical achievements existed in the past. There is a mass of know-how which we have only partially re-discovered today" (von Daniken 1971: vii). Like many other popular writers, von Daniken assumes that all that lies between *us* and *them* is knowledge quite like our own that has simply become lost in time. But such an assumption is too easy, too superficial, and too egocentric to serve as the basis of a methodology for studying the lines; for it relies solely upon the things and ideas of the present world projected onto the world of the past without justification. What compels us to deny that the culture of others can create ideas we had not contemplated? Have we become so narcissistic that we can admire no motives for collective human action other than our own?

Why, then, another book about Nazca? First of all, because so many ideas and so much information about Nazca need to be corrected. Old explanations offered for the lines must be re-examined in the face of new evidence. Second, because much that has been written about the Nazca lines is too long on speculation and too short on documentation. Though we have run the risk of overwhelming the reader with factual data, we have done our best to separate and organize the data into a set of useful appendices. And, third, because too little information about those cultures that resided on the south coast of Peru in the past appears in the literature about the lines. We need to rephrase our questions about the Nazca lines so that the answers can be couched in a pan-Andean framework. The Nazca lines must be rendered a part of what anthropologists call the cultural *insistence* of these people, the sum total of the defining qualities of a particular culture that identify it as unique and distinctly recognizable from all others (Ascher and Ascher 1981: 38).

This book tries to place the problem of the

origin of the Nazca lines in an appropriate cultural perspective. It is a compilation of cross-disciplinary research by archaeologist, anthropologist, and astronomer—each of whom attempts to pose queries about the lines that can be addressed from within the confines of the fields within which they were trained. At the same time, by continually consulting with one another across traditional disciplinary boundaries, throughout several years of collective research on the pampa, the contributors gradually have been able to broaden their perspectives.

Because the surveys for the surface ceramics and the taxonomy and measurement of features on the pampa reported here are relatively complete, the investigators could employ statistical methods with a measure of confidence lacking in the works of our predecessors. One outcome of this research is the suggestion that not all the activity on the Nazca pampa took place at the same time. Different motives may have resulted in different features.

Finally, the problem of who constructed the lines and why is referred to other material evidence in the immediate cultural and ecological environment. Thus, we have investigated the possible relationship between the lines and the great ceremonial center of Cahuachi which overlooks the lines from the south bank of the Nazca River. We also have paid attention to specific features in the natural environment. One chapter deals with colonial documents that pertain to land and water use in the fertile river valleys adjacent to the barren desert upon which these colossal geometrical features were etched. It is by addressing these cultural and ecological questions that we are able to offer a sensible set of motives for people of the Nasca culture to cross the pampa and engage in ritual activities upon its surface.

How, then, shall we "get the Nazca lines we deserve?" Our goal is not to decode the hidden mystery of these enigmatic features, but rather to offer a testable set of hypotheses about why they were made there—ideas that we believe make sense in the context of what we know about the real people who lived, and still live there today.

ACKNOWLEDGMENTS

Though the individual contributors have separately expressed their gratitude to those who assisted them in their research, the editor would like to thank Warren Wheeler for his excellent work in reproducing many of the photographs taken from other sources that appear in the text, and, for their bibliographic and editorial assistance: Elizabeth Ferrigno, Jennifer Schaeffer, and Catherine Weise, all of Colgate University, Bonnie DeGroat for bibliographic typing, and most especially, Lorraine R. Aveni, who helped edit, organize, and type several versions of the draft.

**A. F. Aveni**
**Hamilton, NY**
**March 1989**

# TABLE OF CONTENTS

# Introduction

I was first attracted to the lines while on a pleasure trip in August 1977 with my colleague R. T. Zuidema of the University of Illinois. We had just concluded our second of a planned series of Earthwatch expeditions to Cuzco, where we had been mapping the system of radial lines (*ceques*) which the Inka employed to organize their highland capital. We thought it a good idea to experience our annual descent to the coast by driving the Andes in a rented car. Nazca seemed an attractive place to visit for all the usual reasons. Flying over the figures and examining Maria Reiche's maps and photographs, we were struck by her references to a multitude of lines that appeared connected to star-like or spoke-like patterns. We saw large numbers of lines, some narrow, others very wide, often a dozen or more converging upon particular places. Using a magnifying glass, we were able to trace lines on the photographs that connected one point to another on the pampa.

Formally and structurally, if simplistically, these linear features conjured up a vivid reminder of the general description of the *ceque* system of Cuzco which we had been tracing over the landscape. Zuidema's studies had revealed that a radial element lay at the heart of the design and layout of Cuzco. The Spanish chroniclers tell us that 41 *ceques*, literally visual straight lines, emanated from the Coricancha (Temple of the Sun) and passed outward over the horizon. These *ceques* were delineated by 328 *huacas* or sacred places distributed throughout the landscape. The rather complex plan of the *ceque* system served to define the hierarchical organization of Cuzco. It was based upon kinship and social status, as well as religious and economic principles and Inka concepts of space and time, for the *ceque* system also was a calendar used to tally the days of the civic, agricultural, and religious cycles. At the same time, it served as a device to incorporate an orientation calendar that utilized important points in the natural and man-made environment.

The linear hierarchical nature of the *ceque* system also appears in the design of the *quipu*, or knotted string scheme, used by Andean people to keep records. In a general way, one can liken the *ceques* to the primary cords of the *quipu*, and the *huacas* to the knots thereupon. Indeed, we are told by one chronicler that the plan of the *ceque* system of Cuzco was recorded on a *quipu*.

The expression of hierarchical organization through a radial plan serves as one of the defining parameters of Andean mental systems. Radiality may be as much an element of Andean insistence as the tactile form of writing or the style of monumental architecture they developed. The appearance of radial networks on the floor of the Nazca desert offered us a clue to a possible way of understanding the lines that employed a pan-Andean concept.

As the fieldwork in Cuzco proceeded, the idea of making a structural comparison between Cuzco and Nazca remained an ever-present possibility. Finally, in 1981, on an Earthwatch-funded trip to Nazca with Tom Zuidema and Gary Urton, we began to become familiar with the ecology and the surface of the pampa, as well as with the sort of data it harbored that might be related to an exploration of the structural similarity between *ceque* lines and Nazca lines.

Meanwhile, in the spring of 1980, Gary Urton, with whom I had already shared a common interest in problems of Andean astronomy and calendar, began joint research with me on a project that consisted of collecting and examining all extant maps and photographs, as well as a large body of literature about the pampa. These efforts resulted in the generation of a number of testable hypotheses relating to the orientation of the lines. Urton and I cast these into the form of research proposals which were jointly funded by the National Geographic Society, the Wenner Gren Foundation, and Earthwatch. Thus, we were able to carry out more detailed studies on the pampa during the period 1981–1984. During a significant portion of this three-year interval (1982, Sept–Dec), Urton resided in the Nazca area and on the south coast in general. Urton and I did joint fieldwork on the pampa in January 1982 as well as in the summer of 1984. In addition, I spent January 1983 working on the pampa, having received support during that period from the OSCO Fund.

Reading and reviewing the body of literature on Nazca, I was surprised to learn that only a handful of investigators had ever ventured out onto the desolate surface of the pampa to look at the lines close-up. Had we become so conditioned to viewing them from the air, the way they were "discovered" by the outsiders who first flew over the pampa in the 1920s? Had the myth that they were meant to be seen from above become established dogma? I also found that the many explanations offered for the existence of the lines actually can be reduced to relatively few basic categories. Believing that any serious investigation ought to take advantage of the work that has preceded it, I offer in Chapter I of the present text a critical review of the Nazca literature. In it, I attempt to classify both the types of figures one finds on the pampa and the hypotheses that various investigators have proposed to account for them. To my knowledge, such a thorough review had not been attempted previously and I believe the present one has served the useful function of separating out what can and cannot be taken seriously about the lines.

Straight line features dominate the pampa. The so-called animal figures, though a curiosity, are highly localized and almost incidental in terms of the work effort involved in production. Our study was directed mainly to the mapping and detailed description of the linear features that cut across the 200 square kilometers of pampa surface. Concentrating on the radial aspects of these Nazca geoglyphs, we proceed to a physical description of the radial line centers and member lines. In Chapter II, I present and analyze all the relevant data that we collected over several

seasons of fieldwork on the pampa. Distinct from all other studies, our program incorporated a thorough examination of the lines from the ground, while aerial photography played an auxiliary role. The data include locations, dimensions and directions of the several hundred features we were able to trace out on the ground as well as the more prominent lines visible on aerial photographs which could not be detected at ground level. My goal in Chapter II is to recount the progress of these studies and to utilize the data we collected to test the several hypotheses that had been sorted out in Chapter I. I conclude that there are patterns suggestive of concepts of order present in the construction of the lines.

Making no pretenses about having discovered the secret of the pampa, nor any claims about having decoded the lines, I attempt to relate the perceived concepts or patterns to the various hypotheses. What was the motive? I argue that there is a multitude of answers to myriad questions that can be asked about the several kinds of activity that took place on the pampa more than a thousand years ago. Phrasing the most interesting and important questions has been my principal goal. It now seems clear that this activity was related to a concern about the flow of water and possibly also about the flow of time in the Nazca environment. Also, there is little doubt that the lines were intended to be walked upon.

The study of the archaeological remains on the surface of the pampa is vital to an understanding of why the Nazca lines were constructed. To add to the list of surprises encountered in reviewing the past studies, we discovered that no one had ever undertaken a thorough examination of the surface upon which the geoglyphs resided. Chapter III is a condensation of parts of the dissertation of Persis Clarkson (University of Calgary) on the surface archaeology of the pampa. Working with us on the project since 1981, she was quick to emphasize the importance of obtaining a sound chronological record of the artifacts that remain on the pampa surface. Accordingly, she has logged more time on the

Nazca desert than anyone else connected with our project.

One of the most significant conclusions of her ceramic study is that the biomorphic figures and the straight lines may represent unrelated activities attributable to cultures of different periods living about the pampa. This result agrees with that part of my own study of the superposition of lines and figures, based upon an examination of aerial photographs and reported in Chapter II.

Gary Urton is an Andean anthropologist who had undertaken ethnographic studies on the cosmologies of contemporary people residing in the mountain villages in the vicinity of Cuzco. Having linked both ancient and modern Andean concepts of cosmic order to the way in which people comprehend and interact with the ecological parameters of the immediate environment in which they live, he believed that a significant part of our inquiry about the Nazca lines ought to include the study of land and water utilization in the fragile coastal desert environment of the Nazca drainage basin. Though there was little documentation to be found in Nazca, his detective work in the archival sources in Lima turned up a number of post-Conquest written documents that told of how the land and water were treated in the vicinity of the pampa shortly after European contact. As he began to perceive that the information in these documents bore a potentially significant relationship to the activity on the pampa, he developed Chapter IV of the present text. Here, Urton explains how these documents suggest that a scheme of social organization, not unlike that which prevailed in Cuzco, existed in the region around the pampa. This scheme is shown to be consistent with the need for people to travel across the zone in which the lines exist, and Urton argues that such travel may have been related to the construction and use of the lines. He attempts to relate the Nazca line phenomenon to his other contemporary ethnological studies in the community of Pacariqtambo, also near Cuzco. His discussion of the ritual sweeping or cleansing of long, thin strips of the plaza at Pacariqtambo prior to important festivals provides us with a reasonable hypothesis for the maintenance of the Nazca lines. Each strip was assigned to specific kin groups that farm the land around the village. Urton's essay serves as an excellent example of how ethnographic analogy can be used to help us understand past events.

Pure luck added another archaeological dimension to our Nazca studies, which ultimately resulted in Chapter V. Shortly after we began our surface study of the pampa, we learned that archaeologist Helaine Silverman of the University of Texas had begun a program of excavation on the large ceremonial center of Cahuachi, located on the south bank of the Nazca River fronting one of the heaviest concentrations of line centers. What better way to learn whether a connection might have existed between Cahuachi and the Nazca lines than to ask her to address that very question in the context of her research program? Fortunately for us, not only did she express a willingness to do so, she also became absorbed with some of the ideas on ethnographic analogy discussed by Urton. Utilizing archaeological and ethnographic data, Silverman argues that Cahuachi was, at a late stage of its occupation, a pilgrimage center and that its plaza may have experienced ritual cleaning, not unlike the plaza at Pacariqtambo and perhaps the Nazca lines.

Chapter VI, on the astronomy of the Nazca lines, is somewhat specialized, but very important in certain segments of our research program for it is related to one of the most well-known hypotheses that has traditionally been invoked to explain them. Recognizing the pitfalls that lie in the dependence upon one person's interpretation of a large mass of data, I asked British astronomer Clive Ruggles (who had worked with us during our 1984 Earthwatch field season) to perform an independent analysis upon the alignment data we had collected since 1981. His access to and facility with the superior computing facilities at the University of Leicester offered us the opportunity to push the statistical approach to the limit. My second reason for asking Ruggles to write this chapter was that I wanted to see how a researcher of British Megalithic astronomy would approach the problem of the Nazca lines. Both the lines and the British Megalithic structures have been interpreted as astronomical artifacts, and for both, indigenous written evidence that directly alludes to their function simply does not exist. While Ruggles's study of the astronomical orientation of the Nazca lines offers some parallels to mine in Chapter II, some significant differences are apparent. Therefore, Chapter VI should be of special concern to the reader who is interested in archaeoastronomy in general.

Finally, our project could not have been completed at a sufficient level of detail without the assistance of the invited team of investigators from the University of Minnesota Remote Sensing Laboratory, who were joint recipients of our 1984 Earthwatch grant. Bill Johnson, Doug Meisner, and Gerry Johnson provided us with the most complete collection of low-altitude photographs now available for documentary research that covers the entire pampa between the Nazca and Ingenio Rivers. While we will never be able to preserve *in situ* the delicate features of the pampa that have fallen victim to natural and man-made forces as well as to the ravages of tourism, a complete set of high quality photographs such as those used in the present study is the next best fall-back position. While Mayanists have the photographic essays of Maudslay and Maler to reveal a more pristine state of the Maya inscriptions, no thorough pictorial record of the markings on the pampa has existed up to the present. To make the reader more familiar with the pampa, I thought it necessary to make available in an appendix at least the mosaic photo which this team has pieced together from 213 separate pictures obtained from low-altitude overflights. Beginning with a photograph of the pampa taken from the space shuttle, their brief, descriptive Chapter VII, which discusses how their own survey photos were obtained, outlines the contribution that aerial photography can make to archaeological studies. In this context, it is worth remembering that Paul Kosok's (1965) magnificent photographic study of the ecology of coastal Peru first brought the lines to the attention of the world and provided the initial impetus for their serious study.

# Notes On Contributors

*Anthony F. Aveni* is Russell B. Colgate of Astronomy and Anthropology at Colgate University. Originally trained in Astronomy (Ph.D. University of Arizona), since 1970 he has confined his research interests to the astronomies of PreColumbian Mesoamerica and Peru, a subject in which he has authored/edited several texts.

*Persis B. Clarkson* is Research Associate at the Athabasca University, Alberta, Canada, having completed her Ph.D. Dissertation on the surface archaeology of the Nazca pampa in 1985 at Calgary University.

*Gary Urton*, Associate Professor of Anthropology at Colgate University (Ph.D. University of Illinois) has done ethnographic work in highland and coastal Peruvian communities. He is the author/editor of both texts and articles on ethno-astronomy, calendrics, and symbolism of contemporary Andean cultures.

*Helaine Silverman* is Visiting Assistant Professor at the University of Illinois Institute of Latin American Studies, having completed her Ph.D. in Archaeology at the University of Texas (1986).

*Clive L. N. Ruggles* is Lecturer in the Computing Studies Unit of Leicester University (England). His original training is in astronomy (Ph.D., University of Oxford) and in the past ten years he has published numerous articles in the field of British Megalithic astronomy. He edits the British Journal Archaeoastronomy.

*Gerald W. Johnson* is Professor in the Department of Civil and Mineral Engineering, University of Minnesota, Minneapolis, Minnesota 55455.

*Douglas E. Meisner* has been Vice-President of Interscan, 430 First Avenue North, Minneapolis, Minnesota 55401 and was formerly with the Remote Sensing Lab, University of Minnesota.

*Mr. William L. Johnson* is Technical Specialist in the Faculty of Forest Engineering, State University of New York, College of Environmental Science and Forestry, Syracuse, New York 13210 and was formerly with the Remote Sensing Laboratory, University of Minnesota.

PHYSIOGRAPHIC DIAGRAM OF

## South America

By Guy-Harold Smith

### The Geographical Press

(Formerly of COLUMBIA UNIVERSITY)

a division of

**HAMMOND**
INCORPORATED
MAPLEWOOD, NEW JERSEY 07040

# I. An Assessment of Previous Studies of the Nazca Geoglyphs

A. F. Aveni

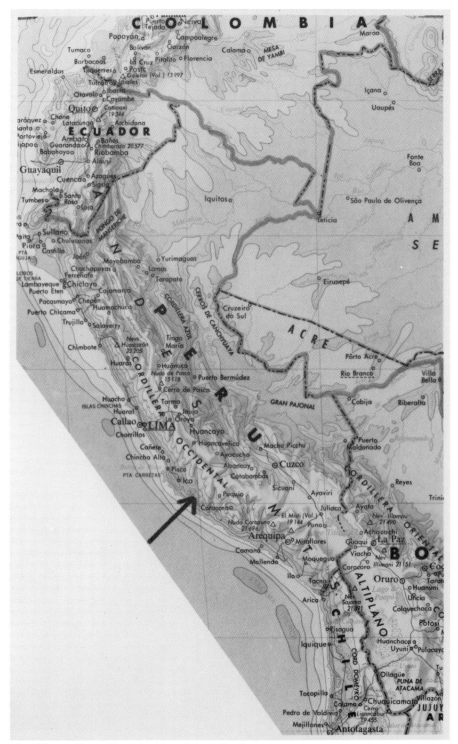

Fig. I.1a.  A Map of the west coast of Peru showing the location of Nazca.

## INTRODUCTION

The western portion of the continent of South America beyond the Andes consists of a narrow coastal strip 4000 km long, averaging 200 km in width, that geographers term a warm, foggy desert. The most arid portion of this region runs from northern Chile (the Atacama Desert) to southern Peru, where moisture from the Pacific Ocean is blocked by a thin mountain chain between desert and coast (frontispiece and Fig. I.1a). Here measurable rainfall occurs on the average of once in several years. The desert terrain consists of rough tablelands carved by deep lush gorges that connect the high Andes with the coast. These inter-riverine lands, totally unfit for any form of life, are strewn with angular broken pieces of stone[1] and marred by *quebradas* or stream beds that have lain dry for centuries, having been produced by ancient flooding that brought huge quantities of water down from the Andes in relatively short periods of time.

One such gorge is that carved by the Rio Grande River, 400 km south of Lima. About 50 km from the Pacific, at an altitude of 500 m above sea level, several tributaries join to form the Rio Grande: the Vizcas, Santa Cruz, and Rio Grande from the north, the Ingenio from the east, and the Nazca from the southeast (Fig. 1b). Each runs about half the year (in the summer months from November to February), thus providing a verdant contrast to an otherwise dull landscape. It is in this region that the Nasca culture flourished 1500–2000 years ago. Between the valley strips irrigated by the Ingenio and Nazca rivers lies an elevated dry plain—called the pampa by the Peruvians.[2] Criss-crossed by *quebradas* running generally NE to SW, the pampa consists of a 220 km² triangular-shaped region bounded on the north by the Ingenio River, on the south and west by the Nazca River and on the east and northeast by the foothills of the Andes at the base of which runs the Pan American Highway (Figs. I.1b & I.1c).

It is on this ancient alluvial plane that most of the features variously called the Nazca *geoglyphs, ground drawings, markings,* or simply *lines* appear.[3] From an airplane, the markings appear as a tangled mass overlapping and intersecting one another, rather like the remains of an unerased blackboard at the end of a busy day of classroom activities (Fig. I.1d). Among the forms represented are trapezoids, rectangles, straight lines, spirals, concentric ray systems, and zoo- and phyto-morphic shapes, among them several birds, fish, a monkey, a spider, and a flower, as well as several other life forms, the identification of which is not universally agreed upon (cf. Fig. I.4). Some of the trapezoids[4] are immense, often measuring a kilometer or more on their longest side.

1. These consist of flat, angular rock fragments of a centimeter up to chunks as large as half a meter in diameter. For a full discussion of their composition and size distribution, see Hawkins 1969: 6–8.
2. The northern edge of this zone (long. 75°08′W, lat. 14°42′S) is variously named Pampa San José, Pampa de los Incas, or Pampa del Calendario on modern maps—no doubt because of the presence of the Nazca lines that have long been interpreted to possess calendric importance. The southern and eastern zone nestled against the foothills of the Andes is called Pampa Cinco Cruces and the western zone, along the Nazca River bank, the Pampa Majuelos. For convenience, we will refer to the entire zone between the Ingenio and Nazca Rivers as the Nazca Pampa. In fact, the region is not perfectly flat but instead, consists of several folds creased by NE- to SW-flowing tributaries of the Nazca River; however, nowhere along the pampa does the ascent grade exceed 1 percent. Also, throughout we will use the terms Nazca when referring to the place, Nasca when referring to the culture. Other spellings, e.g., Wari, the culture; Huari, the place, are intended to be consistent with those employed in a majority of the published literature. Concerning the terms Nazca and Nasca, Menzel (1977: 71–72) states that "The spelling 'Nazca' crept into common use through error, and is historically and linguistically incorrect, as noted by Rowe" (Menzel, Rowe, and Dawson 1964: 8). According to the latter reference: "This name is often spelled with a 'z' in the archaeological literature. The 'z' spelling came into use in the middle of the nineteenth century through an erroneous analogy with the spelling of 'Cuzco'. Until that time, the name was spelled with an 's' in every written account, from the earliest chroniclers on. Since the 'z' spelling has come into use through an error in very recent times, and since 's' and 'z' reflect earlier differences in pronunciation, we prefer to use the historically correct 's' spelling". I am indebted to Helaine Silverman for this historical research.
3. While the highest density of figures can be found on the pampa between the Ingenio and Nazca Rivers, many figures also appear on the desert to the north, especially near Ica and Palpa (Rossel Castro 1977). Large figures of one sort or another can be found as far north as the Santa River Valley (Wilson 1988) and as far south as the Atacama Desert (Iribarren 1968; Nuñez 1976).
4. Not all these so-called trapezoids actually fit the mathematical definition of that figure. Rather, they can be described more appropriately as truncated triangles, the apex angle of which appears clipped off and transformed into an extended line (see discussion in Chap. II).

Fig. I.1b. From a LANDSAT satellite; only a few faint lines and the Pan American Highway, along with other roads (the heaviest features) are visible on the area of the pampa that we surveyed (framed). The Pacific Ocean lies at the lower left.

Fig. I.1c. On a 1:50,000 U.S. Dept. of Defense photograph, several large features are discernible at the NE corner of the pampa. (U.S. Defense Intelligence Agency)

Fig. I.1d. A low altitude S.A.N. photograph reveals a confused maze of criss-crossing lines. Note the damage caused
by wheeled vehicles. (Servicio Aerofotografico Nacional, Peru)

Most animals are much smaller, usually of decametric dimensions. But it is the lines, many up to several km long and ranging in width from that of a narrow footpath up to several meters, that form by far the largest share of the drawings.

While the lines generally appear as stark light-colored features on a dark background on aerial photographs, it is not widely known that large numbers of them are visible, though often with some difficulty, from the ground. Ascending any of the small peaks or dunes that circle the pampa, particularly on the north and west, one is presented with a detailed view that can be the equivalent, over a limited range, of that which can be perceived from the air (Fig. I.2).

The Nazca figures might properly be termed etchings for they were constructed by a subtractive process. The etching process was achieved by removal of the black-colored rock fragments and topsoil from the floor of the pampa. These broken, angled pieces had been coated over several millennia, long before Nasca occupation, by desert varnish, a dark layer consisting of manganese and iron oxides deposited there by aerobic microorganisms (Dorn and Oberlander 1981a). As one can see in Fig. I.3, the difference in darkness between the exposed and unoxidized sides of a given piece of rock is quite noticeable. Removal of this dark surface material rendered visible the underlying unoxidized layer, which is composed largely of coarse sand. The contrast was further heightened by the presence around each etching of a black rim or border created by the detritus (clearly visible in Fig. 2) that was neatly deposited there by the builders of the lines. These hummock-shaped piles of rock fragments range in height from a few

Fig. I.2a. An improbable view of the Nazca lines, from one of the many low hills that ring the pampa.

centimeters for the smallest figures to a meter or more for the largest.

As Hawkins's (1969: 5–8) consultants have stated, the region of the pampa has stabilized and there has been little natural reworking of the material present there since human habitation. Today, wind erosion is minimal and water erosion practically non-existent, except for the rare occasions when El Niño, the tropical weather pattern that occasionally descends to these latitudes, brings rainfall to the area (Craig 1968: 12). Consequently, many of the features, though etched nearly two millennia ago, have remained in their original condition, as wind-blown sand passes back and forth over the lines, continually cleaning the surface and keeping the angled fragments that define the lines well exposed. On the other hand, over the past half-century "human erosion," resulting from inquisitive tourists motoring on the Nazca pampa, has done more damage to the drawings than nature has wrought in the millennium-and-a-half since they were created (see, e.g., Photo Appendix, Fig 2).

One of the frustrating problems in trying to determine the origin and purpose of the Nazca ground etchings is that few signs of past human activity exist on the pampa to suggest a method or purpose for constructing the lines. One could never be sure who made them or when, though most people tended to assume all were created at the same time for a single purpose. Still, other artifacts besides the etchings themselves remain and these man-made features will be dealt with in detail in Chap.

Fig. I.2b. Another Nazca line seen from the ground.

Fig. I.3. Sample fragment from the Nazca pampa: Exposed side coated with desert varnish (left); Underside uncoated (right).

III. Large artificial cone-shaped mounds or cairns up to 1 m high and several meters wide, consisting of broken stones and desert clay, can be found at the bends of some of the zigzag figures or at the ends of certain trapezoids and atop some of the focal points of groups of the lines. In many cases these piles are strewn with broken pottery fragments. Often smaller piles of stones are seen in groups of 50 or more near the borders of some figures. Sometimes, evenly spaced stone piles are found in the interiors of what appear to be incomplete figures (see Figs. 22c and 22d in Chap. II). Usually these piles are separated by about an arm's length. They may have been formed in the clearing process and their condition might suggest a division of labor for removing the top layers. If a group of individuals in fixed squatting positions picked up and stacked all the randomly strewn fragments within their reach, then a series of such evenly spaced piles might be expected to result. Perhaps another set of laborers dealt with the task of removing these piles by placing their contents in some sort of portable container. Thus, Figure II.5c may represent a feature that was in the process of being constructed. In support of this hypothesis, we find in that figure (on the right side) a cleared zone adjacent to one in which the accumulated piles had not yet been removed. Farther on, the remainder of the figure seems to have been outlined on one side, though the clearing process had not yet begun when the builders evidently abandoned it. This construction hypothesis conflicts with the generally accepted assumption (Hawkins 1969: 10) that surface fragments were removed with a rake. The existence of such an implement is unsupported in the archaeological or ethnohistorical record anywhere in Peru, though admittedly the absence of evidence cannot be taken as a strong argument against the use of such tools.

Concerning the ceramic record on the surface of the pampa, there are widely conflicting reports and we must defer a detailed discussion of the problem to Clarkson's chapter on the surface archaeology of the pampa. Surface pottery sherds exhibit a great variety of rec-

ognized types. Hawkins (1969: 15) reports that he collected pottery fragments over three strips of the pampa surface about 2 km long and 5 km wide on the eastern end of the Pampa de los Incas (west of the Pan American Highway), the most figure-cluttered region of the pampa. From his traverses he calculated a surface density of about $17,000/km^2$ over this region. He extrapolated these results to imply that the equivalent of 225,000 vessels lay over the entire pampa. But his result is misleading for at least two reasons; first of all, the NW corner of the pampa is much more heavily cluttered with markings (cf. Photo Appx, Fig. 2) and secondly, pottery fragments in general usually are found to be non-uniformly distributed. Most of the sherds collected by the Hawkins group date from Nasca periods 3 and 4 (100 BC–AD 100) of the Early Intermediate Period (Rowe and Menzel 1967: ii–iii); much smaller populations are attributed to periods as early as the Nasca 2 phase (200 BC) of Early Intermediate and as late as Poroma 4 (AD 1200) of the Late Intermediate Period. At best such information provides us only with an upper limit to the date of construction of the particular line upon which material is found and it cannot be taken as evidence that people of Nasca 3–4 constructed all, or even any of the lines. The results reported by Clarkson in Chapter III of this volume conflict with this interpretation. She actually found very few sherds associated with these periods, but it must be emphasized that she surveyed a different region of the pampa. Surprisingly, prior to Clarkson's survey, no systematic study of surface archaeology on any large segment of the pampa between the Ingenio and Nazca basins had ever been undertaken. This brief description of the remains on the pampa can be amplified in detail if the reader consults our bibliography. In this chapter it is our intention to introduce the reader to the Nazca lines through a critical analysis and survey of the corpus of literature that deals with various hypotheses which have attempted to account for their origin.

While no signs of permanent habitation exist on the pampa, life must have abounded in the river valleys that border it. Indeed the popular myth that there was no one around to build the Nazca lines can be readily dispelled. Archaeological studies of the habitation sites surrounding the pampa are scarce, but some data do exist. In 1957, W.D. Strong published the results of the Columbia University expedition in 1952–53 (see his paper for a bibliography of earlier surveys and excavations in the area).[5] His group undertook a limited surface survey at 81 sites in the valleys of the tributaries of the Rio Grande and of the valley to the north. It is in these fertile areas that the people who etched the ground drawings surely must have lived. Strong excavated at a few of the sites, the most notable being Cahuachi (Kawachi), a ceremonial center consisting of a complex of colossal adobe pyramids adjoined by extensive burial grounds. Strong's stratigraphic sequence displays a continuous record of development of the Nasca culture from evolution out of the Early Paracas style up to the breakdown of the Nasca tradition, with a takeover, perhaps by military conquest (Rowe 1956), by the Tihuanacoid (highland) culture—over 1000 years of continuous activity. Between the Paracas period and the Middle Nasca period, architecture evolved from mounds and wattle-and-daub units to the pyramids typified by Cahuachi, which Strong has assigned to an interval between the Late Paracas phase of the Early Horizon Epoch and the Late Nasca phase of the Early Intermediate Period (see Chap. III, Fig. 5); thus chronological assignment is contemporaneous with the latest date for the lines according to Hawkins's survey but it does not overlap with Clarkson's results. (For further chronological details, the reader is referred to Chap. V on Cahuachi.) In an unpublished 1957 Master's thesis, Robinson (n.d.) refined and extended the work of Strong with surface archaeological studies at 111 sites more closely concentrated about the Nazca basin. His descriptions and catalog of pottery types discovered at the riverine sites provide solid information for future workers who might survey the pampa.

In addition to the limited archaeological data that pertain directly to the pampa, we also have information about the nature and form of the geoglyphs themselves, thanks mostly to the enduring labors of Maria Reiche. Some of the drawings are pictured in various editions of her book, *Mystery on the Desert* (1949a, 1968b) and larger numbers appear in Kern and Reiche (1974). The contours of most figures can be described by a single unbroken line that never crosses itself. For example, one of the largest of the animal figures is a bird[6] (probably a stylized cormorant) with a long zigzag neck (Fig. 4i). The entire figure extends nearly one-third kilometer and can be traced from the air or walked on the ground by following the unicursal line, over a kilometer in length, that defines it. The line that traces the spider monkey (Fig. 4e) emanates from a zigzag geometrical form and begins to outline the figure near the genitals; it describes the delicate arched figure of the body, then the tail, a labyrinthine spiral that coils and then uncoils to form the thick base of the tail. Finally, it returns to where it entered, at the back of the monkey, before going off and becoming lost in the surrounding maze of lines.

The purely geometrical figures are much larger in number and extent. They are spread over the entire pampa, while most of the biomorphs are concentrated in a 10 km$^2$ strip of land along the southern bank of the Ingenio River. Long lines seem to criss-cross the pampa (Fig. 1d). Sometimes they run in pairs, climbing straight up and over low hills (Fig. I.5). Near the modern Hacienda Cantalloc SE of Nazca, one linear motif variously called the "whip" (Reiche 1969: 58), "needle and ball of wool" (Morrison 1978: 57), or "fishing rod" (von Breunig 1980: 211) consists of a long triangle, from the pointed end of which a line emanates and runs back and forth over the main figure in a zigzag pattern (Fig. I.6). In

---

5. We are grateful to Dr. T. D'Altroy of the Anthropology Department of Columbia University for making the Strong survey photographs available to us for study and to K. Schreiber (University of California, Santa Barbara) for directing our attention to this valuable resource.

6. The beak alone measures 300 m and the longest feather is 30 m in length.

Fig. I.4. Biomorphic figures on the pampa: a. Condor

Fig. I.4b. Dog

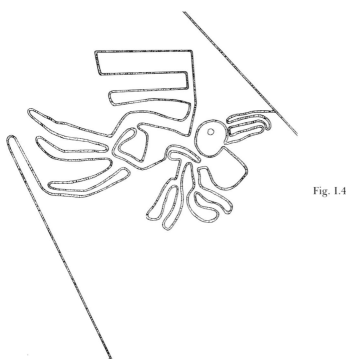

Fig. I.4c. Insect?

Fig. I.4d. Plant

Fig. I.4e. Monkey

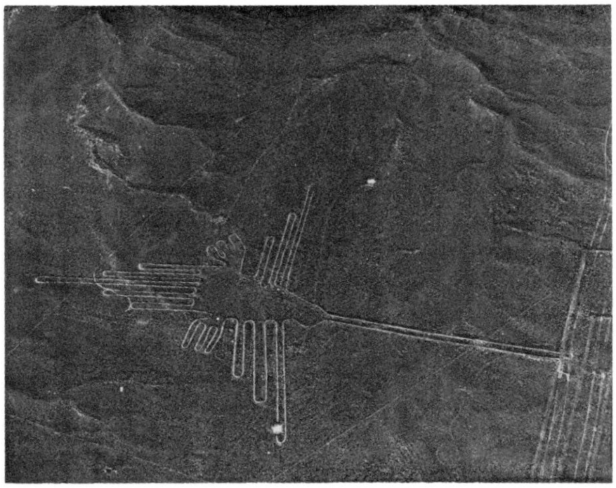

Fig. I.4f. Hummingbird

Fig. I.4g. Shark or Killer Whale

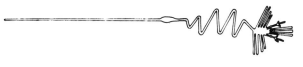

Fig. I.4i. Cormorant

Fig. I.4h. Spider

many other instances (also Fig. I.6), a line zig-zags in saw-toothed fashion across a major figure several times. In still other cases, zigzags are squared off into contours that remind one of the course of opposing parallel lines one makes when plowing a field (see Fig. I.7b). Spirals (Fig. I.7) range from the neatly proportioned figure overlooking the Ingenio ba-

sin (Fig. I.7a) to irregular figures that seem to be box-shaped on the outside and become more rounded as one proceeds inward (Fig. I.7b). Both of these are labyrinths or double spirals that the eye can enter and leave along a unicursal path, but a few appear to be single spirals that coil to a point. A number of the biomorphic figures also exhibit a labyrinthine quality. One begins to trace the figure at a point, passes through it, and then returns to the same point (eg. Fig. 4f).

Finally, there are the *line centers*, a few of which are pictured on Reiche's (1968b: 30) map of the pampa. These have been the primary subject of our Nazca studies and we shall report on them in detail in Chap. II. We have located 62 such centers and more than 750 member lines. Line centers consist of concentric patterns of lines that stretch over a 200 km$^2$ area of the desert floor. Typically, each contains 10 to 20 "spokes" centered on a small natural promontory either overlooking

Fig. I.5. Three parallel straight lines continue their course over a hill. (Courtesy, Evan Hadingham)

a stream or riverbed or lying along the base of the mountains. Many of the departing lines lead to other line centers, but some open into "trapezoids."

## A DISCUSSION OF THE HYPOTHESES

While we have shed some light on how the etchings were constructed and who constructed them, the question that historically has aroused the most attention is "Why were they built?" Professional scholars generally believe that serious and informed studies ought to pay no attention to what the popular literature has to say, but the case of Nazca is a very special one because the popular literature on the subject of the lines has been so extensive that some of the ideas emanating from it have percolated deeply into the interdisciplinary scholarly community.

We spoke in the Preface of von Daniken's explanation for the lines. While we are not concerned in this chapter with debunking his (or anyone else's) writings in detail, a few words about the nature of his approach are worth elaborating.

As he examines the past, von Daniken molds the specter of our ancient ancestors into

Fig. I.6. "Yarn and Needle." (Photo by Marilyn Bridges, 1979, ("Yarn & Needle"; cf. Appendix I)

one that looks more and more like a mirror image of ourselves. Our predecessors thus become demystified when we find that they shared our own ideas, motives, and concerns. We are comforted to know that they were interested in doing the same things in the same ways and we begin to feel less uneasy about cohabiting the same planet with them. A sense of persistence and continuity gives the common person a feeling that perhaps there is something good about today's version of the human race.

But the sense of security von Daniken offers us is a false one, for his study is woefully incomplete. Like many uninformed writers, he commits a sin of omission. Von Daniken simply does not bother to examine evidence about the cultures that produced the artifacts he discusses. For example, his view of ancient man's orientation to the natural world is that of one who does not observe nature for himself. And, this covers most of us, for we live most of the time in an artificially controlled environment. Our immersion in technology has freed us from the need our predecessors once had to observe the sun in order to tell time or to witness the cycle of lunar phases to understand when we can expect faint natural light during the normal hours of darkness. Today we are all quite ignorant of the procedures and tools required to determine the length of the day, month, and year directly or to predict eclipses. When we learn, through the hieroglyphic inscriptions, that the Maya Indians of the Yucatan achieved all these astronomical feats with considerable precision more than 1000 years ago, the interpretation that leaps most readily to mind is that they, like us, must have possessed technological capabilities far in advance of those of most primitive cultures.

By following this confined circular chain of reasoning, von Daniken "discovers" that many aspects of ancient culture were very like our own. Thus, the Nazca lines become runways

upon which astronauts, visiting us from another world, once landed their spacecraft. In another case, he describes certain odd face masks worn by Maya gods on stelae as the space helmets of these visiting astronauts (whose visits evidently were rather widespread).

But what reason have we to assume that extraterrestrial beings in possession of a technology that renders them capable of emigrating across thousands of light years of interstellar space would need runways on which to land once they arrived at their destination, or, for that matter, would even possess a countenance that would need to be inserted into a globular screw-top cover to ward off a noxious atmosphere?

Oddly enough, the Nazca lines first attracted public curiosity when they were revealed from the air by flights made over the pampas of the south coast of Peru in the 1930s. Since then, we have never been able to

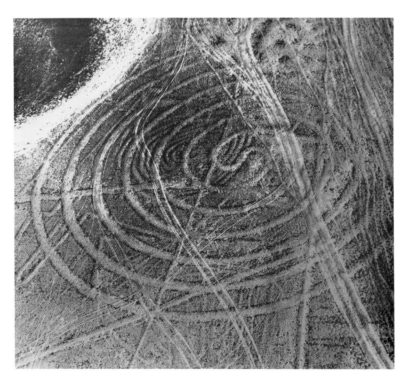

Fig. I.7a. Spiral geoglyph. Courtesy Tom Morrison, S.A. Pictures (Nicky Magge Bruckert)

Fig. I.7b. **Box-shaped labyrinthine spirals.** (Kosok 1965)

get away from the idea that they must be appreciated and understood only when one looks down upon them from above.

Any informed investigation of why the lines were constructed must draw upon the wealth of past studies conducted from different perspectives. In this section, we examine how earlier visitors to the pampa have attempted to answer that question. Rather than review previous studies of the Nazca geoglyphs in a purely chronological manner, we have chosen to subdivide the many attempts to explain the Nazca lines into different categories of hypotheses.

While the studies reported in the present volume are interdisciplinary and seek to explore several potentially interconnected explanations simultaneously, many of the earlier attempts can be characterized as rather monolineal. Thus, it is relatively easy to divide the explanations into five distinct, if not totally unrelated, classes:

A. Calendar and Astronomy
B. Geometry
C. Agriculture and Irrigation
D. Movement or Communication, including Walking, Running and Dancing
E. Artistic Expression

Let us survey the literature on each hypothesis in turn.

*Calendar and Astronomy*

More has been written on the astronomical origin of the Nazca lines than on all the other classes of hypotheses combined. Paul Kosok, a Long Island University historian, was the first investigator to posit an astronomical explanation for the lines. Though it is generally believed that Kosok discovered the lines when he flew over the area, actually they were known to archaeologists including Kroeber and Tello, in the 1920s. T. Mejía Xesspe, a Peruvian archaeological field worker, learned of their existence from Tello and he published the first description of the lines in 1927 (Mejía 1927, reprinted 1940), two decades before Kosok's

Fig. I.8. Kosok's photograph of sunset along one of the Nazca lines on the June solstice. (Kosok 1965)

first publication and nearly 40 years before his book *Life, Land and Water in Ancient Peru* (1965) made the drawings famous.

Kosok included in his book the rather impressive pictorial chapter VI entitled "The Largest Astronomy Book in the World." Here, we find the astronomical hypothesis stated for the first time: "While investigating this region in 1941, I was suddenly struck with the thought that these remains could have had some connection with early calendrical and astronomical observations" (Kosok 1965: 52). While it is not clear whether previous considerations had led him to view the lines in such a perspective, Kosok stated that he was inspired by witnessing, quite by accident, a sunset along the axis of one of the lines. When he realized it was June 21, winter solstice in the Southern Hemisphere, Kosok made his intuitive leap: "With a great thrill we realized at once that we had apparently found the key to the riddle" (Kosok and Reiche 1947: 203; see also Fig. I.8). The lines formed a giant calendar by pointing to important astronomical positions at the horizon.

That the literature on European astro-archaeology had influenced Kosok is clear enough, for he refers to some of the paradigms of Megalithic astronomy in his publications (Kosok and Reiche 1947: 203; Kosok 1965: 53). It should be noted in passing that his astronomical hypothesis was published fully sixteen years before the revival of the astronomical controversy over Stonehenge (Hawkins 1963). Perhaps concerned by the criticism that had fallen upon astronomical orientation theories espoused for other cultures, Kosok was careful to state that one must take great pains to "avoid the errors that have been made in studies of this sort in Egypt and elsewhere" (Kosok and Reiche 1947: 207). Nonetheless, the idea that one might be able to date structures by astronomical alignment seems to have impressed him.[7]

Kosok (1959) gave sociological justification for the astronomical hypothesis by examining, in a rather general way, social developments he believed to have taken place during the earliest periods of Nasca occupation. He reasoned that by developing an advanced agricultural system a tribal society was transformed into an organized, complex civilization. A fuller understanding of astronomy was required "when it became clear to these people that the annual movements of heavenly bodies could be correlated with the annual progress of the seasons, around which the whole productive and social process revolved" (Kosok 1965: 54). The specialty associated with determining the precise nature of these correlations fell to the astronomer-priest class, who ultimately developed it into an esoteric enterprise composed of secret knowledge that could be employed to mystify and impress a naive public. Evidently the calendrical dates that could be determined by the celestial directions of the lines were part of this storehouse of knowledge. Thus, their own deceit provided them with a measure of rigid control over the rest of society. This tired tale of the power hungry astronomer-priest who hood-

winks an unthinking public is familiar to anyone who has read about the purported origins of science among non-Western people. Unfortunately, there is nothing in the story told by Kosok that can be identified with any of the cultural particulars about coastal peoples.

While Kosok felt he gave ample justification for the practical necessity of a calendar in any organized state, little systematic evidence supporting the astronomical orientation hypothesis actually appears in his writing. He did take the trouble to list the most likely solar, lunar, planetary, and stellar alignments that might have been recorded and in several instances he tells us that he took compass readings of alignments and corrected them to true north; but he appears to have undertaken no systematic survey of the lines for astronomical orientation. Instead, we read only general statements like "a number of the lines and roads were found to have a solstitial direction; a few with equinoctial direction could also be identified"; or "various alignments were found to be repeated in many different places . . ." (Kosok and Reiche 1947: 203). Some of these orientations may be the ones later depicted by Reiche (1968b: 75) or only suggested in print (p. 67).

Late in 1941, Maria Reiche, a German-born tutor of mathematics in Lima, was handed Kosok's observations and she drew up several charts for him. Having possessed a prior interest in astronomy,[8] she visited Nazca in December 1941 to witness some of the solstitial alignments. By the end of that year, she and Kosok claimed to have discovered twelve solstitial lines on the pampa (Kosok and Reiche 1947: 204). Though she has worked continu-

7. That the annual shift in the rise-set azimuths (defined from the north horizon point, eastward) of stars is greater than that of the sun was a "blessing in disguise" (Kern and Reiche 1974: 207), for it implied that a technique existed that could provide a relatively accurate chronology for the lines and that could be tested against any dating mechanism based upon cultural data.

8. It is curious that Maria Reiche already harbored astronomical predilections about native Peruvian culture before she ever had heard of the Nazca lines. She writes in the Foreword of her book, *Mystery on the Desert* (1968b: 10). "Shortly after my arrival in Peru in 1932, I came across an article written by the astronomer Rolf Müller about the 'Intihuatanas' (sun observatories) in ancient Peru. This article aroused my interest in the astronomy of the ancient Peruvians and I began to examine some of the ruins and stone structures of the Incas and their predecessors, many of which were probably built for observation of the heavenly bodies and the fixing of important dates throughout the year. When later I came to the coast, I abandoned this study. I did not imagine then, that it would be near the coast that the most important astronomical monument of Peru, and perhaps of the world, would be found."

ously in the region ever since, the amount of material available in print under Reiche's authorship is remarkably scant (see the Bibliography for a complete list of references). Her best-known work (Reiche 1968b) dwells mostly on the description, care and preservation of the figures[9] (particularly on the biomorphic etchings). It adequately reflects her time-consuming and painstaking efforts. Nonetheless, her attack on the problem of the origin and meaning of the lines can be characterized as undisciplined, often speculative, and severely lacking in the utilization of culture-based data.

While Reiche's 1968 book is aimed at a popular audience, the 1949 edition of that work does contain some raw data (Reiche 1949a: 17–22) that deserve to be evaluated critically, if only because the generally acceptable status of her astronomical work persists.

Reiche argued that any agrarian people living in an arid climate would have need of a precise calendar. She suggested that the expectancy of the rainy season in the mountains resulting in the flow of water in the rivers "must have reached to almost a state of fear—To overcome this uncertainty, no effort would be too great—and those who were able to calculate the time, must have attained power and respect among their fellow citizens" (Reiche 1949a: 18).[10] It is surprising that Reiche did not bolster her hypothesis by mentioning that the economy of the region surely must have been delicately tuned to the contrasting ecologies of the coast and the high Andes which border upon one another in the relatively narrow zone of south coastal desert in the Nazca area, a region that undergoes radical seasonal variations (cf. Rossello Truel 1977: 526).

Among those line directions that occur most

frequently, Reiche cited the azimuth range 68°15′–70°10′; in this interval she grouped nine disparate features, among them one of sixteen zigzag segments of a single feature, a line emanating from a trapezoid, one side of each of two trapezoids, one side of a triangle, and four scattered lines. Though Reiche was not careful to separate alignments of lines, geometrical features, and animals, her astronomical calculations relating the alignments to celestial events that took place along this span of horizon seem accurate enough.[11]

Reiche's 1958 paper on the astronomical significance of the monkey figure offers us the most detailed published exposition of her methodology, which as we shall see, incorporates some rather sinuous logic. The monkey may be the only zoomorphic geoglyph that actually can be demonstrated to be connected to geometry. On the basis of its general appearance and a perceived similarity to the arrangement of stars in Leo, Leo Minor, and Ursa Major, she equated the monkey with these star patterns (see Morrison 1978: 55). Her drawing suggests that one and possibly both of the lines emanating from the monkey terminate at the base of a 183-meter-long thin trapezoid, which she calls a "*pista*" or track, which is intersected by sixteen parallel zigzag lines. The zigzags and the *pista* cross at an angle which

---

9. While Reiche has protected the figures by hiring guards to patrol the Pan American Highway, her program of cleaning, sweeping, and reconstructing portions of the lines that comprise the figures has unquestionably and permanently altered the archaeological record.

10. Curiously, Thom and Thom (1978) employ a similar rationale for the astronomical hypothesis for the megaliths of prehistoric Great Britain. This argument is discussed in the context of archaeoastronomical studies in general in a paper by Aveni (1987a).

11. She states that the Pleiades, Scorpio, and "one star in Gemini" (1949a: 18) rose in this direction in AD 500–700 at the latitude of Nazca. Our tables (Aveni 1972) give very close agreement with this result, indicating that the Pleiades rose at Nazca (lat. 14°42′S) at azimuth 70°10′ in AD 500 and at 69°07′ in AD 700. The mountains that ring the NE edge of the pampa are elevated 2° above the true horizon; however, the Pleiades would not have been visible, even in clear skies, until they had attained an altitude of 3°. Our calculations have taken this local anomaly into account. Similarly, the setting point of Antares in Scorpio gives excellent agreement with the reversal of this direction (azimuth 248°15′–250°10′), which Reiche cited, but we find that the two brightest stars in Gemini fall more than 10° out of this zone.

Two other general directions represented by a significant number of lines are said to be 4°–10° and 15°–20°, which she suggested could have been aligned to the stars belonging to the Big Dipper if extended to the north, or to Achernar, the eighth brightest star in the sky, if one looks south. According to our tables, Achernar set between azimuths 196° and 200° between AD 1 and AD 500. The Dipper stars rise over a rather wide range which, nevertheless, does encompass the area of the NE horizon that she mentions. Incidentally, all three of the azimuth zones Reiche discussed (4°–10°, 15°–20°, and 68°–70°) fall within the generally NE to SW trend we have indicated for lines associated with line centers (see, e.g., Chap. II, Fig. 5)

Reiche claimed to be symmetric about the N-S meridian. Therefore, she concluded, these two directions could have been employed to mark the rising and setting points of the same star(s). Since the north star, the northern pivot of celestial motion, is not marked in the sky, these directions could have been used to find true north.[12] We find that the directions quoted by Reiche (31° to 31½°E and W of N) coincide with the rise-set limits that she suggested for Benetnasch (= Alkaid = η Ursae Majoris), the 2nd-magnitude star at the tail end of the Big Dipper, in AD 1000 over a 3° elevated horizon.[13] This coincidence may have led her to compare the figure of the monkey with a configuration of stars in that vicinity of the sky. Thus the stars Phecda (γ), Megrez (δ), Alioth (ε), and Mizar (ζ) were said to form the monkey's arms while the stars of Canes Venatici would represent the head, and Leo and Leo Minor the tail. If we superpose the relative positions of these stars from a sky map upon the monkey figure, we find that while they do fall in the general locations she indicates, any resemblance to the actual figure must be regarded only as fanciful. Reiche also noted that the star η Ursae Majoris would have made its first annual pre-dawn appearance[14] about 30 days before the December solstice, which we note occurs about the time of the commencement of the rainy season.

Other animal figures that Reiche associated with astronomical groupings or directions include the bird-with-the-long-neck, which was said to point "in the solstice direction" (Reiche 1968b: 26), the hummingbird, which aligned with the December solstice sunrise (p. 41), and the spider, believed to represent Orion (Reiche personal communication, 1981; Morrison 1978: 78). She also related one of the whale figures (p. 54) to the December solstice

sunset, evidently because the sun on that date set over it as viewed from a starlike center that she said was connected directly to the figure by a line; however, she provided neither details nor any reference to whether the ethnohistoric record mentions the existence of such constellations.

The influence of the Kosok–Reiche astronomical theory of the Nazca lines continues to be both deep and widespread. Virtually every work dealing with Nazca since the time of Kosok has at least alluded to a possible astronomical function for the lines and many authors uncritically accept the hypothesis as true (cf. Lumbreras 1974: 126; Pezzia 1979: 114–123). It is unfortunate that Reiche's astronomical writings have received little detailed critical assessment. We find that even though her astronomical calculations are generally correct, it is difficult to view Reiche's hypothesis in a favorable light. She never clearly states a set of criteria either for selecting the features she measures or for choosing the astronomical phenomena that she utilizes in seeking matches for the alignments. Worse still, she almost totally excludes from her arguments any evidence derived specifically from Nasca culture studies. Without appealing to the data of ethnohistory, ethnography, iconography, or archaeology, how can one hope to arrive at an explanation that can be tested by reference to observable evidence?

Rossel Castro (1947, 1959, 1977) also cites the astronomical orientation hypothesis as the likely explanation for certain classes of lines—namely, those that are connected with the starlike centers. He identified the complex we call Line Center No. 35 as the "Observatorio de Kawachi" (1977: 225),[15] for which he has published a map (1977: Fig. XVII) showing 22 lines. For a number of these, he suggests matching astronomical directions, including the June and December solstices and the equinoxes. The zones in-between these lines are alleged to have indicated solar sta-

12. She says nothing about the possibility that the spiral monkey tail might indicate a motion about the north pole, an idea later suggested by Hawkins (Morrison 1978: 56).
13. In this instance, a rare one, Reiche (1958: 286) quotes latitude, refraction correction, horizon altitude, and the stellar declinations that matched the line azimuths.
14. Hereinafter referred to as heliacal rise. The heliacal set date is the last day of appearance in the west after sunset.

15. His nomenclature is misleading. The line center is no nearer Cahuachi (which lies 6 km to the SW) than several other such centers that can be recognized on the bank of the Rio Nazca opposite the pyramids (see Chap. II, Fig. 1b).

tions on other important days of the year, but he never fully discusses the matter (1977: 229) and therefore it cannot be analyzed in detail. Furthermore, his data are incomplete and in large measure, incorrect.[16]

Hawkins's work (1969; 1973; 1974a,b; 1975) stresses a more systematic approach to the astronomical orientation theory of the lines. Some of his more recent efforts are reported in Morrison (1978).[17] Fresh from establishing the astro-archaeological methodology that led to his conclusion that Stonehenge was intended as an astronomical observatory and computer to predict eclipses (Hawkins 1963), Hawkins seems to have become attracted to the lines by Tony Morrison, then a BBC photographer. He recognized the lines as offering "an opportunity to apply the principles of astro-archaeology [defined by Hawkins 1966: 2] to an ancient pre-literate construction" (Hawkins 1969: 2) (author's brackets).

Hawkins concentrated his efforts on a 5 m by 2 km strip in the region where the Pan American Highway approaches the south side of the Ingenio Valley, the zone of heaviest concentration of figures and the place where most of the biomorphic figures are located. He undertook six expeditions to this site for a total of 19 days spread over a 12-month period. One such expedition, of eight days' duration, incorporated a ground survey. Most of the alignment data were gathered from photogrammetric surveys, which Hawkins convincingly demonstrates are accurate to 0.1° (Hawkins 1969: 22–24). The data he collected consisted of alignments on 21 trapezoids and 72 linear features centered on two sites in the aforementioned area. While Hawkins has not published a record of precisely which lines he

had measured, he kindly provided the author with a map made by Servicio Aerofotografico Nacional of Peru from which he selected lines for his study. It contains somewhat more than half of the total lines visible in aerial photographs of the same region of the pampa fronting the Ingenio River on the south. Hawkins's photogrammetric survey was carried out using this map, but plans to increase the accuracy with a detailed ground survey never materialized for various reasons (pp. 22–24).

What Hawkins would regard as satisfactory confirmation of the astronomical hypothesis can be gleaned in the following statement from his final report to the National Geographic Society:

> At the commencement of the investigation, we set up a rational criterion for testing a particular hypothesis. We would expect to find all, or a vast majority of the lines, to be explained in terms of a particular type of astronomical alignment. That is to say, we would expect all the lines to be satisfied by some unified postulate such as the rising and setting of the sun and/or moon at key dates in the calendar, or the rising and setting of the brighter stars . . . no matter what hypothesis is finally adopted, we must expect an almost total explanation for the lines; otherwise, we have the unsatisfactory situation of explaining only part of the construction work and leaving the "why?" for the remainder of the lines unanswered (Hawkins 1969: 27).

Such a reductionist strategy hardly can be expected to result in decisive conclusions, especially since there is good ethnohistoric evidence that astronomy appears as a component but is hardly ever the sole factor in the design of any Native American sacred structure. For example, in the *ceque* system of Cuzco, Cobo (1956 [1653]: 169–187) indicates that socioeconomic, religious, and calendric dictates all appear in the design and layout of the system. Some *ceque* lines, such as those directed to the December solstice or anti-zenith sunset positions, clearly functioned as astronomical sight lines (Zuidema 1981b; Aveni 1981a), but others were intended to lead to mountains, bends in rivers, water sources, or other points of rit-

---

16. Concerning the raw data, our survey of Line Center 35 shows 40 lines, not 22, and several of our alignments disagree with Rossel Castro's by 3° or more. We find no evidence for either claimed solstitial or equinoctial orientations. Moreover, the means by which he acquired his data are unclear; for example, he quoted alignments that appear to have been obtained from magnetic readings (p. 226) to the impossible accuracy of an arc second (1/3600 of a degree!). Later, he appears to have attempted to establish a precise baseline by witnessing a sunset (p. 228).

17. Some of these articles, along with those of Reiche, have been reviewed by Isbell (1979a, b) from the archaeological perspective.

ual significance in the environment. Therefore, any statistical approach based on a single-cause hypothesis stands in direct contradiction to the ethnohistoric record. While it offers a seemingly direct approach capable of generating a corpus of data that may be dealt with statistically, Hawkins's method can be quite barren when it comes to results.

What about the selection of astronomical phenomena Hawkins utilized as targets to compare with the alignments? He proposed as a test the four extreme rise-set points of the sun and the twelve lunar extrema used in his original study of Stonehenge (Hawkins 1963). In addition, he also chose the rising and setting points of the 45 stars brighter than magnitude 2.0 plus the brightest star of the Pleiades, which, though nearly a magnitude fainter than the dimmest object in the sample, he justified for inclusion "because of its acknowledged importance in pre-Columbian culture" (Hawkins 1969: 29).

Following the approach outlined above, Hawkins defined the problem so that he could arrive at either a "yes" or "no" answer to each astronomical question. Were there more "hits" on the chosen astronomical targets by the alignments than one would expect if the matter were left to pure chance? According to his analysis, the answer was "no"; consequently, he found the astronomical hypothesis wanting. In fact, for any time period he selected, Hawkins found no significant coincidences (Hawkins 1969: Fig. 3). Eliminating the fainter stars from the sample, he discovered that once again a purely random distribution law for the line azimuths was indicated. It was clear that the astronomical test applied at Stonehenge had proved negative on the sample of alignments drawn from the pampa; Hawkins concluded that the lines showed no solar, lunar, planetary, or stellar preference and that they "as a whole cannot be explained as astronomical nor are they calendric" (1969: 40).

Several criticisms can be made of Hawkins's study. First, he identifies significant astronomical phenomena largely from the perspective of a northern high latitude observer. Such

phenomena cannot be assumed to be the same as those that would be important to a person living in the Southern Hemisphere, especially in tropical latitudes (Aveni 1981b). Moreover, the sky events he chose constitute but one of a large number of possible sets. He does not include in his selection the rising and setting position of the sun on the day of its passage through zenith. Since Hawkins's study, we have reason to think that the points of intersection of the horizon and the southern Milky Way, where named dark-cloud and star-to-star constellations are located, are of great importance among contemporary Andean cultures because the Milky Way is considered to be a celestial continuation of terrestrial rivers. In a number of cases the heliacal rise and set times of the dark-cloud constellations occur at dates in the calendar that correspond to the commencement of important periods in the life cycles of the animals they represent (Urton 1981a). While Urton's recent ethnographic studies have revealed other examples of Southern Hemisphere celestial constructs, no attention was given in Hawkins's study to ethnographic and ethnohistoric information on ancient South American culture, which, though admittedly sparse in the decade of the '60s when Hawkins conducted his research, was not entirely unknown (cf., e.g., Lehmann-Nitsche 1928 and references in the post-Conquest chronicles cited therein).

While Hawkins did use the extreme positions of the sun at horizon as possible targets, he never examined orientations for other dates in the solar year that conceivably might have been of specific agricultural or religious importance. Indeed, the care and precision of Hawkins's methodology in testing alignments, though praiseworthy, nonetheless may have deflected readers from any critical commentary about either its thoroughness or most especially its relevance to Andean culture concepts. Whether it be evaluated on the grounds of the inappropriateness of the set of astronomical possibilities examined, the small percentage of the area of the pampa it encompassed, or the types of features that were eventually surveyed, the negative results of the Hawkins survey cannot be regarded as the final word on any astronomical hypothesis for the origin of the lines.

Morrison's book (1978), which incorporates Hawkins's investigations, is a useful source for general information and references, but unfortunately it excessively glamorizes the scientific detective work, focusing as much upon the sleuths as upon the mystery. Inexplicably, considerably more attention is given to the Pleiades and the solstice in this text (pp. 48–49) than in Hawkins's original study. Certain features actually are labeled as astronomically oriented as if to imply that an astronomical solution to at least a part of the Nazca puzzle had been reached. For example, we find bizarre interpretive labels, such as "The Great Rectangle-Plaza of the Pleiades" (p. 58) and "Plaza of the Sun" (p. 59). The former, one of the largest trapezoids on the northern part of the pampa, is so labeled by Morrison on a copy of Hawkins's map, evidently because Hawkins found the Pleiades aligned with the two rock cairns at opposite ends of the figure in AD 600–700. It happens that this date closely matches the radiocarbon date (AD 610) assigned to the remains of a wooden post found nearby. On the same map, adjacent to a triangular extension of another long trapezoid, appear the words "Rising of the Pleiades (610 AD ± 30 years)". A third feature, a series of parallel lines, is termed "Grid of the Pleiades" by Morrison. A similar "Grid of the Sun" lies to the east. One edge of the long trapezoid called "Plaza of the Sun" is indicated to be pointing to the rising sun on the June solstice. Three more long lines are labeled solstice pointers. One of these lines passes across the wingspan of one of the bird figures, the condor, "which could be argued to be a 'special' marker and the line therefore highly significant" (p. 63). Two other lines are simply marked "North-South" lines. Unfortunately, all these labels, applied to the chosen few among a small number of randomly oriented lines, simply appear in the text without discussion. To anyone but the most careful and cautious reader, it would appear from this figure that the case for astronomically oriented Nazca lines is proven

unequivocally. But later, following a repeat of Hawkins's 1969 statistical discussion, Morrison adds the qualifying statement that "A few were good candidates for sun calendar markers—the entire maze was not a vast sun-moon-star calendar" (p. 62). Then Morrison expands this restricted result to a more general statement: "Gerald Hawkins had confirmed that the computer results would not support a time-clock-calendar theory" (p. 64). Given these confusing details, one can see why the ultimate outcome of Hawkins's survey has been to discourage serious investigators from looking further into the astronomical hypothesis.[18] Paradoxically, two different stories are being told. Astronomy remains firmly entrenched within the Nazca lines at least in the public eye and popular works such as those of Morrison and Reiche have contributed to that belief (cf. Schumacher 1983).

Reviewing the literature, one is struck by the simplistic character of the astronomical explanations for the Nazca lines that have been advanced thus far. Each investigation asks the same question; namely, do the lines point to astronomical phenomena on the horizon or do they not? Each investigator seems driven by a methodology that assumes the astronomical problem can be solved in a straightforward manner devoid of other kinds of evidence. Perhaps such an approach only serves to illustrate the nature of the scientific age in which we live. Largely culture-blind, most investigations consistently avoid any discussion of agriculture, rainfall, irrigation, or other seasonal or periodic activity that might have had an impact on the lives of the people who lived adjacent to the Nazca pampa. It is difficult to imagine that these kinds of approaches to what surely must be a very complex problem can ever offer us anything of substance.

18. Indeed, few others have entered the celestial arena. Rossello Truel (1977) proposed a connection between astronomically oriented lines and circular structures but gave no details, referring only to unpublished manuscripts. Likewise, Fung (1969) associated the structure called the Templo de las Haldas with an astronomical observing function, again without providing a detailed argument. Illescas Cook (1952) and Waisbard (1977) have offered even more exotic comparisons between celestial and terrestrial constructs.

*Nazca Geometry*

What we will call the geometrical hypothesis for the origin of the Nazca geoglyphs suggests that, at least in part, the lines were produced as a cerebral exercise. Thus, the drawings are said to reflect a knowledge of geometry that is discoverable through the precision in the execution of their contours and in the existence of one or more units of measurement encapsulated within their proportions. Though little has been written about it separately, geometry in the Nazca drawings is often a rider on the astronomical hypothesis. Perhaps this is because we think of geometry and astronomy in the Western scientific sense as purely esoteric pursuits that go together.[19]

In the rare but revealing 1949 edition of *Mystery on the Desert* and in a short paper published in Lima two years later (Reiche 1951), Reiche revealed a few tantalizing details of her geometrical hypothesis. She states that five trapezoids (we are not told which ones) exhibit widths at one end of 66–66½ yards (1949: 5), while diameters of 42 and 84 yards were found in at least five more (p. 6). In the 1951 paper the dimension 45.6 m (49.9 yards) and its integral and half-integral multiples are said to repeat six times, both in segments of animal figures and in the widths of "*pistas*" (p. 224), literally "trails" or "tracks." On the same page we learn that 32.6 m and its double also occur frequently, as do several multiples of 26.7 meters. The latter occurs at least ten times, several examples being cited in the long-necked bird figure. For example, this is the length of the bird's beak as well as of its feet, its tail, and half of its wingspan. The 10th multiple of 26.7 is the length of both the entire bird and "segments of many of the zigzag lines" (pp. 224–225, author's translation). The 20th and 30th multiples also are encountered frequently. In her 1968 work, Reiche (1968b:

58) stated that 1.10 m may be a possible standard unit. Still later (Kern and Reiche 1974), she settles on a standard length of 32.5 cm, a unit which she suggests could have been derived by placing a string between thumb and index finger and extending it to the inner part of the elbow (p. 12).[20] Most of the biomorphic figures are said to have been reproduced as precise scale models based upon such a unit. Curves allegedly were made by connecting circular segments of radii that are multiples of this basic unit, each portion having been laid out by cords tied to stakes at different centers of curvature.

It is very difficult to check Reiche's results for at least three reasons. There is, first of all, a lack of information about precisely which figures she examined. Worse still is her eclectic manner of reporting the many units of length to which one might attribute significance. Finally, the non-uniformity of selection criteria for those parts of figures being measured and contrasted endows the whole argument with an *a priori* quality. Nonetheless, the hypothesis of the use of measuring units based upon parts of the body is not unreasonable.

Reiche's method of constructing curves is demonstrated pictorially for the non-linear portions of the condor (Kern and Reiche 1974: Figs. 64–66) as well as for a few other geoglyphs (Fig. 59). In most of these cases, in order to reproduce the figure one must not only vary the length of the string used to construct it but also constantly shift the position from which one swings the arcs. In this regard, Reiche's method exhibits the same intangible quality of arbitrariness as that elucidated by Thom (1971: Chap. 6; 1978: 18) for constructing the egg-shaped megalithic circles.

The spiral tail of the monkey is said to be executed by joining segments of arcs of radii of 32.5 cm and multiples thereof (Kern and Reiche, 1974: Fig. 42); however, in a more recent publication (Spencer 1983) she is said to advocate a 38-cm unit. Here she also proposes the idea that the figures were first

---

19. This hypothesis, too, finds its place in the megalithic rings of the British Isles, as is evidenced in the following statement by Thom (1967: 27): "They were intensely interested in measurement and attained a proficiency—only equalled today by a trained surveyor. They concentrated on geometrical figures which had as many dimensions as possible arranged to be integral multiples of their units of length . . . the basic figure of their geometry, as of ours, was the triangle."

---

20. Our study of line widths offers no strong support for the reality of any of these units (see Ch. II, Fig. II.4).

drawn on pieces of starched cloth with chalk: "Some would have had to be quite large to be detailed enough. The body of the monkey, for example, would need to be at least two meters long to be enlarged with accuracy" (p. 7). The transcription of the planned figures to the pampa would have proceeded by swinging compass arcs of various multiples of the 38 cm unit using poles and ropes. Offering no evidence, she claims an angular measuring unit of 15° or 1/24 of a circle. A number of individuals, including Morrison (1978: 190) and the author have witnessed Reiche demonstrate this technique on the spiral located on the pampa of Cantalloc, just east of Nazca (Kern and Reiche 1974: Fig. 27) (cf. Appx. I).

Reiche also seems to have invented an imaginative way of combining the astronomical and geometrical hypotheses (Spencer 1983: 8). Analyzing the spider figure, she finds that its abdomen can be approximated by a dozen linked arc segments whose radii total 147.5 units of 38 cm length. She recognizes this total as an integral multiple of the cycle of lunar phases (thus, $5 \times 29\frac{1}{2} = 147.5$). But unlike the Rosetta Stone, there is no explanation for why this relationship should exist or how this information might have been used. Evidently, the abdomen of the spider is supposed to harbor secret astronomical information in its numerologically based construction. This exercise stands as a singular example of a presentist attempt to decode an ancient puzzle that may not even exist. The analysis is quite arbitrary and utilizes no information about the culture that produced it. Moreover, there are many sets of mathematical curves that can be enlisted in order to sketch close approximations to the arachnid's bulbous rear-end, which, upon close inspection, gives all the indications of a free-form drawing.

In order to test some of the basic tenets of the geometrical hypothesis, we sought to make a precise map of a spiral during our 1981 July Earthwatch field season at Nazca. In Appendix I, we analyze the Cantalloc spiral based upon data we collected at the site. We conclude that there is no evidence to suggest that the people who constructed this particular spiral utilized a knowledge of precise geometry and mathematics. This is not to suggest that the construction was either haphazard or totally unplanned. In our extended discussion in the Appendix, we offer some particulars of a possible construction method that began to suggest itself once we had examined the figure in some detail.

By mapping and examining a Nazca figure close up, we can learn something about the construction process. But other questions remain: Just how difficult is it to construct a geometrical figure on the pampa? How much precision and pre-planning are required and what sort of labor force must be mounted to complete the task? And, does one really need a blueprint in order to proceed? In June 1984 at the suggestion of Peter Spry-Leverton (ITV, London), we designed an experiment employing a group of twelve Earthwatch volunteers that was aimed at seeking answers to these questions. The experiment, filmed by Spry-Leverton under the title "Mysteries of Peru," consisted of drawing our own Nazca figure on the spot, with no written plan and a minimum of technology. We selected a heavily rock-strewn segment of a remote region of the pampa, about 1 km east of the Cantalloc figure. Our "Nazca line," for which we drew up no map in advance, was to consist of a rectangular strip about 15 times as long as its width[21] and aligned on a distant mountain peak. We intended to attach to this linear segment three inter-connected, leftward-turning circular arcs as follows:

(a) a segment approximately one-sixth of the arc of a circle in length and of radius 8 times the width;

(b) a segment approximately one-half of the arc of a circle in length and of radius equal to one-half that of segment (a);

(c) a segment approximately one-half of the arc of a circle in length and of radius equal to two-thirds that of segment (b);

Thus, the figure which started out straight, would then appear to coil up (see Fig. 9).

---

21. The metric width turned out to be 0.7 m.

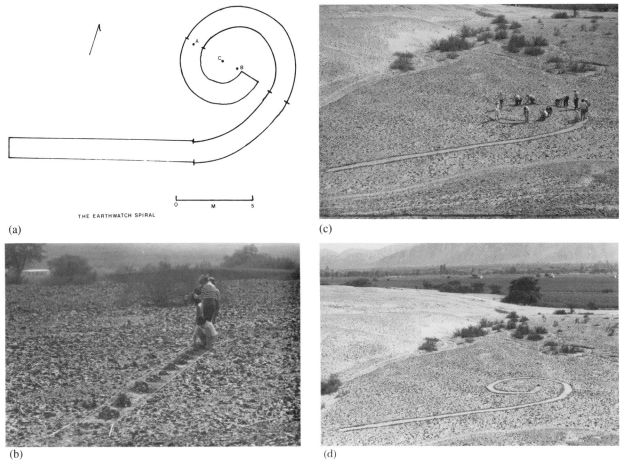

(a)

(b)

(c)

(d)

Fig. I.9a–d. (a) The Earthwatch Spiral: A controlled experiment in the design and execution of a Nazca line. Points A, B & C represent the centers from which the arc segments were ruled. (b) & (c) The work team at two phases of the operation. (d) The finished product.

We used two persons, each holding a vertical straight stick, to align our linear feature with a distant mountain as viewed by a third observer who simply instructed the other two to move their sticks laterally until they lined up with the mountain. Once the alignment was fixed, we measured one pace as the base width, fixed this length on a piece of string, and then connected points on the ground along the baseline between the two sticks with a second piece of string 15 times as long as the first. We measured off the radii of the arcs in unit lengths of the string and swung them from points in such a way that the arcs represented a reasonable continuation of the segments to which they connected. Having strung off the entire area, we then divided our labor force into two shifts. Members of the first shift squatted an arm's length apart within the pe-

rimeter of the figure and proceeded to gather debris within their reach, stacking the pieces in neat piles. Recall the argument that the first step in cleaning a line may have consisted of making such neat piles—thus the reason for the piling exercise. Workers of the second shift removed the material from the piles to form a neat edge to the figure. They were supervised by two individuals who arranged themselves along the borders of the figure but outside of it. This "edging" operation was conducted entirely by naked-eye approximation with the supervisory personnel offering the corrective instructions only when the edging appeared to be uneven.

The cleared area totaled 31 square meters and the task was completed in 90 minutes, with everyone working at a leisurely pace. When we completed the exercise, we erased the figure by recovering the entire area in ten minutes. The photographs of Figure 9 reveal our "home-made Nazca line" to be at least as precise as the Cantalloc spiral of Appx. I. The exercise demonstrates that neither a complex technology nor a sophisticated knowledge of classical geometry detailed through a "blue-print" is required to construct such a figure. Moreover, the amount of labor is surprisingly small. Extrapolating from our work record, we conclude that a force of 100 persons working 10 hours per day could have cleared 2000 square meters of the pampa in two days. This is equivalent to a good-sized (200 m × 10 m) trapezoid. The sizable trapezoid associated with line center No. 30 (see Appx. II, Fig. 1b.) could have been cleared in less than a week by the same team. Indeed, given a work force of 10,000 (and inspired by a sound work ethic), all the features on the pampa could have been constructed in a matter of a few years.

For completeness, other references to geo-metrical hypotheses deserve mention. A more extreme use of geometry with diffusionist implications is given by Scholten D'Ebneth (1959), who suggested that it is possible to in-fer directions and proportions evident in Nazca geometry over the globe to the Andean highlands and even to Mesoamerica.

Precision in the execution of geometry also enters into Rossel Castro's (1977) garbled combination of explanations for the lines. He states that the arrangement of the figures was planned and that much precision and perfec-tion exists in the trapezoids and triangles, yet he does not report on any survey of these works that test his ideas.

The notion that considerations of precise geometry are contained within the Nazca lines is indeed tantalizing, especially when one ob-serves them from the air. Yet, aside from our work on the Cantalloc spiral, no systematic study, not even one comparable to Hawkins's modest astronomical data collecting and anal-ysis, ever has been undertaken with a view to-ward examining whether geometrical sets of rules might exist there. Our survey and anal-ysis of a single spiral ought not close the door to further discussion.

And, finally, our suggestion that the Nazca lines are not stupendous feats of engineering that required vast investments of energy ought not detract from the need to explain the origin of these unique and curious desert markings. As Clarkson remarks at the end of her chapter, perhaps the very act of making them was of ultimate importance.

*Agriculture and Irrigation*

The most important commodity in Nazca is water. The pampa that contains the Nazca lines is bordered by two of the principal trib-utaries of the Rio Grande and *quebradas* cut-ting across the pampa drain water from the high Andes into the Nazca River. In this nar-row coastal strip between the high Andes and the Pacific Ocean where it almost never rains the precious liquid plummets from 3000 meters to sea level. It is difficult to imagine any coastal world view in which water, its ori-gin, movement, and function would not play a central role. As Urton (n.d. c: 17) has re-marked, "One of the predominant 'themes' of virtually every conversation with informants in Nazca or Ingenio is rain and the amount, or lack, of water in the rivers." At the practical level, the seasonal and long-term variations in the flow of these descending waters are vital to the survival of coastal inhabitants. The recog-nition of such variations by the local inhab-itants offers both a starting point and a ratio-nale for the study of coastal calendars (Urton 1982[22]). Urton (n.d. c: 2) tells us that the locals employ scintillation and subtle color changes of the stars as well as the orientation of the first lunar crescent to foretell rain. According to one of his informants, nearby Cerro Blanco once spewed water from its summit and one still can induce water from the mountains by carrying a vessel of foaming sea water to a hill above Nazca and sprinkling it on the ground (p. 11).

---

22. In this work, Urton gives a thorough discussion of coastal fishing and agricultural cycles and their possible relation to the development of astronomy and calendar. In our analysis of the line centers (Chap. II), we refer to some of these hypotheses.

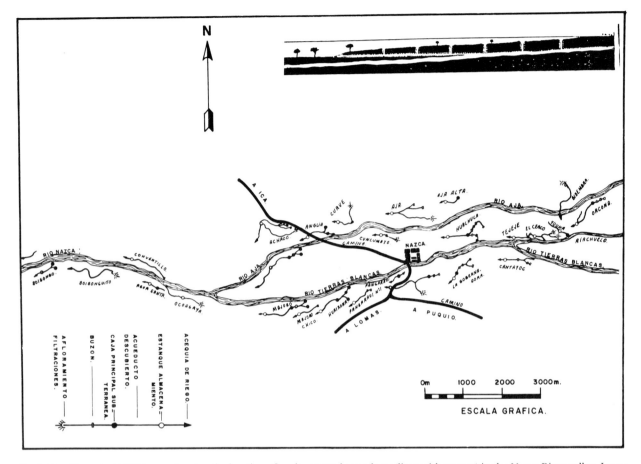

Fig. I.10a. Gonzalez' (1978) map showing the location of underground aqueducts (lines with arrows) in the Nazca River valley. Inset: Cross-section of one of these.

One of the earliest discussions of the Nazca lines in a hydrological context appears in an article on irrigation systems by Mejía Xesspe (1927). Enjoining the linear concepts of canals and roads, it is aptly entitled "Acueductos y caminos antiguos de la hoya del Rio Grande de Nazca." In this important article, Mejía, who had excavated with Tello in Nazca in the 1920s, surveyed the archaeological record relating to a complex system of subterranean aqueducts and underground wells (*puquios = pukios*) which apparently were used for irrigating the southern tributary valleys of the Rio Grande drainage system (i.e., the Nazca, Taruga, and Kopará Rivers); this is the region to the east and south of the pampa on which most of the geoglyphs are found.[23] The sub-

Fig. I.10b. A view of one of the vertical perforations possibly used by workers to descend into the stone-lined puquios in order to clean them.

terranean irrigation system (Fig. I.10a) is composed of stone-lined canals, some of which

---

23. However, in nine separate drawings, Mejía (Fig. 6, I–IX) displays linear features lying in the same general vicinity as the subterranean canals. There can be no doubt that one of the

features (VIII) is the Cantalloc figure discussed in Appendix I. It is situated a few kilometers east of the underground systems.

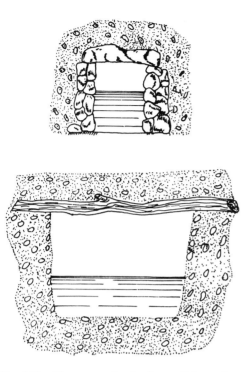

Fig. I.10c. *Transverse sketch of two of the underground tubes: Upper—through a sandy surface; Lower—in less porous conglomerate.* (Gonzalez 1978: Fig. 4)

measure up to 500 meters in length, punctuated by vertical shafts (Fig. I.10a inset), also stone-lined (Fig. I.10b, c), that connect to the surface. Whether these apertures, which are spaced about 20 meters apart on the map, were used for ventilation and/or for workers to descend into the canals for the purpose of cleaning them (as Mejía suggests) is not clear. These subterranean *puquios* flank each of the rivers and run up the intermontane alluvial fans from which they drain off ground water. According to Gonzalez (1935, reissued 1978), certain rules regulated the sharing of the water among the various proprietors of the land surrounding the rivers; many of these systems are still in use today. Specific instructions indicate which channels are to be opened to particular parcels of land on various days of the month. In Chap. IV, Urton reports on his discovery and analysis of early colonial documents that indicate that a similar temporal division of water rights according to the Andean *mit'a* system (cf. Chap. IV and Appx. III) existed at least at the time of the first Spanish

settlement of the Ingenio Valley. These actions supply a motive for local people to trek across the pampa in an organized and prescribed manner.

Mejía's and Gonzalez's discussions of the underground irrigation network provide evidence for a high level of hydraulic engineering in the Nazca area in pre-Columbian times and offer eloquent testimony to the surveying and engineering skills of the indigenous populations. While neither of these investigators directly connected the underground aqueducts with the Nazca ground drawings, there is an implied similarity. Both sets of features are linear, one lying above the ground and the other below. Some underground aqueducts even pass beneath the river. As we shall see in Chap. II, the potential connection between the Nazca lines and the use of water is strengthened by the discovery that most of the star-like patterns we call line centers are located along the river banks, tributaries, and at the bases of the mountains from where the drainage proceeds.

Rossel Castro (1977: 209–216) has carried the Nazca line function further into the realm of the practical. Just as the subterranean aqueducts (which he calls "*galerias filtrantes*") subdivided the land below ground into an irrigation network, so too did the geometrical figures parcel out the land above ground, he claimed.[24] Thus, Rossel Castro conceived the drawings to be a direct part of an irrigation plan. He suggested that even today, the land around Nazca is divided into trapezoids or triangular parcels (called "*kollo*" in Quechua) that resemble the shapes and dimensions of Nazca ground drawings. A typical plot is said to be 800 meters in length and to range in width from 80 to 100 meters. Often these "*acequias*"

---

24. Rossel claimed to have discovered one such plot or "*parcela*" on the pampa; however, he does not specify its location. On the fertility of the pampa soil, this personal communication from Persis Clarkson: "I spoke at length with a British-Peruvian farmer (born and raised on a hacienda in Peru) who has a grape farm near Nazca; he says the soil on the pampa is quite good for agricultural purposes. I don't claim that he meant all of the pampa, but he did point to the plowing northwest of line centers No. 3 and 4 [see Chap. II, Fig. 3(3/4)] as indication that people are willing to farm the area as soon as the government irrigation project comes through" (17 January 1984).

connect the apex angle of a triangular plot to a water source and the land is heaped up around the border to conserve moisture within the parcel so that a more fertile crop can result. On the basis of our examination of 1:2000 SAN aerial photos of the Nazca drainage basin, we are unable to confirm his suggestion. In ancient times, Rossel contends, the pampa may have been a verdant one, for once the parcels were laid out, the infertile soil native to the pampa was removed and replaced with more enriched loam.[25] That the huge geometrical figures are all located close to the rims of the river valleys is said to provide strong evidence for the case that some Nazca figures physically served an agricultural function. Moreover, contends Rossel, many of the animal figures located near and often between the large geometrical features possess agricultural significance. For example, the spider is a symbol of fecundity and the vulture is the precursor of rain. Still another figure is identified with an algal plant ("*varec*") which is used as fertilizer.

Could the pampa have been cultivated? Craig (1968: 98–100) has referred to certain devices (dew traps and fog brooms) by which people living in a foggy desert environment have been known to secure limited amounts of water, but he concludes that such techniques could hardly have been employed to irrigate even a modest percentage of the pampa.

In the final analysis, there is no real archae-

ological evidence to support the hypothesis that the pampa ever was farmed; nonetheless, it may be worth noting that Maria Reiche expended a great deal of effort in the 1960s blocking attempts on the part of the government to irrigate a portion of the pampa in the vicinity of the animal figures. Indeed, in our own survey work, we often encountered portions of the pampa where ground drawings had been plowed over and the land planted within the past decade. But usually these fields lay very close to the major river valleys.

Recently, Schreiber and Lancho (1988) have conducted a study of the *puquios* flanking the Nazca drainage basin. Though they reach their lowest levels in November and December, just prior to the annual rainfall in the mountains to the south and east, these wells always were found to contain some water. Employing geological data, they have determined that surface water in the Nazca area disappears about 5 km upstream from the town of Nazca and reappears 10 km downstream, thus necessitating the use of the underground irrigation system in the region in-between at some period during the history of the Nasca culture.

They have dated the *puquios* to Late Nasca times on the basis of the existence of early habitation sites exclusively in the area where surface water was available. Furthermore, they suggest that a settlement shift took place during the later period that can be related to the construction of the underground irrigation system (between Nasca 4 and 8, most likely during Nasca 5, a period during which other significant changes in the Nasca culture also are alleged to have taken place).

T. Settle (personal communication) first called our attention to the general similarity between the Nazca subterranean aqueducts and the Persian *qanat*s. Glick (1970) shows a cross-section of a *qanat* (p. 183) bearing a striking resemblance to Mejía's diagram (p. 561, Fig. 2). According to Glick, *qanat* technology diffused as far as Spain in the twelfth century and thence to the New World. Are the Nazca aqueducts definitely of pre-Hispanic origin, in which case they would constitute a remarkable

---

25. In this connection, Craig (1968: 96–98) has drawn attention to an interesting series of radial lines that may have been associated with irrigation in the Pisco valley, 150 km northwest of the Nazca pampa. Six lines radiate from a point in the desert tentatively identified as "a pillar of adobe rubble" (p. 96). Craig states that "If followed a sufficient distance outward from a point of origin, they would ultimately intersect one of the major irrigation canals at a point where the canal makes a distinct change in direction" (pp. 96, 98). While this conclusion is borne out in an accompanying map (p. 57), it is not clear whether the lines are physically connected to the bends in the system. Craig posits that the markings may have been related to the surveying process that led to the construction of the irrigation system. In June 1984, Urton and the author, assisted by Earthwatch volunteers, explored the relatively sandy pampa between the Pisco and Chincha River Valleys immediately east of the Pan American Highway in a failed attempt to find Craig's line center. However, we were able to discern several lines which we followed on foot. These terminated in a group of line centers flanking the banks of a tributary of the Chincha. Thus, we conclude that the phenomenon of line centers is not unique to the Nazca pampa (see Chap. II for a further discussion of this interesting parallel).

example of independent invention, or might they have resulted from diffusion? Though she has not dated them archaeologically, Schreiber has examined the technological and constructional differences between *qanats* and Nazca *puquios* and though her work has not yet been completed, she offers the opinion that the Spanish likely did not build them and that therefore they must be of pre-Columbian origin.

While dealing with the theme of water and Nazca, one must not overlook the important work of Reinhard (1983a,b; 1985a,b; 1987). Utilizing ethnographic and ethnohistorical data, he clearly establishes enduring relationships among water, fertility, mountain worship, and mountain deities all over the Andes and particularly the south coast. Drawing on some of the data we present in Chap. II, he speculates that some of the Nazca lines may have played a role in fertility rituals by connecting particular points in the irrigation system with central places of worship. Our detailed analysis of the straight line features in Chap. II are not in disagreement with his general hypothesis.

Given the evidence, much of it admittedly circumstantial, one has the impression that water—its properties, seasonality, and the need people in this extremely arid region must have possessed to obtain it—could well have played a role in the orderly distribution exhibited by the line centers. As we shall learn in Chap. II, lines cross-cross the zone in-between the rivers and they emanate from centers that seem to have been located deliberately near water sources. But to this point, no one has been able to elaborate in detail a specific hypothesis that can be thoroughly tested and evaluated. Further probing of the ethnohistoric documents may be the only potential means of leading to a more substantive discussion about precisely how the lines could have been tied to the flow of water.

*Movement, Communication, and Travel: Lines Intended to be Walked Upon*

". . . in ancient times before the Incas there were in this land other people called Viraco-chas—and they made roads that we still can see today, some narrow like a street [road] with walls on each side" (Monzón 1881 [1586]: 210) (author's translation).[26]

Anyone who sets foot on the pampa will realize immediately that whether astronomy or hydrology, or both, played a role in the design and layout of the Nazca lines, they surely were intended to have been walked upon. The chronicler's statement leaves little doubt that roads were of considerable importance in ancient Peru and that they extended all over the highlands and the coast. Hyslop's (1984) survey and detailed description of Inka roads offer us a number of possibilities for exploring structural similarities between Inka roads and the Nazca ground drawings.

One characteristic roads and lines have in common is the straightness of their trajectory. Particularly over the coastal deserts, the roads are known to pass straight over intervening hills (Fig. I.11a). For example, the major prehistoric road between Batan Grande and Guadelupe extends 90 km maintaining an orientation between azimuth 343° and 350°.

The Inka roads in the desert environment were not simply trails; rather, they often exhibited low walls or piled debris at their boundaries (Fig. I.11b). Hyslop discovered that one technique for indicating constructional changes in coastal road segments was to erect stone piles at the end of each sidewall (Fig. I.11c). Thus, as it leaves the southeastern edge of the Chicama Valley bearing 140° (magnetic), the ancient road suddenly widens from 28 meters to 58 meters. A pair of rock piles, one on each side of the road, mark the spot. Over the next 300 meter segment, the road gradually assumes the shape of a trapezoid as it narrows to a width of 30 meters. Hyslop likens this aspect to the trapezoidal drawings on the Nazca pampa (Hyslop and Urrutia 1980: 14). It should be noted that rock cairns often are located at the ends of trapezoids that are attached to lines emanating from line centers.

26. For an additional description of the Royal Road on the coast, see Cieza 1962 (1553): 182–183. Hyslop (1984: 266) discusses references to coastal roads in the Inka chronicles. See also Urton, this volume.

Fig. I.11a.  Pre-Columbian coastal roads and Nazca lines share many features: Inka straight road going over a hill in the Jequetepeque valley. (Courtesy J. Hyslop)

Thus, one's walk from a Nazca line center sometimes terminates at the wide end of a trapezoid (Fig. I.11d). Keeping the same width, the Chicama road abruptly bends and bears 135°. The sudden widening, alteration of direction, trapezoidal shape, and delineation of the basal end of a trapezoid are all structural features of the geometrical figures on the Nazca pampa.

Another feature common to Nazca lines and Inka roads is that often one finds pairs or even groups of parallel features. Hyslop described and illustrated a road segment on the southern entrance to the Zaña Valley that consists of three parallel lines separated by hummocks of detritus (Fig. I.11e). The possible use of such a road had been described by Gutiérrez de Santa Clara (1963 [1599?]: 248–249):

Two collateral roads were on both sides of the (coastal) royal road and they too had two strong and wide walls. And when the Inka passed on these roads, he went on the middle one and was followed by those who were responsible for carrying his litter. They were 600 men who alternated carrying it on their shoulders. There were

also many important Indians of his royal court who accompanied him. They were carried by many Indians on their shoulders because they were great lords and chiefs of different peoples who were given permission to travel in a litter . . . The other multitudes of Indian workers and bearers went by the other two adjoining roads. And none of them passed to the middle road unless the Inka called them . . . .
  Hyslop (1984: 261–262), translation by Hyslop

These similarities between some of the structural features of certain of the Nazca lines (cf. Fig. I.5) and Inka roads cannot be overlooked. As we shall argue in Chap. II, a straight segment of the Inka road system appears to enter the hills just north of the pampa. It may be at least partially traceable across a part of the pampa. And one of the structures found by Urton on the pampa may have been an Inka *tambo*, or resting place.

One of the earliest descriptive terms to be applied to the lines, *"camino religioso"* (Mejía 1927), places the road hypothesis in a more religious and somewhat less economic framework. In the same vein, Mejía also refers to the

Fig. I.11b. The low walls surrounding an Inca road resemble the piled detritus that forms the borders of the lines. Compare with Fig. 2. (Hyslop)

lines as "*seqe*" (line, ray). His analogy, together with our recognition of the great abundance of interconnected ray-like patterns of lines on the desert, provides us with a fundamentally Andean perspective on the study of Nazca features. The recognition of this hidden similarity allows us to look elsewhere in the Andes in order to formulate concrete hypotheses for the structure and function of the lines on the pampa.

Though we shall discuss the *ceque* system in more detail in Chap. II, a brief allusion to it is appropriate at this point. The Quechua word *ceque* (= *seqe*), defined as a ray or line (Cobo 1956 [1653]: II: 169) is related to an important concept of social, political, economic, and ceremonial order in the Andes during Inkaic times. The chronicler Cobo informs us that in the Inka capital city of Cuzco, 41 *ceque* lines radiated out from the ceremonial center of the city, the Temple of the Sun (Coricancha), to the horizon. Along the *ceques*, 328 holy sites, or *huacas*, were located. In addition to organizing the space within the valley of Cuzco, the *ceques* and *huacas* delineated in detail the structure of the irrigation system as well as the hierarchy of socio-political groups and marriage classes (Zuidema 1964). That certain *ceque* lines were also intended to be moved upon or walked over will be established in Chap. II.

The responsibility for administering the *ceques* was assigned to kinship groups in an alternating pattern of three that proceeded systematically around the horizon in each individual quarter or *suyu* according to the proximity of descent of the group from pure royal blood. The method of naming the *ceques* in the various quarters of the city also incorporated the story of the descent of the Inka royal line from the earliest times up to the founding of Cuzco. Zuidema's more recent works (1977a,b; 1981a,b; 1982a,b,c) along with that of the author (Aveni 1981a) have established that the *ceque* system also served as a calendar used to count the days of the solar and lunar years by a tally of the *huacas* and *ceques*. It also incorporated a complex sighting scheme related to a horizon calendar that included pillars erected for the purpose of marking the days by the changing position of the sun on the horizon as sighted from different points within the *ceque* system.

The picture that emerges from our studies of the *ceque* system of Cuzco is that the concept of radial lines converging on a center was the fundamental organizing principle of the great Inka capital. In Chap. II, we shall further develop the analogy of the *ceque* system as a general Andean model upon which to base certain arguments pertaining to the organization of linear radial patterns of the etchings on the Nazca plain.

As one might expect, there are other pan-Andean concepts that can be associated with convergence, divergence, or with a division of things—one into many. One artifact incorporating this principle is the *quipu*, an array of-

Figure I.11c. A pair of Cairns mark the point of widening of an Inka road. (Hyslop)

Fig. I.11d. On the pampa, a similar pair of markers (arrow) serve to indicate the crossing point of two large geometrical features near line center No.37. (U. of Minnesota)

knotted strings which served as a primary medium of expression and communication in pre-Inkaic times. Indeed, Kosok (1965: 59–60) and Morrison (1978: 127–129) have noted the formal structural similarities between the *quipu* and the Nazca lines.

The concept of dividing or splitting things hierarchically is very important in Andean culture. The verb *rakiy,* which is widely and variously employed, expresses the action of dividing a single thing into two or more parts or branches (Fairchild n.d.). In contemporary communities, this term receives rather widespread use as a way of describing the parcelling of land (Urton 1981b: 42, 139, 140) or the branching of a primary irrigation canal into secondary channels. *Rakiy* describes the way a tree divides into branches. But the term is also employed in the social arena to describe aspects of separation by gender and discontinuity. It also is the point of union that forms the dialectical forces of the social universe so common in the Andes: death and life, past and future, male and female. The terms *mallcu, tinkuy,* and *chuta* (*chhiuta*) (Urton 1984 and Chap. IV, this volume) in one way or another

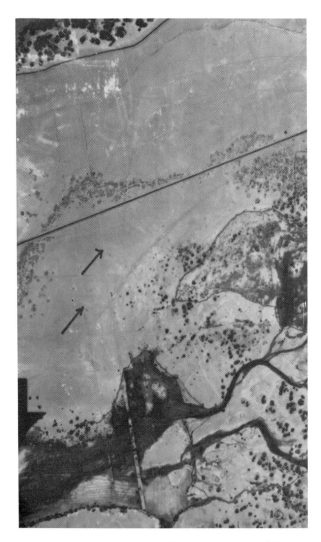

Fig. I.11e. Three roads (marked by arrows) run parallel to one another. (Hyslop)

Fig. I.11f. Cairn at the end of a long Nazca trapezoid (E. Hadingham)

also refer to the concept of splitting or dividing things.[27]

By mentioning these diverse examples, it is not our intention to advocate specifically that

---

27. Urton's (1984) recent work on *chhiuta* employed as a ritual in contemporary Pacariqtambo for the division of labor in cleaning or preparing the space of a plaza or an irrigation channel offers a more solid connection. For example, the sweeping of the plaza of Pacariqtambo results in well-defined parallel strips, each having been cleaned by a pre-assigned kinship group.

In the Inka ruins of Quebrada de la Vaca on the coast about 100 km south of Nazca, there is an enclosure, one end of which may have served as an elite burial chamber. The open plaza facing the vaults is divided into horizontal strips each of which is edged or defined by a line of stones, the whole resembling at least in a general way the reworked surface of the pampa. It measures 840 meters in length by 100 meters wide and "had been plowed and fertilized in its interior" (Rossel 1959: 355). (For details, see the discussion in Urton, Chap. IV, this volume.)

the Nazca lines were employed formally to divide things, much less to suggest what they divided; rather we only intend to establish that the organizing principle of splitting or dividing according to hierarchical principles was very common in Andean social life. Pathways that pass outward from a center represent one concrete physical manifestation of this concept.

In several drawings, Mejía compared "*seqe*" shapes and arrangements within different areas of the Rio Grande de Nazca. He concluded that there are primarily two forms of *seqes* (lines): one is composed of a series of wide, geometrical plaza-like areas, the other of narrow lines that extend for considerable distances across the pampa. The formal typology of Nazca lines developed by Mejía still is basically sound, although there is a certain danger in labeling them "*caminos*" (roads) until the functional implications of that term in relation to Andean cultural and ritual behavior have been investigated more systematically. Nonetheless, Mejía's early observations remain important in the discussion of the forms and possible functions of the Nazca lines.

Walking on the lines is the central theme of a rather ingenious, though not very wellknown study by University of Trujillo (Peru) archaeologist H. Horkheimer (1947). This Peruvian investigator spent more than two months on and about the pampa and was particularly intrigued by the triangle-trapezoid features, which he calls "*plazoletas*." The triangle, he argues, would have been the natural form that best fit a landscape contoured by stream systems with many tributaries and at the same time allowed the figures to converge at a single point.

The essential components of his theory are:

(1) The trapezoids were intended as places of assembly for sacred reunions of cults of the dead. Different groups met on different trapezoids depending upon who their descendants were;

(2) The lines passing into the trapezoids were genealogical lines that provided information about the origin and kinship among the various cults that were united on the "*plazoletas*". Here, though he does not mention it, Horkheimer draws a parallel with the *ceque* lines of Cuzco;

(3) Upon the biomorphic figures sacred dances were choreographed that related to the worship of the dead. Given the Inka penchant for preserving and parading around their ancestors and the preponderance of ritual dance among Andean peoples, this theory applied to people living on the coast a millennium earlier sounds fairly reasonable. Like the Egyptians, the people of Nazca could have utilized the wasteland beyond their cultivable space for the worship of their ancestors.

But can any of these hypotheses be tested? Horkheimer offers us as pivotal evidence the statement that many lines tie the *plazoletas* directly to tombs and that several groups of these triangular cleared areas converge on tombs. However, at least one of the examples he cites turns out to be a line center that we have mapped (his Fig. 23 may be compared with our Ch. II, Fig. 3 (16/17)). However, there is not the slightest evidence of any burials in the vicinity; as far as we know, no archaeological excavations have been undertaken at any of these sites.

It is possible that Horkheimer has identified as "tombs" the cairns that one often finds at the line centers. Clarkson (this volume) reports that in the several instances in which looters have unpiled the stones and dug as much as a meter below the surface, she finds not a single trace of human remains or adornments having been scattered about as one does

among the looted burials around Cahuachi. Therefore, it seems likely that the cairns on the pampa were not associated with burials. It is true, as Horkheimer states, that many lines cross burial places at the interface between the pampa and the valley. In fact, line center No. 33 (Chap. II, Fig. 3-33) appears to have been built alongside the cemetery site named Pacheco; but given that there are over 200 burial sites on the rim of the Nazca–Ingenio Valleys and nearly 1000 lines leading across the pampa, any implied association between lines and burials must be shown to hold up statistically.[28] In spite of the lack of evidence, one senses something reasonable in a pan-Andean sense about Horkheimer's hypothesis. Walking long, straight imaginary lines in a prescribed way according to the rigorous laws of kinship is very much a part of Andean insistence, as we shall reiterate when we discuss the *ceque* system of Cuzco later in this text.

A more detailed argument on the possible ceremonial function of the lines is offered in Morrison's text (1978: 131–149). He documented the importance of straight ceremonial roads in the Andes in general. Particularly revealing is his reference to the work of Metraux (1934) on the pathways of the Chipaya (Cípaya) Indians, an Aymara people of highland Bolivia. These pathways converge like spokes on a wheel on isolated chapels, leading the walker straight to them without regard to the roughness or incline of the ground. Metraux's description bears a strong resemblance to the line centers that we discuss in Chapter II (cf. especially Morrison's illustration on p. 158). It is interesting, Morrison points out, that Metraux calls these features "paths." The description of similar features on the Nazca pampa as "lines" appeared only with the advent of aviation and aerial photography.

The chapels, called "*Mallcu*" (*Mal'ku*), after the earth spirits who were venerated there

---

28. There is one documented case of a likely association between lines and burials, but it does not occur on the pampa. We are indebted to T. Patterson (field notes 28/vii/61) who reports isolated trapezoidal markings on the desert near Cerro Soldado in the Ica River valley, the north ends of which terminate in a cemetery. Sherds collected at the site date it to Ocucaje phase 7-9 and Nasca 4-5.

through offerings, consist of conical piles of stone and earth of about the same dimension as the stone cairns often found associated with Nazca geometry. They are said to represent the effigies of various earth spirits, and each has its own name. These *Mallcu* lie on straight lines 5 to 15 km from the nearest village and pilgrims journey there to place offerings in chambers at their bases.

Several contemporary lines connecting shrines are pictured and described by Morrison (1978: 156–163). One of his Aymara informants told him that just before a fiesta held on January 2, the worshippers would proceed to a "*capilla*" to fast. They would encircle the shrine on their knees. Later, when the fast was broken, they would shatter the bowls that once contained their food and present it to the shrine as "*jik'illita*" (money fragments). Morrison also found many instances among the Aymara of pathways called "*T'aki*" that led to shrines at the top of the highest hills, intermediate shrines having been established along the path, particularly where shallower hills intervened. However, the custom of erecting a "*calvario*" or Christian cross on the highest hilltop in sight of a village may be of colonial origin.

Another example of the radial road principle has been reported at the Inka and pre-Inka complex of La Centinela in the Chincha Valley just north of Nazca (Wallace 1971). Hyslop has commented (1984: 313) that the straight roads extending out from the large adobe pyramid "should make any Andean archaeologist wonder about their relationship to Inca ceque principles." He followed the four paths that led outward to kilometric distances from the structure. One path led across the pampa to the Pisco River Valley passing a number of scattered stone piles along the way (shrines along the road?). Remains of corn, fish bones, and a few pieces of textile lay scattered among the stones. Three of the four roads gave access to habitation sites, thus supporting the notion that they were of practical, economic importance rather than purely ritualistic. Finally, Reinhard (1987: 22–25) cites a number of instances in Bolivia and Chile where straight lines lead up to the tops of hills.

In some cases these hilltops are employed as places for the presentation of offerings to adjacent high mountains which often were regarded as water sources.

Among the more imaginative explanations for the Nazca lines that can be classified under the path or runway hypothesis is that of von Breunig (1980). He proposed that the lines were constructed for the purpose of running competitive races. As odd as this idea might seem at first glance, the initial hypothesis that led to it seems reasonable enough: that "connection between two points specially [sic] if these points were kilometers apart most likely involved human beings, either in terms of walking or running" (p. 210). Actually, there is plenty of evidence in the chronicles that ritual walking, running, or dancing were important in ancient Peru (see references in von Breunig 1980: 219 and Aveni 1980a: 269; also Nabokov 1981; Rossel Castro 1977: 185). Also, we know that in Inka times, there were 400 runners who ran on the *ceque* lines of Cuzco.

To support his hypothesis, von Breunig undertook a series of measurements on the much-overworked Cantalloc spiral geoglyph. He claimed that the curved pathways were banked in such a way that could have resulted from continued running over them. Specifically, his measurements indicated that soil from the depressed center portion of the track became heaped up on the outside portions of the curves, a condition that could have resulted from the action of a runner's feet as he changed direction on the curve. Our examination of the Cantalloc spiral does not bear out his conclusions.[29] Von Breunig then evolved his running thesis to Olympian proportions by positing a scenario that begins with local races and ends in a set of national games involving fully athletically garbed participants (replete with team-shirts and head

---

29. The degree of precision claimed by these measurements seems incredible. His charts of vertical profiles of the curved portions of the figure show differential soil depths of 10 cm—much larger than we have ever witnessed. Also, it should be noted that the figure he studied is among those most well trod upon by modern tourists. On the other hand, Urton and the author have observed pathways within a large number of Nazca lines that may well be ancient remains (see Chaps. II and IV).

gear), all of which are said to be depicted on Nazca pottery.

Though von Breunig's idea as stated and argued is open to wide criticism, it has served to fuel the notion that movement back and forth over the lines may have been an important activity and that perhaps investigators have tended to devote too much attention to the geometrical and astronomical hypotheses. We shall discuss this idea of movement further in the next section, but in a slightly different context, namely that of artistic expression.

*The Nazca Lines as Works of Art*

"From the ground, Nazca is totally incomprehensible, yet from the air one gasps with astonishment—and that is what fascinates modern man. . . . To appreciate Nazca one *must* be airborne above the plains."

Woodman 1977: 11

With that sweeping ethnocentric statement began a modern hot air balloon odyssey over the lines that has attracted much public attention. The quote also reveals the domination of the visual over all the other senses in our culture. But "to appreciate" is not necessarily synonymous with "to understand" and as we have argued earlier in this chapter, we may be deluding ourselves if we believe that by flying over the lines and gazing at them, we can even begin to understand why they were constructed.

Ever since the lines were revealed to the public eye, they have been considered from an aerial viewpoint. In fact, they were "discovered" from the air. The oft-used descriptive words "line" or "ground drawing," even the structurally preferred term "etching," evoke the visual mode of perception that remains wedded to the history of the study of the lines. Thus, whether we study these features from the ground or from the air, it would be difficult to omit the visual artistic element from consideration in our discussion.

Minimalism in conventional Western art strives to offer a succinct message with few lines on the canvas. Sculptor Robert Morris (1975)

has suggested that the apparent economy in creating and delineating a few basic classes of abstract shapes by the simple process of removal is a characteristic shared by the Nazca lines and twentieth century environmental art. There is a certain public aspect about the way the Nazca artist treats the open space of the desert and its surrounding mountains that one can regard as similar to the way the minimalists of the 1960s exhibited a desire to communicate their own logic to the public via the great works of nature—a form of emotional dialogue between the individual and his fellow humans. Smithson's "Spiral Jetty" in the Great Salt Lake is but one example that can be offered for comparison (Kern and Reiche 1974: Fig. 144).

In the Nazca environment, the artist achieves a mediation between the flat and the spatial: "The further down the line one looks, the greater its definition. Yet the greater the distance, the less definition of detail. The lines are both more general and more distinct as lines in direct proportion to the distance focused by the eye. The gestalt becomes stronger as the detail becomes weaker" (Morris 1975: 31).

That the Nazca geoglyphs may have been meant to be comprehended through some non-visual mode was already hinted at in the previous section. There we revealed some of the arguments and evidence that the Nazca lines were designed to be moved over, or walked upon. Perhaps one ought to sense the monkey or the hummingbird not by seeing it from the air, but rather by walking (or running) upon it. Thus one would perceive with the body every sinuous turn in the labyrinthine tail or the delicate curvature of each individual fragment of avian plumage.[30] Like negotiating a curve on a highway, one lives through it from beginning to end, even though symbolically one may see it repre-

30. This explanation of non-visual perception of a Nazca figure by a person on the surface of the earth does not preclude the possibility that the figures also might have been intended to be viewed by the gods above, a rationale advocated for many of the giant effigy forms that fit the description of "earth art" (Kern and Reiche 1974). While there is no cultural evidence to suggest that the latter purpose was intended, one is hard pressed to know what sort of evidence to look for either to support or to refute such a hypothesis.

Fig. I.12a. Lines and figures often seem to fit perfectly into the natural spaces that frame them: Low level view of a portion of the Cantalloc "Yarn and Needle figure." Cf. Fig. 6 & App'x. I)

Fig. I.12b. The tail and wing features of this partially obliterated bird figure radiate just to the edge of the pampa.

Fig. I.12c. Large trapezoid. Note the stream bed tangent to the right side.

sented in flat-space on a highway sign as one approaches it (Morris 1975: 38).

Conkey (1980: 234) offers a holistic principle from paleolithic art that we might apply to the Nazca geoglyphs. The subtractive nature of the creation process on the pampa is rather like that involved in certain sculptured paleolithic forms wherein the artist seems to function not to apply a decoration or pattern to a given space or material but rather to liberate a preexisting form from the medium that surrounds it. The term "etching" seems particularly appropriate for such a process. For the Eskimo artist, recognizable shapes already can be seen or felt in an untouched piece of stone, bone, or antler and these shapes direct the artist in his work:

As the carver holds the unworked ivory lightly in his hand, turning it this way and that, he whispers, 'Who are you! Who hides there!' And then 'Ah, Seal!' He rarely sets out to carve, say, a seal, but picks up the ivory, examines it to find its hidden form, and if that's not immediately apparent, carves aimlessly until he sees it, humming or chanting as he works. Then he brings it out: Seal, hidden, emerges. It was always there; he did not create it, he released it, he helped it step forth

(Carpenter 1973: 59). Chunks of ivory, cave or canyon walls are the matrices out of which patterns are derived; one may also view the carved boulders of Monte Alto, Guatemala (Chaves van Dorne 1973) in this way. In the high Andes, the mammoth carvings of natural rock on the hillsides surrounding the north of Cuzco provide another possible example, while in the highlands of Central Mexico, Malinalco's buildings, carved out of solid rock, offer yet another (Marquina 1951).

The art hypothesis argues that the constructors of the Nazca lines recognized particular images in the spaces between the capillary-like empty tributaries that cross the pampa and that they sought to articulate them by carefully removing certain portions of the desert pavement. As we remark in our discussion of the spiral etching near Cantalloc (Appendix I) and as can be noted in Figure I.12a, this figure seems to fit perfectly into the space that contains it. Note that the bends and kinks in the zigzag portion of the figure proceed just to the end of the elevated surface. The same holds for the bird figure in Figure I.12b, whose bulbous tail-feathers penetrate just to the edge of the pampa surface. Therefore, the shape of the frame defined by the dark region between the surrounding *quebradas* may have had something to do with dictating the overall shape of the figure. It only remained for the earth movers to sketch in the zigzag and outline the contours of the compressed labyrinthine spiral. Other examples can be found in which a Nazca figure fits neatly into a natural space (cf. Fig I.12c). Also, in the map of line center No. 35 (Chap. II, Fig. 3(35)), note that line no. 1 opens into a trapezoid precisely at the place where a *quebrada* turns outward, away from the line, after running parallel to it for some distance. The stream bed forms a neat border on the eastern side of the surface upon which the geometry has been etched.

While one can point to a general association between zigzag figures and the flow of water across the pampa, at least one other writer (Rossel 1977: 220–222) has tied the choice of this form to textile art. He contends that the back-and-forth component of certain figures represents the warp and weft of textile weaving. A good example is the figure on the Pampa Sacramento just north of Palpa (Fig. I.7b) in which one sees sets of parallel zigzag lines (like those adjoining the monkey geoglyph in our Fig. I.4e) etched across the pampa in two directions at right angles to one another. Near Arequipa in southern Peru, there is another geoglyph that strikingly resembles a textile (see Kauffmann-Doig 1969: 525), though the chronological provenience of the figure is not at all clear.

On the subject of Nazca geoglyphs as a form of artistic expression, W. Isbell (1978) reminds us that many of the animal species etched on the pampa also can be found in Nazca ceramics.[31] Nasca wares, collected mostly from

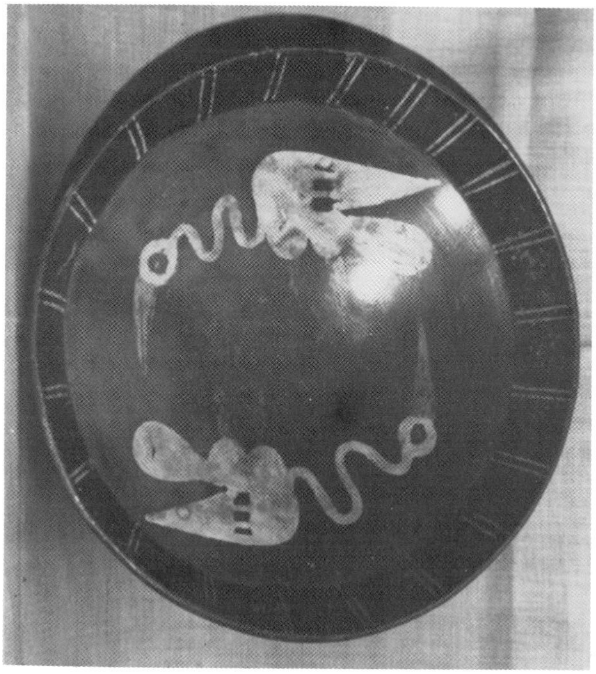

Fig. I.13. Bird-with-a-long-neck on a pot; compare with the biomorphic Nazca geoglyph in Fig. 4i. (Museo Regional, Ica)

mortuary sites near Nazca, date from about 200 BC to AD 600 and fall into several chronological classes. Isbell pictures several Nazca pots on which the animal effigies bear a distinct resemblance to shapes found on the pampa. These include the killer whale (or shark), monkey, lizard, and frigate bird. One vessel in the regional museum at Ica is particularly striking because it displays the figure of a bird (probably a cormorant) with a long zigzag neck that looks very much like an exaggerated bird geoglyph etched on the pampa (cf. Figs. 4i and I.13). Like the biomorphic, figural drawings on the pampa, in nearly all instances the figures on the ceramics are outlined in black.

In a lengthy unpublished work, Yung (n.d.) has identified by species a number of animal figures on the basis of comparison with photos of native South American animals. She proposed an interesting explanation for the highly exaggerated lines that comprise some of the

---

31. Isbell (1978) offers economic determinism as an explanation for the lines. He suggests that they were created as a means of keeping people occupied—a gigantic work project, much like the WPA of World War II. But he never really addresses at a specific level what purpose the lines themselves served. Thus, he puts the cart before the horse when he states that they were

---

"harmoniously a product of social mechanisms for regulating the balance between resources and population" (p. 150). Moreover, no calculation is offered of the amount of energy expended in producing the final product.

figures, contending that the form of the figure may contain information about the behavior of the animal that was known to the builders. For example, she tied the zigzag shape of the neck of the cormorant figure to the motion of the animal when executing an underwater dive in search of fish (Murphy 1936: 872). Urton (personal communication) has remarked that the zigzag shape also mimics the vibratory motion of the animal's neck when he consumes a whole fish. Thus it may be possible that from a study of the biomorphic etchings, we can learn something about the nature of the animal world as perceived by the people who constructed the figures.

CONCLUSIONS

We began this review with the assumption that any informed discussion of the Nazca geoglyphs could benefit from the information and ideas that have emanated from a host of studies conducted both on and off the pampa over the past half-century. In this introductory chapter, we have attempted, with a critical eye, to summarize the relevant literature on the subject and to synthesize and evaluate some of the more important works. We believe that many previous investigators have erred in seeking single, causal explanations for the lines and that too often they have failed to incorporate evidence based upon cultural traits and concepts that existed among the cultures who inhabited that ecologically delicate zone between the coast and the highlands in which the Nazca lines are found.

It is significant that alone of all the ancient artifacts of Peru, the problem of the lines has been tackled almost always from a non-Andean point of view. Research strategies generally have been ethnocentric and have incorporated only a minimum of conceptual information derived from the culture groups which inhabited the region. Perhaps this is because the lines hold the potential to astonish us, as Woodman implies, and we only wish to be astonished, not to explain and understand. Because the lines have attained the status of

"wonder of the world" owing to their repeated reference in the public literature, they also seem to have been labeled "untouchable" by the serious researcher. One is reminded of the course of study of planetary astronomy in the wake of Percival Lowell's Martian Canal hypothesis around the turn of the century. Nearly a generation passed before the professional community of astronomers would turn a serious eye back toward the surface of Mars. Paradoxically, as a result of these developments, the lines, known to tourists from every part of the world, actually have received little serious attention from Andeanists.

Rather than dealing with previous studies in chronological order, we thought it useful to classify and describe them by hypothesis category. Such an exercise offers an excellent means for synthesizing our own research, which is delineated in other chapters of this volume, with the various categories of meaning that have been proposed for the lines. The discussion of the Nazca geoglyphs in the context of one particular hypothesis (e.g., that they were forms of artistic expression), does not preclude the possibility that they also may have functioned at another level (e.g., that they reflected astronomical knowledge). Indeed, we have tried to show that plausible cases can be made for a combination of hypotheses. The lesson implicit in this review may be that too often we see in the lines only that which we are trained or oriented to perceive, or what is most familiar to us. Just as Stonehenge was viewed as a work of precise engineering by engineer Alexander Thom, so, too, the Nazca lines became mathematical entities for mathematics teacher Maria Reiche, and works of earth sculpture for artist Robert Morris. One has the sense that we must stretch to reach beyond our own disciplinary perspectives to comprehend them. The fullest, most satisfying explanation of the etchings on the Nazca pampa will come only when we can shape a collective informed viewpoint derived from the labors and thoughts of all those researchers who have contemplated them most deeply.

## II. *Order in the Nazca Lines*

**A. F. Aveni**

## ORIENTATION AND SOURCES OF INFORMATION

In Chapter I we attempted to review the history of previous investigations of the Nazca lines. There we discovered that one pitfall encountered by many of our predecessors was that perhaps they tended to view the problem of the Nazca lines too monolineally, i.e., they sought a single answer to the engaging question: What is *the* purpose of the Nazca lines? Many assumed a single explanation would suffice for all the observed properties of all the features on the pampa. But there is also a second problem. Most people who visit the pampa tend to view each man-made mark upon it as if it were related to every other mark. In the absence of studies on relative dating, this might seem the simplest, most efficient approach to any study of these curious desert etchings. But can one assume the chalk marks that remain on a classroom blackboard at the end of a busy day were put there at the same time or that they contain the same message?

A close look at the pampa reveals that the surface contains an extraordinary amount of detail, with many figures overlapping and obliterating others. One has the distinct impression that at some time in the past an enormous amount of human activity must have taken place there. Many different morphological categories of features exist upon the desert floor and there is no reason to assume all of them were put there either at the same time or for the same reasons. We find it useful to distinguish among three major classes of Nazca etchings:

(a) Biomorphic (zoo- and phytomorphic) figures—Representations of living animal (the majority) and plant forms. Most of the animals are birds and fish;

(b) Geometry—Abstract forms consisting of triangles, trapezoids, rectangles, spirals, zigzag or meandering patterns, usually made up of straight line segments; and

(c) Straight lines, these being the dominant form.[1]

Our[2] attention was first attracted neither by the highly visible plant and animal figures, nor by the intriguing trapezoids and spirals that had so often enticed other investigators out onto (or over) the pampa. Instead, we were captivated by the long straight lines. We noticed, upon examination of Reiche's map of the northern part of the pampa fronting the Ingenio River, that many lines seemed to converge in what Reiche had called "star-like centers" or "networks" (Reiche 1949a: 31, 36, 48; see esp. map on p. 30). We were able to sharpen our recognition of these "line centers" and particularly to note some interconnections among them after we made an enlargement of one of Reiche's maps (Kern and Reiche 1974: 1) and removed all the features belonging to the morphological classes defined above, *except for the straight lines.* Thus we found, stretched over a 50 sq. km strip of desert floor bordering the south bank of the Ingenio River, four spoked patterns from which a total of 88 lines emanated (or converged). In fact, we failed to trace a single line that did not connect to at least one of these focal points. Moreover, when we followed some of the lines on the ground, we noticed that they seemed to be directed toward other recognizable star-like centers on the other side of the pampa, some of which had been depicted on Reiche's other maps (1949a: 11). However, these other maps, unlike the de-

---

1. Large-scale, man-made phenomena appearing on the pampa have variously been called *drawings, ground drawings,* geoglyphs, figures, features, and most commonly, simply *lines.* We have suggested that they might be called *etchings,* a term that at least describes the process of removal by which they were made. Concerning the geometrical etchings, the word *trapezoid* is a misnomer. Most Nazca trapezoids closely resemble triangles, except that the apex angle often is clipped off and the missing portion replaced with either a triangle of smaller apex angle or, more often, a long, thin rectangle (cf. Fig. 11). Composite trapezoids consisting of combinations of these forms also occur. Geometrical features are sometimes called *plazoletas, pistas* or *avenues* in the literature, as if to suggest a purpose for their use.

Abstract geometrical shapes, such as spirals, zigzags, or other shapes that cannot be identified with any life forms also exist. Often these categories merge, e.g., one figure consists of the head of an insect that degenerates into a series of parallel lines. One also can cite instances in which lines become tied to zigzag patterns that are either saw-toothed (Chap. I, Fig. 6) or that consist of sets of parallel lines joined into a continuous meandering pattern via links at the ends (Chap. I, Fig. 4e).

2. Because a number of individuals have contributed directly and at different stages to the work contained in the present chapter, the collective "we" shall be employed throughout (see also Preface and acknowledgments at the end of this chapter).

tailed plan of the strip of land bordering the Ingenio River, had been sketched at a highly reduced scale, thus exhibiting only the major features.

We were struck by the general resemblance of these line centers to descriptions of the *ceque* system of Cuzco and to the general theme of radiality which seems to be very strongly ingrained in the Andean cultural heritage, a topic we shall discuss in some detail in the next section. Now, as we mentioned in Chap. I, Mejía Xesspe (1927; 1940), the Peruvian archaeologist, already had applied the term *ceque* (*seqe* = line) to the Nazca lines, though not in the specific context of visible lineations that focus at a point. Rather, he had likened the lines to roads, a subject that we also shall explore later in this chapter.

We also recall that the resemblance of the hub-spoke pattern to the *ceque* system is cited, in rather general terms, by Morrison (1978: chap. 5), who mentions Metraux's (1934) early reference to contemporary radial pathways that connect Aymara places of worship in the Bolivian highlands. No doubt encouraged by his appreciation of Hawkins's work, Morrison also hypothesized that the centers might have been astronomical observing stations. Indeed, some of our early work with the extant Nazca maps and photographs on the relative positions of the four centers had tended to support such an idea.

When we closely examined the photographs then available to us, we were surprised at the sheer number of straight lines that crisscrossed every frame we inspected, yet we could find only little descriptive detail about these features in the literature. So much attention had been devoted to the zoomorphic figures, while widths and lengths of lines had scarcely been tabulated. No one seemed to know where most of them began or ended. But these straight features constituted by far the majority of the labor effort and resulting surface area that had been etched out in ancient times. Moreover, we had visible evidence on the photographs that interconnecting patterns of lines existed. What was the extent of this patterning? Did a discoverable concept of

order lay behind it? If so, what principle(s) of organization might have been involved in the construction of the lines and line centers? Specifically, could the patterns we were beginning to observe be conceptually related to a social system we know already existed in Cuzco and which also took the form of radial expression? Because of the incompleteness of data on the lines of Nazca, we simply needed more information about the lines in order to frame answers to these basic questions concerning possible concepts of order in the Nazca lines.

Having divided the Nazca features into several distinct forms and recognizing that one of these forms (the straight line) appeared to be both the most widespread and potentially patterned, we decided to undertake fieldwork on the pampa. Originally, our survey was directed specifically toward answering the following questions about the line centers:

(a) What are the characteristics of the foci of the line centers? Are they on level ground or are they elevated? What topographic features might have led to the selection of these points? Are there any features of human origin associated with the centers?

(b) Can the lines that connect the centers be characterized as visual lines, i.e., is it possible to view a given center from another along a connecting line?

(c) Do the lines extend over the river basins or do they stop at the edge of the bluffs overlooking the drainage, as Reiche's maps seem to imply?

(d) To what extent are the extant maps both accurate and complete with respect to the lines?

(e) Was astronomy a factor in the establishment of either the directions of the lines or the alignment of one center relative to another?

(f) Do the calendar dates that might be associated with any of the alignments to solar rise/set positions possess any significance?[3]

Our plan for retrieving information that

3. We were motivated to ask astronomical questions (e) and (f) because the hypotheses about astronomy and calendar dominated the literature on the Nazca lines at that time (cf. Chap. I).

might enable us to formulate answers to these questions was fairly straightforward:

(1) Obtain all the aerial photographs and maps available over the region between the Nazca and Ingenio Rivers and the Pan American Highway, where most of these features are located. Fig. II.1a illustrates the area in which we proposed to collect the data. The stock of photographic and topographic information concerning the pampa lying between the Ingenio and Nazca Rivers consisted of a 1:25,000 topographic map provided by the Instituto Geografico Militar[4] along with S.A.N. (Servicio Aerofotografico Nacional) low altitude (approximately 1:10,000) survey photos of the river valleys that include the territory lying within 1 or 2 km of the Nazca River bed. The photos do not cover the region in the middle of the pampa between the two rivers, but rather extend to only about 30 percent of the region that attracted our interest. S.A.N. also provided isolated shots of some of the more dramatic features at scales ranging down to approximately 1:1,000. The latter constitute about 2 percent coverage of the pampa and they are the pictures with which most readers may be familiar for they appear in the Reiche, Kosok, and Kern and Reiche texts as well as in other popular works. Also, special overflights commissioned by Hawkins produced a 1:2,000 topographic map of a 10 sq. km strip tangent to the south bank of the Ingenio Valley, where most of the zoo- and phytomorphic figures are laid out. Later, we were fortunate to secure the survey photographs (1:30,000) of W. D. Strong as well as all available unclassified photos of the area from the U.S. Department of Defense (1:50,000).[5] While very helpful, these photographic resources failed to provide us with sufficient detail of all portions of the pampa. Accordingly, we invited the team from the

University of Minnesota Remote Sensing Laboratory to undertake the survey that they reported upon in Chapter VII. The areas within our zone of interest covered by the various sources are indicated in Table 1;

(2) Trace out the lines and line centers visible in the aerial photographs and modify the Kern and Reiche maps to give a more representative view of the linear remains on the desert floor;

(3) Locate the line centers on the ground and investigate their general makeup. Set up a surveyor's transit at each center. Take alignments with an astronomical fix of all lines visible from the ground that depart from the center. Transfer all the transit measurements to the map;

(4) Take measurements of the altitude of the horizon in order to determine: (a) whether any lines departing from the centers might point to distant topographic features (a property that certain *ceque* lines are known to exhibit); and (b) elevation corrections that might be necessary in the astronomical calculations.

Descriptions and measurements of the lines from ground-based observations are extremely rare and even when we find such references, the detail is both sparse and disorganized. Reiche (1968), who has done most of the ground-based work, has focused mostly on the biomorphic figures and the geometrical proportions and astronomical orientation that might be incorporated therein. The studies of Horkheimer (1947), Mejía (1927; 1940), and Rossello Truel (1977) also were essentially ground-based, but all were relatively spotty in their coverage and unsystematic in their approaches. Rossel Castro (1977) mapped at least one line center with the transit but, as we suggested in Chapter I, he did a rather poor job, leaving out a number of lines and using only a magnetic compass to fix the directions of alignment.

Hawkins (1969), who produced the most detailed photographic survey of a well-defined small segment of the pampa, evidently did little more on the ground than to establish an azimuthal baseline for a photo-

---

4. We express our gratitude to Servicio Aerofotografico Nacional (Lima, Peru) for selected aerial photos. We are grateful to Peter G. Park, Freedom Information Officer of the U.S. Dept. of Defense, for making the Defense Intelligence Agency photos available. Also, thanks to Gerald Hawkins for sending us a large-scale map of the zone he surveyed.
5. Prepared under the direction of the U.S. Department of Defense and published by the U. S. Army Topographic Command.

---

**TABLE 1**
**PHOTOGRAPHIC & MAP RESOURCES EMPLOYED IN THE PRESENT INVESTIGATION OF THE NAZCA LINES**

| PHOTOGRAPHS | TOTAL AREAL COVERAGE OF THE PAMPA (sq. km) | PRINT SCALE | DATE | SPECIFIC AREA COVERED |
|---|---|---|---|---|
| W. D. Strong Survey, Columbia University | 250 | 1:30,000 | 1952 | Rectangular area, corners marked roughly by 60x10, 50x05; 73x90, 70x80 on IGM Nazca, Palpa, and Tunca Hacienda 1:50,000 sheets. |
| Servicio Aerofotografico Nacional (SAN) | 10 | 1:5,000 | 1954–1960 | Widespread selected areas. |
| Reiche & Kern-Reiche (SAN) | 10 | Various, down to 1:2,000 | 1950s & 1960s | Widespread selected areas, mostly centered on 75x87 on IGM Nazca 1:50,000. |
| U. S. Defense Intelligence Agency | 175 | 1:50,000 | 1955 & 1963 | Three rectangles, corners marked by 1) 81x72, 81x77; 90x72, 90x77; 2) 61x85, 61x07; 67x85, 67x07; 3) 92x61, 92x53; 61x05, 53x05 on IGM Nazca, Palpa, and Tunca Hacienda 1:50,000 sheets. |
| Instituto Geografico Militar (IGM) | 250 | 1:50,000 | 1956 | Entire pampa. |
| Hawkins (SAN) | 3.5 | 1:2,000 | 1968 | 2.5x1.3 km strip along S bank of Rio Ingenio. |
| University of Minnesota Remote Sensing Laboratory | 150 | 1:10,000 & 1:5,000 | 1984 | Parallelogram, corners marked by 60x02, 60x88; 74x89, 74x77 on IGM Nazca, Palpa, and Tunca Hacienda 1:50,000 sheets. |
| University of Minnesota Remote Sensing Laboratory | 2 | 1:2,000 | 1984 | Centered on 97.5x61.5 on IGM Tunca Hacienda 1:50,000 sheet. |
| MAPS | | | | |
| Ministero de Agricultura (Ica) | 250 | 1:25,000 | 1955(?) | Entire pampa. |
| IGM | 250 | 1:50,000 | 1962 | Entire pampa. |

---

grammetric aerial survey of a thin strip of the pampa; however, he did collect ceramics in a surface survey (see Chap. III for a detailed discussion). Even though Hawkins's survey map is presented at a relatively expanded scale, it is still incomplete, as we learned when we discovered additional features and a greater wealth of detail to be visible from the ground than he had mapped from the air.

Even with all the aerial photographic resources at our command to help locate lines and line centers, we felt it vitally important to collect basic data *on the ground*, though we often could refer back to the maps and aerial photos to assist us. Our reasons for this ground-based strategy are manifold:

First, the lines were made on the ground by human beings. Second, if one is concerned with the directions of the lines, the most direct and accurate method of data collection would consist of making ground-based measurements with the transit using an astronomical fix.[6] Third, this ground-based survey method means that the visible horizon can be viewed and measured directly, thus allowing for ele-

---

6. Essentially, this means the alignments surveyed are referred to readings taken on some astronomical object, usually the sun. By taking a simultaneous reading of the time, one can refer the resulting map of a set of features to *true north*, which is far more reliable than the ever-changing (and quite different) north given by the magnetic compass. For a discussion of the method, as well as of the pitfalls entailed in the use of the magnetic compass for survey maps, see Aveni 1980b: Chap. II, Apps. E and G and Aveni 1981a).

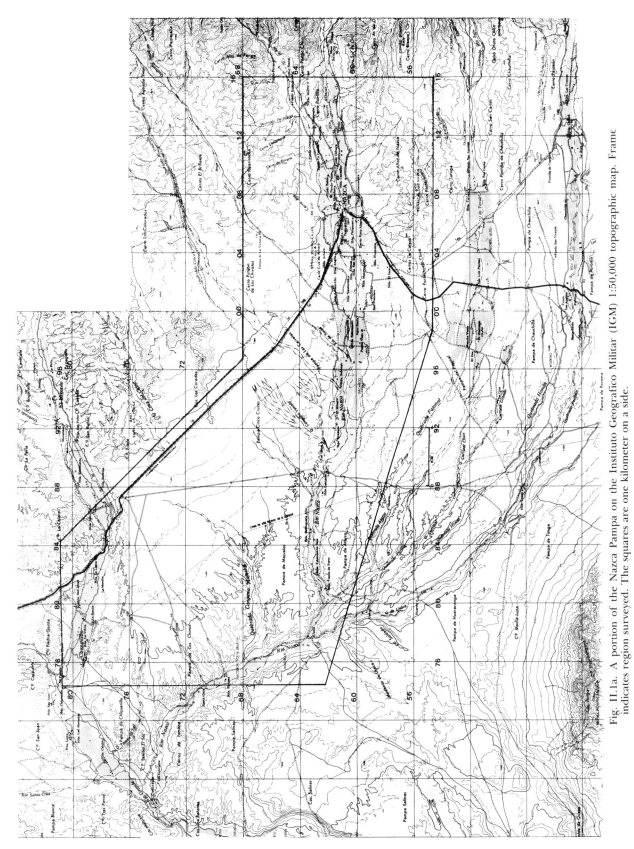

Fig. II.1a. A portion of the Nazca Pampa on the Instituto Geografico Militar (IGM) 1:50,000 topographic map. Frame indicates region surveyed. The squares are one kilometer on a side.

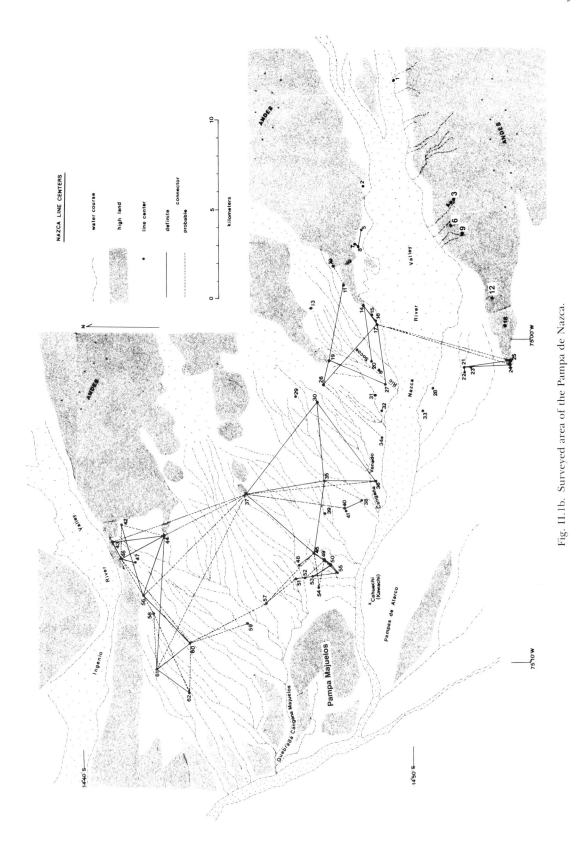

Fig. II.1b. Surveyed area of the Pampa de Nazca.

vation corrections affecting possible astronomical orientations to be assessed without recourse to photogrammetry or other secondary techniques. Also, working on the ground, one has a better sense of whether the local topography might have influenced the placement and/or orientation of certain features.

Finally, ground-based work forces the researcher to spend long periods of time in the vicinity of each feature, where subtle details might be perceived. Thus a great deal of our time was occupied walking the lines, many of them to their termination points. As a result, we could examine and record cultural remains along the way, and study at close range the superposition of features, items which could be examined only superficially on the aerial photographs.

On our first field trip in July 1981, we proceeded to test some of the ruler-and-compass propositions that we had derived from our initial study of the aerial photographs. We had planned during this particular expedition to: (a) locate and map the four centers we had noted on Reiche's map (Nos. 44, 56, 58, and 61 on our Fig. II.1b); (b) collect information with the transit on the alignments and basic dimensions of the member lines; (c) describe the physical features at the horizon toward which the lines were directed; and (d) obtain as rich a qualitative description of each line as possible by walking it.

Once we arrived at Nazca, our plans were immediately altered by the discovery of a fifth line center (No. 35 in the present nomenclature), one we indeed had expected might exist, for we could already notice the apparent convergence of lines off the southeastern edge of both Reiche's and Hawkins's large-scale maps. When we began walking some of the lines adjacent to the Pan American Highway in order to approach center No. 35 from the east, we also discovered centers No. 30, 37, and 11.[7] On the last day of our first month

in the field, we found center No. 19, thus bringing the total to nine well-documented, mapped line centers spread over 50 square kilometers of desert floor.

With but nine candidates recorded, a remarkable likeness among these centers of radiating lines already began to appear. Examining our data, we were able to enhance our definition of "line center" by realizing that all these features shared some specific characteristics, thus:

A *line center* consists of one or several natural hills or mounds often topped by one or more piles of boulders and from which several lines of various widths emanate. Most centers are found to be situated in that part of the pampa where the last hill can be seen to descend from the mountains and, like a finger, project westward out onto the flat surface. Many centers are located on small hills shaped by the Nazca and Ingenio drainage. All seem to be situated on quite prominent headlands from which one can see a considerable distance.

Since we had found a few line centers on the banks of the Ingenio River, we began to wonder whether the banks of the Nazca River also might be dotted with such features. If so, was the frequency of occurrence of centers higher near the denser areas of settlement or near ceremonial places, such as the site of Cahuachi on the south bank of the Nazca River? Also, did the density of centers decrease as one moved northward onto the relatively featureless terrain of the pampa between the Nazca and Ingenio Rivers? Thus, the bank of the Nazca River became the starting point for our next field season and our questions became more refined. If we found line centers there, we planned to proceed with a systematic survey on foot that gradually moved northward out onto the pampa from the north bank of the Nazca River. This would be the only way to determine once and for all whether results concerning the number and degree of interconnectedness of line centers, derived from a concentrated search around the rim of the pampa, might be spurious.

7. The last was located well away from the region of investigation originally proposed, on an adjacent pampa fronting the Río Socos, a tributary of the Nazca River. Thus, we decided to extend the survey zone. Also, we later discovered that some of these centers had indeed already been indicated on Reiche's small-scale sketch maps.

Before moving on to a discussion of the data that we collected in order to try to resolve some of these questions, it is necessary to divert ourselves in order to acquire useful information already present in the record of Andean culture that relates to linear patterns and especially to a single remarkable system incorporating concepts of social order based upon lines organized in a radial pattern—the *ceque* system of Cuzco.

## RADIALITY IN ANCIENT ANDEAN SYSTEMS OF THOUGHT

Of all the reasons that might be given for the success of the Inka empire, one that must be regarded quite seriously is the strict order that attended every aspect or component of it. Thanks to the writings of the Spanish chroniclers, the Inka capital of Cuzco is one of the few places in the ancient Andean world on which we have any reliable data about how cities were planned and organized. As the work of Zuidema (e.g., 1964; 1977a; 1981b; 1982b) and others (Duviols 1967; Rowe 1979a) on the principles of organization of Cuzco has demonstrated, highland concepts of both time and space are inextricably bound to religious, social, and political organizing principles in the structural plan of the city. These principles can be understood only in their totality; they lose their meaning once we attempt to break them down into separate spheres of concern. Moreover, the system is *radial* in its basic layout, a form that seems very special and important in Andean society, and it is precisely this property of the Nazca lines that attracted us.

In this section, we examine briefly the chroniclers' descriptions of the city of Cuzco to reveal how time, space, and social principles were incorporated into the Inka scheme of radial organization. One hopes this examination of a system which is historically recorded will generate more definitive ways of comparing the details of Cuzco's structure with the radiating lines at Nazca. In this task we shall follow rather closely the descriptions, analyses, and notational schemes developed by Zuidema.

Cuzco is situated in latitude 13½°S (about 1°N and 2½°E of Nazca) at the junction of two rivers in a high (alt. 3240 m) mountain valley in the central Andes. The city is segmented into halves called Hanan- (northwestern, upper) and Hurin- (southwestern, lower) Cuzco, and each half into two sectors, or *suyus* (see Urton's paper (Chap. IV) for a discussion of the concept of *suyu*). However, none of these four regions occupies a 90° segment of a circle. The principle rationale for dividing the city has to do with the watershed environment rather than with any considerations of pure geometry. The boundaries between *suyus* demarcate the flow of underground water in the Cuzco valley. They were intended to serve as an organizing principle to delineate water rights to those who live in the various kin-related groups called *ayllus*. These people receive, by right of birth, the underground water directly from their ancestors who are believed to reside within the earth. The four major roads leading out of Cuzco serve as the dividing lines among the *suyus*, which extend to the remotest domains of the Inka empire. Cuzco itself was called Tawantinsuyu (= four quarters) by the Inka. *Suyus* were ranked, as were the kinship groups who lived within them, the organizing principle generally having to do with whether they were located up- or down-river.

As revealed through the descriptions of the chroniclers, the *ceque* system seems to have been a mnemonic device built into Cuzco's natural and man-made topography that served to unify ideas about religion, social organization, hydrology, calendar, and astronomy. Attesting to its general importance, the chronicler P. Bernabe Cobo in his *Historia del Nuevo Mundo*, completed in 1653 (1890–95: Book 13, chaps. 13–16), has given us a thorough description of the system. It appears to have consisted not only of *suyus*, but also a number of imaginary radial lines of sight that were grouped zonally according to their location within each of the four *suyus* that went out in more or less intercardinal directions. These *ceques* emanated from the Coricancha (mistakenly called by the Spaniards the Temple of the Sun [see Fig. II.2a]). Actually this was the most important temple of ancestor worship and was related as much to the underworld as it was to the heavens. Cobo lists nine *ceques* associated with each of the quadrants: the northeast (centered around the district named Chinchaysuyu), southeast (Antisuyu), and southwest (Colla-suyu), while 14 were associated with the northwest (Cuntisuyu) quadrant, making a total of 9 + 9 + 9 + 14, or 41 lines.

According to Cobo's description, each *ceque* was traceable by a line of *huacas,* or sacred places in the landscape. These *huacas,* which number 328 in all, according to the interpretation of Zuidema, are said to be temples (natural or man-made), arrangements of stones, bends in rivers, fields, springs or other natural wells called *puquios,* hills, even impermanent objects such as trees. In most cases, the water theme and its association with the agricultural calendar are given extreme emphasis.

For example, "The seventh (huaca of the 8th ceque of the Chinchaysuyu quadrant of the city) was called Sucanca. It was a hill by way of which the water channel from Chinchero comes. On it there were two markers as an indication that when the sun arrived there, they had to begin to plant the maize. The sacrifice which was made there was directed to the sun, asking him to arrive there at the time which would be appropriate to planting, and they sacrificed to him sheep, clothing, and miniature lambs of gold and silver" (Rowe 1979a: 27 [author's parentheses]). Note the rather concrete information about both the flow of water and the sky in this particular passage.

According to Cobo, each *ceque* was assigned one of a set of three names that represented the social classes that tended to them:

(a) *collana:* "First or most prominent", said to be maintained and worshipped by the primary kin of the Inka ruler, that is, by the aristocratic class;

(b) *payan:* worshipped by his subsidiary kin, formed by the union of *collana* men with non-*collana* women who were chosen as subsidiary wives;

(c) *callao:* tended to by that segment of the population not related to the ruler.

The assignments on the hierarchy of worship rotated sequentially as one proceeded from one *ceque* to the next, all the way around the horizon in a clockwise direction in the northern *suyus,* counterclockwise in the south.

The arrangement and classification of *ceques* in a social context are not only very orderly but also quite detailed. They include a vast amount of information about the interrelationships among Cuzco's various social classes. At the risk of oversimplification, the following general categories of social information can be enumerated:

(1) The placement of *ceques* in various quadrants conveys information about the various kin groups (*panacas*) deriving from the royal bloodline around the Cuzco valley. Each *panaca* was said to have originated from the primary descendants of an Inka ruler. The arrangement of *ceques,* therefore, also conveys information about the history of the mythical descent of rulership in Cuzco up to the time of its founding by real leaders claimed to have descended from them;

(2) The systematic arrangement of *ceques* pertains to the relationship among groups belonging to a specific territory (*suyu*) in the capital, even if all the members necessarily do not possess blood ties;

(3) The organization of ritual and work activities, particularly having to do with agriculture and irrigation, also was regulated by the *ceque* system, e.g., representatives of each of 40 families drawn from the *suyus* participated in the ritual plowing that took place annually in the plaza of Hurin-Cuzco, each delegate plowing a designated portion (Zuidema 1977b: 236–237). Even rules for the servicing and maintenance of the irrigation canals were specified by the order of the *ceques* (Sherbondy n.d.);

And finally, as Zuidema (1964: 51) has shown,

(4) The arrangement of *ceques* in the four *suyus* also delineates information on marriage classes.

In sum, the *ceque* system may be considered a rather complex kinship map based upon residence and ancestor worship in a radial and quadripartite geographic framework.

From Cobo's description, Zuidema and the author have attempted to map the system by undertaking a thorough reconnaissance of the Cuzco landscape. We found, indeed, that several *ceques* could still be traced today and that these did not deviate from a straight line by more than a few degrees (Fig. II.2b).

Upon attempting to map the system, we had occasion to trace *ceque* lines that pass straight over the high-relief topography of the Cuzco valley to distant invisible horizons. For example, in the case of the *ceque* containing the *huaca* Sucanca (described above), we discovered the most remote *huaca* at a distance of 13 km from the Coricancha after we followed the *ceque* radially outward over six consecutive hills, each one blocking the view of the next. We traced the *ceque* with our transit all the way to its termination point, a *huaca* called Collanasayba, which we were able to identify in the landscape on the basis of Cobo's written description of it. This rock outcrop, adjacent to some old Inka walls, was located at a prominent bend in the river that flows down from the mountains. Cobo tells us that the terminal *huacas* of many *ceques* lay at positions where the water flow changed directions. Collanasayba would have been an ideal place to throw offerings brought from Cuzco into the river, a practice often referred to by the chroniclers.

Some of the published work of Zuidema (1981b; 1982b) and the author (Aveni 1981b) on the location of astronomical sightings in the *ceque* system is based upon descriptions of Inka astronomical principles given by several chroniclers. The ethnohistoric, astronomical, and archaeological evidence has led us to the conclusion that the Inka sighting schemes made use of several observation points in the environment of Cuzco from which particular *huacas* along the horizon were employed to mark the positions of important celestial objects at key times of the year. By direct sighting of sunrises and sunsets over named *huacas*,

the Inka could preserve, without the necessity of writing as we know it, a record of the most important dates of the tropical year. If we are to invite detailed comparison with Nazca, we must understand something of the astronomical concepts and sighting methods that survive in the ancient Andean record, even though they might emanate from a time and place somewhat removed from Nazca.

When discussing the role of astronomical alignments in the *ceque* system, we must emphasize that astronomical sight lines seem to be related to certain *huacas* of particular *ceques;* but not every *ceque* and *huaca* are necessarily related to astronomy. This is a very important point to keep in mind if we wish to begin to make comparisons between Nazca lines and the *ceque* system. Contrary to Hawkins's assumption (see Chap. I, p. 19), we should not employ the working hypothesis that all the lines need to test out as astronomical. Again for want of space, we shall attempt only to summarize the general role of astronomy in the *ceque* system. We invite the interested reader to explore the abundant and detailed literature on this subject (Zuidema 1977; 1981b; 1982b; Aveni 1981b and references cited therein).

Objects sighted at the horizon by the Inka included the sun at the solstices, and on the zenith and anti-zenith passage dates, the bright stars $\alpha$ and $\beta$ Centauri (called by the Inka the "eyes of the llama" constellation), the Southern Cross, and the Pleiades (a *collca* or storehouse). Many of the stellar alignments can be connected with dates of heliacal rise and set of these objects,[8] these events having served as timing devices to mark the agricultural and ritual calendar. The following alignments can be traced specifically in the environment of Cuzco:

---

8. One of the fundamental timing mechanisms utilized in Cuzco (Zuidema 1981b) is based upon a scheme that associates the movement of the sun throughout the year with that of the stars, the horizon serving as a reference. As the sun changes its position relative to the stars over the course of the year, stars can be seen to make their first and last appearance at the ho-

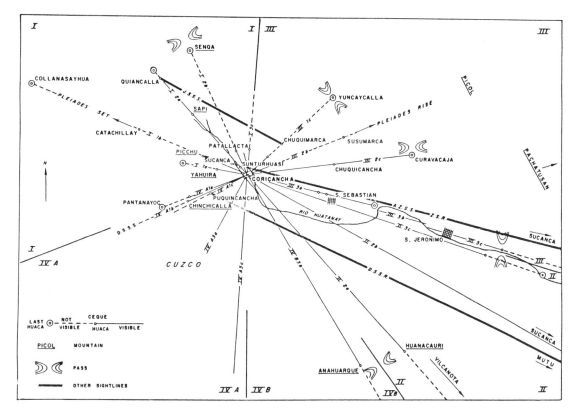

Fig. II.2a. left. Coricancha, center of the *ceque* system. Church of Sto. Domingo is built over a remnant of the Inka wall (dark structure at the bottom).
Fig. II.2b. below. Map of the valley of Cuzco with some of the *ceques* delineated. Roman numerals indicate the four divisions of the city. (Zuidema 1982b)

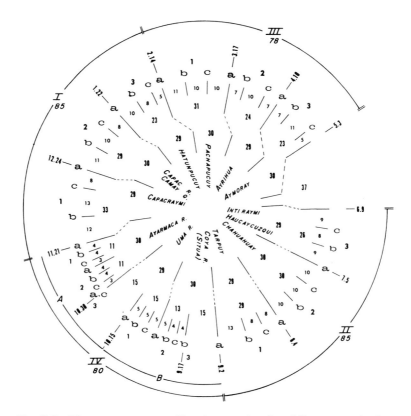

Fig. II.2c. The *ceque* system considered as a *quipu* that delineates a calendar. Numbers of *huacas* per *ceque* are given inside the alphabetic letters which indicate rank (*collana*, *payan*, or *callao*) according to worship by various kinship groups. Names of the lunar months are printed at the center. (Zuidema 1982b)

(a) The 13th *ceque* of the Cuntisuyu (SW) quadrant (*ceque* IV$_A$1b in Zuidema's 1964 scheme) functioned as an astronomical sight line to the setting sun at the December (sum-

---

rizon at various times during the annual cycle. Because the dates are reckoned with respect to the position of the sun, we term the apparitions and disappearances the *heliacal risings* and *settings*. Four such timing events may be recognized, two of which take place when a star is rising (i.e., on the eastern horizon) and two when it is setting (on the western horizon) (Aveni 1972). The intervals between these timing events have the following characteristics:

(a) The time between the first rising at morning twilight to the last visibility on the opposite (eastern) horizon in the evening twilight. At the end of this period, the star is visible the whole night;

(b) At the middle of this generally brief period between visibility on the eastern horizon at dusk and at the western horizon at dawn, the star reaches its greatest altitude at midnight;

(c) This interval is marked from visibility on the western horizon at dawn to the last day on which the star is visible in the west after sunset;

(d) The time between last visibility in the west after sunset and the first visibility in the east before sunrise constitutes a period of invisibility.

mer) solstice (labeled D.S.S.S. in Fig. II.2b). A pair of man-made pillars mentioned by Cobo likely served as the foresight, the observer having been situated in the Coricancha, 3 km to the NE where he could witness them framing the sun against the skyline on the hill Chinchincalla;

(b) The June (winter) solstice sunset position also was marked by a pair of pillars at the visible horizon (J.S.S.S. in Fig. II.2b). These constituted the *huaca* of Quiangalla (*ceque* 6, *huaca* 9 of Cuntisuyu; Zuidema number I2a), a hill by the side of the road to Yucay. In this case, the astronomical sight line was not a *ceque*. Instead, the observer stood on another *huaca*, Chuquimarca (IIIlc), of another *ceque* to make the observation;

(c) The December solstice sunrise point (D.S.S.R. in Fig. II.2b) was observed in a similar manner from a *huaca* of another *ceque*. It was related to a mountain (Mutu) to the SE of

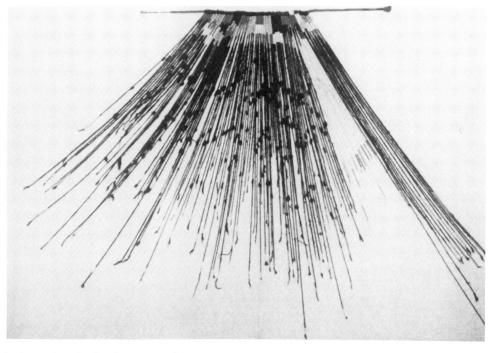

Fig. II.2d. Andean *quipu.* (Regional Museum of Ica). Courtesy Persis Clarkson.

Cuzco that served to orient one along the direction of a pilgrimage undertaken by priests at the time of the solstice; the course took one up the Vilcanota River toward its point of origination. (A down-river pilgrimage also took place at the June solstice, the time in the annual cycle opposite the December solstice.) At the end, about 100 km from Cuzco, sacrifices were offered to the place where the sun was born. This up-river direction, extended radially from Cuzco, passes through the island of Copacabana in the center of Lake Titicaca, thus following the mythic course of the god Viracocha, who led forth the sun out of the underworld;

(d) One of the most important calendrical determinations associated with astronomical alignments in Cuzco was the traditional date of the start of the planting season, a day occurring in mid-August when the sun arrived at its position opposite the zenith (the anti- zenith).[9] There is evidence that this day

was incorporated into the *ceque* system via the reversal of a much longer alignment to the rising sun on the day it passed the zenith. This straight line in the landscape, connecting sun positions at horizon on the days of zenith and "anti-zenith" passage (Z.S.R. & A.Z.S.S. in Fig. II.2b), was a reflection in horizontal space of the vertical/anti-vertical dualism that is such an important part of Andean ecology and cosmic thought (B.J. Isbell 1978: 197–220). An anonymous chronicler (Maurtua 1906 [1570?]) describes the passage of the sun by the four pillars on Cerro Picchu around this time of year. The pillars, only two of which Cobo mentions, were the Sucanca of the 7th *huaca* of the 8th *ceque* of Chinchaysuyu quadrant (IIb) that we described earlier and that overlooked Cuzco from high on the NW horizon. The observer stood somewhere in the present-day Plaza de Armas, a few hundred meters from Coricancha, and watched the sun set. Note that again in this case *the ceque* itself was not the sight line, and that the center of the *ceque* system was not

9. The usual term, "nadir," for the point opposite the zenith, is somewhat misleading for it usually carries the unwarranted notion that the Inka conceived of the universe as a spherical framework, the nadir being a point in three-dimensional space co-equal with the zenith. We prefer the term, "anti-zenith,"

which is intended to connote the time in the seasonal calendar that was the reciprocal of that when the sun passed overhead.

always the point from which the observations were made. More likely, the sighting station was the *Ushnu*, "a fountain of well-worked stone one estado high" (Maurtua 1906: 150–152) that once stood in the plaza. Sightings also were made from the Suntur-huasi, a large cylindrical building with a cone-shaped roof that the chronicler Guaman Poma describes as an observatory with windows. Evidently the time for planting in different elevations in that vertical environment of Cuzco was marked out by the day-to-day horizontal course of the sun across the row of pillars. It should be noted that the planting dates in the Valley of Cuzco coincide closely, though not precisely, with one of the sun's anti-zenith passage dates.

We believe that the recognition of the importance of these dates in the agricultural season and the discovery that they coincided with one of the signal, conveniently visible celestial phenomena in the environment of Cuzco probably led the Inka, or more likely, their predecessors, to regard the two as going together—thus, the metaphoric association between both man and the sun penetrating the earth;

(e) In a similar manner, the association of planting, water, irrigation, and the Pleiades star group probably developed when people recognized an approximate equivalence between the period of absence (about 40 days) of the prominent star group from the sky and the time from the end of the harvest to the beginning of the next planting season. Thus, we found that the west wall of Coricancha and its principal doorway were oriented to the Pleiades' rise position, a direction which is also traced by *ceque* III2b (Zuidema 1982: 212–215). The star group would reappear along this *ceque* line about 6–9 June to signal formally the commencement of the month of planting. There is also a western orientation incorporated into the *ceque* system to mark the point of disappearance of the Pleiades 40 days earlier;

(f) The celestial llama is another important astronomical construct represented in *ceque* alignments. Its body is formed by the dark cloud called the Coalsack near our constellation of the Southern Cross (Zuidema and Urton 1976; Urton 1981), and its eyes are represented by the bright stars $\alpha$ and $\beta$ Centauri. This llama also has been intimately associated with the agricultural calendar in highland Peru. Each month of the year, one hundred llamas of different color categories (white, brown, and "multi-colored") were sacrificed. The animals were brought to Cuzco in great numbers for this ritual. For example, the chronicler Molina tells us that in September (the month of planting), large numbers of animals due to be sacrificed in the next year were brought in from the fields where they had grazed during the post-harvest season. A schedule of llama-sacrifices associated with the heliacal rising and setting as well as upper and lower culmination[10] of the llama constellation also is implied (see Zuidema 1982: 225 and elsewhere for a more detailed discussion of llama rituals connected with agriculture). In the *ceque* system, the rising and setting points of the llama's eyes are neatly framed by the boundary *ceques* of the southernmost *suyu* ($IV_A/I$ and $IV_B/II$ in Fig. II.2b). These stars and only a few other bright stars visible from Cuzco have the special quality of being perpetually visible.[11]

Finally, the *ceque* map can be viewed not only as a directional device that points to significant horizon events but also as a solar calendar with each *huaca* representing one-day clusters of *ceques* that signify both lunar sidereal and lunar synodic months[12] (Fig. II.2c).

10. I.e., the dates when at morning or evening twilight the constellation stands at its highest or lowest position in the sky.
11. These are the so-called "quasi-circumpolar" stars (Zuidema 1982b: 210); they are visible for at least a brief period of time on every night of the year *even though they are not circumpolar*. Therefore, they exhibit the capacity to be employed as time markers throughout the year. It has been argued that such stars may have been recognizable as a unique class of celestial objects in the astronomy of Cuzco.
12. The synodic month is that measured by the lunar phases (approx. 29½ days), while the sidereal is that indicated by the movement of the moon with respect to the stars (approx. 27⅓ days). The numbers of the *ceques* (41) and the *huacas* (328) imply a calendrical significance associated with the sidereal month interval; for example, $2 \times 41 = 82$, or three sidereal lunar months ($3 \times 27⅓$), while 328 is exactly equal to 12 lunar sidereal periods. It was these coincidences that first led Zuidema (1977a) to explore the possibility that not only spatial directions

The Inka adjusted these month periods slightly in order to force them to correspond to significant periods in the agricultural cycle, such as the time of plowing, planting, the appearance of water, and harvesting. There was much concern that certain feasts and ritual activities be celebrated during a period commenced by a named full moon. This is not unlike our antiquated habit of beginning the harvest during the month initiated by the appearance of the Harvest Moon or of opening hunting season with the Hunter's Moon. The 12 months of the lunar synodic calendar were divided among the population of Cuzco and vicinity in such a way that each socio-political group was assigned the responsibility to tend to the ceremonies and sacrifices performed at the *huacas* that were associated with their particular month of the year in the calendar-counting scheme.

The description of the *ceques* and their linear radial hierarchical structure is reminiscent of Andean *quipus* or knotted string recording devices. The *quipu* (dust jacket) constituted a tactile form of language—rather like Braille. A typical *quipu* consisted of a thick cotton cord (the primary cord) from which were suspended thinner subsidiary cords, each containing clusters of knots according to a decimal system. Hierarchically, the cords may be likened to *ceques* and the knots to *huacas*. Often, additional cords dangled from the subsidiaries, the hierarchical scheme sometimes reaching the 5th order (Conklin 1982; see also Ascher and Ascher 1981 for other examples). Yet the *quipu* was capable of carrying more information than Braille-like writing for it also included a visual element. In many cases, the cords exhibited different colors and color combinations and alternating directions of twisting of the component fiber.

The importance of the *quipu* is well attested to in the chronicles; for example, Guaman Poma (1980 [1584–1614]) discusses and illustrates the duties of *quipu-kamayoc*, or *quipu* specialists, and Garcilaso de la Vega's (1966

[1609]) lengthy writings on the subject leave no doubt that one of the primary functions of the *quipu* was accounting. According to the chronicler Matienzo (1967 [1567], ch. XXXVI), the original description of the *ceque* system was transcribed from a *quipu*, though we have no direct evidence that the *ceque* system itself was conceived as a *quipu*.

Do any of the calendric principles evident in the *ceque* system of Cuzco turn up in other Andean frameworks? Recently, Urton and Aveni (1983) studied potential astronomical orientations of some of the major ceremonial centers on the coast of Peru. We found quite good correlations between the horizon positions of the Pleiades and the facing directions of major structures at Batan Grande, Pacatnamú, Huaca de la Luna, Chavín (not really a coastal site), and Chan Chan. A somewhat weaker correlation, but still a positive one, was found between the zenith/anti-zenith sun directions and buildings at Cerro Sechin, Paramonga, Tambo Colorado, and Cahuachi. The last two sites are situated on the south coast; Cahuachi (cf. Fig. II. 1b) lies rather close to the Nazca lines (also see Chap. V by Silverman). The doorway of the Huaca del Loro, a Late Nasca period round structure, includes a range of azimuths that would have neatly accommodated the rising position of both the anti-zenith sun and the Pleiades. At Tambo Colorado, the convergence of two astronomical sight lines, one involving the zenith sun, focuses on the point of the nearby horizon where one attains the last glimpse of Tambo passing out of the valley along the road to Cuzco.

Urton's (1982) studies of coastal calendrics, based on ethnographic and ethnohistoric documents, reveal a continuity between the calendars present there and those used to regulate activities in the highland region. But, as one might expect, the ecology of the desert coast and the delicate transitional region between coast and highland (where Nazca is located), with its markedly different seasonal pattern, results in a slightly different way of ordering temporal events. Marine cycles, periodicities relating to the flowering of the landscape, and

_____

but also time periods determinable from astronomical observations might have been integrated into the *ceque* system.

the availability of water are among the most important environmental correlates in these calendars.

Among those groups exploiting resources in the higher reaches of the coastal valleys, Urton finds more complex calendars that reflect the impact of a number of ecological zones (Urton 1982: 233–235). He has been able to relate satisfactorily the appearance and disappearance of the Pleiades to combined agricultural and fishing cycles in some of these communities. He notes that the anti-zenith sun passage (10 April) in the Moche/Huanchaco calendar of the north coast coincides with the beginning of the disappearance period of the Pleiades. The use of the Pleiades' period of absence from the sky as a rough indicator of an interim period of ecological significance and the tying of these phenomena to zenith/anti-zenith sun passages is reminiscent of the calendar of Cuzco. Urton also finds considerable evidence for the use of the heliacal rise/set of Orion's Belt, the Southern Cross, and several dark cloud constellations as timing devices within these subsistence calendars. In each instance, he suspects there were "seasonal boundaries that formed the 'core' periodicities" (e.g., the periodicities in the flow of river water), upon which more elaborate calendars, related to the exploitation of more diverse ecological zones, must have been built. "A coastal society's ability to efficiently coordinate the resources and human activities of its river valley would have been a determining factor in the relative success or failure of its cultural tradition" (Urton 1982: 244–245).

Before we end the discussion of the general structural properties of the *ceque* system and return to the lines on the pampa, we should discuss some of the subtle constructional nuances of the arrangement of *ceques* and their *huacas* that actually mirror what we find on the pampa. For example, there is some evidence in the *ceque* system of Cuzco for two major structural features that we also find (and will later describe in detail) on the pampa:

(a) the linkage of radiating lines to points (evident on the pampa in the map of Fig.

II.1b) that also serve as centers of emanation; thus, in the *ceque* system:

(b) the chain-linking of features in a linear pattern, such as is illustrated in Fig. 11, wherein one finds an alternation of line-triangle-line-triangle line, etc. proceeding in one direction across the pampa; thus, in the *ceque* system:

In connection with the first property, Cobo, in his description of the *ceque* system, uses the notion of principal *huacas* to imply that they are central to a hierarchical arrangement. For example, Huanacauri (Zuidema 1981b: Fig. 26.5), one of the *huacas* of the *ceque* system (the 7th of the 6th *ceque* of Collasuyu), was also one of the most sacred mountains in the environment. It is referred to by Cobo (Rowe 1979a: 47) as: ". . . the oldest which the Inkas had after the window (cave) of Pacaritampu, and where the most sacrifices were made . . . ." Huanacauri is also the starting point of a pilgrimage that took place in the month containing the June solstice and was intended to celebrate the birth of the sun. It was conducted over a complex 21-stop course described by Zuidema (1981b: 330–331). This pilgrimage proceeded in a linear direction that followed the Vilcanota River upstream to a place known to the Spanish as La Raya or "dividing line" (also called the village of Vilcanota, after House [*nota*] of the sun [*villca*] in Aymara) What is also interesting about this straight line course is that it points in the general direction of SE, the region of the December solstice sunrise. One of its stopping points, Omotoyanacauri, may have been the place from which the Inka precisely observed the December solstice sunrise from a sun temple (Puquincancha) in Cuzco proper (Zuidema 1981b: 331). There is some evidence (Zuidema 1981b: Fig. 26.4) that this straight line emanating from Huanacauri may have continued well past Vilcanota, all the way to the Island of the Sun in Lake Titicaca where the sun was alleged to have been born and from whence the Inka were alleged to have come.

Let us deal next with the second property, that of the linking together of *ceques*. In tracing certain *ceque* lines across the landscape, Zuidema (e.g., 1981b: Fig. 26.6) has remarked about a few instances in which some groups of *ceques* with separate and distinct names seem to fit together in a kind of chain link pattern. Certain of these *ceques*, in particular the terminal ones of Antisuyu and Cuntisuyu, clearly do not begin at Coricancha; rather they commence close to a position where a neighboring *ceque* terminates—thus, the 8th *ceque* of Cuntisuyu quadrant (Zuidema No. IV$_A$3a,c), half of which was named Callao and the other half Collana. It was clearly formed of two linear chains of *huacas* linked together, though "the whole of it had 15 guacas" (Rowe 1979a: 57), an unusually large number of *huacas* for a single *ceque*. The first *ceque* of the Cuntisuyu quadrant, IV$_B$3b, exhibits similar properties. Also, it bears the unique name of Anahuarque (the others are either Collana, Payan, or Callao).

It is curious that both these doubled *ceques* appear in the Cuntisuyu quadrant which, unlike the other *suyus*, possesses 14 rather than the usual 9 *ceques*. Other structural peculiarities also are evident in this quadrant. For example, it seems to have been divided in half spatially, one zone being comprised of 7 *ceques* containing 43 *huacas*, the other consisting of 7 *ceques* and 37 *huacas*. The latter zone contains a large number of consecutive *ceques* with small numbers of *huacas*, thus: 3, 4, 4, 3, 4, 4 which immediately follow the rather overpopulated *ceque* IV$_A$3a,c.

Finally, a group of three *ceques* is linked together in the Antisuyu quadrant (the 7th, 8th, and 9th; III3a,b,c). At least the topographic and documentary evidence makes clear the fact that the *huacas* of all three do not commence close to Coricancha. Rather, those of *ceque* III3b begin where those of III3a leave off, etc., all well outside the valley of Cuzco. One wonders whether the topography might

have played a role in the naming system for these *huacas*, since they stretch out end-to-end. They go in the direction where the valley of the Huatanay River becomes rather narrow. There is a stricture, a narrow pass called Angostura, 20 km SE of Cuzco through which these linked *ceques* pass (cf. Zuidema 1981b: fig. 26.6). Moreover, these *ceques* are associated with the primary solar alignment in Cuzco that was used to demarcate the planting season; namely, that between Cerro Picchu, immediately to the west of Cuzco, and Tipon (Pucara), 26 km to the east. As we stated earlier, the alignment points to the rising position of the sun on the day of its passage through the zenith, if one looks from west to east, or in the opposite direction to the sunset on the anti-zenith passage date. Therefore, a detailed reading of Cobo's description makes it clear that the *ceque* system of Cuzco was not purely radial with a single emanation point and that some of its peculiarities are not unlike those that we shall encounter when we examine the Nazca lines and line centers in detail.

This brief review of the *ceque* system of Cuzco and Andean astronomy and calendars in general is indispensable as a background to exploring the Nazca lines with the goal of determining whether they fit into recognized patterns of cultural insistence in Peru. A knowledge of these patterns from other work on the ancient cultures of Peru offers us one means of raising sensible questions about why the Nazca lines might have been constructed. We realize from this examination that, if we intend to study the lines for possible astronomical orientations, we need to pay special attention to the concepts and phenomena that already had attained widespread use in the calendars which we know existed at and since the time of the Conquest. Are there orientations in the Nazca lines to the Pleiades and the sun at the zenith and anti-zenith passages, as well as at the solstices, or to the celestial llama? Orientations to stars that bear a specific functional relation, such as in their heliacal rising and/or setting to a key period in the solar calendar, might also be expected to have been of some importance in the development of any

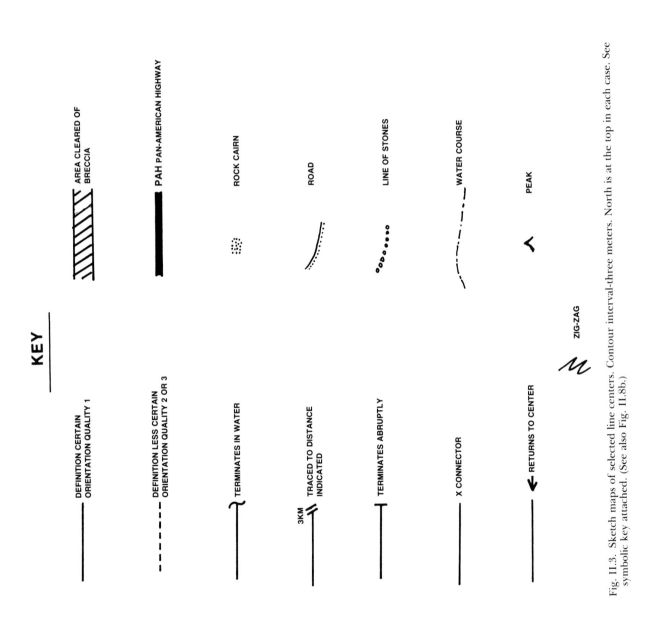

Fig. II.3. Sketch maps of selected line centers. Contour interval-three meters. North is at the top in each case. See symbolic key attached. (See also Fig. II.8b.)

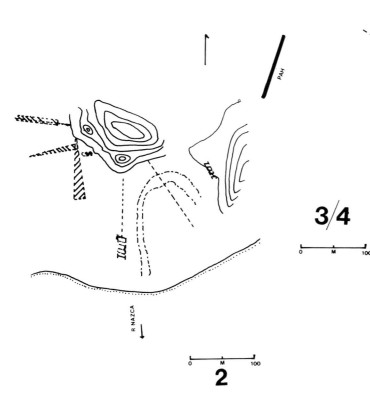

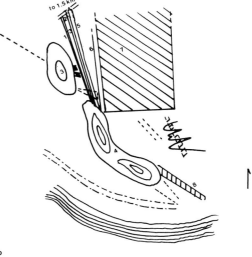

Fig. II.3(3/4).

Fig. II.3(2).

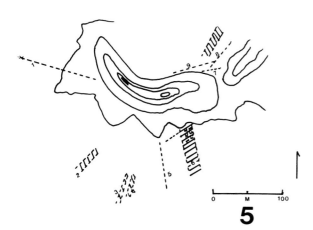

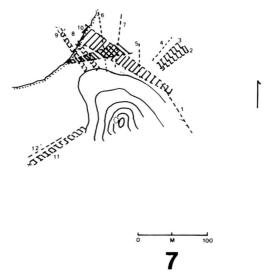

Fig. II.3(5).

Fig. II.3(7).

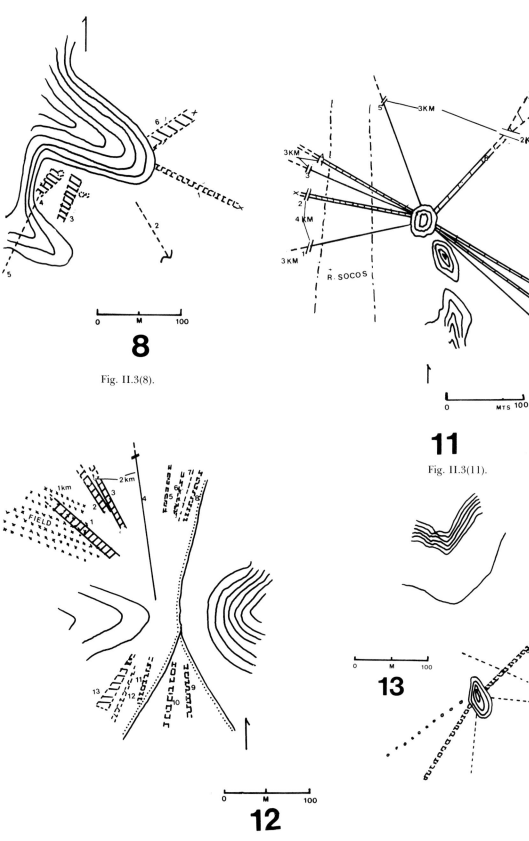

Fig. II.3(8).

Fig. II.3(11).

Fig. II.3(12).

Fig. II.3(13).

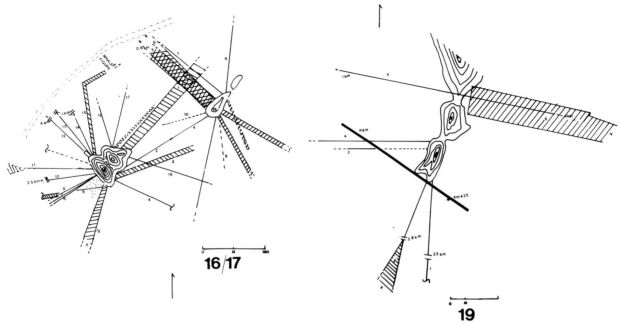

Fig. II.3(16/17).

Fig. II.3(19).

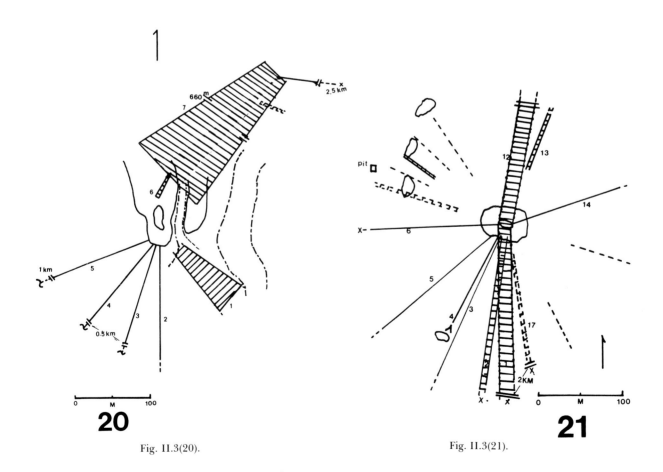

Fig. II.3(20).

Fig. II.3(21).

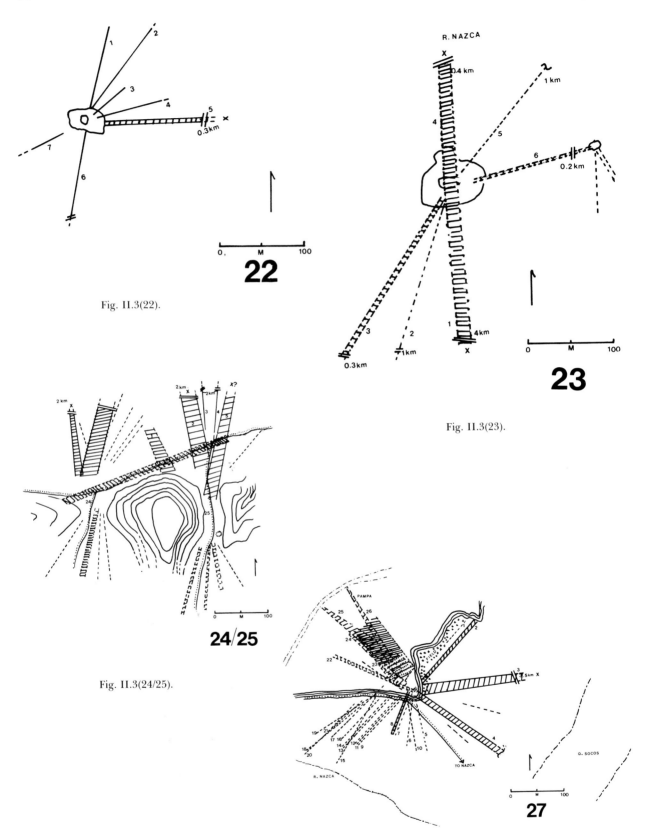

Fig. II.3(22).

Fig. II.3(23).

Fig. II.3(24/25).

Fig. II.3(27).

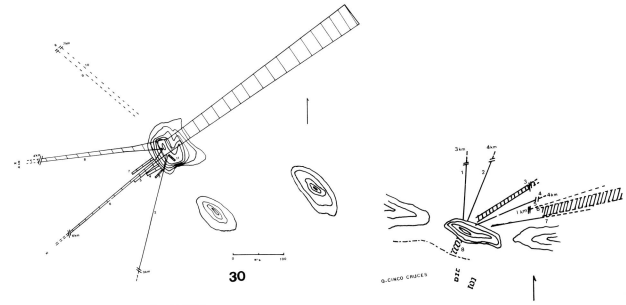

Fig. II.3(30).

Fig. II.3(31).

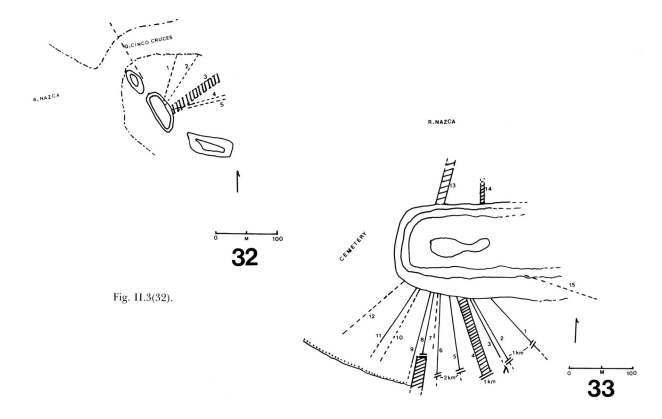

Fig. II.3(32).

Fig. II.3(33).

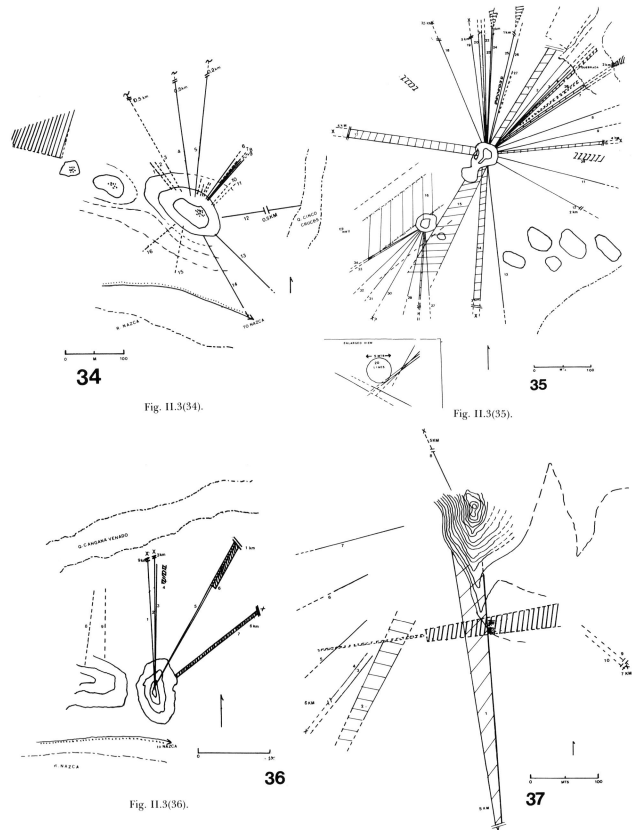

**34**

Fig. II.3(34).

**35**

Fig. II.3(35).

**36**

Fig. II.3(36).

**37**

Fig. II.3(37).

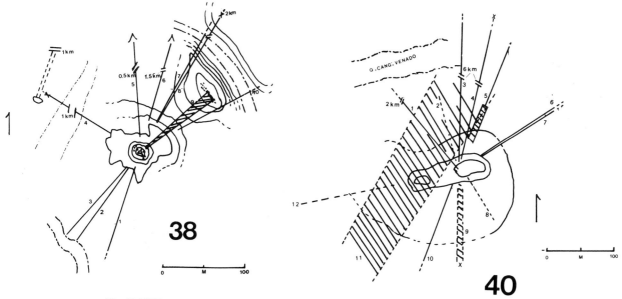

Fig. II.3(38).

Fig. II.3(40).

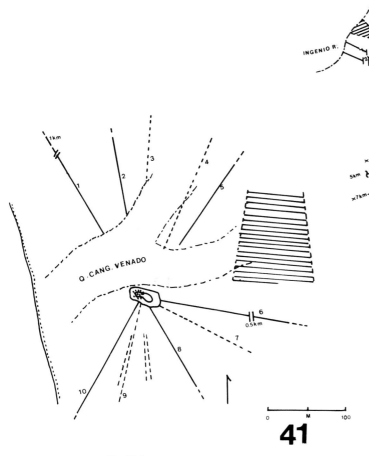

Fig. II.3(42).

Fig. II.3(41).

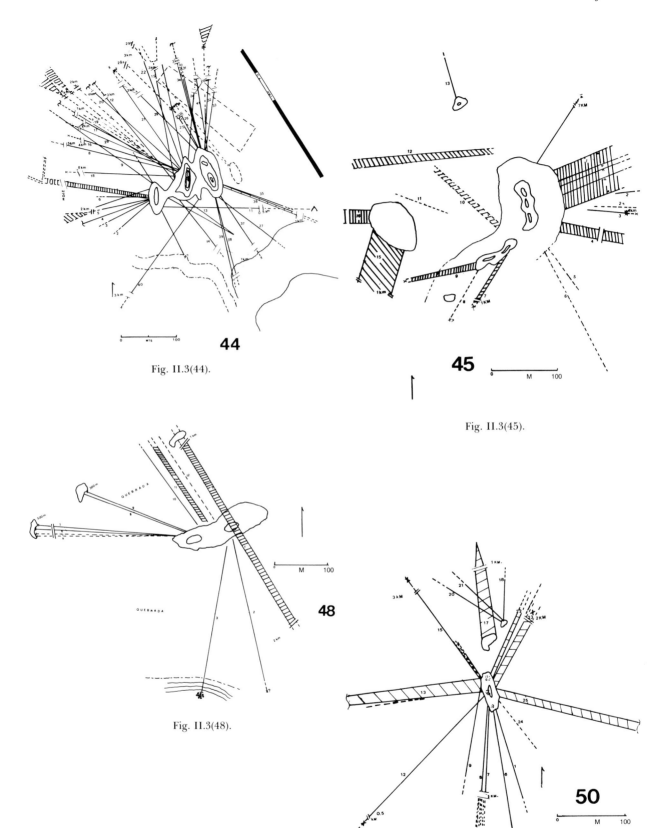

Fig. II.3(44).

**44**

**45**

Fig. II.3(45).

**48**

Fig. II.3(48).

**50**

Fig. II.3(50).

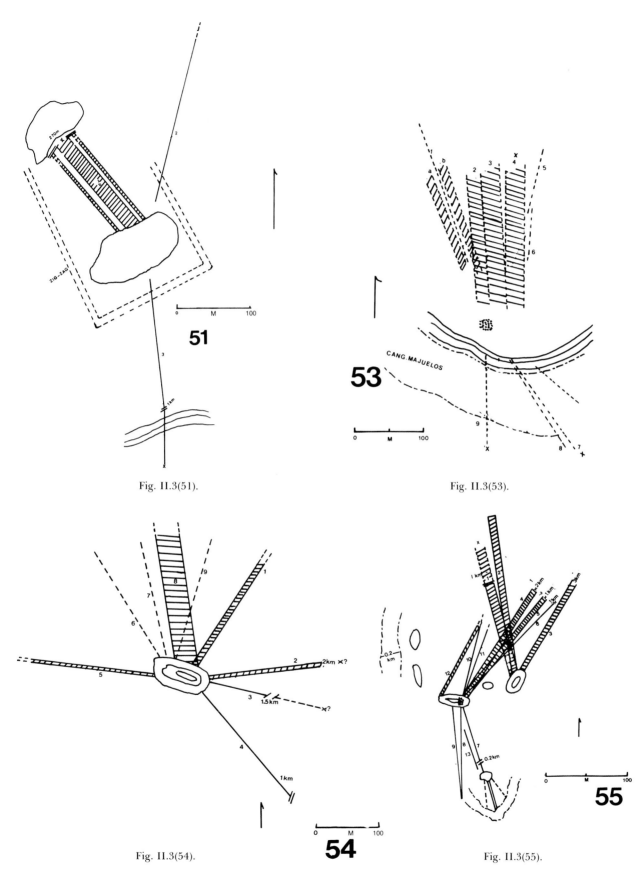

Fig. II.3(51).

Fig. II.3(53).

Fig. II.3(54).

Fig. II.3(55).

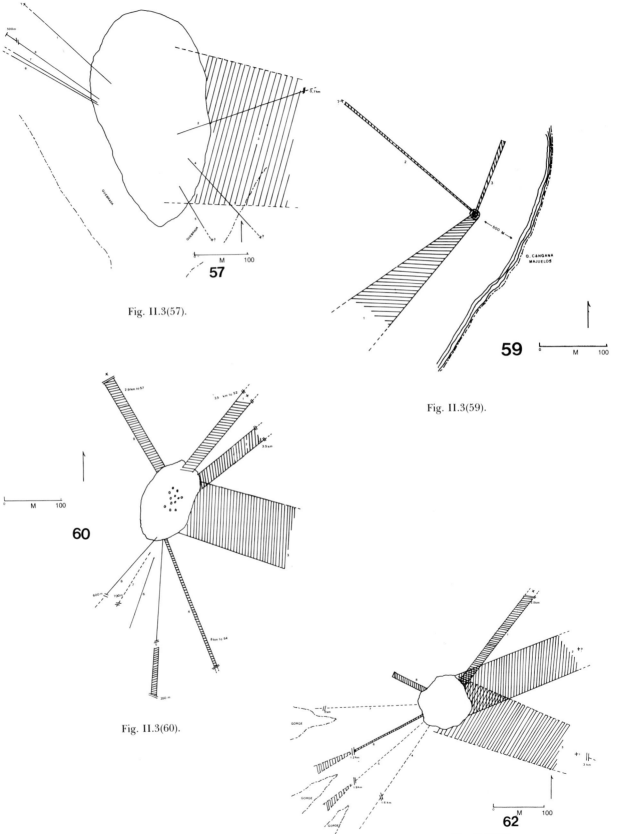

Fig. II.3(57).

Fig. II.3(59).

Fig. II.3(60).

Fig. II.3(62).

Nazca calendar. Whether these stars were quasi-circumpolar might be noted in particular.

Rituals associated with the *ceque* system time and again stress the relationship between people and water. That the termination points of many *ceque* lines are found over the tops of hills well out of sight of Cuzco carries the straight line aspect of *ceques* far beyond the realm of that which is immediately and directly visible; yet, linearity and straightness are the overriding structural principles of the system. Do the Nazca lines behave this way? The association of *ceque* lines with bends in rivers suggests to us that we might explore whether the desert etchings are related to the river channels and ancient irrigation canals in and around the pampa.[13] Many features of a given part of the *ceque* system can be connected with the topography in its immediate vicinity, but some *ceques* are tied to places and events far beyond—e.g., there is the association between a *ceque* aligning with the December solstice and a pilgrimage undertaken along the Vilcanota River, which, as we stated, was followed upstream on a more or less straight line toward the direction of Lake Titicaca. Can we find the same sort of distant associations for the Nazca lines? In this case we have no documentary evidence in the written record, but we can note carefully where a line begins and ends, whether the location of distant peaks and other prominent places in the large-scale landscape correlates with an extension of that line. Information about kinship, social organization, and Nazca mythology is totally absent from the record that remains on the Nazca landscape; therefore we can argue only by analogy with what we see in Cuzco, such as the grouping of *ceques* into particular numerical categories. But such argumentation is justified by the possible continuity over time and space of certain concepts inherent in the system that one also finds em-

ployed in textiles dating from the Middle Horizon (Zuidema 1977a: 221–226), as well as in the organizational schemes of pre-Inka centers such as Chavín and Tiahuanaco (Reinhard 1985b).

As we report on the analysis of the data from the pampa, we shall do so with this background information foremost in our minds and we shall attempt to analyze our data in such a way as to test specific hypotheses that can be generated by this background material.

## LINES AND LINE CENTERS: THE DATA BASE

The area on the map of Figure II.1a enclosed by the Ingenio and Nazca Rivers and the Pan American Highway at the base of the Andes is 220 sq. km in extent. Within that area[14] we accomplished the following:

(1) We walked the area and mapped any line centers extant. We estimate that we are 90 percent certain of having noted all the line centers in this region;

(2) We mapped each center by making measurements with a tape and surveyor's transit of the dimensions and orientations of the general region upon which the lines converge, usually a natural hill;

(3) We located and described features of possible human origin at each center;

(4) We measured (usually with the surveyor's transit and astronomical fix) the orientation of the member lines;

(5) We measured the widths and determined (on foot, where possible and with the aid of aerial photography), the points of termination of the lines;

(6) We provided a sketch and/or a photograph at a scale of 1:1,000 or less, of the vertical view and a 360° horizon panorama of each line center, including the line features going out from each center.

---

13. Zuidema (n.d., b) also has referred to another theme in the Inka calendar that likely had a long tradition, namely the use of panpipes in ritual drinking. He argues that in the Nasca, and later in the Wari culture, these instruments were played by an earth deity at the commencement of the agricultural season when water flowed in the rivers and irrigation canals.

14. The area surveyed includes not only the region bounded by the two rivers and the Pan American Highway, but also crosses to the south bank of the Nazca River and up several of the valleys of its tributaries. We extended the survey in this manner when it began to appear that the lines were not confined to the main pampa alone. This also was apparent from Reiche's maps. When we recognized that a few etchings existed on the narrow alluvial fans on the north side of the Ingenio River, we decided to include that region in the survey as well.

## TABLE 2 BASIC PROPERTIES OF NAZCA LINE CENTERS

| Number | Coordinates | Number of Lines Narrow | Number of Lines Broad | Connecting Line Centers | Notes |
|---|---|---|---|---|---|
| 1 | 1941–III 145611 | 6 | 0 | | 1, 2 |
| 2 | 1941–III 085629 | 2 | 5 | | 2 |
| 3 | 1941–III 078579 | 2 | 3 | | 2, 3 |
| 4 | 1941–III 079578 | 6 | 2 | | 3 |
| 5 | 1941–III 062630 | 6 | 5 | 8 | 2 |
| 6 | 1941–III 064579 | 3 | 0 | | 1, 4 |
| 7 | 1941–III 053635 | 6 | 7 | 8 | 2 |
| 8 | 1941–III 052632 | 2 | 4 | 5, 7 | 2 |
| 9 | 1941–III 059573 | 4 | 0 | | 1, 4 |
| 10 | 1941–III 042647 | 11 | 9 | 11? | 1, 2 |
| 11 | 1941–III 031642 | 4 | 5 | 10?, 19 | |
| 12 | 1941–III 023555 | 7 | 6 | | |
| 13 | 1941–III 019659 | 6 | 2 | | 2 |
| 14 | 1941–III 018628 | 8: | 2: | 16, 17, 20 | 1, 4, 5a |
| 15 | 1941–III 013624 | 6 | 2 | | 1, 4 |
| 16 | 1941–III 012623 | 5 | 6 | 17 | |
| 17 | 1941–III 009622 | 14 | 6 | 14, 16, 24?, 25?, 26, 27 | |
| 18 | 1941–III 008549 | 5 | 0 | | 1, 2, 5a |
| 19 | 1841–II 988649 | 8 | 1 | 11, 26, 27 | |
| 20 | 1841–II 988624 | 4 | 3 | 14 | |
| 21 | 1841–II 985572 | 10 | 7 | 22, 23, 24, 25 | |
| 22 | 1841–II 982571 | 6 | 1 | 21 | |
| 23 | 1841–II 985568 | 2 | 4 | 21, 24 | |
| 24 | 1841–II 986546 | 8 | 4 | 17?, 23 | |
| 25 | 1841–II 989545 | 4 | 6 | 17?, 21 | |
| 26 | 1841–II 974653 | 9 | 2 | 17, 19, 34? | 1 |
| 27 | 1841–II 976618 | 17 | 9 | 17, 19 | |
| 28 | 1841–II 973590 | 3 | 0 | | 1, 4, 5b |
| 29 | 1841–II 969669 | 5 | 0 | | 1, 4 |
| 30 | 1841–II 965656 | 8 | 3 | 35, 36, 37 | |
| 31 | 1841–II 969623: | 5 | 3 | | |
| 32 | 1841–II 961619: | 5 | 1 | | 1, 2 |
| 33 | 1841–II 960595: | 11 | 4 | | 6 |
| 34 | 1841–II 945619 | 21 | 0 | 26? | |
| 35 | 1841–II 921652 | 20 | 20 | 30, 36, 37, 38?, 45 | |
| 36 | 1841–II 921623 | 7 | 3 | 30, 35, 37? | |
| 37 | 1841–I 913696 | 8 | 2 | 30, 35, 36?, 40?, 43?, 44?, 45, 56?, 61? | 7 |
| 38 | 1841–I 910630 | 9 | 1 | 35?, 40 | |
| 39 | 1841–II 903651: | 6 | 0 | | 1, 4, 5b |
| 40 | 1841–II 906641 | 9 | 3 | 37?, 38 | |
| 41 | 1841–II 904640 | 13 | 1 | | |
| 42 | 1841–I 896770 | 10 | 0 | 44?, 46?, 56 | |
| 43 | 1841–I 886775 | 3 | 5 | 37?, 44, 46 | 1, 8 |
| 44 | 1841–I 890744 | 47 | 3 | 37?, 42?, 43, 46, 56, 61 | |
| 45 | 1841–II 881658 | 7 | 9 | 35, 37, 48?, 50, 54?, 55?, 57? | |
| 46 | 1841–I 878769 | 16 | 4 | 42?, 43, 44, 47, 56?, 60? | 8 |
| 47 | 1841–I 875762 | 14 | 3 | 46 | 8 |
| 48 | 1841–II 874667: | 10 | 2 | 45? | |
| 49 | 1841–II 877652: | 3 | 1 | 50?, 52?, 54?, 55? | 1, 2 |
| 50 | 1841–II 875648 | 16 | 5 | 45, 49?, 53, 55 | |
| 51 | 1841–II 867668 | 2 | 1 | 53, 57? | |
| 52 | 1841–II 867663: | 8 | 4 | 49? | 1, 2 |
| 53 | 1841–II 867659 | 7 | 5 | 50, 51, 55 | |
| 54 | 1841–II 861655 | 5 | 4 | 45?, 49? | |
| 55 | 1841–II 870645 | 11 | 6 | 45?, 49?, 50, 53 | |
| 56 | 1841–I 856756 | 24 | 4 | 37?, 42, 44, 46?, 58?, 60 | 8 |
| 57 | 1841–II 852685 | 7 | 1 | 45?, 51?, 60? | |
| 58 | 1841–I 847750 | 13 | 9 | 56?, 61?, 62? | 8 |
| 59 | 1841–I 841696 | 1 | 2 | 60? | |
| 60 | 1841–I 830729 | 3 | 6 | 46?, 56, 57?, 59?, 61?, 62? | |
| 61 | 1841–I 815749 | 23 | 3 | 37?, 44, 58?, 60?, 62 | 1, 8 |
| 62 | 1841–I 802729 | 3 | 5 | 58?, 60?, 61 | |

[1] No sketch map.

[2] No tabulations; uncorrected magnetic readings only.

[3] Multiple center consisting of two or more hills 100 m or less apart.

[4] Identifiable only on aerial photographs on which it appears as an apparent concentration of lines, but not visible at ground level; no readings of alignments.

[5] Heavily eroded, (a) mostly as a result of proximity to the Pan American Highway; (b) due to relative absence of rock fragments.

[6] The so-called Pacheco cemetery site is adjacent.

[7] Because of extensive stream erosion on its W side, the connectors from centers 40, 44, 56, and 61 cannot be followed all the way up to this center.

[8] Readings adopted from maps of Hawkins (1969) and Kern & Reiche 1974, Fig. 1, pp. 1–3).

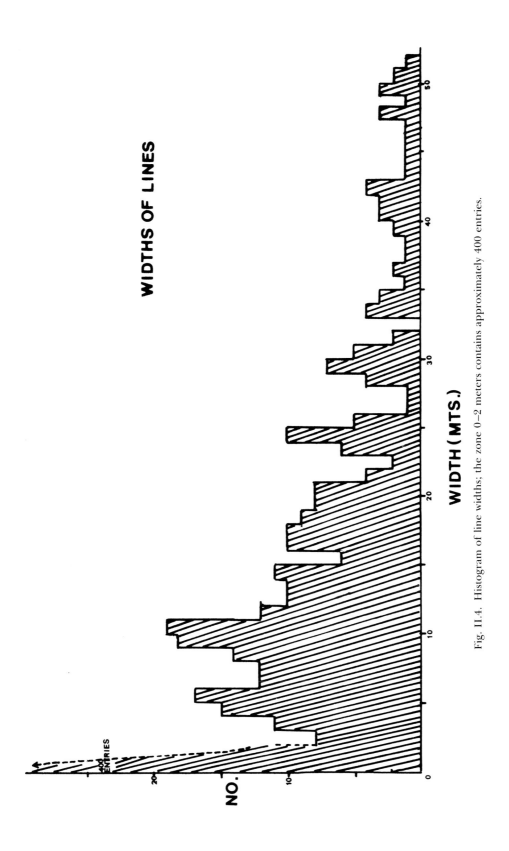

Fig. II.4. Histogram of line widths; the zone 0–2 meters contains approximately 400 entries.

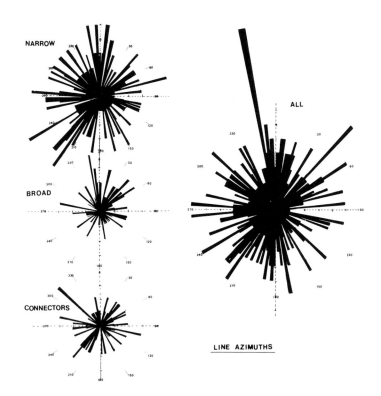

Fig. II.5. Histograms showing the frequency distribution of the alignments of all lines of quality Classes 1 and 2:

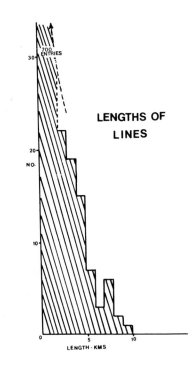

Fig. II.6. Frequency distribution of lengths of Nazca lines; the zone 0–2 km contains approximately 700 entries.

We discovered that once a line departs a center, several alternatives, some of them combined, may result (the figures in parentheses give the approximate percentage of occurrence of a particular alternative):

(a) It may terminate at a tributary or one of the small dry *quebradas* that flow into the tributaries (3 percent), or at one of the major rivers (9 percent) (Total: 12 percent);

(b) It may lead to another center (22 percent);

(c) It may terminate abruptly in a featureless region of the pampa (less than 1 percent). (It is difficult to tell in most of these relatively rare cases whether the termination was the result of unfinished work);

(d) It may terminate at a peak that is not a line center (4 percent);

(e) It may become lost either in a confused agglomeration of other man-made features or in regions of the pampa where erosion superceded the line (approx. 45 percent). In most such instances, we successively lost and recovered the line several times before it finally vanished from our view;

(f) It may develop sharp kinks and bends, often acute angles, thus zigzagging across the pampa before terminating in any of the other ways listed (7 percent);

(g) It may lead to (or feed into) one of the large geometrical figures (10 percent). In most such cases the geometrical figure will be delineated by *quebradas* or tributaries. We shall discuss the nature of these occurrences later.

We have attempted to illustrate symbolically on the sketch maps of selected line centers (Fig. II.3) what happens to a given line once it departs a line center.

Having performed the aforementioned activities over several field seasons, we were able to identify 62 line centers that fit the definition of that term as given above. These are labeled in their approximate locations on the map of Figure II.1b, which also shows the lines that connect a given center to other centers. On this map, a *solid* line represents a definite connector, either walked or traced on a photograph (or both). Some of the more

prominent centers are labeled on the survey photograph of the pampa in the Photomosaic (Appendix IV). A *dotted* line represents a likely, but less certain, connector. In Table 2 we list the centers according to a location-by-number system that proceeds from the east toward the west in kilometer squares arranged in columns going from the north to the south, as delineated on the Instituto Geografico Militar 1:50,000 topographic maps (Fig. II.1a). In column 2 of this table, we give the location of each line center in a Universal Transverse Mercator system in which the first four digits and Roman numeral indicate the map sheet number and the last six digits give the location on the sheet. The first two numbers of the last six digits (the easting) denote the vertical grid line as printed on the map, and the third number pinpoints the location to the nearest 100 meters east of the vertical line; the fourth and fifth numbers refer to the printed horizontal lines on the map, and the last number signifies the location north of this horizontal line. Thus, the position of a given line center is specified to 100 meters in both grid latitude and longitude. In the third and fourth columns we tabulate, respectively, the number of narrow and broad lines attached to the center.

Widths of individual lines vary but if we take averages,[15] we find that the overwhelming majority are less than one-half meter wide—just wide enough to walk on. In virtually all cases we find pathways incorporated within them. The most common line width, that of over half the lines, is a little over one-third meter. Concerning precise data on the narrower lines, 25 measurements on 12 lines yielded an average width of 0.39 m ± 0.07 m (probable error), which might be related to a standard unit of measurement.[16] The histogram of Fig. II.4 shows the width distribution

---

15. The widths of a few of the wider lines vary by too large an amount to permit averaging. For example, the line that connects center No. 45 with No. 37 is 1.9 m wide at a distance of 0.8 km from No. 45. It narrows to 1.5 m at 1.3 km, to 1.7 m at 2.0 km, then narrows further to 1.2 m at 2.3 km, and finally to 1.0 m at 4.2 km, or approximately 1 km from center No. 37.
16. This is a fair approximation to the distance between the elbow and the tips of the fingers extended, which is attributed to Reiche (Spencer 1983) as a possible unit of measurement based on human proportions.

## TABLE 3
### TRANSIT READINGS OF AZIMUTHS[1] OF LINES EMANATING FROM LINE CENTERS

| Line Center No. | Line No. | Azimuth | Notes |
|---|---|---|---|
| 4 | 1 | 340°04′ | |
| | 2 | 340°38′ | |
| | 4 | 343°26′ | |
| | 5 | 343°50′ | |
| | 6 | 345°33′ | |
| | 7 | 353°59′ | ● |
| | 8 | 120°20′ | ● |
| 11 | 1 | 257°20′ | |
| | 2 | 280°20′ | To 19(line bends) |
| | 3 | 292°05′ | |
| | 4 | 298°07′ | |
| | 5 | 338°35′ | |
| | 6 | 43°18′ | ● |
| | 7 | 118°55′ | |
| | 8 | 123°45′ | |
| | 9 | 129°57′ | |
| 12 | 1 | 310°08′ | ● |
| | 2 | 328°48′ | ● |
| | 3 | 332°52′ | ● |
| | 4 | 353°11′ | |
| | 5 | 06° | |
| | 6 | 11° | |
| | 7 | 18½° | |
| | 8 | 19½° | |
| | 9 | 175½° | ● |
| | 10 | 188° | ● |
| | 11 | 194½° | ● |
| | 12 | 203½° | ● |
| | 13 | 207½° | ● |
| 16 | 1 | 117°34′ | ● |
| | 2 | 145°26′ | ● |
| | 3 | 188°10′ | |
| | 4 | 239°31′ | To 17 |
| | 5 | 304°50′ | ● |
| | 6 | 306°23′ | ● |
| | 7 | 304°29′ | |
| | 8 | 02°15′ | |
| | 9 | 175° | |
| | 10 | 256½° | |
| 17 | 1 | 42°35′ | ● |
| | 2 | 59°31′ | To 16 |
| | 3 | 69°12′ | ● |
| | 4 | 111°11′ | |
| | 5 | 198°45′ | To 24 or 25? ● |
| | 7 | 239°09′ | |
| | 8 | 240°22′ | |
| | 9 | 258°49′ | |
| | 10 | 262°26′ | To 27 |
| | 11 | 265°34′ | |
| | 12 | 311° | To 26 |
| | 13 | 318°40′ | |
| | 14 | 332° | |
| | 15 | 348°59′ | To 14(sharp bend) ● |
| | 16 | 337°36′ | |
| | 17 | 06°06′ | |
| | 18 | 102°39′ | |
| 19 | 1 | 185°47′ | |
| | 2 | 204°18′ | To 27 (line bends) ● |
| | 3 | 271°31′ | |
| | 4 | 269°44′ | |
| | 5 | 280°27′ | To 26 |

### TABLE 3 (Continued)

| Line Center No. | Line No. | Azimuth | Notes |
|---|---|---|---|
| | 6a | 100°01′ | To 11 (line bends) ● |
| | 6b | 99°32′ | |
| | 6c | 104°00′ | |
| | 6d | 100°15′ | |
| 20 | 1 | 137°14′ | ● |
| | 2 | 180°40′ | |
| | 3 | 198°37′ | |
| | 4 | 219°32′ | |
| | 5 | 248°43′ | |
| | 6 | 33°42′ | ● |
| | 7 | 55°18′ | To 14 (line bends) ● |
| 21 | 1 | 178°49′ | To 24 ● |
| | 2 | 186°34′ | To 23 ● |
| | 3 | 204°10′ | |
| | 4 | 207°53′ | |
| | 5 | 229°31′ | |
| | 6 | 266°19′ | To 22 |
| | 12 | 09°38′ | ● |
| | 13 | 19°47′ | |
| | 14 | 71°08′ | |
| | 17 | 168°11′ | To 25 (slight bend) |
| 22 | 1 | 13°57′ | |
| | 3 | 54°50′ | |
| | 4 | 74°27′ | |
| | 5 | 87°01′ | To 21 ● |
| | 6 | 190°08′ | |
| | 7 | 243°50′ | |
| 23 | 1 | 178° | To 24 ● (bends) |
| | 2 | 201° | |
| | 3 | 215½° | ● |
| | 4 | 0° | To 21 ● |
| | 5 | 43° | |
| | 6 | 78½° | ● |
| 24 | 1 | 354°21′ | To 23 ● (bends) |
| | 2 | 14°59′ | ● |
| 25 | 2 | 348°24′ | To 21 ● (slight bend) |
| | 3 | 357°54′ | |
| | 4 | 07°25′ | |
| | 5 | 15°30′ | To 17? ● |
| 26 | 1 | 133°30′ | To 17 |
| | 2 | 100°17′ | To 19 |
| | 3 | 177°58′ | |
| | 5 | 219°30′ | |
| | 6 | 224°01′ | To 34? |
| | 8 | 260°17′ | |
| | 9 | 223°32′ | |
| | 10 | 192°11′ | |
| | 14 | 222°44′ | |
| 27 | 2 | 42°40′ | ● |
| | 3 | 82°24′ | To 17 ● |
| | 4 | 122°49′ | ● |
| 30 | 1 | 56°05′ | ● |
| | 2 | 196°04′ | |
| | 3 | 224°10′ | |
| | 4 | 242°40′ | |
| | 5 | 232°10′ | |
| | 6 | 233°15′ | To 36 |
| | 7 | 237°10′ | |
| | 8 | 264°42′ | To 35 ● |
| | 9 | 313° | To 37 |
| | 10 | 313° | To 37 |
| 31 | 1 | 06° | To 26? |
| | 2 | 26° | To 19? |
| | 3 | 50° | ● |

(Continued)

## TABLE 3 (Continued)

| Line Center No. | Line No. | Azimuth | Notes |
|---|---|---|---|
|  | 4 | 71° | To 17? |
|  | 5 | 75½° |  |
|  | 6 | 80° |  |
|  | 7 | 85° |  |
|  | 8 | 207° | ● |
| 33 | 1 | 135°45' |  |
|  | 2 | 148°52' |  |
|  | 3 | 151°46' |  |
|  | 4 | 159°13' | ● |
|  | 5 | 172°17' |  |
|  | 6 | 183°32' |  |
|  | 8 | 191°48' |  |
|  | 9 | 196°15' |  |
|  | 11 | 215°01' |  |
|  | 13 | 15°58' | ● |
|  | 14 | 01°56' | ● |
| 34 | 4 | 354°30' |  |
|  | 5 | 07°50' |  |
|  | 6 | 40°02' |  |
|  | 7 | 43°28' |  |
|  | 8 | 43°36' |  |
|  | 9 | 45°07' | To 26? |
|  | 12 | 85°36' |  |
|  | 13 | 133°56' |  |
|  | 14 | 152°35' |  |
| 35 | 1 | 32°35' | ● |
|  | 2 | 39°46' |  |
|  | 3 | 43°32' |  |
|  | 4 | 44°49' |  |
|  | 5 | 47°13' | ● |
|  | 5a | 51° | ● |
|  | 6 | 55°48' | ● |
|  | 7 | 56°24' |  |
|  | 8 | 69°33' |  |
|  | 9 | 76°51' |  |
|  | 10 | 84°38' | To 30 ● |
|  | 11 | 104°03' |  |
|  | 12 | 118°56' |  |
|  | 13 | 173°33' |  |
|  | 14 | 184°24' | To 36 ● |
|  | 15 | 210°24' | ● |
|  | 16 | 237°26' | ● |
|  | 17 | 280°16' | To 45 ● |
|  | 18 | 337°25' |  |
|  | 19 | 352°50' | To 37 |
|  | 20 | 356°35' |  |
|  | 21 | 358°21' |  |
|  | 22 | 359°42' |  |
|  | 23 | 03°04' |  |
|  | 24 | 03°19' |  |
|  | 25 | 13°46' |  |
|  | 26 | 16°19' |  |
|  | 27 | 176°59' |  |
|  | 28 | 185°04' |  |
|  | 29 | 195°00' |  |
|  | 30 | 211°06' | To 38? |
|  | 31 | 220°01' |  |
|  | 32 | 227°07' |  |
|  | 33 | 239°04' |  |
|  | 34 | 239°10' |  |
| 36 | 1 | 357°03' | To 37? |
|  | 2 | 359°44' | To 35 |
|  | 3 | 0°30' |  |
|  | 4 | 28°03' |  |
|  | 5 | 25½ |  |

## TABLE 3 (Continued)

| Line Center No. | Line No. | Azimuth | Notes |
|---|---|---|---|
|  | 6 | 29°22' |  |
|  | 7 | 53°11' | To 30 ● |
|  | 8 | 357°40' |  |
|  | 9 | 06°10' |  |
| 37 | 1 | 172°45' | To 35 ● |
|  | 2 | 209°00' | ● |
|  | 3 | 223°15' |  |
|  | 4 | 221°33' | To 45 |
|  | 5 | 229°55' |  |
|  | 6 | 246°02' |  |
|  | 7 | 255°40' |  |
|  | 8 | 335°22' | To 44? |
|  | 9 | 133° | To 30 |
|  | 10 | 133° | To 30 |
| 38 | 1 | 198°31' |  |
|  | 2 | 216°00' |  |
|  | 3 | 222°05 |  |
|  | 4 | 301°29' | To 40 (sharp bend) |
|  | 5 | 356°13' |  |
|  | 6 | 16°56' |  |
|  | 7 | 30°59' |  |
|  | 8 | 31°41' | To 35? |
|  | 9 | 53°41' | ● |
|  | 10 | 61°56' |  |
| 40 | 1 | 322°12' |  |
|  | 2 | 348½° |  |
|  | 3 | 04°31' |  |
|  | 4 | 16°03' | To 37? |
|  | 5 | 26°06' | ● |
|  | 6 | 58°35' |  |
|  | 7 | 60°40' |  |
|  | 8 | 163½° |  |
|  | 9 | 183°03' | To 38 ● |
|  | 10 | 204°13' |  |
| 41 | 1 | 328°39' |  |
|  | 2 | 349°14' |  |
|  | 5 | 65°29' |  |
|  | 6 | 101°24' |  |
|  | 7 | 118° |  |
|  | 8 | 148°44' |  |
|  | 9 | 194° |  |
|  | 10 | 210°13' |  |
| 42 | 1 | 249°33' | To 56 |
|  | 2 | 258°26' |  |
|  | 3 | 265°04' |  |
|  | 4 | 272°51' |  |
|  | 5 | 280°50' |  |
|  | 6 | 293°37' |  |
|  | 7 | 296°25' |  |
|  | 8 | 301°56' |  |
|  | 9 | 350°14' |  |
|  | 10 | 262° | To 46? |
| 43 | 1 | 135½° |  |
|  | 2 | 153½° |  |
|  | 3 | 167½° | To 44 |
|  | 4 | 168° | To 44 |
|  | 5 | 169½° |  |
|  | 6 | 156° | To 37? |
|  | 7 | 193½° |  |
|  | 8 | 237½° | Bisector of trap.; to 46 |
| 44 | 1 | 152°53' |  |
|  | 2 | 230°40' |  |
|  | 3 | 245°27' |  |
|  | 4 | 250°45' |  |

(Continued)

TABLE 3 (Continued)

| Line Center No. | Line No. | Azimuth | Notes |
|---|---|---|---|
| | 5 | 258°46′ | |
| | 6 | 272°16′ | |
| | 7 | 280°46′ | ● |
| | 8 | 283°49′ | |
| | 9 | 306°13′ | |
| | 10 | 327°58′ | |
| | 11 | 92°54′ | |
| | 12 | 321°21′ | |
| | 13 | 124°26′ | |
| | 14 | 140°49′ | |
| | 15 | 349°07′ | |
| | 16 | 288°59′ | To 56 |
| | 17 | 298°50′ | |
| | 18 | 274°04′ | To 61 |
| | 19 | 299°51′ | |
| | 19a | 300° | |
| | 19b | 300½° | |
| | 19c | 303° | |
| | 19d | 310½° | To 47 |
| | 20 | 313°38′ | |
| | 21 | 326°40′ | To 46? |
| | 22 | 341°48′ | |
| | 23 | 349°34′ | |
| | 24 | 07°52′ | |
| | 25 | 328°52′ | |
| | 26 | 333°40′ | |
| | 26a | 334° | |
| | 26b | 339° | |
| | 27 | 127°30′ | |
| | 28 | 294°39′ | |
| | 29 | 316°00′ | |
| | 29a | 312° | |
| | 29b | 318° | |
| | 30 | 347°52′ | To 43 |
| | 31 | 347°52′ | To 43 |
| | 32 | 05°30′ | |
| | 33 | 11°09′ | To 42? |
| | 34 | 344°13′ | |
| | 35 | 109°29′ | |
| | 36 | 109°43′ | ● |
| | 37 | 145°34′ | To 37? |
| | 38 | 164°00′ | |
| | 39 | 166°08′ | |
| | 40 | 216°05′ | To 57? |
| | 41 | 351°22′ | |
| | 42 | 355° | |
| 45 | 1a | 73°42′ | 5 lines, 3 of which can be measured, |
| | 1b | 75°13′ | run the length of |
| | 1e | 74°13′ | this trapezoid. ● |
| | 2 | 84°49′ | |
| | 2a | 97°49° | |
| | 3 | 100°16′ | To 35 |
| | 4a | 105°43′ | Pair of lines in |
| | 4b | 108°24′ | trapezoid ● |
| | 5 | 148°36′ | |
| | 7 | 216°08′ | To 50 ● |
| | 8 | 215°41′ | To 55? |
| | 9a | 265°46′ | Two lines in trap.; |
| | 9b | 261°50′ | to 54? ● |
| | 10 | 317°35′ | ● |
| | 12 | 273°06′ | ● |
| | 13 | 349°47′ | |

TABLE 3 (Continued)

| Line Center No. | Line No. | Azimuth | Notes |
|---|---|---|---|
| | 14 | 39°44′ | To 37 |
| | 15 | 203°57′ | ● |
| | 16 | 275°54′ | ● |
| 46 | 1 | 57½° | Bisector of trap.; to 43 |
| | 2 | 77° | |
| | 3 | 83° | |
| | 4 | 164½° | Parallel |
| | 5 | 165° | pattern |
| | 6 | 164° | (zigzag) |
| | 7 | 165° | |
| | 8 | 164° | |
| | 9 | 164° | |
| | 10 | 163½° | |
| | 11 | 180½° | |
| | 12 | 189 | Double line returning on itself |
| | 13 | 200½° | To 47 |
| | 14 | 208° | |
| | 15 | 220° | To 60, bending |
| | 16 | 235½° | |
| | 17 | 235° | Zigzag |
| | 18 | 238½° | |
| | 19 | 239° | |
| | 20 | 269° | Bisector of trapezoid |
| 47 | 1 | 3½° | |
| | 2a | 20½° | To 46 |
| | 2b | 20½° | To 46 |
| | 3 | 56½° | |
| | 4 | 57° | |
| | 5 | 58° | |
| | 6 | 69½° | Trapezoid |
| | 7 | 256½° | |
| | 8 | 257½° | |
| | 9 | 265° | Zigzag |
| | 10 | 273° | Linked to 11 |
| | 11 | 275½° | Linked to 10 |
| | 12 | 278° | Linked to 13 |
| | 13 | 278° | Linked to 12 |
| | 14 | 278½° | |
| | 15 | 309½° | |
| | 16 | 317° | Zigzag across no. 6 |
| | 17 | 348° | Bisector of trapezoid |
| 48 | 1 | 148°34′ | To 45? ● |
| | 2 | 168°06′ | |
| | 3 | 191°26′ | |
| | 4 | 270° | |
| | 5 | 271° | |
| | 6 | 272°11′ | |
| | 7 | 273°09′ | |
| | 8 | 289°23′ | |
| | 9 | 290°14′ | |
| | 10 | 323°28′ | |
| | 11 | 324°51′ | ● |
| | 12 | 326° | |
| 50 | 1 | 161°05′ | |
| | 6 | 169°20′ | |
| | 7 | 181°55′ | |
| | 8 | 184°29′ | |
| | 9 | 188°56′ | |
| | 12 | 224°46′ | To 55 |
| | 13a | 262°17′ | ● |
| | 13b | 259°00′ | |
| | 15 | 322°58′ | To 53 |
| | 16 | 325°35′ | |

(Continued)

TABLE 3 (Continued)

| Line Center No. | Line No. | Azimuth | Notes |
|---|---|---|---|
| | 17a | 349°33' | ● |
| | 17b | 349°33' | |
| | 18 | 351°02' | |
| | 20 | 204°17' | |
| | 21 | 221°05' | |
| | 22 | 23°50' | ● |
| | 23a | 34°01' | To 45 ● |
| | 23b | 30°51' | |
| | 24 | 138°56' | |
| | 25 | 104°14' | ● |
| 51 | 1 | 321°12' | To 57? ● |
| | 2 | 10°48' | |
| | 3 | 174°19' | To 53 |
| 53 | 1 | 335½° | ● |
| | 1a | 339½° | |
| | 1b | 339° | |
| | 2 | 352½° | ● |
| | 3 | 352° | ● |
| | 4 | 355° | ● To 51 |
| | 5 | 13½° | |
| | 6 | 04° | |
| | 7 | 143° | To 50 |
| | 8 | 144° | |
| | 9 | 165° | To 55 |
| 54 | 1 | 33°51' | ● |
| | 2 | 84°16' | To 45? ● |
| | 3 | 103°00' | To 49? |
| | 4 | 136° | |
| | 5 | 278°48' | ● |
| | 6 | 333° | |
| | 7 | 352°54' | |
| | 8 | 19° | ● |
| | 9 | 25° | |
| 55 | 1 | 343°07' | To 53 ● |
| | 2 | 350°45' | ● |
| | 3 | 31°59' | ● |
| | 4 | 34°56' | To 45? ● |
| | 5 | 41°02' | To 49? ● |
| | 6 | 44°54' | To 50 |
| | 7 | 161°34' | |
| | 8 | 180°15' | |
| | 9 | 194°56' | |
| | 10 | 16°19' | |
| | 11 | 21°35' | |
| | 12 | 31°50' | ● |
| | 13 | 160°22' | |
| 56 | 1 | 10° | |
| | 2 | 12° | |
| | 3 | 46½° | |
| | 4 | 55° | |
| | 5 | 57½° | To 46? |
| | 6 | 59½° | To 46? |
| | 7 | 62° | |
| | 8 | 70½° | To 42 |
| | 9 | 110° | To 44 |
| | 10 | 134° | To 37? |
| | 11 | 168° | |
| | 12 | 196° | |
| | 13 | 221½° | To 60 |
| | 14 | 249½° | To 58? |
| | 15 | 255° | |
| | 16 | 266° | |
| | 17 | 277½° | |
| | 18 | 289½° | |
| | 19 | 295° | |

TABLE 3 (Continued)

| Line Center No. | Line No. | Azimuth | Notes |
|---|---|---|---|
| | 20 | 345° | |
| 57 | 1 | 311°24' | To 60? |
| | 2 | 73°56' | |
| | 3 | 103° | ● |
| | 4 | 137°20' | To 45? |
| | 5 | 148°38' | To 51? |
| | 6 | 299°16' | |
| | 7 | 300°42' | |
| | 8 | 304°24' | |
| 58 | 1 | 15° | |
| | 2 | 43° | |
| | 3 | 65° | To 56? |
| | 4 | 90½° | |
| | 5 | 120° | |
| | 6 | 173½° | |
| | 7 | 210½° | |
| | 8 | 229° | |
| | 9 | 241° | |
| | 10 | 249° | |
| | 11 | 267° | To 61? |
| | 12 | 289° | |
| | 13 | 294° | |
| | 14 | 310° | |
| | 15 | 323° | |
| | 16 | 331° | |
| | 17 | 348° | |
| 59 | 1 | 228°26' | ● |
| | 2 | 310°30' | To 60? |
| | 3 | 21°57' | ● |
| 60 | 1 | 41°47' | To 56 ● |
| | 2 | 50°16' | ● |
| | 3 | 106°01' | ● |
| | 4 | 157°40' | ● |
| | 5 | 183°47' | |
| | 6 | 199°24' | |
| | 7 | 212° | |
| | 8 | 222°43' | |
| | 9 | 329°01' | To 61 |
| 61 | 1 | 16° | |
| | 2 | 47° | |
| | 3 | 53½° | |
| | 4 | 62½° | |
| | 5 | 65° | |
| | 6 | 68½° | |
| | 7 | 76° | |
| | 8 | 86° | |
| | 9 | 95° | To 44 |
| | 10 | 108½° | |
| | 11 | 116½° | To 37? |
| | 12 | 133° | |
| | 13 | 151° | To 60 |
| | 14 | 163½° | |
| | 15 | 189° | |
| | 16 | 208½° | |
| | 17 | 215° | |
| | 18 | 218½° | To 62 |
| | 19 | 226° | |
| | 20 | 231½° | |
| | 21 | 248½° | |
| | 22 | 265° | |
| | 23 | 283½° | |
| | 24 | 306° | |
| | 25 | 323° | |
| | 26 | 347½° | |

(Continued)

TABLE 3 (Continued)

| Line Center No. | Line No. | Azimuth | Notes |
|---|---|---|---|
| 62 | 1 | 39°30′ | To 61 ● |
|  | 2 | 67°23′ | To 58? ● |
|  | 3 | 107° | To 60? ● |
|  | 4 | 215° |  |
|  | 5 | 229° |  |
|  | 6 | 242°26′ | ● |
|  | 7 | 267° |  |
|  | 8 | 294°53′ | ● |

[1] Readings quoted in whole or half degrees are either magnetic readings corrected on site or are taken from Hawkins' survey map. In either case they are determined to be accurate to 1°. (These are represented as dotted lines in Fig. 2.) (Quality 2). The accuracy of all other readings, which were made with the surveyor's transit and astronomical fix, is limited by the straightness of the feature, usually ± 5′ minutes of arc (Quality 1). These appear as solid lines in Figs. 2. Quality 3 readings (error ± 2°), which also appear as dotted lines, are not tab- ulated.

[2] A dot in the Notes column indicates a wide feature.

of broader lines; it indicates that a deficiency of lines falls in the width range of 2 to 3 m; accordingly, we have employed this discontinuity to define a broad line as any line wider than 3 m. Beyond 3 m, the number of lines increases to a maximum at approximately 10 m, then falls off dramatically with increasing width, the widest measuring up to about 50 m. Additional discernible peaks appear at 5, 10, 24, and 29 m. None of these correspond to the various integral units mentioned by Reiche and discussed here in Chapter I. Geometrical figures, which often appear attached to lines, range in maximum width at the base from several up to 200 m and possess mean widths between 60 and 70 m; therefore, the widest lines (often called "avenues" in the literature) associated with the line centers rival the trapezoids and triangles.

When narrow lines terminate in triangles or trapezoids, we regard the two as separate features, e.g., a narrow line connected to a trapezoid. Using this classification scheme for our 62 line centers, we thus tabulate 762 lines, 538 of them as narrow and 224 as broad—the later constituting about 30 percent of the sample. Consequently, we can state that each center contains on the average a dozen lines, but some contain twice as many or more, e.g., for center No. 44, we mapped 50 lines. In very few cases do we find centers for which the number of broad lines rivals the narrow ones, and there

are a few examples of smaller centers (e.g., Nos. 2, 7, 23, 25, 43, 45, 60), where broad lines constitute the majority of features.

In the fifth column of Table 2, we list the other centers to which a given center is connected by a line that either we walked or that we could follow quite discernibly on one or more of the aerial photographs. We note that most centers are observed to be connected to others, usually in their vicinity, but there are some long-distance connectors (e.g., No. 61 to No. 44, a distance of over 6 km).

There is no question that the data on connectors are incomplete and that stream and wind erosion are the dominant factors contributing to the loss of the record; they account for the number of connectors labeled with question marks in Table 2. In a number of instances we would follow a line that appeared to go in the direction of a distant center only to lose track of it upon entering one of the many dry washes that cross-cut the pampa in a NE-SW direction. Thus we suspect that line center No. 37, situated on one of the most badly eroded parts of the pampa, may have been connected to a large number of other centers. The centers located on the south bank of the Nazca River east of Cahuachi also are badly eroded, having been constructed in a soft, sandy area that is impoverished in the desert-varnished rocks that make up the main pampa.[17] Therefore, the maps of these centers reflect lines that could be traced only a little way out before they faded into invisibility. This unfortunate circumstance, coupled with the extensive agriculture in the valley and its immediate environs, has made it possible to trace only a single example of a line that we can be sure crosses the Nazca River and continues on the other side.

In the opinion of Clarkson (personal communication), the visibility of the lines etched in the soil along the south bank of the Nazca River seems satisfactory enough in most places to reveal any lines that could have been continued across the river from the north bank;

17. This can be taken to imply that the appearance of a dark, fragment-strewn surface of pampa is not the sole motivation for constructing an etching.

however, she suggests that it is possible that agricultural activity both in the recent as well as in the distant past may have effaced lines that once crossed the river bed. We find a number of instances (e.g., centers No. 24, 25, 33) in which lines depart a center located near the edge of the river bank and head directly for the river. These features fade from view as they reach the fertile valley. Therefore, it may be that some of the lines were intended to be directed toward features/activities occurring in the valley a relatively short distance away (see Appx. II, Fig. 6b bottom, arrow, for an excellent example of a huge trapezoid feature that plunges straight into the river and resumes on the other side).

Table 2, together with the set of figures (Fig. II.3), offers the reader a detailed description of the complex physical environment of a given line center. For want of space we are unable to give a full transcription of our field notes, wherein we describe each center in great detail. However, in Appendix II we have singled out a representative sample of line centers for fuller description. In Table 3, we list, by line center number given in Table 2, the alignment of each measured member line that goes out from its center.[18]

The reader who elects to undertake our guided walk across the pampa in Appendix II ought to consult closely the relevant maps of Fig. 3 that serve to delineate the extent of the principal lines emanating from these centers,

and the points of contact in the landscape that one can reach by walking on the lines. Using Fig. II.1b and the aerial mosaic (Photo-Appendix, Fig. 2) we shall see that lines from a given center often conduct the traveler rather far across the landscape.

ANALYZING THE NAZCA LINE DATA

Originally we set out to answer the question: Do patterns exist in the Nazca lines? To attempt to answer that question, we phrased several more specific questions and then determined that we would need to collect certain types of data by employing an essentially ground-based strategy. Perceivable patterns can serve as evidence for formulating new questions relating to the unifying principles of order in the construction and use of the lines. In the final portion of this chapter, we shall try to view the problem of whether order is present in the lines by attempting to sort the data so that we can deal with our broader query in more specific terms, thereby raising an even more precise set of questions that we could not have raised before—questions that might have escaped us because we had not yet become familiar enough with the pampa to ask them. We shall deal with our data in a structural type of analysis in three separate discussion categories.

*(1) Ecological Order*

We ask: Is there any evidence that the location of hills, the general nature of the skyline, rivers and their tributaries, soil types, agriculture and irrigation, etc. on and about the pampa, might have played a role in the builders' decision about where to locate and how to construct lines and line centers, the directions and lengths of lines, or the number and type of lines?

*(2) Astronomical Order*

Are the lines astronomically oriented? Historically, this is one of the problems upon

---

18. We placed the alignment data in three quality classes: *Class 1* (error ± 5 arc minutes), which applies to lines very clearly traceable, is obtained from transit readings based on an astronomical fix. For *Class 2*, with less easily discernible lines (error ± 1°), the orientation was determined with a magnetic compass and then was corrected by bringing the transit to the line center and obtaining the astronomical fix by measuring the orientation of one or more of the lines. Lines of these classes appear as solid lines in Fig. 3. Included as dotted lines in Fig. 3 are additional fainter lines for which the alignment data are of *Class 3* (error ± 2°). For this class, only magnetic compass readings were taken. These were converted to true (astronomical) readings by the additive correction: True Azimuth = Magnetic Azimuth + 3°40' ± 40' (probable error), which was determined from a series of magnetic and astronomical readings taken with both transit and compass by Aveni and Urton at a single arbitrary location in the middle of the pampa.

For certain centers, we have tabulated the line azimuth as read from Hawkins's photogrammetric survey map, which we obtained from a selected sampling of lines, the azimuths of which we determined with the transit to be accurate to 1° (quality Class 2).

which great emphasis has been laid. Recall (Chap. I) that more literature has been generated on the astronomical hypothesis for the origin of the Nazca lines than on all other hypotheses combined. Therefore, the many astronomical questions that can be raised deserve close examination.

*(3) Order with Respect to Other Cultural Remains*

This broad category overlaps slightly with Chapter III by Clarkson, who is concerned primarily with the archaeological remains on the pampa. Here we shall deal specifically with whether the lines and line centers are correlated with other categories of etchings and large-scale remains on the pampa such as the biomorphic figures, the geometry, and the widespread system of pre-Columbian roads in Peru.

Before we begin to test hypotheses about the lines, let us summarize the general extent of the data we have collected and, at the same time, introduce histograms (Fig. II.5), upon which all the alignments are plotted. These histograms will prove useful in the forthcoming discussion.

As stated earlier, we have tabulated 762 lines emanating from 62 centers. Of these, 224 (29 percent of the sample) are classified as broad and 538 (or 71 percent) are narrow lines. We know of but a single example of a straight line feature that is demonstrably not tied to one of these centers (see Fig. II.18). We have measured the alignments of 505 lines at quality level 2 (see Note 18, this chapter) or better, and this is the sample entered into our histograms; it consists of 126 broad and 379 narrow lines. The longest of these lines is over 9 km and there are 20 over 5 km in length (see histogram of Fig. II.6). The shortest is a small rectangle atop center No. 30 (15 m long and 2 m wide).

The average *traceable* length of a line from a sampling of centers is 1.3 km. Therefore, the total length of all lines etched on the pampa is slightly more than 1000 km, surely a lower limit when we realize that human activity, as

well as wind and stream erosion, have erased perhaps one-third to one-half or more of what might have been visible originally. It would not be an exaggeration to suggest that over 2000 km in total length of lines, representing a cleared area of 6½ million sq. m, once had adorned the 220 sq. km surface of the Peruvian desert between the Nazca and Ingenio Rivers.[19] These estimates include neither the trapezoids connected to lines that emanate from line centers, nor the isolated trapezoids, both of which we will treat in a later section.

Of the 62 line centers on the survey map of Figure II.1b, 45 are known to be connected to one or more other centers via 113 connector lines. Connector lines are no more heavily represented within the broad category, there being 32 broad and 81 narrow connector lines; i.e., 14 percent of all broad lines and 15 percent of all narrow lines measured are connectors. The average number of lines per center is about 12, but some centers contain double or more this number. Center No. 44, a very prominent peak jutting far out into the NW corner of the pampa, has the largest population of lines with 50. Center No. 35, in the middle of the pampa, has 40; center No. 61 has 26. By contrast, centers No. 51 and 59 possess only three lines apiece.

*The Nazca Line Centers and the Ecology of the Pampa*

There seems to be no question that line centers and lines attached to them constitute the most abundant morphological class of figures etched on the pampa. Lines intertwine and interconnect like a complex network over the entire pampa.

Our long-distance views (cf. Fig. II.1) of the locations of the line centers and lines associated with them verifies one fact we had already begun to anticipate fairly early in the

19. The estimate is made as follows: Using the histogram of widths, we determine the median width of narrow lines to be about 1 m and that of the wide lines to be about 14 m. Then we compute a total area in narrow lines of 1.00 sq. km and in wide lines of 5.39 sq. km for a total of 6.39 sq. km.

investigation: that the placement of the line centers might have something to do with the location of mountains and of surface water. We find that with few exceptions, the centers are located *at the bases of hills that penetrate the pampa from the mountains and along the elevated rim of the pampa that border the two principal river valleys and their tributaries.* We found few centers in the middle of the pampa. Centers No. 35 and 45 are two notable exceptions and it may be significant that both of these exhibit numerous lines, many of which connect to other centers.[20] These centers are positioned atop natural hills generally elevated barely a few meters above the pampa surface and, like most centers, they are visible from several kilometers away on a clear day. Often the centers are composed of clusters of hills with most of the lines radiating from the hill possessing the greatest elevation (cf. Nos. 30, 38, 44). In particular, note in Figure II.1b that centers No. 14, 15, 16, 17, 27, 34, 36, and 38 overlook the Nazca River from its north bank while centers No. 43, 46, 56, 58, and 61 appear on the high bluffs above the south bank of the Ingenio. Centers found at the tips of the finger-like projections of mountain chains out onto the pampa include Nos. 11, 19, 30, 37, 42, and 44. In Fig. II.7a, b, we employ a larger scale than the general map of Figure II.1b, to locate several centers with respect to the local topography. We also found a few centers on the south bank of the Nazca River, which opens onto the Pampa Atarco (e.g., Nos. 21, 22, 23, 33). Center No. 33 may be especially noteworthy because a few of its lines overlie the cemetery site of Pacheco. Moreover, most of the lines from center No. 33 radiate southward onto the open pampa, though a few go northward toward the Nazca River. These are traceable only a few tens of meters to the point where they enter the cultivated strip bordering the river. We suspect that the relative sparsity of desert-varnished fragments on the Nazca River's south bank may render invisible

any ancient lines that might have been constructed there.

A close examination of Fig. II.1b reveals that many line centers seem to have been established *along the broader tributaries* that pass from the mountains onto the pampa; line centers No. 1, 2, 3, 4, 6, 7, 8, 9, and 13 are examples at the upstream (east) end of the pampa. Also, a number of centers seem to have been deliberately located within view of tributaries that connect the main pampa with the river valleys. Selected examples include Nos. 40, 41, 45, 49, 50, 52, 54, and 55 on the north bank of the Nazca River. It is important to note that all the line centers (from No. 62 on the west to No. 42 on the east) that are found on the high bluffs above the south bank of the Ingenio River are situated on tributaries that flow not into the Ingenio, but into the Nazca drainage about 10 km to the SW and on the other side of the pampa. There are no line centers on the north bank of the Ingenio. The same is true of the centers located on the south bank of the Nazca River. In fact, all the centers are tied exclusively to the Nazca River drainage. While the frequency of occurrence of line centers along the north bank of the Nazca River is high, it diminishes drastically once one passes the general region of Cahuachi going downstream. This diminution could be attributable to the generally fragile nature of the sandy Pampa Majuelos and the canyon-like channels and chopped-up landscape of the Majuelos tributary in this region, both of which offer a very different landscape from that of the main pampa. Also, this is a much less productive area agriculturally (ONERN 1971).

There is an unusually high concentration of centers on the north bank of the Nazca River immediately opposite Cahuachi, as can be seen in Fig. II.1b. There, we find nine centers clustered in a square about two kilometers on a side, the highest concentration of radiating lines anywhere on the pampa. Following the member lines, we find no correlation between the position of the pyramids and the directions of these lines; however, a general associ-

---

20. Center No. 45 has 16 lines, of which seven are connectors. Center No. 35 has 40 lines, of which five are connectors. Recall that the average number of lines per center is 12; the average number of connectors is two.

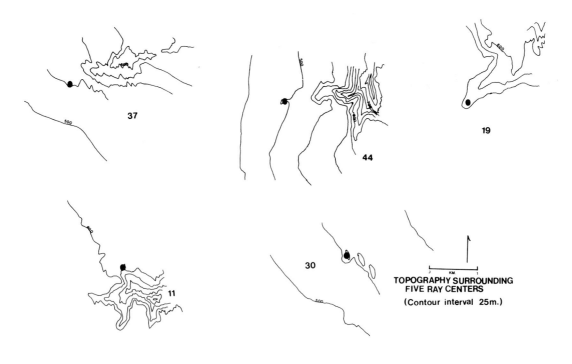

Fig. II.7. The location of specific centers (filled circles) relative to local topographic features, traced from IGM 1:50,000 maps. Inset: aerial view of one of these, No. 11 (cf. Fig. II.3(11)). In each case, the center lies at the end of a finger-like chain of hills that intrudes onto the pampa (arrow).

Fig. II.8a. Zigzag features. On this heavily worked zone of the pampa, zigzag and bent lines seem to wander chaotically across the desert surface, often reflecting off the *quebradas*. (Servicio Aerofotografico Nacional [SAN] Photo 6511-A-2-44)

ation between Nazca lines and that great ceremonial center may exist (as Silverman argues in Chap. V, this volume).

The association between line centers and water in general can be further refined. We have noted earlier that at least one, and often many more, large trapezoidal features are connected to line centers. Often a line becomes a trapezoid a long way from a center. While the lines emanating from centers usually cut across the dry *quebradas*, the large trapezoids attached to lines seem to be situated in the spits of elevated land that lie in between. Frequently their axes lie parallel to the direction of the flow of water, a fact we will verify quantitatively later, when we discuss the Nazca geometrical etchings in some detail. Take, for example, the lines attached to center No. 11, which lies on a hill that juts out onto the pampa containing the Rio Socos. Examining Figure II.3(11) and Photomosaic (Appendix IV), we note that lines 1 through 5 cross the

pampa of the Rio Socos and cut the river at nearly right angles. But line 6 proceeds to a distance of 2 km from the center toward the direction of the immediate source of the river in the mountains. It opens up into a huge trapezoid over a kilometer in length. Other large trapezoids that are associated with line centers and whose axes lie along the direction of flow of water include 4-7; 17-1 and 5; 20-7; 35-6, 23, 24, 25, 15, 16; 37-1; 38-9; 45-1; 52-3; and 55-1 and 2. Trapezoid 30-1 (see the oblique aerial photograph of Appx. II, Fig. 1a), like so many of these features seems to fit neatly onto the elevated land between pairs of parallel flow patterns. Were such areas the only spaces ample enough to contain these giant figures with the assurance that they would not be eroded by floods? We shall return to this question later.

Next, let us look more closely at the hills that extend in finger-like patterns down onto the pampa from the northeast (Fig. II.7). We

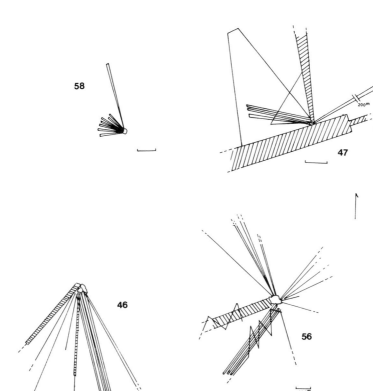

Fig. II.8b. Line centers associated with "saw-tooth" and parallel-line zigzag patterns. Often the lines repeatedly conduct the walker away from the center and then back again.

find that nearly half (46 percent) of the lines associated with these hills lie within ± 30° of the axis of the peninsula that protrudes out onto the pampa. If lines radiated randomly from the tip of a given hill, we would expect to find only 8½ percent so aligned (see the maps of centers No. 30, 37, and 42 in Fig. II.3 for a particularly striking illustration of this focusing effect). These results give the impression that in a typical center, the interaction between the two end points represented by a line is related to a phenomenon or activity lying in the general direction of the open pampa or on the other side of the pampa as seen from the protruding finger, or vice-versa. Not surprisingly, the axes of these fingers generally lie along the prevailing direction of the flow of water down from the mountains, across the pampa, and into the Nazca basin.

What of those lines that do not connect center-to-center (78 percent of the sample) or center-to-trapezoid (90 percent)? Unfortu-

nately, many lines—nearly half of them—are impossible to follow onto the pampa because of the heavy erosion. We see them disappearing into *quebradas*, or the large tributaries, many only to reappear faintly on the opposite bank. Some can be followed across the ancient natural waterways as though they might have preceded the erosion features and then become partially eroded by them, but, in general, this length seems unlikely because geological evidence shows that most flooding episodes occurred in remote antiquity. On the other hand, as we stated earlier, a few lines, perhaps 3 percent, we can actually be assured do terminate in *quebradas* (examples include 27-2, 38-2, and 3; and several lines from centers Nos. 42 and 44 that end abruptly at the Ingenio River). Other lines (7 percent) seem to bend and reflect off the boundary between pampa and river valley (a host of examples is visible in the photo of Fig. II.8a). Some of these bent lines develop into zigzag patterns and still others return to the same center whence they departed (Fig. II.8b). Often one finds a bent line that splits into branches as it goes along (44-7 is a good example).

Up to this point, we have begun to become fairly convinced that *the immediate tangible environment, i.e., the region within meters, tens and perhaps a few hundred meters of a line or line center, is a significant determinant of its placement.* But what can we say about the wider environment of the pampa and its relation to lines? If the direction of flow of water is correlated with orientation, we should examine how the direction to the sea or the direction to the intersection of the Nazca and Ingenio Rivers (the Rio Grande), both invisible points from the pampa, might relate to the lines. The nearest shoreline of the Pacific Ocean, an environment whose denizens are represented in the marine figures etched on the pampa, lies 70 km from the pampa in direction 240° (cf. Photomosaic (Appendix IV); this is the same as the direction of the water flow across the pampa), while the intersection of the rivers lies in the direction 270° (measured from north toward the east) with respect to the line centers on the Rio Ingenio's bank and 290° with respect to the group residing on the bank of the Nazca River. Of the three directions, Fig. II.5 reveals that only the first may show a marginally significant correlation with respect to line azimuth. Eleven lines are situated in azimuth 239° ± 2°, four more than expected on the basis of chance coincidence. However, if we single out the locations of this sample of lines, we find that they spread out relatively evenly over the pampa.

Andean ethnography and ethnohistory are filled with information about the importance of mountain peaks that overlook most sites (cf. Reinhard 1987), but in the case of Nazca, we know all too little about the relative importance of the hills that ring the pampa, save for the prominent white mountain (that actually resembles a giant sand dune) lying to the east (though Reinhard also mentions Cerro Tunga). Urton's (n.d. c) ethnographic work in the area suggests Cerro Blanco (elev. 2078 meters) was very important in local rites for

inducing the rains; it lies at azimuths 90°–120° as sighted by an observer moving from the southern to the northernmost regions of the pampa. Reinhard (1987: 16–17) offers evidence from the chronicles that this mountain was worshipped as a means of providing water and controlling meteorological conditions at least a few hundred years prior to the Spanish occupation of the Nazca valley. Shifting our frame of reference within this 30° sector, we actually detected an underabundance of lines compared to what we would have expected from a random distribution. From centers No. 3, 4, 6, 9, 21, 22, 23, 24, and 25, those nearest Cerro Blanco (though the peak would not be visible), we found not a single line out of a sample of several dozen to be oriented to within 5° of the direction to Cerro Blanco. From centers No. 11, 14, 15, 16, 17, 19, 20, 26, 27, 30, and the Nazca north bank group located on the bluffs above the Ingenio, only three lines visually pointed to within 5° of the azimuth of Cerro Blanco (120°). Given the overwhelmingly negative results, we wonder whether the builders deliberately *avoided* aiming lines at Cerro Blanco.[21]

_____

21. Ruggles's analysis (Chap. VI) produces the same conclusion. In a more rigorous statistical approach, he determined the orientation to selected points of possible significance in the landscape, with respect to the position of each individual line center, whereas we grouped line centers and employed averaged positions, an action we felt was justified by the relatively large distance between the centers and the topographic points. Nevertheless, most of the large-scale trends Ruggles reports upon in his paper, particularly the avoidance of east, the dominance of north in the histogram for all lines, and the NE skew in the distribution of broad features, also can be seen graphically in our Fig. II.5.

Concerning the relationship of Nazca lines to the environment, we should enumerate the unpublished observations of Josue Lancho, a Nazca schoolteacher and local official who has worked extensively in the archaeological zone of Cantalloc. Readers of Chap. I will recall that this place lies well off the main pampa in the little tributary valley 3 km west of line center No. 1 in Figure II.1b. He claims that "All of the geoglyphs of triangular form face towards the farthest part of the hills, the most prominent of which is 'The White Hill, the highest dune of all the Americas'" (Lancho n.d.). The first half of his statement lends independent corroboration to our discovery that the large geometrical figures line up with the water flow, but the second half is inconsistent with what we and Ruggles found on the pampa. Lancho also contends that three lines start from a point (possibly a line center we had not recognized) and are directed toward the locations of three man-made aqueducts of the type we discussed in Chapter I. He accompanies his one-page text with a sketch map that includes three lines showing them connected to three aqueducts on the banks of the Tierras Blancas River. Given the evidence, we are unable to judge

*Astronomy and the Nazca Lines*

The major points to be derived from reviewing the literature mentioned in Chapter I are that an analysis of the Nazca line alignments for astronomical orientation must be particularly thorough and that before we can adopt any astronomical hypotheses as facts, we must have supporting evidence that is statistically significant. If any of the lines functioned as astronomical indicators, then what can we hypothesize as possible targets?

The ethnographic and ethnohistoric evidence discussed in an earlier section of this chapter suggests that some possible orientation schemes related to agriculture and ritual could have been employed by the Nazca line builders, and surely we should look for correlations involving these concepts. But can we first seek any other general indications of astronomical orientation? For example, the range of the horizon between azimuths 65°–115° and 245°–295° is roughly that through which the sun moves on its annual course. That the Nazca system of agriculture might have employed a solar orientation calendar is quite reasonable and Urton's (1982) study of the calendars of the coast gives us a working set of solar dates to search out. Extending this zone by 5° at either end, we would include the range of horizon through which the moon and planets pass. Another zone of possible significance, also suggested by Urton's ethnographic work, is the region over which the centers of the four quarters of the Milky Way intersect the horizon: marked by azimuths 60°, 122°, 238°, and 300° (Urton 1981b: 164). At the most general level, we can seek matches for all our alignments (to within a 1° tolerance, assuming an elevation of the horizon of 3°)[22]

with the directions of the rising and setting of the brightest stars, the solar and lunar horizon extremes, and special stars and star groups that Andean people might have sought out, such as the aforementioned Pleiades and α and β Centauri. The points of sunrise/sunset on the day of zenith and anti-zenith passage and the cardinal directions also ought to be checked. To reduce the error spread, we should utilize only those lines for which our measurements are precise (i.e., quality classes 1 and 2; see Note 22, this chapter). Supportive data for the stellar orientations might be expected to exist not only in the ethnographic and ethnohistoric record but also in the form of functional calendric relationships. For example, are the heliacal rise-set dates of stars that are found to match line azimuths also significant in the solar calendar?

At first glance, except for the avoidance of Cerro Blanco to the east and a piling up around the north, our histograms (Fig. II.5) showing distributions of line directions in horizontal space seem rather unrevealing; however, a closer look indicates that there are a number of azimuth ranges, some of them wide and others narrow, where line directions might appear to stack up, particularly in the total sample:

(a) 347°–17° (passing through 0°): 71 lines, or about 14 percent of the total measured, fell in this wide zone (we would expect 42 in a random distribution); the direction exactly opposite (167°–197°) has only 47 entries. Of these 71, 18 were broad and 53 narrow. Eighteen were connectors, all about what we would expect on the average. This pack of lines seems to have its greatest concentration toward azimuths 347° to 352°, where 17 lines fall, more than double the number anticipated. Six lines lie between 349° and 350°. The centers from which lines belonging to this azimuth category emanate are relatively evenly spread across the pampa, but we do note that lines linked to four very large trapezoids are among the features that fit in this narrow az-

---

whether these aqueducts are part of a single system. Since the lines seem to terminate well before they reach the aqueducts, it may be that they were intended, like so many lines we traced on the main pampa, to end in the river. We did not check out the locations of those points.

22. A one-degree difference of elevation at the latitude of Nazca results in a difference in the azimuthal shift of the sunrise/set positions due to horizon elevation of less than 20 minutes of arc (cf. Aveni 1980b: 117–118), i.e., about two-thirds of the solar disk. Because we found the altitude of the horizon to vary by no more than one degree from a mean of 3° and because a large portion of our data are of quality Class 2 (see discussion,

note 1 to Table 3), we have adopted a mean of 3° for the horizon elevation throughout our analysis.

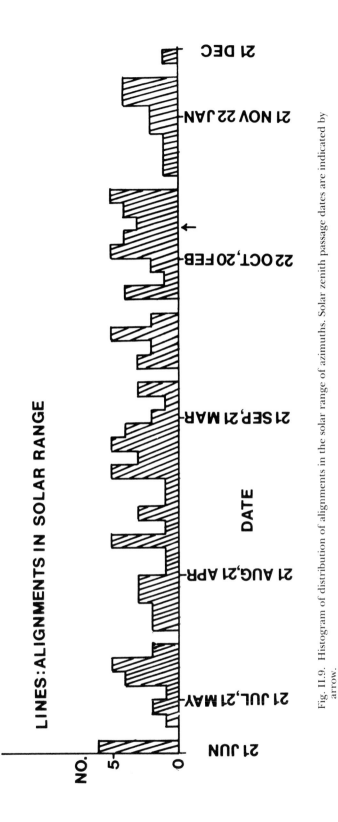

Fig. II.9. Histogram of distribution of alignments in the solar range of azimuths. Solar zenith passage dates are indicated by arrow.

imuthal band. We find no astronomically significant events in this region except to note that it is close to the general south-north direction. Also, azimuth 350° corresponds roughly to the direction to the adjacent pampa north of the Rio Grande on which one finds many of the same types of features as those that appear on the main pampa;

(b) 215°–225°: For this region we tabulated 26 entries (15 expected). Four of these are broad and 22 are narrow; there are 10 connectors. For the opposite direction (35°–45°) we listed only 16. The peak occurs at 215°–217° in which interval nine lines were tabulated (six between 215° and 216°). We find nothing unusual about the collection of centers from which this cluster of lines emanates, and there are no astronomical events occurring there to which we can attribute any significance.

There are no other broad zones within which we find significant clumping. Looking at narrower zones, we find slight excesses in 43°–44°, 279°–280°, 259°–260°, 216°–217°, 170°–171°, 56°–57°, and 16°–17°.[23]

We withhold discussion of the 259°–260° samples until later in this section because they may be related to other solar positions, namely, sunset on the day of zenith passage (279°–280° corresponds to sunset on anti-zenith passage). We can discover nothing of significance for the remainder.

Let us apply the most general test of the frequency of matching of alignments with azimuths in the zone of the horizon traversed by the rising/setting sun. Given our sample, we would expect 140 lines to fall in this range by pure chance. In fact, we find 123 (56 on the east, of which 18 are broad and 38 are narrow, and 67 on the west, of which 12 are broad and 55 are narrow). There were 15 connectors in the east and 13 in the west group. Some centers, e.g., Nos. 11, 30, 37, and 42, exhibited a rather large percentage contribution to that zone.[24] Our results are in basic agreement with

Hawkins's conclusion: that there is no general solar or lunar orientation principle followed by the lines taken as a group. However, the reader must be reminded (cf. Chap. I) that Hawkins employed a different sample of lines.

Next, we look only at the alignments that fall within the solar zone and we deal with them as a separate sample. We do this with complete justification because we realize that astronomy (and particularly solar orientations) may be only a *part* of the system, just as has proven to be the case in the *ceque* system of Cuzco.

In Fig. II.9, we display the distributions of alignments in the 65°–115° and 245°–295° zones (the solar zone). Of course, every alignment in these zones must coincide with sunrise/sunset on a particular pair of dates in the tropical year. The graph is composed of 123 alignments of quality classes 1 and 2, and we judge that the spread over this region may be non-random. Though there is no obvious clustering tendency precisely at the solar zenith and anti-zenith sunrise/sunset azimuths, 22 alignments (50 percent above the anticipated number) are grouped in the 5° range representing the period 22 Oct–2 Nov and 10 Feb–20 Feb of the solar calendar. This zone

---

23. We note that all but one of the lines in the 16°–17° sample emanate from the SE corner of the pampa.
24. If we extend the solar zone to include the moon and planets, we obtain for the full sample of 505 entries a total of 140 "hits" (168 anticipated). Looking at the distribution plots of broad features only and connectors only (Fig. II.5), we find above-average concentrations of broad features at:

| | |
|---|---|
| 31°–35° | (6 of 10 features are broad) |
| 41°–44° | (5 of 10 " ) |
| 82°–85° | (4 of 5 " ) |
| 278°–281° | (5 of 8 " ) |
| 348°–351° | (5 of 12 " ) |

The heaviest concentration of connectors can be found in the zones:

| | |
|---|---|
| 39°–45° | (6 of 16 features are broad) |
| 82°–88° | (4 of 9 " ) |
| 100°–101° | (3 of 4 " ) |
| 133°–135° | (3 of 6 " ) |
| 203°–205° | (3 of 6 " ) |
| 215°–217° | (4 of 9 " ) |
| 262°–267° | (5 of 10 " ) |
| 280°–281° | (3 of 5 " ) |
| 310°–314° | (5 of 10 " ) |

Twenty-seven connectors fall in the solar zone. In the lunar zone, we find 31, about the number expected due to randomness in either case. Likewise, for the Milky Way–horizon intersection zone, we find 350 (365 anticipated) lines falling in this region. The only Milky Way extreme that may show a significant correlation is 205° (SSW).

includes the 100°–105° azimuth range for sunrises and the 255°–260° azimuth range for sunsets.[25] Solar zenith passages in Nazca occur on 2 Nov and 10 Feb. This raises the possibility that some of the alignments may have served as a warning device in anticipation of the spring (Nov) zenith passage, which correlates very well with the time one finds water running in the canals. Interestingly enough, this very prediction was advanced by Kosok (1965: chap. 5) in the form of a hypothesis that the lines might point to sunrise/sunset dates during the season of water flow across the pampa (see the seasonal rainfall chart for the pampa in Chap. III, Fig. 3 this volume); however, he did not link these events with solar zenith passage. Recall the evidence from Urton's work supporting the importance of the zenith passage dates in the calendar. Also, note that the peaks in our histogram fall several days either side of the zenithal passage dates, thus supporting the notion that observations leading up to a significant solar event, perhaps with attending rituals, took place. Such anticipatory observations seem quite reasonable among cultures developing agricultural timing mechanisms and indeed, there is a precedence for their use in other native American horizon-based astronomies (Zeilik 1985; McCluskey n.d.).

We also find (in Fig. II.9) a sharp peak of six lines falling close to the June solstice, while a dearth of lines correlate with the December solstice. All the lines in the solstice sample are narrow and particularly long; two of them emanate from the same center.

We also looked at individual centers in the light of the above orientation criteria. Some turned out to yield strong correlations, while others were found to give rather poor ones. Leaving the interaction between astronomical targets and alignments to pure randomness, we would expect that, given the total of 30 targets utilized in the present study, with a ±2° window for each and without target overlap, we should find 120° or 33⅓ percent of the

horizon to be impinged upon by lines. Thus, one alignment picked at random would exhibit a one-out-of-three chance of an astronomical match-up.

Utilizing our data, we find matches in 34 percent of the instances. Thus, this statistical test also gives us reason to believe astronomical planning was not a general part of the design and layout of all line centers taken together. But, as we argued above, this conclusion does not rule out an astronomical function for some of the centers or part of the system. (Recall the analogy of the *ceque* system.) For example, center No. 11 is among those that possess many more astronomical orientations than we would expect; furthermore, the objects to which the lines are oriented seem to bear a calendrically functional relationship to one another—that is, the phenomenon of the appearance and/or disappearance of these objects could have been used as timing devices to mark specific points in the solar calendar. Finally, one of the lines (no. 1) points to within 2° of sunset on the day of zenith passage. Given the evidence, we must regard line center No. 11 as one of the best cases for an astronomically oriented line center. Moreover, its outlook toward the open pampa to the west would have given a commanding view of the sky.[26]

---

25. Of the 22, 12 go east and 10 west. Six are broad, and four are connectors. The lines belonging to this group emanate from centers spread all over the pampa.

26. Specifically, line no. 4 points to within 1° of the bright star Arcturus's set in AD 500 (best fit AD 650). Now, it turns out that Arcturus underwent heliacal rising (see Aveni tables [1972], event A) within one day of solar zenith passage in AD 500 (same date for AD 650). Therefore, there may be a functional relationship between the appearance or disappearance of this star and the appearance of the sun to back up the alignment. Line 11-1 aligned with Rigel (1¾° error) in AD 500 (an exact fit in AD 000). Rigel underwent heliacal event C seven days after zenith passage in AD 500 (one day after in AD 000). Thus, a Rigel alignment and related solar event also fit both date and direction in AD 000. Capella's rise direction fits exactly in AD 500 with the direction of line 11-6. Heliacal event B for this star happened within five days of anti-zenith sunset in AD 500 (exact in AD 750). Capella underwent event A on June 2 in AD 500 and we have another alignment at line center No. 11 that fits that direction: line 11-3 points within ½° of sunset on that day. Finally, line 11-2 points to sunset on 18 Apr and 26 Aug. The former lies close to the date when Arcturus underwent event C. Therefore, *altogether for line center No. 11, we have three stellar alignments, all of which can be related (over an admittedly broad range of time) to the timing of solar events; furthermore the spatial directions to all three of these events are indicated by lines from the same center.* The later dates for these events (AD 500–750) are more consistent with the archaeological record. Finally, Urton (personal communication) has noted that the direction of outlook also corresponds

Fig. II.10. One of the many instances in which a line from a
line center covers over a figure. Looking eastward along line
42–9 toward line center No. 42, the small peak projecting out
onto the pampa from the mountains (arrow).

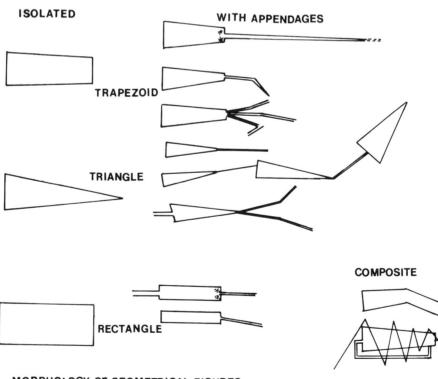

**ISOLATED**                    **WITH APPENDAGES**

**TRAPEZOID**

**TRIANGLE**

**RECTANGLE**                                    **COMPOSITE**

**MORPHOLOGY OF GEOMETRICAL FIGURES**

Fig. II.11. Morphological classification of geometrical shapes etched on the pampa.

Fig. II.12. It is common for a line from a line center to lead into a trapezoid. Note that the trapezoid terminates in one of the *quebradas* that crosses the pampa. (SAN. Photo 0-28273)

Fig. II.13. Region of gigantic trapezoids (one of them covers a bird). Several large figures about the northern rim of the pampa, where it falls off into the Ingenio basin (bottom left)

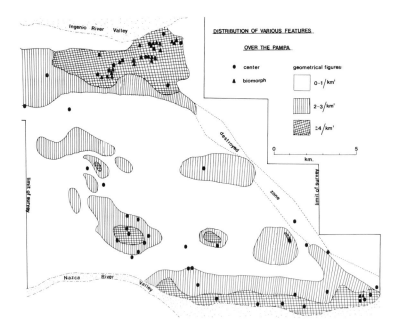

Fig. II.14. Distribution of various types of features over the pampa. Note that practically all the biomorphs are confined to a small area on the south bank of the Ingenio River.

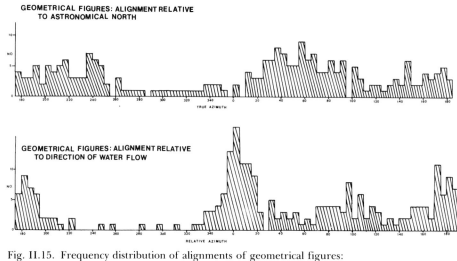

Fig. II.15. Frequency distribution of alignments of geometrical figures:
(a) With respect to astronomical north.
(b) With respect to the direction of flow of water across the pampa (upstream = 0°).

Finally, let us examine the frequency of matching of alignments with specific astronomical targets. We tabulated the number of lines that fit the direction of stellar, solar, and lunar events to within 1°. With a window of ±1° per target, one can anticipate, due to randomness, 5.5 hits on a rise/set position of a single object given our sample of 505 lines. The total number of hits on all targets would be expected to be 165. For time AD 000, we tally 183 hits and for AD 500, 194 hits, the latter of which corresponds with the best evidence we have for dating the lines by other means. The relatively late dates of AD 1000 and 1500 yield a total of 166 hits and 182 hits, respectively.

We must exercise caution in our interpretation of the stellar alignments because of the relatively rapid change of azimuth of star rise and set with time (up to 1° per century). Nev-

_____
to the principal direction of travel out of the Nazca valley and toward the Ingenio valley in general.

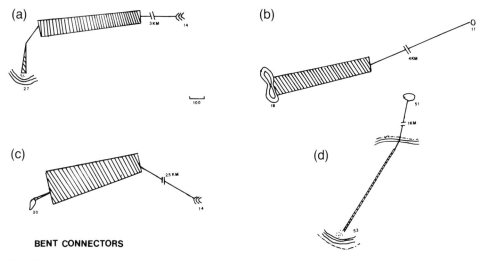

BENT CONNECTORS

Fig. II.16. Some examples of connecting paths between centers comprised of linked or angled segments rather than straight lines: (a) 27 to 14 (b) 19 to 11 (c) 20 to 14 (d) 53 to 51

Fig. II.17. This Inka road south of the Jequetepeque valley closely resembles the wide Nazca lines. (See also Chap. 1, Fig. 11) (J. Hyslop)

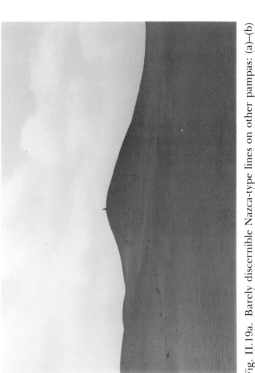

Fig. II.19a. Barely discernible Nazca-type lines on other pampas: (a)–(b) Trapezoids lead up to hilltops overlooking the Chincha River valley.

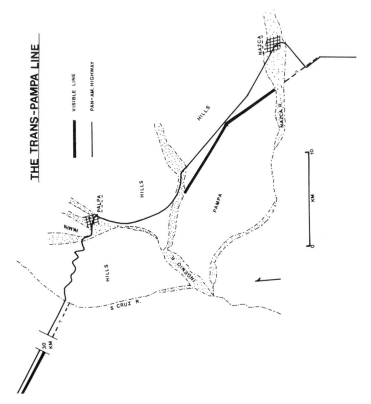

Fig. II.18. The trans-pampa line and the continuation of the Inka road north of the pampa.

Fig. II.19b.

Fig. II.19c. A cairn located atop one of the hills.

ertheless, adopting a date of AD 500, we find a relatively high frequency of hits for the Pleiades, the zenith sun, and α and β Centauri, which are known to have been of some significance in Andean skylore. Canopus, of which we have heard no mention in skylore, but which happened to possess very nearly the same declination and consequently the same rise/set azimuths as α and β Centauri, also is found to score high.[27] Rigel, Capella, Regulus, and two of the lunar extremes are targets for which no real ethnographic base appears in the literature and their appearance on the high side of our tabulations may be due to coincidence, especially since there is an equal number of stars for which we have no ethnographic basis and which score quite low (Vega, Spica, Fomalhaut, Betelgeuse, Altair, Procyon, Aldebaran, ε Orionis).

We cannot impose the same narrow windows when dealing with the Milky Way horizon intersection points because the former is such a wide configuration. If we widen the window by several degrees, we do note a possible excess of alignments in the directions of three of the four centers of the quarters of the Milky Way (122° excepted).

Our analysis, if somewhat tedious, reveals that astronomy, though largely lost in the data, may nevertheless be faintly present. Though there are no obvious clustering tendencies that can be directly attributed to astronomical factors, sky phenomena that were recognized and that possessed meaning in the coastal environment seem to turn up in the alignments. Given the nature of Andean astronomical concepts as revealed in the *ceque* system of Cuzco, we should expect to find that if the Nazca lines and the *ceque* lines are even remotely comparable, then the astronomical and calendrical structural determinants would be mixed among the other criteria, such as water flow, that we already feel certain were employed at least in part to determine the layout and orientation of lines on the pampa.

Of the possible astronomical orientations

revealed in these studies, it is no surprise that one of the more prominent turns out to be that most important of all dates in Andean calendrical systems, the day the sun crosses the zenith.

We are pleased to have loaned all our data to Clive Ruggles of the Computing Studies Unit at the University of Leicester (see also Note 21), who offered to perform a rigorous analysis of it employing his excellent facilities. For an alternative study of the possible role of astronomy in the planning of the lines, the reader should consult Chapter V, which can then be compared with the present section of this work. Our experiment demonstrates that significant differences can result when different methodologies are applied to basically the same data set. One will note that there are points of agreement in the general results as well as a number of specific differences. For example, Ruggles's detailed analysis of the Pleiades' dates and orientations reveals a greater potential importance for that star group than we have indicated. While our study suggests that center No. 11 may possess the highest frequency of astronomical orientations, his results single out center No. 44. Finally, there is some disagreement in our comparative lists of the best target stars one ought to employ. While some of our differences can be attributed to the ways in which one can interpret statistics, others stem from different assumptions about what azimuth range constitutes a "hit" and what epochs one uses. Perhaps the lesson to be learned from a close comparison of the two studies is that we should be very cautious about jumping to any specific astronomical conclusions. Nevertheless, both studies reveal the likelihood that astronomical concepts are embedded somewhere within the scheme.

*Order with Respect to Other Cultural Remains*

**The Lines and the Other Features on the Pampa**

Our strategy for studying the problem of the origin and meaning of the Nazca lines has consisted of collecting and analyzing data on a

---

27. Canopus is also the second brightest star in the sky.

single type of feature. Recall that at the outset of this chapter we defined a line as a carefully constructed *straight feature* with a border consisting of the detritus removed in the etching process. Having isolated and examined straight lines as a class, we learned that nearly all of them emanate from centers consisting of natural hills. We determined that the lines were almost surely walked upon (recall that many have footpaths within) and that the act of walking may have been associated with the water flow because the lines began and ended at centers that were located at significant points on the pampa with respect to the passage of water over it. Astronomical orientations probably played a role in the plan of some line centers, but if astronomy was connected to the design scheme, it must have been only part of the total picture.

In order to obtain a clearer understanding of the meaning of the lines, we must now place them back into their appropriate context as but one category of the cultural remains that adorn the pampa. Thus, we raise the question: Is there any connection between lines/line centers and the other remains of human origin on the pampa? Does the detailed information we have gathered in our survey of the lines shed any light on these other remains and, by looking at the other data, can we obtain a better understanding of why lines and line centers were built?

The other remains to which we shall refer in this section are the other Nazca etchings: the geometrical features such as triangles, trapezoids, and the abstract figures, especially the famous biomorphic figures. The subject of the traditional archaeological remains, such as ceramics, cairns, rings, and other standing structures, will be dealt with in the chapter by Clarkson, but we will mention the pre-Columbian roads here because they represent one category of cultural remains that bears a distinct resemblance to the Nazca straight lines.

There exist some three dozen examples of biomorphic Nazca figures that can be classified more precisely into zoo- or phytomorphic

etchings, mostly the former.[28] Practically all of them are located in a relatively small area that covers about 5 percent of the pampa on the eastern half of its NW corner (see Fig. II.14, in which triangles represent the plant and animal figures, while the cross-hatched regions show the heaviest concentration of large geometrical figures). These labyrinthine figures seem to have been constructed in the same way as the linear features, but it may be significant that they were built on an entirely different scale from the lines, the figures being much smaller in extent than either the lines or trapezoids.[29] In fact, not a single one of these figures is visible on the photomosaic provided in the Photomosaic (Appendix IV).

In most cases, a given figure can be traced by a unicursal line that never crosses over itself. This fact indicates that they may have been intended to be walked upon rather than viewed from on high, though one cannot rule out the possibility that both motives were intended. If most of the figures were to appear physically connected to straight lines and line centers, then it would be possible to propose that lines and biomorphic figures possessed a related meaning. The archaeological record can help us here. On the basis of the ceramic data, Clarkson has suggested that the lines may have been later features (see Chap. III). But, can we find, simply by looking at them, any examples of lines that run on top of or obliterate underlying animal figures or animal figures that overlie the lines? Unfortunately, in her zeal to preserve these features, Reiche has swept many of them so thoroughly clean that it is difficult to answer this question. However, a few of the figures have lain relatively untouched.

It has been suggested that the animal figures and the geometry are related (Kern and Reiche 1974: 1–2), but we find it more likely

---

28. Kern and Reiche (1974: 38) list 32 figures of which only four or five could conceivably represent plants. About half of the animal sample are birds (see Chap. I, Fig. 4). In addition, there appear the well-known monkey, spider, fox, some fish, and a lizard. (See Clarkson [n.d.] for the possible identification of some of the more enigmatic composite figures.)

29. Excluding the 125-m-long bird-with-a-long-neck, all the figures are less than 100 m in length.

that these two morphological types of pampa etchings are unrelated physically and functionally and that instead they may represent activities undertaken by entirely different groups of people at different times.

Are the biomorphic figures and the geometry oriented in the same direction? On her map of the lines (Kern and Reiche 1974: 2), Reiche shows only eight biomorphs and about 20 trapezoids. The latter seem to align in the general directions 15°–195° and 70°–25° (passing through 0°). Two animals align in the first direction, while the remainder more or less fit the second, so there may be a weak correlation in this regard. On this map, the geometry—like the line centers—is shown to be concentrated along the north bank of the Nazca River and on the high bluff overlooking the south bank of the Ingenio River. If the biomorphic figures and the geometry were intended to be associated with one another, why, then, do we find practically none of the former among the geometrical figures that are situated at the southern end of the pampa?[30]

We believe the issue of connectedness of different morphological types can be resolved only through a case-by-case examination. In our analysis we have referred to two separate categories of figural drawings in the discussion:

(i) Those which appear to be connected either to a zigzag pattern, a trapezoid, or to one or more straight lines;

(ii) Completely isolated open or closed figures.

Finally, we cite figures that are demonstrably covered over by lines. (Fig. II.13 is an excellent example of this category, in which a trapezoid obliterates a large section of a bird-like figure[31]; see also Fig. II.10.)

We were unable to cite a single example of an untouched biomorphic figure when examined either from the air, from the ground, or both, that covers a linear feature. The high incidence of occurrence of such figures near large geometric drawings and lines often is taken to imply a connection between the two,[32] but a closer look at these figures reveals that, in many cases, the connection is imagined.[33]

Still, a few definite connections between zigzag lines and biomorphs can be established. For example, there is no doubt that the Monkey figure is connected to a complex linear pattern. It starts and ends in zigzags, one form of which contains 16 parallel lines intersected by a thin trapezoid (cf. Chap. I, Fig. I.5). These two geometrical elements, when added to the double labyrinthine spiral, are precisely the same components one finds in the purely abstract Yarn & Needle geoglyph near Cantal-

---

30. Zuidema (personal communication) pointed out that the pan-Andean radial quality, so prominent in the line centers and in the *ceque* system of Cuzco, also is discernible in the biomorphic etchings. For example, he notes that the tail feathers, wings, and legs of the condor (Chap. I, Fig. 4a) all converge at a point at the center of the body of the animal. Therefore, one may suggest that lines and biomorphs are physically related in the sense that they possess similar structural characteristics.
31. In the discussion that follows, we refer to these figures with an "R" followed by their number given on the map in Kern and

Reiche 1974: 2. All other figures are labeled "KR", for Kern-Reiche, followed by the number of the photograph on which they can be found in that text. Figures which Reiche suggests are connected to zigzag patterns by virtue of the way she has drawn them on her map (Kern and Reiche 1974: 2), include the Plant-like figure (R18), the Monkey (R7), the Spider (R16), and the Aerodynamic Bird (KR 69). Those she regards as being connected to trapezoids or triangles consist of the Fox (R8) and the Condor (R14). (A straight line clearly overlies the Condor; cf. Morrison 1978: 60.) The Aerodynamic Bird (KR 69), as well as the Insect (or Bird?) (R19), is interesting in the present instance for, while neither is connected to a zigzag pattern, each appears to exhibit the zigzag pattern within the confines of its construction. Indeed, the Insect(?), except for its head, degenerates into an abstract zigzag rectangular form. The crest of the Pelican's head (upper right corner of map) also is made up of a zigzag pattern which, if isolated from the remainder of the figure, scarcely would be discernible from many of the purely abstract zigzags that appear on the pampa. (Views of some of these biomorphs can be found in Chap. I, Fig. 4.)
32. E.g., Kern and Reiche 1974: 133 Note 5, 134 Note 12, 136 Note 37; Reiche 1949: Fig. 66; Reiche 1968: 58.
33. Take the Plant-like figure (R18). The oblique angle photograph (KR 47) shows that the so-called connecting line actually cuts across the main stem of the figure, continuing beyond its north side, a segment which Reiche does not show in the map of Kern and Reiche 1974: 2, though it does appear in the drawing (KR 37). The line shown connecting the Condor (R14) to a trapezoid is, in fact, part of a tail feather that happens by chance to border upon the trapezoid. The line tracing the tail feather returns back toward the bird design, making it, in effect, a closed figure and not an open one, dangling by a line from the end of the trapezoid, as Reiche portrays it on the map. The Spider (R16) actually is not connected to any lines, though two lines do cut across and apparently over it. However, these lines are among a group of 18 that emanate in all directions from our line center No. 47, and it is likely only due to chance that they intersect the body of the Spider (cf. Hadingham 1987: 102).

loc (Chap. I, Fig. 6), as Morrison (1978: 57) has pointed out.[34]

On the contrary, the number of animal and plant drawings that can be demonstrated to be totally untied to lines and geometry is rather considerable.[35]

One fact we cannot emphasize enough in the present analysis is that, *of the several hundred lines we have mapped or traced* over the five-year period 1980–1984 we worked on the pampa, *not a single one was found to lead to or terminate within a biomorphic figure.* The archaeological evidence discussed by Clarkson and the photographic and ground survey data reported in the present chapter seem to work strongly against the hypothesis that biomorphic figures and lines were related functionally.[36]

In every instance where we have made observations at ground level of lines and zoomorphs crossing over one another, and when we can be certain that the biomorph has not been swept or cleaned in modern times, the linear feature always seems to overlie the biomorph. Note for example the figure of the bird submerged by trapezoids in Figure II.13. On the other hand the hummingbird (Fig. 4f of Chap. I) stands out above the linear features only because it has been swept clean in the past quarter century. We conclude that the zoomorphic figural drawings were part of an

earlier, rather more localized tradition, likely engaged in by people who lived primarily in the portion of the Ingenio Valley nearest that small section of the pampa where these figures appear. Ceramic evidence, as well as the forms that appear on the pottery, suggests we might attribute these developments to earlier phases of the Nasca culture (see Clarkson's detailed discussion on this point in Chap. III).

The association between the lines and geometry is entirely different, as we shall see in the next part of this section. We believe the rare examples where contours forming the zoo- and phytomorphic figures tie in with geometry are either whimsical or fortuitous.

### Lines & Geometry

The large geometrical figures cover a greater area of the pampa than the straight lines and the zoomorphic figures combined. We recognize three basic morphological shapes (see Fig. II.11): trapezoid, triangle, and rectangle, though the term "trapezoid" usually is employed to designate all three. Some of the figures stand alone, but more often an appendage consisting of a narrow line seems to shoot out of the apex (Fig. II.12), frequently running for a kilometer or more before terminating in a line center or in another geometrical figure. The appended line keeps a constant width in some cases, while in others it gradually narrows, being of maximum width at the point where it links up with the narrow end of the trapezoid (Fig. II.11). If one walks such a trapezoid beginning at its wider base, one finds that after moving some distance over the figure, it abruptly narrows; at this point the walker enters the long, thin appendage, the entry-way usually being marked by a pair of rock cairns (cf. Fig. II.12).

Given the widespread occurrence of these curiously shaped figures and their apparent relationship to the line centers, at least based on a cursory examination of the qualitative data, we felt compelled to conduct a quantitative survey of the photographic data in order to determine the number and frequency of figural shapes, sizes, and directions of align-

---

34. The connection between the Fox (R8) and a (bent) line also appears to hold up in the photographic evidence (KR 50), as does that between the Hummingbird (KR 80) and a second Spider (R12). The Flower (R17) shown in KR 105 and another in KR 107 are clearly attached to a trapezoid and a zigzag pattern, respectively.

35. A partial list includes the closed figures and consists of the Bird-Plant figure (R18), the Weedy Plant No. 2 (R15 and adjacent figure), the Bird-with-a-long-neck (R25), the Plant (R12), and a trio of whales (KR 95 = R10, KR 98 = R22, and KR 100), the last of which, it may be recalled, is transected by an angled line that emanates from line center No. 17, that line appearing to pass *over* the animal figure. Among the open figures in the disconnected category, we find the Pelican (KR 81), the Lizard (also in R18), and the Whale (KR 102). There are several clearcut examples of straight lines that lie on top of animals. These include the birds (R6, KR 35, R15), the Plant (KR 78, right side), and an indefinable form (KR 212); also a bird-like figure that we discovered along line 42-9 (see Fig. II.10). The spirals KR 29 and 30 and the Great Double Spiral (KR 35) (Fig. II.13) also are overlain by lines.

36. Morrison's (1978: 77) study confirms this conclusion. On this issue, Reinhard (personal communication) notes that some lines also obliterate other lines and that it is possible that these earlier lines were contemporaneous with the biomorphs.

Fig. II.20a.  Three views of the plaza at Quebrada de la Vaca (see Urton, Chap. IV).

Fig. II.20b.

Fig. II.20c.

ment. A ground survey at the level of detail that we conducted on the line centers was ruled out because of the sheer volume of data confronting us. Accordingly, enlargements of the 213 photos that comprised the mosaic (Appendix IV) were scanned with a 10× ocular containing a scale calibrated to 0.1 mm and safely readable to 0.05 mm (which corresponds to a resolution of 60 cm on the floor of the pampa). The shape of every geometrical feature that we could identify was placed into one of the categories illustrated in Fig. II.11; width and length measurements also were taken. The orientation of each figure relative to both true north and to the approximate direction of the flow of the nearest *quebrada* or tributary was determined with a large protractor placed over the photograph and oriented by astronomical fixes taken at ground level.[37] For that part of the pampa situated between the northern limit of our photo survey and the Ingenio basin, we employed the photographs

and maps of Hawkins (1969), Reiche (1949a: Fig. 23), and Kern and Reiche (1974: 1–3). The resolution on Hawkins's thin survey strip was actually somewhat higher than ours (10–20 cm), while that on the Reiche materials was about the same (50 cm). This means that a number of smaller features likely went undetected over the small region that we studied. However, because an abundance of geometrical features occurs at the south bank of the Ingenio, we felt that we needed to obtain at least some quantitative information about the number and type of figures located there.

Our survey revealed a total of 227 geometrical figures, each possessing an area in excess of 12 square meters. However, we can cite a few examples that were discovered in the ground survey that had even smaller areas, so we must stress once again that our estimates of the number and total area of the pampa etched out in trapezoids constitute only a lower limit. Altogether, these figures represent the removal of 3.79 million square meters of broken stone—about 1.9 percent of the entire pampa. Accordingly, a typical geometrical feature possesses an area somewhat in excess of 16,000 square meters. Since it is generally about 10 times as long as it is wide, this "mean

37. This operation is admittedly less accurate than determining the alignment relative to astronomical north, but our experience demonstrated that it could be achieved to less than a 5° uncertainty in all cases—enough to test the hypothesis that, in the layout of the geometrical figures, attention was paid to the water flow directions.

trapezoid" would consist of dimensions of 40 × 400 meters. But the range of figures we actually encounter is considerable. For example, 12 features possess areas lying between 300 square meters and the limit of resolution of our survey, while at the other end of the spectrum, there are 34 features with areas in excess of 30,000 square meters and 24 with areas larger than 45,000 square meters. The largest geometrical figure is 156,000 square meters in extent. It lies among 13 others that overlook the southern bank of the Ingenio, a place that may accurately be termed "the land of the giant trapezoids" (Fig. II.13). Within that narrow strip, which comprises less than 10 percent of the pampa, we find more than half the features of truly large dimension. Most of the other figures are located relatively close to the Nazca River. Fig. II.14 offers a graphic demonstration of the similarity in the distribution of geometrical figures (heavy concentration areas cross-hatched) and line centers (solid circles) over the pampa. The smaller figures generally can be found as one progresses farther out into the pampa. Therefore, both the density and size of figures are considerably less in mid-pampa, a region where it would have been relatively more difficult to sustain a work force for an extended length of time. Clearly then, the most ambitious clearing projects seem to have been undertaken relatively close to the habitation areas. Whether this resulted from convenience alone or perhaps because of the importance given to the region where the water is overtaken by the desert, we cannot say.

It is possible to link physically a majority (58 percent) of the large figures to the line centers and a significant portion (29 percent) to other geometrical figures (see, e.g., Fig. II.8a). Often one finds "chain links" of trapezoids, each being joined to a neighbor hundreds of meters away by a straight line, the whole giving the appearance of a march of figures going across the pampa (Fig. II.11, middle).

Let us look next at the breakdown by morphological category. Trapezoids proper comprise 62 percent of all the geometrical figures we examined. At least one connecting appendage was detectable in 59 percent of that sample—a figure which once again must be regarded as a lower limit. Appendages may have existed that we simply could not detect either because of the heavy state of deterioration of the pampa or the resolution limit of our photographic survey. We were able to connect up these trapezoids to line centers in 31 percent of the sample, the short end of the trapezoid facing the line center about two-thirds of the time. Nearly always the trapezoids are linked to the centers either directly (Fig. II.3(16/17), (27), (30)) or via an appendage varying in length from tens of meters to over two kilometers (Fig. II.3(19), (42), (44)).

Triangles comprised 27 percent of the sample, appendages having been traced from 81 percent of these. Triangles were linked to line centers about as often as were the trapezoids and generally in the same manner. Rectangles were relatively rare; they made up only 9 percent of the sample and some, but certainly not all, of these may well have been trapezoids with the two long sides very nearly parallel. The highest percentage of cairns was detectable on the trapezoids. These stone piles appear in 29 percent of the cases, usually at the short end of the trapezoid at the point where the appendage emanated (Appx. II, Fig. 7). On the other hand, less than 10 percent of the triangles exhibited cairns. Viewing them from ground level, one has the feeling that these cairns may have been intended to direct the attention of a person situated within a geometrical figure to the point from which the appendage emanated, a point that might be more obvious to someone standing within a triangle than inside a huge trapezoid. Similar cairns are known to mark the boundaries of Inka roads as well as the points where they suddenly change in width (Hyslop 1980; and Appx. II, Fig. 4). We shall have more to say about this similarity in the next section.

Finally, Figures II.8a, b and II.11 illustrate some of the rarer figures that do not fit our simple tripartite morphological classification scheme. These "composite" figures consist of compound shapes such as part-trapezoid/part-triangle or triangles-and-trapezoids with many lines of various widths entering and leaving at different points.

We have seen that some definite patterns emerge from the assembled data on the geometrical figures. Only a few well-defined types of figures occur and often they are physically connected either to one another or to the line centers. But can any order be discovered with respect to the distribution of their directions in space? To determine the answer to this question, we consult the histograms of Figure II.15.

Figure II.15a shows the directional distribution of the axes of the geometrical figures about true north, the angle measured being that between north and the extension of the axis of the figure taken from its wider through its narrower end (or point). Unlike the histograms for the lines (Fig. II.5), which show a distribution closer to random, the data for the geometrical ones show definite peaks and valleys. The heaviest directional concentration seems to lie between 10° and 120°, peaking in the range 55°–60°. A secondary peak at 235° lies in the middle of another heavily populated zone between 190° and 250°. On the other hand, very few figures are aligned in the space between 265° and 10° (passing through zero). The phenomenon that might account for such skewed behavior is revealed when we examine a map of the topography of the pampa such as Figure II.1a or b. Note that the general direction of the flow of water across the gently sloping pampa is NE to SW, though it varies a bit as one shifts locations about the pampa.

To investigate whether this relation might be sharpened, we made a second histogram based upon the measurement of the angle formed by the axis of a geometrical figure and the direction of flow of water. In each case, the angle was measured on the photographs, to an estimated accuracy of ± 5°, with respect to the direction taken by the nearest definable water course. We defined the direction opposite the flow (upstream) as zero. The results, which appear in Fig. II.15b, illustrate quite dramatically the correlation between the orientation of the geometry and the flow of wa-

ter. Sharp peaks occur at 0° and 180° (width at half-maximum about 15°) with about 60 percent of the figures pointing up and 40 percent downstream. The region between 215° and 335° (centering on 275°) represents one of the cross-stream directions (looking generally NW); it is a virtual zone of avoidance. Note how effectively all three of these regions are translated from and sharpened with respect to Fig. II.15a.

Horkheimer (1947) had observed that many trapezoids seemed to line up along the direction of water flow. As the reader will recall in our review of his studies in Chapter I, Horkheimer explained the triangle-trapezoid shape as the one that would logically be chosen to fit readily into the spaces between the tributaries on the pampa, especially if a pattern of converging figures was desired. His explanation also would account for the correlation we find between figural axis and flow of water.

While there are practically no figures aligning with the cross-stream direction looking NW, the SE cross-stream direction is not devoid of data but instead displays a rather sizeable secondary peak (between 95° and 100°). In view of the general cardinal symmetry with respect to water flow exhibited in the rest of the diagram, this result seems rather perplexing and we can offer no obvious explanation for it.

To illustrate the dramatic difference between the two distributions that lie at right angles to the upstream direction, in Figure II.15b we note that the axes of only five trapezoids lie within a 90° zone centered on the direction of 270° measured clockwise from upstream; on the other hand, 56 trapezoids fall in a similar zone centered on the direction 90°. This cross-flow correlation suggests to us that the directions of alignment of these trapezoids were being selected deliberately to correspond to the movement of water and not simply employed as a matter of convenience to fit with the landscape contours, a possibility which we raised earlier.

We speculate that the builders, by this cross-flow direction, may have intended to establish some sense of local direction or "handedness" with respect to water flow. Suppose the trapezoids had been intended as modes of conveyance and that a walker moved along the appendage into the space of the trapezoid. It may have been desirable, for whatever reason, to approach the terminal point of the figure, i.e., the bank of the *quebrada,* in such a way that the upstream or water source direction would be on the walker's right but never on the left; conversely it would have been forbidden to have the upstream direction to one's left and the downstream to the right. On the other hand, if we assume one started at the wide end of the trapezoid and walked out of it by proceeding along the axis and into the appendage, we would need to reverse all the indicated directions. This hypothetical principle may be illustrated by looking at the trapezoids flanking the south bank of the Ingenio (Fig. II.13). Their wide ends abut the northern terminus of the pampa just where it drops off into the Ingenio basin (lower left of photo near spiral figure). Upstream lies to the left and slightly upward; therefore these trapezoids correspond to the 90° orientation in Figure II.15b.

The trapezoids in this area constitute about 40 percent of the sample, and it should be noted that, as there is a much smaller pampa surface on the north side of the Ingenio, there would have been less of an opportunity to construct trapezoids that align in the direction 270°. Admittedly, this might account for a portion of the skewed distribution we have noted but there are numerous examples of this strange cross-flow orientation phenomenon in mid-pampa; consequently, we are inclined to believe that we are witnessing in our data some sort of directional principle to which the builders consciously adhered. Thus, the same general sort of order, an ecological order, lies hidden in the geometrical figures as well as the lines and we can begin to extract it when we examine the figures carefully and in detail.[38]

---

38. Ruggles's result that the directions of wide lines also relate to the flow of water (Chap. VI) suggests to us that at least this particular category of lines and the geometrical figures in general resemble one another in their layout.

One fact that has become very clear from our study is that not all lines emanating from the centers go radially outward to their points of termination. Others return to the center from which they started, and still others reflect back and forth in a seemingly random way, often becoming lost in the confused maze that one finds out on the pampa. Many of these lines are very difficult to trace, but the substantial number that can be documented leave little doubt that lines and zigzag patterns are generically related, particularly at the north end of the pampa. Let us illustrate and discuss a few of the more well-documented cases (see Fig. II.8b).

Line centers No. 46, 47, 56, and 58 all contain lines that turn around and go back to their points of origin. Center No. 47 consists of 18 lines, but a closer look reveals that line no. 11 actually is connected to line no. 10 at its extremity, as are lines no. 12 and 13. These lines come to an abrupt halt at the periphery of an earlier(?) parallel zigzag pattern 350 m west of the center; then they reverse their directions and go back to the center. Line no. 9 extends outward some 200 m and then sharply veers off at a 55° angle from its original direction. The bend occurs at about the location of the Spider. This line continues along until it intersects and disappears within a large N-S facing trapezoid. A zigzag pattern overlays line no. 17, which is actually a trapezoid 650 m long and 70 m wide at the base, with its apex angle impinging on the center. The pattern begins and ends at almost the same place at the wide end of the trapezoid; it crosses the trapezoid four times as if to guide the walker through the complex and back to its point of origin. The whole geometrical figure bears a distinct resemblance to the Yarn & Needle (or Fishing Rod) figure at Cantalloc (Appendix I, Fig. 1b). All together, then, about half the lines associated with center No. 47 possess some non-radial aspect.

Center No. 46 also has a similar type of arrangement. Here, a series of radial lines (no. 4 through 9 and 12) turn out, upon close inspection, to be a connected zigzag pattern that repeatedly leads back to the emanation point.

Line no. 46-17, like 47-9, bends sharply and goes into a trapezoid. One can trace it across the trapezoid as it becomes a saw-toothed zigzag line that cuts the trapezoid several times before becoming lost. In the case of center No. 58, no less than 10 lines are actually observed to be paired and connected with their next-door neighbors, thereby taking our hypothetical walker out and back several times. And finally, center No. 56 possesses at least four traceable examples of radiating lines that turn into zigzags cross-cutting a trapezoid.

The aforementioned centers all lie close to one another along the southern bluffs overlooking the Ingenio and they are the only examples that exhibit this "direct return" aspect. Was this the result of local fancy or the exercise of stylistic liberty on the part of the builders? Perhaps the rules to which one adhered in fashioning these line centers were quite flexible. At least, we do not find these parallel lines directly tied to the centers in other areas of the pampa.

At the southern end of the pampa, line centers No. 16 and 17 are among those possessing non-radial lines. For example, examine the wandering paths of lines no. 17-15 and 16-6, both described in our "walk across the pampa" in Appendix II. In each case, the intent may have been to return the individual to the center, but this is not achieved in the most direct manner possible. Instead, one first must wander, making sharp bends several times, for more than a kilometer in each case, before heading back to the start.

Fig. II.16 illustrates some line centers with sharply deviated lines that lead from one center to another rather than back to the point of origin. In these cases, the lines are kilometers long and they lead into the apex angles of large trapezoids from the wide ends of which other lines extend outward to the other line centers.

In conclusion, one corollary that emerges about connector lines is that *not all the line centers are connected to other line centers by the shortest line that can be drawn between them*. In still other examples (several at center No. 44), lines lead outward to decametric distances, bend sharply,

and go along until they disappear, usually at a major water source. All in all, one out of fifteen features we have identified with line centers have such bends at some point in their courses.

### Lines as Roads

The similarities between the structure of Nazca lines and Andean roads in general is too obvious to go unnoticed. In Chapter I, we referred to comments by the chroniclers alluding to large ground features along the coast. However, one cannot tell from the chroniclers' descriptions whether the object of each reference is an Inka road or a Nazca line (see also Chap. IV by Urton). Not only are the clearing, edging, and dimensions of many of the lines that we have examined on the pampa similar to parts of the Inka road system, but also our discussions with Hyslop and an examination of his work (Hyslop 1984 and earlier references cited therein) have revealed that there are instances in which roads have properties very much like lines—e.g., they take on trapezoidal proportions (Hyslop 1980: 4) and there are often cairns at the points where changes of width occur. For example, Hyslop has reported specifically (personal communication, August 1982; field notes of August 1979) that a section of road in the Chicama Valley about 1 km west of the Pan American Highway, 4 km after it leaves the southeastern edge of the Chicama Valley, leads into a trapezoid 300 m long, 58 m wide at one end, and 38 m wide at the other. The wider end, which lies toward the valley, is marked by a pair of piles of sand and rock precisely at the point where it narrows into a road 28 m wide that takes the traveler into Chicama (see Chap. I, Fig. 11, which illustrates this as well as other similarities between Nazca lines and Inka roads).

In line center No. 37 we find an excellent example of the crossing point of a pair of trapezoids being marked by two cairns (Fig. II.3(37) and Chap. I, Fig. I.11d) and along the connector between centers No. 17 and 27 we recall that cairns marked the half-way point, which also happened to be the point of descent into a steep *quebrada* from which one would have had great difficulty following the line (Appx. II, Fig. 7).

The remarkable straightness of both Nazca lines and Inka and pre-Inka roads provides an additional index of the likeness between them (Hyslop 1980: 4–5) (Fig. II.17 and Chap. I, Fig. 11).

We found one linear feature that incorporated two very long straight segments that cut all the way across the eastern side of the pampa. This is the region flanking the mountains where one would anticipate a deviation inland away from the relatively arid coastal zone that would provide inclement travel conditions (Hyslop 1984: 245). It was the only linear feature we mapped that we could not trace to a line center. We call this unusual feature the "trans-pampa line"; it appears to be a segment of a road that transects the pampa in the NW-SE direction. It is clearly visible on the photomosaic as well as in the LANDSAT photo (Chap. VII, Fig. 1a) and it is also represented in the map of Fig. II.18. Varying in width between 10 and 100 m, it can be traced on the photographs for a distance of 15 km, from the place where it leaves the Nazca drainage basin going northwest (portions of it actually are visible within the cultivated area of the Nazca Valley) through a narrow pass formed in that portion of the foothills containing center No. 37. (The Pan American Highway also runs through this pass.[39]) The discovery of Inka remains and even a possible *tambo* alongside the trans-pampa line near center No. 37 support the possibility that this line was, in fact, a continuation of the Inka coastal road.

During our 1983 field season, we devoted some attention to an examination of the subject of pre-Hispanic roads near Nazca. At Hyslop's suggestion, we measured the alignment of an Inka road that flanks the Pan American

Highway between KM 340 and KM 360, south of Lima (about 20–30 km NW of the border of the area in which we were working). We wondered whether this road, which Hyslop had traced on the ground over a considerable distance down the south coast, might have connected with the trans-pampa line.

Our analysis indicated that the direction of the road over the 12 km interval between the two locations at which we made our measurements is 25°22' to 28°36'S of E (or N of W),[40] a variation of about 3°; this variation in orientation is typical of that reported by Hyslop for roads on the north coast (Hyslop 1980). Extending imaginary lines from each of these two points in the given directions, we found that one direction intersected the Ingenio Valley just north of the pampa lying between the Ingenio and Nazca Rivers, specifically at a point where the Pan American Highway approaches the pampa (see Fig. II.18). Later, in fact, we were able to trace this road on the 1:50,000 IGM aerial photos to within 6 km of the heavily etched pampa east of Palpa and to within 12 km of the northern border of the pampa on which we had been pursuing our studies. As Figure II.18 reveals, a continuation of this road to the SE is parallel to and nearly coincident with that segment of the trans-pampa line that lies on the northern end of the Pampa de Nazca.

Knowing already of the existence of lines on the small pampa near Palpa 20 km to the north of our area—the one lying between the Rio Grande and the Rio Palpa—and having been motivated to investigate a reference to a line center on the pampa adjacent to the north bank of the Pisco River about 175 km NW of Nazca (Craig 1968: 97), we set out in the field season of June 1984 to explore the possibility

39. Another example where the Pan American Highway runs along the vestige of a Nazca line can be found at KM 457, about 5 km south of Nazca. The road named Leguia that cuts N-S across the pampa in the direction of Cahuachi also may be a Nazca line that was converted to a modern road (see Silverman, Chap. V, p—). It begins at the kink in the Pan American Highway, where it enters the Ingenio valley (Fig. II.1a).

40. We made alignment measurements with the transit at two different locations along this road, thus:

| Directions of an Inka Road Near Nazca | | | |
|---|---|---|---|
| Location | Lat. | Long. | Azimuth |
| KM 358 | 14°26'S | 75°29'W | 115°22'–295°22' |
| KM 346 | 14°23'S | 75°35'W | 118°36'–298°36' |

that line centers and lines in general also might be found on some of the many other pampas that lie between the E- to W-flowing rivers that comprise the coastal watershed.[41] While the problem of the nature of lines on other pampas and in other guises must await a complete and thorough separate study, at this stage we can securely establish that Nazca lines as we know them are not unique to Nazca. In fact, they may be more visible there only because of the unusual nature of the elevated desert between the Ingenio and Nazca Rivers. It is practically the only pampa along the entire coastal strip that is heavily laden with large, angled bits of debris. When these varnished chunks are removed and piled up, the patterns they reveal are both easily visible and quite durable.

We walked the length of the pampa between the Pisco and Chincha valleys. Though this terrain is quite sandy, we discovered several lines, most of them 10–50 meters wide. In a few instances, the enclosed area was framed not by a space resulting from the removal of the fragmentary debris within it, but rather from the addition of material from well outside to form the border; i.e., these figures are more like "negative Nazca lines," rather than etchings. Still the forms are the same. Wide avenues lead up to dunes that overlook the river valleys (Fig. II.19). In the center reported by Craig (1968: 97) in the Pisco valley, six lines are said to emanate from a single point, each terminating at a bend in a local irrigation canal (see Chap. I, Note 25).

Urton (Chap. IV) has noted that the trapezoidal form of the Nazca lines and their method of construction also can be seen in a trapezoidal plaza fronting a burial chamber at Quebrada de la Vaca, a large site located on the seashore at Chala, 175 km SE of Nazca. Improving upon a map originally published by Engel (1982), (Cf. Fig. IV.7), Urton spent considerable time at the site looking at the re-

mains and making orientation measurements. The plaza (45 × 30 m) is divided along its lesser dimension by eight parallel strips that are split into groups of four by a pathway which enters the plaza on its seaward side. At the other end of the plaza lies a series of 16 chambers (eight to a side), which, though looted, still contain a sizable quantity of human remains (Fig. II.20). Urton has likened this way of dividing the space of the plaza to the manner in which contemporary Quechua people in highland Pacariqtambo make their "*chhiutas*", or sweep out the space of the central plaza. Each *ayllu* is assigned the duty of caring for its own strip of the plaza at Pacariqtambo and must prepare that space for all festival occasions. These duties include not only sweeping the designated area clean, but also painting or decorating the section of the wall bordering the plaza at the end of the cleared strip. Evidently, the decorating can be done as each *ayllu* sees fit, without regard to the action undertaken on a neighboring strip. Accordingly, the back wall of the plaza often is seen to resemble a patchwork quilt of different colors of paint, sizes of bricks, and types of roofing, each reflecting the individuality of a particular group. While the width of the strips at Pacariqtambo is indicated by marks along the wall, at Quebrada de la Vaca the spaces are permanently delineated, as are the Nazca lines, by precisely straight rows of stones.

The alignment of these strips is also of interest. Urton had determined from corrected magnetic compass measurements that they pointed roughly to the zenith/anti-zenith sunrise dates. In 1984 we confirmed these measurements with the transit. The averaged orientation of 257° or 13°S of astronomical west points to sunsets on 16 Feb. and 27 Oct. The zenith/anti-zenith dates at Quebrada de la Vaca, 5 Feb, 7 Nov, occur within two weeks of these dates. But the zenith/anti-zenith dates at Cuzco (12 Feb, 31 Oct) lie even closer. Therefore, it is possible that at least one aspect of the Inka calendar was adhered to by that bureaucratic organization when the building at Quebrada de la Vaca was constructed. Unfortunately, we cannot be sure that the construction

---

41. Wallace's (n.d.) study of Chincha Alta offers us another parallel to the line center in the vicinity of Nazca. He has noted the existence of a number of radial pathways that departed from a large pyramidal complex.

of the main edifice and its plaza can be precisely dated to the Inka period.

## SUMMARY

Our goal at the start of this chapter was to determine whether any patterns might exist within the chaotic-looking mass of lines and figures that stretches across the 200 sq. km of pampa between the Ingenio and Nazca River Valleys, and if so, whether any concepts of order on the part of the builders that might underlie such patterns could be suggested. Our strategy lay in identifying distinct morphological classes of geoglyphs and then concentrating mainly on the straight lines, both because they constituted the largest volume of features, and they appeared to be physically connected. Once we adopted this procedure, the universal radial character of the lines began to reveal itself.

The task of explaining what we find on the pampa is complicated by the absence of pre-Columbian written texts and a dearth of other cultural information that might pertain to these curious features. In such a situation, one must resort to an argumentation by analogy with other, perhaps not unrelated, Andean cultures, as well as to a stronger dependence upon results gleaned from statistical procedures. Both of these alternatives have proven helpful to us in the present work. Also, we have not ignored the studies of our predecessors on the pampa over the past five decades—people from disciplines and with approaches that often differ from ours.

To summarize, it may be helpful to review the evidence we have uncovered about the possible function and meaning of the Nazca lines within the context of the five categories of hypotheses proposed in the literature on the subject reviewed in Chapter I.

We cannot retreat from the hypothesis that Nazca lines were roads or pathways, at least in a broad sense. There seems to be much that implies the lines were intended to be moved over, i.e., either walked, run, or even danced upon. But walking simply to get from one place to another could not have been all that was intended, for some of these lines are much wider than they needed to be to serve as simple footpaths and others much too short and narrow to take anyone a considerable distance with comfortable posture. We found a significant number of the lines that we measured and walked to bear a distinct resemblance to Andean coastal roads, with regard to their straightness, method of edging, and the positioning of cairns and other markers. Moreover, deviations from rectangular to trapezoidal edging were found in both cases. Fossil pathways, likely of early origin, still exist on some of the wider features.

Arguing by analogy, we cited other Andean constructions of a radial character, e.g., pathways reported by Wallace at Chincha Alta and by Metraux in the Bolivian highlands. Meanwhile, Morrison had discovered that pathways, not unlike some of the broad Nazca features, were still used in certain dance rituals. But in our search for the meaning of the Nazca lines and line centers, we appealed most strongly to the *ceque* system of Cuzco, the dominating feature present in the physical and built landscape that denotes concepts of order and organization. We learned that these radial, though invisible, lines were walked upon and, like some of the lines from the Nazca centers, they occasionally were bent (see Rowe 1979b: 232 and Zuidema 1981a: 168). Like the *ceque* lines, the Nazca lines do not assume the most advantageous path across the landscape. Instead, they climb up over hills and pass deep down into the perpetually dry *quebradas* as if ordained to be straight for some overriding ritual reason. But to suggest that the Nazca centers and lines are similar in form to the *ceques* of Cuzco does not imply their functions were precisely identical. We found that at Nazca the meaning behind these straight lines can perhaps best be understood by appealing to the agriculture and irrigation hypotheses.

Specifically, we discovered that the vast majority of lines that could be traced with certainty connect important points that delineate the flow of water across the pampa: e.g., bends in rivers, dunes overlooking the banks of the rivers and their tributaries, or the last hill by which one descends down onto the pampa as one approaches from the Andes. The large geometrical figures, many of which are connected to the lines, also exhibit orientations related to the flow of water.

The documents dating from the early post-Conquest period (discussed by Urton in Chap. IV and reproduced in Appendix III) are testimony to the attention given the vital matter of controlling and utilizing water in this delicate ecological transitional zone between the coast and the mountains. Consequently, it comes as no surprise to find that water occupies such a prominent place in the local cosmologies. The lines may have been related, at least in part, to some sort of ritual process or procedure associated with summoning the rare precious liquid up from its underground and down from its high mountain sources, a function also implicit in Cobo's description of the use of the *ceque* system. Recall that in the *ceque* system of Cuzco, many lines terminate where the water changes its direction and that at such locations one must cast sacrificial objects into the water. Routes of pilgrimage often proceeded along *ceque* lines that paralleled water sources. Finally, a connection between astronomy and irrigation is present in the ritual sacrifices of llamas of different colors, which symbolize the lunar months of the year, in order to bring water.

We believe the choice of locations for the centers was more than a matter of practical convenience. Except for the far western extremities of the pampa and the region south of the Nazca River, the rocky quality of the surface is essentially homogeneous. Given the relative infrequency of water flow across the pampa, one cannot argue that the dunes were the best locations for making geoglyphs simply because they were nearest a water source for the laborers. On the other hand, high points do have the advantage of offering the builder-user a view of where the feature is pointing or what it leads to. And, finally, our evidence supporting the careful, controlled fitting of the lines and geometry, along, as well

as perpendicular to, the water-directed contours of land between fossil *quebradas* further suggests a sense of deliberate planning.

Realizing the amount of attention paid to it in the literature, we believe the astronomical hypothesis has been greatly reduced in force as a result of both our study and that of Ruggles (Chap. VI). We attempted to analyze all the possibilities for astronomical orientation of the lines that we could imagine in the context of those astronomical phenomena that are known to occur in southern tropical latitudes. There is much practical evidence to argue against a general astronomical use for the lines: the prevailing haze around the horizon and the unusually great lengths and widths of some of the lines. On the other hand, we had already discovered from our earlier work that astronomical orientations were a part of the *ceque* system, one of the circumstances that motivated us to study Nazca straight lines in the first place. Our data analysis revealed that the lines, taken as a whole, probably had nothing to do with astronomy, but this result is exactly what we should have expected based on a comparison with the *ceque* system. Of the many inquiries we conducted in connection with the astronomical hypothesis, it may be significant that we found a marginally positive result on one celestial phenomenon that converges with the agriculture-irrigation hypothesis. Thus, we believe it possible that some lines emanating from the centers were deliberately oriented to the sunrise positions on or slightly before one of the two annual passages of the sun across the zenith. This occurs at the end of our month of October and it coincides very closely with the expectation of the arrival of water in the *quebradas,* and in the linear underground channels that had been constructed to convey water to the fields in the valleys that flank the pampa. Following these events, the fields would be planted.

Symbolically, this alignment also makes sense because it can be related to the dualistic notion of summoning water from above (the mountains) and below (the earth) by appealing to the vertical and anti-vertical aspects of the sun at this time of year. Precisely the same dualistic representation has been argued for Cuzco (see Aveni 1981b for a summary). In this case, the line between sunrise on the zenith and sunset on the anti-zenith passage dates appears prominently in astronomical orientations that were used to express the agricultural calendar.

While we found several important fragments of the old astronomical hypothesis to be retrievable, our fabrication of the "Earthwatch Spiral" (see Chap. I, Fig. 9) led us to the conclusion that the lines certainly were not massive feats of engineering, an opinion expressed by earlier workers (Hawkins 1973: 104). Nor can we support the notion that the lines were intended to reflect a precise geometry or metrology resembling that of the classical world. Further, our measurements of the Cantalloc Yarn & Needle figure (Appendix I) offer little evidence either for a precise unit of measurement or for the construction of figures through the use of multiples of a quantized unit.

There can be no doubt that pure artistic expression was a part of the story of what remains on the pampa. Rather than visual art, a tactile form of sensation may have been involved in part of the construction of the biomorphic figural drawings which, according to both Clarkson's and our own evidence, were fashioned, probably by a different sub-culture, long before the straight lines. The idea of "sensing" the animal figures by walking over them likely had nothing to do with lines and line centers; at least our evidence weighs against these two types of construction having any physical connection with each other.

In sum, then, were we to reformulate a hypothesis most consistent with the data, it would be a hybrid of the walking, the agricultural, and the astronomical hypotheses reviewed in Chapter I. Accordingly, we would suggest that the Nazca lines and the associated geometry were intended, at least in part, to be walked over in some complex set of rituals that pertained most likely to the bringing of water to the Nazca valley and perhaps to associated mountain worship. Both Morrison

(1978) and Reinhard (1987) have discussed contemporary walking or dancing on lines in connection with mountain or ancestor worship. Reinhard's booklet demonstrates particularly well the ritual roles mountains in the Andes played as sources of water and controllers of meteorological phenomena. In certain instances at Nazca, it is possible that the ritual may have stressed a connection with the calendar by way of lines directed to a point of appearance of the sun at horizon on the day it passed overhead, an event that took place at about the time when the water usually appeared in the canals. Other elements of the *ceque* system, such as ancestor worship and kinship information, are simply not retrievable from the type of Nazca data we have collected, but Urton's Chapter IV on documents and ethnology from the post-Conquest period in this area strongly implies such an association. Finally, it may be helpful to recall that in Cuzco the *ceque* system was intended primarily as a map of the water entitlements derived from one's ancestors, who literally owned the earth and lived within it.

We have learned that the maze of lines and figures etched in a seemingly confused array across the desert floor is neither whimsical nor chaotic. At least a portion of the rapidly vanishing features that we can still see today offers evidence of the expression of certain ideas and beliefs of the people who lived in the delicate ecological framework of the south coast of Peru. As is always the case when information is lacking, we have found it necessary to labor very hard to push open the door of the past but a crack in order to illuminate, even if only in the dimmest light, the patterns of behavior of a culture still all too unfamiliar to our Western minds.

## ACKNOWLEDGMENTS

The collective "we" used throughout this chapter includes a number of individuals and institutions I wish to thank, not only for their cooperation, but also for their interest and encouragement. I shared an early interest in the lines with Tom Zuidema, with whom I had been working at Cuzco. In 1981 (10–31 July), I was joined in my studies by Gary Urton, who had a profound impact on their direction. In 1982 (5–25 January), 1983 (3–27 January), and 1984 (1–14 January), Urton and I conducted much of the survey work described in this chapter, having been assisted in the field by both Earthwatch volunteers and Colgate University students. The periods of study with Urton were supported by joint grants from the National Geographic Society, the Wenner-Gren Foundation (Grant No. 4175), the National Science Foundation (Grant No. BNS81-02336), and Earthwatch. The OSCO Fund also funded studies conducted by the author, when he was assisted by Colgate students. Meanwhile, Urton resided in Nazca from De-cember 1981 to January 1982 and October to December 1982, walking and taking magnetic compass readings on selected lines as well as performing his ethnographic investigation. Persis Clarkson assisted us on a number of aforementioned occasions and, with Jonathan Damp, she explored and discovered several new line centers during the period May–Sept 1982, when she resided in Nazca. During the 1984 season, the group from the University of Minnesota Remote Sensing Laboratory joined the investigation team.

Permission to work on the pampa was generously granted by the Instituto Nacional de la Cultura, in Lima. The Instituto Geografico Militar and the Servicio Aerofotografico Nacional provided maps and photographs.

# III. The Archaeology of the Nazca Pampa: Environmental and Cultural Parameters.

**Persis B. Clarkson**

## INTRODUCTION

While the Nazca geoglyphs were discovered in the 1920s, very few attempts have been made to correlate them with substantiated data on the makers of the geoglyphs and the reasons for their construction. In fact, much of the literature on the Nazca geoglyphs is shrouded by presuppositions that have not been adequately verified in the field. Finally, there has been a lack of any attempt to tie these ideas in with people or cultural systems. Because the geoglyphs are a human creation, they must be considered within the context of the anthropological entity from which they derive.

In 1982 I began a research project to document the archaeological remains on the Nazca pampa in an attempt to bridge the gap between what is and is not known about the geoglyphs. Knowledge of the archaeological remains present on the pampa and in association with the geoglyphs can help augment an understanding of the nature and age of the geoglyphs. This basis of information can be compared and combined with that derived from other disciplines, such as astronomy, ethnography, agriculture, iconography, and mythology to determine how the geoglyphs fit within a cultural system.

The archaeological remains of the Nazca pampa are described and interpreted here on the basis of the criteria described above. The study of the prehistory of the Nazca pampa requires an understanding of the environment as well as the prehistory of the Nazca region in general. These are presented as a background to the discussion of the culture history of the pampa.

*Environmental Parameters*

There are three marked natural features of the Nazca region: the Andes, the pampa, and the river valleys (Fig. III.1). The Andes rise abruptly from the pampa, with the highest local point, Cerro Blanco (2070 m), standing in marked bright contrast to the dark brown color of the surrounding mountains. The dis-tinctive peaks provide familiar landmarks for the traveler in the region, and several of them, such as Cerro Blanco, play a key role in local mythology (Reinhard 1987). The Andes are always visible to some degree, except on extremely hazy days. Chains of peaks descend and jut onto the pampa on either side of the main drainages (Fig. III.2).

The pampa (alt. 400–600 m a.s.l.) is bordered on the northeast, east, and southeast by the Andes, and on the south, southwest, and northwest by river valleys. It is a vast alluvial-fluvial fan that slopes away from the Andes toward the Nazca River. The terrain of the pampa is generally smooth or gently undulating, being broken by numerous *quebradas*, or washes, that cut southwest, becoming markedly deeper and wider as they approach the Nazca River. Beneath the layer of dark colored siliceous volcanics (Marvin, in Hawkins 1969: 5–6) that cover most of the pampa are fine soils of moderate agricultural potential (ONERN 1971).

The Nazca Valley stands in abrupt and verdant contrast to the brown pampa. This rich agricultural strip has been the economic base of the region for at least two thousand years. Cotton, tobacco, corn, grapes, barley, and a variety of legumes, squashes, melons, and tubers are among the many crops grown here today. Prehistorically, there is direct evidence from archaeological sites adjacent to the Nazca valley and indirect evidence from depictions in ceramics and cloth found in the Nazca region to indicate that crops such as peppers, corn, beans, lucuma, yuca, cotton, and gourd were grown. However, the Nazca region receives less than an average of 6 mm of precipitation per year (Fig. III.3), and water in the channel of the Nazca River flows an average of only a few days per year (Fig. III.4). Subterranean water originating in the Andes is a year-round dependable source for the region. This water source was tapped by precolumbian inhabitants of the Nazca region with the construction of horizontal artificial tunnels, known locally as *pukios*, that connected the subterranean water to the surface where it emptied into a *kocha*, or reservoir.

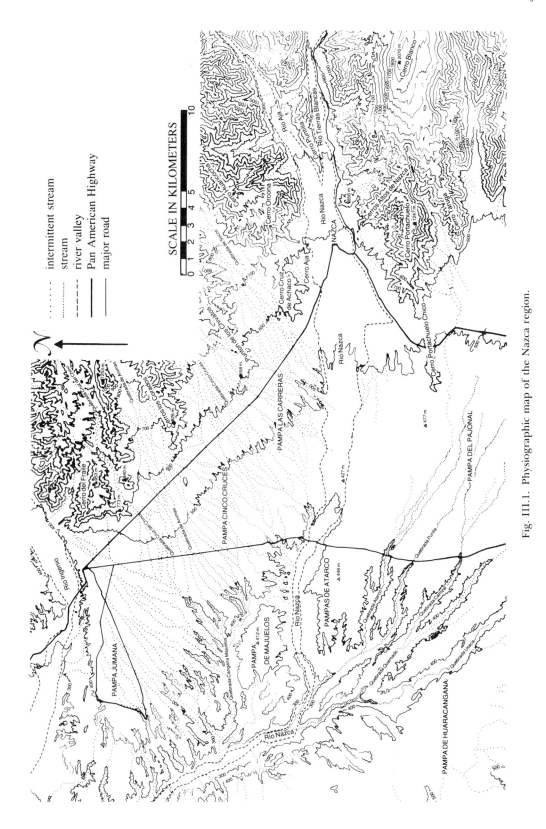

Fig. III.1. Physiographic map of the Nazca region.

Fig. III.2. The mountain ridges of Puntón Los Chivatos separating Quebrada Cinco Cruces on the left from the Quebrada de Socos on the right, spread onto the pampa. View is toward the northwest and the Andean massif.

The *pukios* were constructed in a zone of the Nazca drainage where little or no water flows in the river bed due to "climatic, topographic, and geologic factors" (Schreiber and Lancho 1988). Recent fieldwork by Schreiber indicates that the earliest settlements in the *pukio* zone date to phase 5 of the Early Intermediate Period (see Fig. III.5), whereas there are earlier and later settlements in the regions above and below the *pukio* zone where water flows on the surface naturally. Without the existence of over six hundred kilometers of above-ground canals and over two hundred and fifty wells, of which Schreiber (1986: 3) estimates there are at least forty-one precolumbian *pukios*, the Nazca Valley could never support the quantity of agriculture and permanent inhabitants that it does and did.

The aridity of the Nazca region is responsible for the remarkable degree of preservation of many artifacts. Textiles, gourds, and human remains are often found in excellent condition. These climatological conditions also have aided in the preservation of the Nazca geoglyphs.

Rainfall on the pampa is infrequent. Over a nine-year period between 1957–1965 when rainfall was recorded at Majoro station, situated 3.5 km west of Nazca, the average precipitation was 4.53 mm per year (four months out of 108 months were not recorded; one of these had had significant rainfall recorded in other years). In six of those nine years rainfall was less than 2.0 mm per year, and in 1963 23.0 mm out of 24.4 mm fell in the month of January (ONERN 1971 (2): 15). Despite some claims that increasing pollution has caused an increase in the frequency of rain, which in turn is damaging the geoglyphs, rainfall by itself upon the pampa is insufficient to affect them. Furthermore, the coarse matrix of the pampa affords rapid draining: it is rare to see evidence of pooled water in the immediate environs of the geoglyphs. Rather, it is precipitation that falls in the Andes mountains north and east of the Nazca pampa that makes its way to the pampa in the countless rivulets that braid across it. The vast majority of the geoglyphs are constructed on surfaces above the levels where rivulets and rivers flow. In

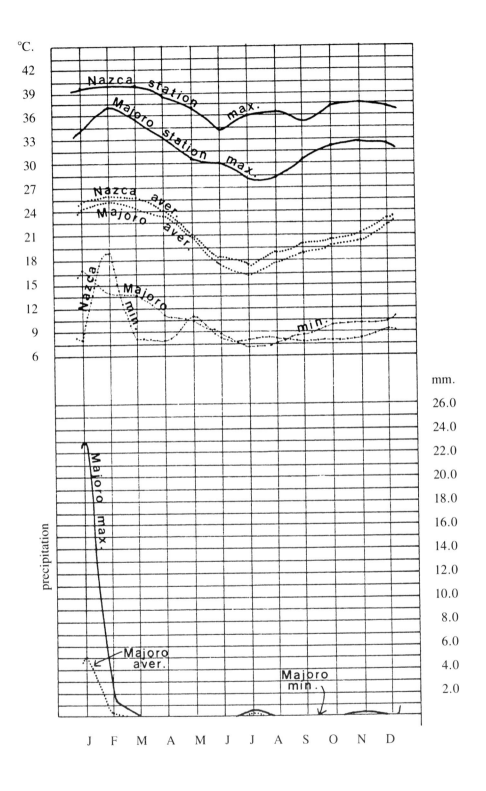

Fig. III.3. Hythergraph: Nazca region.

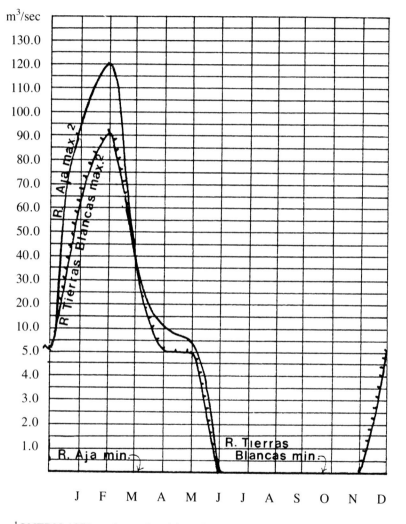

[1]ONERN 1971, volume 2, tables 17 and 18.
[2]maximum instantaneous flow.

Fig. III.4. Monthly river discharge: Aja and Tierras Blancas Rivers[1] (Nazca drainage), 1947–1968.

CULTURAL CHRONOLOGY OF THE SOUTH COAST

| A.D. | RELATIVE CHRONOLOGY | EPOCH | ICA VALLEY (MASTER SEQUENCE) | NAZCA VALLEY |
|---|---|---|---|---|
| | COLONIAL PERIOD | | Ica 10 | (Ica 10) |
| 1500 | LATE HORIZON | | Ica 9 (Inka Influence) | (Inka Influence) |
| | LATE | 8 | | |
| | | 7 | | Poroma |
| | | 6 | | |
| | INTERMEDIATE | 5 | Ica | |
| | | 4 | | Carrizal |
| | PERIOD | 3 | | |
| | | 2 | | |
| 1000 | | 1 | | |
| | | 4 | Ica—Epigonal A + B | Nasca Epigonal |
| | MIDDLE | 3 | Pinilla | Soisongo/Pinilla |
| | HORIZON | 2 | Ica—Pachacamac | Atarco A + B |
| | | 1 | Nasca 9 | Nasca 9 |
| 500 | | 8 | | |
| | EARLY | 7 | | |
| | | 6 | | |
| 100 | INTERMEDIATE | 5 | Nasca | Nasca |
| A.D. | | 4 | | |
| B.C. | PERIOD | 3 | | |
| 100 | | 2 | | |
| | | 1 | | |
| | | 10 | | |
| 500 | | 9 | | |
| | EARLY | 8 | | |
| | | 7 | Ocucaje | |
| | | 6 | | |
| 1000 | | 5 | (Chavin Influence) | (Chavin Influence) |
| | HORIZON | 4 | | |
| | | 3 | | |
| | | 2 | | |
| | | 1 | | |
| 1500 | INITIAL | | Consuelo | |
| | PERIOD | | Erizo | |
| 2000 B.C. | | | | |

Fig. III.5. Cultural Chronology of the Nazca region.

some cases the situation of certain geoglyphs, particularly evident on some trapezoids, shows deliberate and intentional planning by the Nazca constructors to prevent the geoglyphs from being damaged by flowing water (see Chap. I, Figs. 13a, b, c). However, there are instances in which a linear geoglyph is intersected by a water channel. In some cases the geoglyph continues across the channel bed; this continuation may be distinct and clear or it may exist as a faint outline. In other cases there is no line visible where a water channel crosses a geoglyph, although there may be a cairn constructed beside the line on either side of the channel to mark the geoglyph. These cairns are especially useful if one must drop down into a deeply cut channel and cannot keep the line being traveled in view. The presence of cairns and the careful placement of trapezoids indicates that the water channels were well established by the time the geoglyphs were made, and that the Nazca geoglyph constructors made very deliberate choices about the place and form of the geoglyphs.

The other climatological phenomenon of the region to be discussed is wind. Usually there is a gentle breeze which blows constantly across the pampa. Reiche formerly maintained erroneously that the heat reflected from the pampa surface from the sun created a "cushion" that prevented the winds from reaching the pampa surface, and thereby protected the geoglyphs from erosion (Spencer 1983: 4). Currently, Reiche no longer holds this view, and has recognized that the force of the winds is insufficient to dislodge the stones comprising the geoglyphs (Fajardo 1984). On occasion the intensity of the wind increases to the point where the air is full of sand particles that obscure visibility beyond a few meters. I have experienced these winds on two occasions, both times in June, and was forced to wait out the storm for several hours before being able to continue working. The force of these winds was, however, insufficient to pick up or even roll the pebbles and stones that make up the geoglyphs.

Knowledge of the prehistoric climate in southern Peru during the period of human occupation is essential to an understanding of the lifestyle of the inhabitants and the conditions under which the geoglyphs were constructed and used. The prehistoric climate of the Nazca region is poorly known at the present time. Climatological records of the Nazca region have been kept sporadically between 1946 to 1954 and 1957 to 1965. While there are no studies on the past climate specific to the Nazca region, some have been done in various areas of coastal Peru (Craig and Psuty 1968; Richardson 1978) and the Peruvian Andes (Richardson 1978) (see Conrad 1981 for a more complete bibliography of climate studies). The findings broadly suggest no major climatological changes in the last few thousand years, although there is evidence of increased aridity on the coast accompanied by pluvial episodes in the Andes during that time.

*Prehistory of the Nazca Region*

In order to understand the significance of the archaeological remains on the pampa, the general cultural trends in Peruvian prehistory and the results of archaeological research that has been done in the Nazca region must be known. These are briefly summarized in the following section.

Peruvian prehistory is generally divided into six ceramic-bearing periods of discrete time units (Rowe 1962b) called Horizons and Periods, although other systems are recognized (see Lumbreras 1974; Moseley 1983; see Fig. 5). During Horizons, single cultural complexes predominated over large areas, while regionalized subareal styles marked the intervening Periods. The preceramic stage is also divided into six periods; because of the paucity of information on the south coast during this stage, I will treat it as one unit.

The preceramic stage (>9500–1800 BC) is characterized on the coast by subsistence centering around marine resources plus the cultivation of a limited number of plants such as gourd (*Lagenaria siceraria*), maize (*Zea mays*) (Kelley and Bonavía 1963), and cotton (*Gossy-*

*pium* spp.). There are no preceramic sites known in the Nazca region, although two sites on the Tierras Blancas River appear to be aceramic (Clarkson n.d. a).

The ensuing Initial Period (1800–900 BC) marks the appearance of ceramics in Peru, although previously established lifeways appear little affected. The earliest ceramic complexes in South America are known from coastal Ecuador, where the Valdivia pottery dates from 3300 BC, and from Puerto Hormiga on the northwest coast of Colombia, where that pottery has been dated to around 3000 BC. Lathrap (1974) has argued cogently for an inland Tropical Forest origin of these early ceramic styles of South America, based on evidence from the Ecuadorian and Colombian coast, as well as Early Tutishcainyo ceramics from Kotosh on the eastern slopes of the Andes. However, much new evidence of early origins in coastal areas of western South America continues to appear and a Tropical Forest origin need not be categorically accepted (Damp, personal communication). On the south coast the site of Hacha appears in the Acari valley and Erizo in the Ica valley during this time period (Rowe 1963: 202).

The first horizon style, the Early Horizon (900–200 BC) (hereafter EH), is best known from the site of Chavín de Huantar in the northern highlands, although it did not originate there but probably on the coast (Burger 1981). The EH manifestations on the south coast are known as Paracas and Ocucaje, which appear by and large during the later portions of the EH. Paracas is famous for elaborate interment of mummies with large quantities of textiles. There is scanty evidence of EH culture in Nazca; the best comes from the site of Cahuachi on the south bank of the Nazca River, where Paracas sherds were found on and under a huge piece of cloth measuring approximately 7.0 × 50.0 m, and there were also remains of rectangular habitation structures (Strong 1957: 13–16).

In the Nazca region, the site of Cahuachi rose to extensive dimensions during the Early Intermediate Period (hereafter EIP) (200 BC– AD 600), when plazas, stepped pyramids, and cemeteries extended along the Nazca River for over a kilometer (Rowe 1963: 11). Cahuachi was abandoned by EIP 5, although there is evidence of sporadic use after abandonment. Rowe also mentions habitations, although the excavations at Cahuachi by Silverman (Chap. V here) may suggest that domestic refuse is lacking there.

The EIP is synonomous with the Nasca culture when fine polychrome ceramics were produced. The first seriation of Nasca pottery was done by Gayton and Kroeber (1927), wherein it was divided into periods A, X, B, and Y. Later, Kroeber (1956) eliminated X and replaced Y with C. Currently, a nine part seriation devised by Dawson (see Rowe 1960; Pezzia 1968; Proulx 1983) is accepted and used by archaeologists. Further refinements of Dawson's seriation have been made by Roark (1965) for phases 5 and 6 and by Proulx (1970) for phases 3 and 4, while a study by Wolfe (1982) evaluates aspects of Nasca 1–5 ceramics. The ceramics studied by Dawson, Proulx, and others are from gravelots excavated by Uhle in the Ica valley and Kroeber's gravelots collected in the Nazca valley. However, little functional or use-contextual information has been reported for excavated Nasca ceramics (Lothrop and Mahler 1957; Strong 1957).

Descriptive terms also have been applied to Nasca ceramics, with phases 1–4 corresponding to Monumental (approximately equivalent to Gayton and Kroeber's Nasca A), Proliferous corresponding to phases 6 and 7 (Gayton and Kroeber's Nasca B), while Disjunctive equates with phases 8 and 9 (partially equivalent to Gayton and Kroeber's Y or C). Phase 5 is considered transitional between Monumental and Proliferous, while Phase 9 falls within the ensuing Middle Horizon. The distinction between Nasca 1 and the preceding Ocucaje 10 phase of the EH is largely arbitrary (Menzel, Rowe, and Dawson 1964), as many of the EH elements were retained. Some new factors include the addition of paint prior to firing, a wide variety of colors (maroon, brown, red, ochre, orange, buff, cream, gray, and white), and better controlled firing techniques. The motifs of the first four phases are naturalistic, while the "proliferation" of ornamentation in these motifs during phases 6 and 7 often obscures their identity. Roark (1965) suggests that the increased occurrence of trophy heads at this time is a corollary of increased militarism (see also Yacovleff 1932a, 1932b, 1933; Sawyer 1961; Zuidema 1972). Evidence of strong cultural continuity between Ocucaje and early Nasca is also indicated in textiles and burials.

Most of the prominent early EIP sites on the south coast, such as Tambo Viejo, Chocavento, Amato, and Huaroto in the Acari valley, were fortified. It has been suggested that Cahuachi was the center of a small "empire" (Strong 1957; Rowe 1963:12; Lumbreras 1974). This prevailing view of Cahuachi as the seat of a militaristic south coast empire has been challenged recently by Silverman (Chap. V here), who maintains that Cahuachi was a pilgrimage center occupied intermittently for brief periods of time from the EIP to the LIP (Late Intermediate Period). The site of La Estaquería was established during EIP 5 or 6 approximately 5.0 km downstream from Cahuachi. A stepped pyramid lies beside a regular arrangement of wooden huarango (*Prosopis chilensis*) posts reported in rows and columns of 12 × 20 by Tello in 1940; most of these have since been removed over the years by local residents. There is evidence that there were other sites in the Nazca Valley with similar post arrangements (Robinson n.d.: 96–97), including a sacred structure at Cahuachi with offerings of spiny oyster shell (*Spondylus* spp.) and panpipes inscribed on the walls surrounding the post structure (Silverman 1985b). While much of our present knowledge on the Nasca culture comes from cemeteries such as at Cahuachi, La Estaquería, and from Chaviña in the Lomas Valley (Lothrop and Mahler 1957), and gravelots in the Ica Valley (Roark 1965; Proulx 1968, 1970; Menzel 1977), ongoing excavation in the Nazca Valley is revealing Nasca habitation sites buried beneath alluvial and aeolian deposits.

The Nasca culture appears to have maintained ties of some sort with the cultures of the Andes. This is evidenced by llama remains (Strong 1957: 37) and wool, neither of which imply a direct relationship with the highlands, and by coca (Lothrop and Mahler 1957: 6), which may have been imported from the east slopes of the Andes, although some early Colonial documents from the central coast mention locally grown coca. Clearly, there is much more to be learned about Nasca culture.

The second widespread horizon affecting Peru was the Middle Horizon (hereafter MH) (600–1000 AD), which was a blending of aspects from Tiahuanaco in the Titicaca basin of Bolivia and Huari in the Ayacucho highlands, which was also the center of this culture. It has been suggested that Wari culture probably spread through military conquest (Larco 1948; Bennett 1953; Lumbreras 1960) with inherent religious connotations (Menzel 1964).

The ceramic sequence of the MH in the Nazca valley has been described by Robinson (n.d.), and the ceramics appear to share most aspects of those found in the Ica Valley, where they are better known and described. Lyon (1966: 178) has outlined some of the drawbacks to the data base used to analyze the ceramics from the Ica Valley. Here, the sample was small, with the majority coming from private collections. A major problem encountered by Lyon with regard to the lack of utilitarian vessels is one that has been echoed by others for ceramic studies that rely upon material associated with gravelots.

> The sample upon which this study is based consists entirely of vessels with painted decoration. Although some of the burials include undecorated utilitarian ware, the number of utilitarian specimens was too small to permit any useful generalizations. It is obvious, however, that the utilitarian ware throughout the period under consideration is significantly different in form from the decorated ware (Lyon 1966: 178).

Three notable sites date to the MH in the Nazca Valley: Pacheco on the Nazca River, Huaca del Loro on the Tunga River, and Tres Palos II below the junction of the Palpa and

Ingenio Rivers. Ceramics from Huaca del Loro show affinities with EIP 8 ceramics of Ayacucho, suggesting significant contact between Tiwanaku-Wari and Nazca at this early date (Paulsen 1983). The ceramic complexes of Huari, Tiahuanaco, and Nazca all show strong interrelationships up through the breakdown of Wari culture. Three tons of Wari-type ceramics were recovered from subterranean adobe chambers at Pacheco in 1927 by Tello (1940, 1942). The vessels, of which over a hundred were reconstructed from the sherds, appear to have been deliberately smashed, a ritualized behavior that has been documented at MH sites in the highlands as well (Ravines 1968). Among these vessels at Pacheco were giant urns measuring up to 60 cm high. The decoration on them includes depictions of highland cultigens such as tarwi (*Lupinus neutabilis*) and oca (*Oxalis tuberosum*), as well as maize (*Zea mays*). Structures are also depicted on an urn, which Isbell (1977: 48–50) related to the rectangular structures from the Middle Horizon site of Jargampata. He believes such rectangular enclosures "functioned within a complex system of redistribution of goods" (Isbell 1977: 54). Given the important position held by Nazca during the Middle Horizon as a major supplier of cotton for textiles, a respected innovator in ceramics, and the site of ceramic-smashing rituals, it is possible that Nazca was a pilgrimage center as well as being economically crucial to the functioning of the system developed during the Middle Horizon.

With the collapse of the city of Huari (estimated at the end of MH 2B at AD 800), Wari influence gradually faded to the point where regional politics once again appeared. On the south coast, the Ica-Chincha culture emerged as the dominant force during the LIP (1000–1476 AD). Although there are many sites and cemeteries dating to this period in the Nazca region, the main centers lay in the Ica and Chincha Valleys to the north; the influence of the cultures spread as far south as the Acarí valley. The administrative center appears to have been at Tambo de Mora in the Chincha Valley. La Centinela is a large pyramid in the

Tambo de Mora complex from which emanates a radiating system of roads (Wallace n.d. a).

The initial phase of the LIP is typified by "archaism," wherein design elements harking back to as early as the beginning of the MH were reintroduced into or remained within the repertoire in slightly altered ways. Lyon suggests that the alterations in motif elements from MH2 to LIP1 indicate "reinterpretation" or even misunderstanding of the earlier religious art (Lyon 1966: 192).

The two main subdivisions of the ceramic sequence in the Nazca region during the LIP are Carrizal and Poroma. The archaism described by Lyon is present during the Carrizal phase, with some tendencies toward geometric motifs. This tendency becomes prevalent during the Poroma phase, where jars and dishes predominate.

With the defeat of the Chinchas around 1476 by the Inkas (Rowe 1945: 271–272, 279), the Ica-Chincha culture was brought under the domain of the Late Horizon Inka culture (1476–1534 AD). It is possible that the Inkas rebuilt and expanded roads through the Nazca area built during the MH (Hyslop 1984: 273; Isbell and Schreiber 1978: 384), as the magistrate of Rucanas and Soras, Luis de Monzón (1881) wrote in 1586 that there were *caminos* (roads) prior to the Inkas. Aside from the construction of *tambos* (way stations) or other sites such as Paredones in the Nazca valley, evidence of Inka presence in Nazca is sparse. Local developments in pottery during the LH do not reflect Inka presence at Nazca (Robinson n.d.: 161). Two architectural complexes have been reported on the pampa west of Nazca with stone rectangular structures and aryballoid sherds, indicating LH occupation (Clarkson n.d. a: 57; Urton n.d. d: 21); these may be sites reported by Horkheimer (1947: 53). Their location near an irregular linear feature suggests they may have been *tambos* or some other kind of LH structures along an Inka highway.

Inka rule was terminated in 1534 with the conquest by the Spaniards. It is interesting that no reference to the Nazca geoglyphs has been found in Spanish accounts, although continuing research may yet turn up information on this enigma.

## ARCHAEOLOGICAL INVESTIGATIONS IN THE NAZCA REGION

### Background

Specific research on the prehistory of Nazca has focused upon two areas: the river valleys and the pampa. Archaeological survey and excavation in the river valleys have revealed sites from every ceramic-bearing cultural period. Strong (1957), who did the first comprehensive archaeological study of the area from 1952–1953, published data on eighty-one sites in the Ica, Nazca, Lomas, and Chala Valleys, although he noted that there were many more sites that he located. Fifty sites were reported in the Nazca branch, of which Strong excavated seven: La Estaquería, Cahuachi, Trophy Head Cemetery, San Nicolás I, San Nicolás II, San Nicolás III, and Huaca del Loro. All these sites are situated in the river valley, except for the San Nicolás sites which are located on the coast.

It is not possible to determine the methodology employed by Strong to locate and select sites to excavate, as it is not evident in his report or in the distribution of sites. The clustering of sites along river valleys reflects a prehistoric preference for settlement closer to water and cultivable land. It may also reflect the accessibility of sites in this area because the modern roads are also concentrated in and beside the river valleys. Until recently, studies on the geoglyphs focused almost entirely upon the northwest corner of the pampa where the majority (n = 93 percent) of the figural geoglyphs are found.

Robinson's (n.d.) survey also concentrated upon the Nazca river drainage. As with Strong's survey, there is a strong indication that survey was conducted by vehicle, because the map of sites is oriented around roads rather than the natural topography of the region. Robinson reported sixty sites in the area

of the Nazca River, all of which were surface sampled and described.

An important revelation in Robinson's work is the incredible extent of looting that has occurred in the area by *huaqueros* (pot hunters) (Robinson n.d.: 95). He estimated an average of 350 looted burials per site, with a maximum of 5500 at Cahuachi IV. One can only imagine and lament the tremendous amount of information that has been and continues to be lost in this manner.

The geoglyphs were first discovered by the archaeologist Kroeber in 1926 (Rowe 1962a: 404), but he appears not to have been sufficiently interested to pursue an investigation of them. Soon thereafter, the Peruvian archaeologist Mejía saw the geoglyphs, and later published a paper suggesting that the linear geoglyphs were ancient roadways and aqueducts, and compared their form to *ceques* of the Andean highlands (Mejía 1927, 1940). The geographer Paul Kosok, who first brought the Nazca geoglyphs to worldwide attention, suggested that cairns directly associated with geoglyphs were "numerical-calendrical-astronomical recording devices" (Kosok 1959: 15–61; 1965); Reiche (1980: 32) and Kern and Reiche (1974: 124) have suggested that they might be observation posts, altars, and/or burial places, although they offer no proof of this. There have been numerous publications about Nazca geoglyphs concerning their meaning, iconography, and purpose. (See Chap. 1 here for a review of the literature.) Recent renewed interest in Nazca geoglyphs has produced a growing body of documented and interesting research (see Mejía 1940; Kosok 1959, 1965; Hawkins 1974b; Morris 1975; Isbell 1978; Urton n.d. d; Reinhard 1983a, 1986, 1988; Eckhardt 1985; Herrán 1985). Rossel Castro (1977) noted Nasca sherds in subterranean aqueducts running through the Nazca Valley, and dated the Nazca water system between 330 BC and AD 500. Rossel Castro's statement that all geometric geoglyphs are agricultural and irrigation fields is unsubstantiated. Horkheimer's (1947) report of burials associated with geoglyphs is also unsubstantiated. However, Horkheimer (1947: 52–53) did publish a description and photograph of several structures overlying and partially erasing large trapezoids on Cerro Utua in the Palpa Valley (Fig. III.6).

The only field survey of prehistoric artifacts associated with geoglyphs on the pampa was done by the astronomer Gerald Hawkins while he was examining the astronomical hypothesis for the function of the Nazca geoglyphs. Hawkins concluded that the geoglyphs were probably coetaneous with Nasca 3–4 pottery, based on a high incidence of these ceramic types on the geoglyphs. This coincides with the apogee of occupation at Cahuachi. Furthermore, he noted greater quantities of LH sherds on the mesa edge near Ingenio (Hawkins 1974: 22), a factor which might be

Fig. III.6. Outlines of stone structures that were built atop several overlapping trapezoids on Cerro Utua in the Palpa valley. (Photograph by E. Herran G.)

accounted for by two reported LH sites in the Ingenio Valley (Strong 1957, sites 37 and 38).

Thus, while several studies have been made of the Nazca geoglyphs, Hawkins's (1969, 1974) was the first systematic attempt to correlate artifacts with geoglyphs in order to date them. Hawkins's contribution to unraveling the enigma of the age of the Nazca geoglyphs is significant, as it provided "the only quantitative evidence in existence of pottery artifacts on the Nazca desert pampas" (Hawkins 1974: 121). There are, however, several factors which should be considered before accepting Hawkins's confirmation of an EIP/Nasca date for the geoglyphs. First, while Hawkins strove to study the most representative portion of the region (Hawkins 1974: 123), he chose the area of the pampa with the densest concentration of linear and figural geoglyphs (over 90 percent of the known figural geoglyphs on the pampa are situated here). Second, Hawkins's criteria for dating the geoglyphs are based on the most abundant type of pottery. The presence of certain ceramics indicates only that people were crossing the pampa at that time, and provides only a maximum date (or minimum age) for the lines. Finally, the inclusion of only identifiable remains biases the percentages of Nasca ceramics; while Hawkins (1969: 18) notes that 80 percent of the reconstructed ceramics date to Nasca 3 and 4, these ceramics comprise only 35 percent of the total sample of fragments and 26 percent of the "reconstructed" vessels (Fig. III.7).

One attempt to identify the chronological and cultural affiliations of the geoglyphs employed iconographic comparisons of the figural geoglyphs with those of Nasca ceramics (W. Isbell 1978). Hawkins (1974: 136) noted that although the drawing styles were quite different, this may be "a natural result of transferring from the decorating of pottery to a large expanse of desert".

*Cultural Remains on the Nazca Pampa*

The intent of the present research was to document evidence of prehistoric human activity on the pampa, particularly activities as-

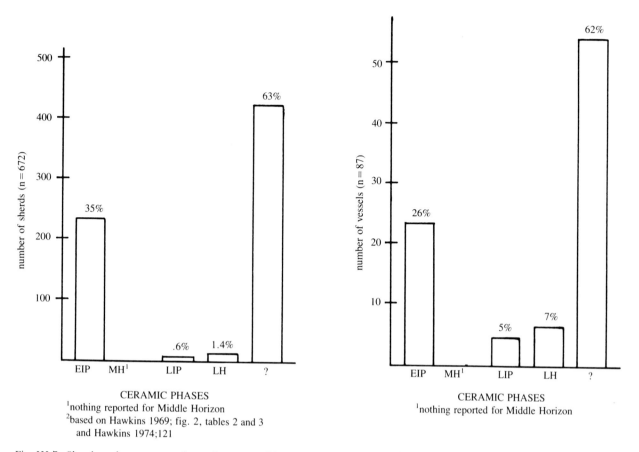

CERAMIC PHASES
[1] nothing reported for Middle Horizon
[2] based on Hawkins 1969; fig. 2, tables 2 and 3
and Hawkins 1974;121

CERAMIC PHASES
[1] nothing reported for Middle Horizon

Fig. III.7. Sherds and reconstructed vessels recovered by Hawkins's survey team.[2]

Timetable of Nazca Fieldwork

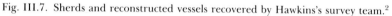

| DATE | CREW | MAN DAYS |
|---|---|---|
| 1981 10–31 July | Earthwatch | 22 × 12d = 264 |
| 1982 31 May–2 August | Nazca Archaeological Project | 2 × 55d = 110 |
| 1983 3–27 January | Colgate University students | 25 × 16d = 400 |
| 1984 31 May–18 June | Earthwatch | 19 × 7d = 133 |
| | | Total = 907 |

Fig. III.8. Nazca pampa survey and timetable summary.

sociated with the creation and/or use of the geoglyphs (Figs. III.8 and 9). This information could then be applied to determining the age of the geoglyphs and their function within the societies that used them.

The focus of the archaeological survey was upon the pampa surrounding the Nazca River (Fig. III.10). The survey area was delimited by natural features that define the flat to gently undulating pampa: the edge of the pampa at the Ingenio Valley in the north, the Quebrada de Taruga in the south, the Andes on the east,

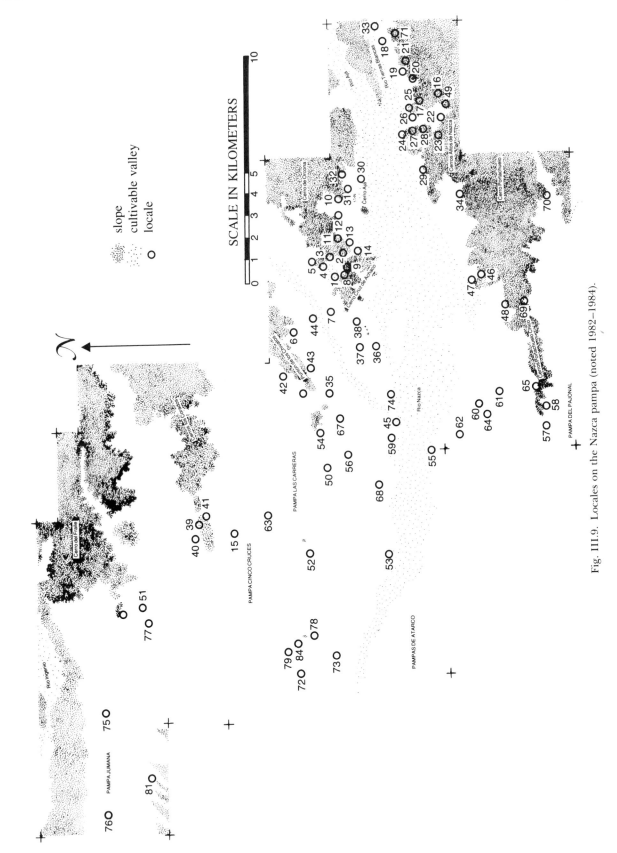

Fig. III.9. Locales on the Nazca pampa (noted 1982–1984).

Fig. III.10. Areas surveyed in the Nazca region.

and the edge of the pampa beside the Nazca River to the west. The six *quebradas* or tributaries that drain onto the pampa from the Andes were also included in the survey because they are natural extensions of the pampa into the mountains. Here, the pampa merges into steep, heavily washed zones from between two kilometers in the Quebrada Cruz del Chino to six kilometers in the Quebrada de Socos upstream from the mouth of the *quebrada*. Access was complete to all areas within the zone described above, except for a 10 × 3 km area in the northwestern corner of the pampa. This is the location of Hawkins's study and the majority of the figural geoglyphs, and ground access is extremely limited by Peruvian law.

The survey was conducted with both random and non-random transects. The greatest coverage of the pampa was achieved with non-random transects, wherein all walking was done within the confines of geoglyphs. Because the geoglyphs criss-cross the entire pampa in virtually all directions, coverage was quite complete. Random surveying was possible where the surface was rocky and not fragile, in areas cut by water erosion (which also cover much of the pampa), and on modern roads that haphazardly cut across many geoglyphs. Complete coverage was made of line centers and the immediate environs, as well as the hills and mountains surrounding the *quebradas*. Fig. III.8 indicates the total effort expended in the survey.

All information acquired was recorded in the field. Cultural remains and features with diagnostic characteristics were described, drawn, selectively photographed, located as accurately as possible on 1:50,000 topographic maps, and described in terms of association with any other cultural features. No collections were made in order to ensure that the data would remain available in context for future research. Furthermore, there was more opportunity to draw meaningful observations with all the material and associations in context.

During the course of the survey, four classes of cultural remains were noted on the pampas

in addition to geoglyphs and line centers: (1) stone circles, (2) cairns, (3) structures, and (4) artifacts. Each of these categories will be described and their context and associations discussed.

The majority of the cultural remains found during the surveys of the Nazca pampa were widely dispersed and few in quantity. Because the term "site" carries with it a connotation of contextual remains indicative of activities, which were lacking in the majority of the material found in the Nazca region, I refer to all "groupings" of cultural remains as locales. A locale can vary in size from an isolated find such as one sherd to a complex of structures and cultural remains. See Fig. III.9 for a plot of the distribution by locales across the area surveyed.

*Stone Circles*

Common features of the Nazca pampa are circular arrangements of fist- to head-sized cobbles, referred to here as stone circles. The shape ranges from completely enclosed circles to semicircles or arcs. Usually, they stand no more than one course of stones high, and there is rarely any evidence to suggest that they were originally higher. Most of the circles measure about 2.0 m in diameter, although they range from 1.0 to 10.0 m (Fig. III.11a and b).

Stone circles are found in the environs of both linear and figural geoglyphs, and are frequently situated within gullies or at the base of low (approximately 1.0 m high) sandy ridges. In addition, they often abut each other. Although they are not always adjacent to linear geoglyphs, they are often (55 percent) within the area described by the extreme limits of the lines from a line center (Clarkson n.d. b: 158). The presence of stone circles is dependent upon the immediate local environment, since no stone circles have been recorded from stone-sparse or stone-free areas except where natural outcrops coincide with the geoglyphs (Fig. III.11 c–f).

All examination of stone circles was limited to surface study, except where *huaqueros*

Fig. III.11a. Stone circles of the Nazca pampa: complete ring.

Fig. III.11b. Arc.

Fig. III.11c. Abutting circles made by gathering stones, adjacent to a low ridge.

Fig. III.11d. Abutting stone circles made by clearing away stones—Nazca valley is visible in the distance.

Fig. III.11e. Stone circles adjacent to a broad linear geoglyph—peak at center in near distance is a line center.

Fig. III.11f. Numerous stone circles dot the pampa in the environs of line center 37 where stone is readily available.

(looters) had dug into them. The interior area is largely free of any debris and usually is full of windblown sand. Artifacts are scarce in and around stone circles, but include pottery, lithics, shell, and bone. Although the presence of artifacts associated with stone circles might be helpful in assessing their chronological, functional, and cultural placement, there is very little absolute evidence that the artifacts are contemporaneous with the stone circles. The majority of the ceramics are utilitarian wares dating to the LIP and LH (Fig. III.12). The relative antiquity of the stone circles is indicated by the manner in which they are deeply and firmly embedded in the soil by aeolian action.

The evidence for the function of the stone circles is elusive. Horkheimer (1947: 59–61) seems to have believed they were burials. There is no published evidence to back this claim, nor have I been able to confirm it from personal observation. Their location within narrow gullies might mean they were used solely during dry periods, or the gullies and low ridges may have served for wind shelter. Winds occasionally blow fiercely across the pampa, and the ridges and gullies are the only natural obstructions to the wind. Furthermore, the majority of incomplete stone circles open to the leeward side. This aspect gained more significance after two occasions in 1982 and 1984 when especially powerful wind storms lasting several hours occurred during fieldwork. Visibility was reduced to a few hundred meters at most, and the stinging sand particles blown about by the wind made it nearly impossible to be without shelter of some sort. Most of the stone circles are large enough for one or more adults to sit inside. The ring of stones may have served as weights to hold down a cloth shelter supported by a post. Temporary shelters of this form and size have been recorded among migrating natives of northern Chile, who use them as shelter against sudden and severe storms in the Andes. On the Nazca pampa, structures of this sort could have provided shelter against the sun or windblown sand.

*Cairns*

From the ground, cairns are the most visible cultural feature on the pampa, and can be seen from nearly every part of it (Fig. III.13). Cairns are made of flat rocks piled one on top of the other, or a neat pile of stones measuring up to a meter in diameter at the base and becoming increasingly narrower toward the top. The average height of cairns is about 1.0 m, with a range of 0.4 to 2.0 m.

Cairns are often situated at the end, intersection of, or beside lines. Not one has been observed in washed out areas, either because they were never built there or because they have been eroded away. Frequently they are found at the edge of a gully beside a line. In this sense, they may have served as a means of keeping on track when a line is not visible, such as through a wash or during sand or dust storms. (See Chap. I, Fig. 11f, for a possible example.) Cairns are also found on hill tops that mark line centers, though not necessarily at a radial point of the center. There is a tremendous number of large cobbles scattered around the top of line centers 50 and 55 (see Chap. II, Fig. 3), suggesting there may have been cairns here at one time. While LC 55 is situated in a stony area of the pampa, there are no stones of the kind found at LC 50 anywhere in the vicinity. One can only wonder at the significance attached to the cairns to have caused people to haul in rocks over a distance often amounting to several kilometers.

The age of the cairns is at present an unresolved question. Ideally, the association of cairns with geoglyphs should provide some indication of relative age. That cairns are situated beside and never within lines suggests the possibility of contemporaneity. However, the presence of cairns where there are no geoglyphs raises additional questions and requires further explanation. Only one cairn of hundreds examined had any associated cultural material, and this was modern. I suspect that many of the hilltop cairns at line centers are modern because of the kind of debris associated with them, and their visibility and accessibility from modern roads and settle-

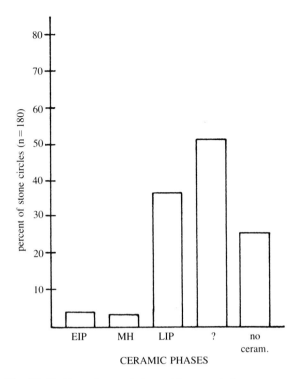

Fig. III.12. Ceramic associations with stone circles.

ments. These factors do not necessarily negate the contemporaneity of line centers with cairns on top, but they do cast some doubts. However, there are known examples of line centers with cairns that are situated some distance from roads and settlements, and are not prominent features on the horizon. These aspects would suggest that the cairns were constructed prehistorically and may be integral to the line center.

*Structures*

Another cultural feature of the pampas are circular and rectangular walled enclosures (Fig. III.14). These structures, made without mortar and of locally available stone, are often found clustered together. The walls are several courses of stone high, measuring up to 1.0 m in height, although there is evidence of collapsed wall sections at some locales, suggesting that the walls originally stood higher. Elsewhere, clusters of rectangular outlines one course of stones high with much loose rock in the environs suggest collapsed walls. These walls may close off a nook in natural

topography, or they may form discrete units of one or more structures.

The majority of structures are near the edges of small pampas on the south side of the Tierras Blancas valley. Two clusters of rectangular structures have been noted on the pampa west of LC 37 (Clarkson n.d. b: 164; Urton n.d. d: 20–21), and Horkheimer (1947) reported numerous clusters of rectangular structures on top of trapezoidal geoglyphs on Cerru Utua near the junction of the Nazca River and the Palpa River (see Fig. 6).

There are very few clues to the age or function of any of the structures. The presence of modern debris and goat droppings within and around walled enclosures in the Tierras Blancas valley shows evidence of use by goatherders, although it is difficult to imagine why they would bring goats into an area totally devoid of vegetation and water. On the pampa west of LC 37, Urton (n.d. c: 20–21) noted aryballoid vessel sherds, and I saw Late Ica sherds at Locale 51. These two clusters of structures lie nearby a unusual linear geoglyph that may have been an Inka road, thus accounting for the LH ceramics associated with the two groups of structures. Finally, Horkheimer identified the sherds found in the structures on Cerro Utua as belonging to the LIP. This has not been checked in the field, but if correct, could provide an upper limit on the age of the linear geoglyphs.

*Artifacts*

Four different kinds of artifacts were encountered on the pampas: ceramics, lithics, shell, and bone. Ceramics comprise the majority of remains, occurring at 78 percent (n = 66) of the locales, while lithics were found at 18 percent (n = 15) of the locales, plus small amounts of shell (6 percent) and bone (2 percent). Since all my surveys concentrated upon surface observation and notation, lightweight and easily decomposed material such as shell and bone might be underrepresented in my sample.

The identified ceramics constitute 37 per-

Fig. III.13a. Cairns are frequently encountered with linear geoglyphs.

Fig. III.13 b.

Fig. III.14a. Structures are generally encountered near valleys (a and b). The features of b include rectangular and circular structure remains, some of which intermingle with a linear geoglyph that extends toward the Tierras Blancas valley in the distance.

Fig. III.14b.

cent of the ceramic sample noted in the field. The majority of these are polychrome Nasca sherds, the best documented ceramics in the area. Ceramics dating to the MH, the LIP, and the LH were also documented on the pampa (Fig. III.15). The smaller percentages of these ceramics are due in part to the absence of published seriations or typologies for these time periods in the Nazca region.

The presence and distribution of ceramics on the Nazca pampas provide the best available clues for the age of the geoglyphs. At the very least, the presence of ceramics in association with geoglyphs, i.e., on, in, or immediately adjacent to the geoglyphs, can provide information on when the geoglyphs were used. Furthermore, the presence of ceramics in association with geoglyphs can serve as indicators of maximum age of the geoglyphs (Fig. III.16).

Nasca ceramics are scattered throughout the survey area, with many of them situated close to the Nazca River, where many Nasca component sites have been documented (Robinson n.d.; Strong 1957) (Fig. III.17). The majority of the identified Nasca ceramics date to early Nasca phases 3 and 4; there are also some Nasca 6 sherds (Fig. 18). Vessel shapes include flaring bowls, cup bowls, round or conical bottom bowls, dishes, straight sided jars, and double spout bottles or collared jars. Thematic motifs represented include trophy heads, fruits, girl's face, fish scales, the Harvester, Mythical Bird, Oculate Being, fish, and decorative elements associated with the Anthropomorphic Mythical Being. All these forms and motifs are typical of the Nazca Valley, except for the fish scale motif (Fig. III.18k), which Proulx (1968: 94) notes is known only from the Ica Valley.

Although eight (13 percent) of the line centers have an identified Nasca component, seven of these line centers are situated within 1.0 km of the Nazca River where the concentration of Nasca occupation is high, and six documented sites (see Robinson n.d.) with an EIP component are situated within 2.0 km of seven line centers with EIP sherds. In addition, Nasca sherds were found at sixteen lo-

cales, fourteen of which are situated within 2.0 km of the Nazca River. Nasca sherds were found on two out of three figural geoglyphs examined during this study. Early Nasca sherds (Monumental) were noted immediately on and adjacent to a "whale" and another unidentified figure situated well outside the figural geoglyph zone of the northwestern corner of the pampa (Figs. III.18e and g). A dense concentration of Nasca 4 and 6 sherds was found atop a white topped mountain projecting onto the pampa at Locale 39 (Figs. III.18k, n, and o). The nature of the deposit at Locale 39 suggests ritual dumping or smashing of fine Nasca polychrome ceramics. The situation of Nasca sherds in association with figural geoglyphs complements Hawkins's survey of the pampa in the densest area of concentration of figural geoglyphs, where he noted a majority of Nasca sherds.

Many of the MH sherds are found near the Nazca and Tierras Blancas Rivers (Fig. III.19). Unlike Nasca ceramics, MH sherds on the pampa are not situated near known MH valley sites. This may be due to destruction of valley sites for agricultural expansion, although some of the MH sherds on the pampa are not near agricultural areas.

The presence of MH sherds on the pampa is extremely meager (Fig. III.20). It is interesting to note that the majority of the identified MH sherds date to epochs 3 and 4, which succeed the collapse of Wari in the Ayacucho highlands at the end of MH2. Locally, these latter phases are known as Soisongo and Nasca Epigonal, which correspond respectively with Pinilla and Ica Epigonal in the Ica Valley. A depiction of a mammal with bent maxilla from an open dish dated to MH3 (Fig. III.20a) can be compared with Pinilla vessels from Ocucaje in the Ica Valley (Lyon 1966: fig. 12a). Open bowl interiors decorated with geometric designs of half stepped-pyramid and semicircles pendant from the rim are common, as are wavy lines. A very eroded sherd displaying disembodied feline heads (Fig. III.22h) may also date to MH3 or 4.

LIP sherds are scattered throughout the entire area of survey along geoglyphs, at line

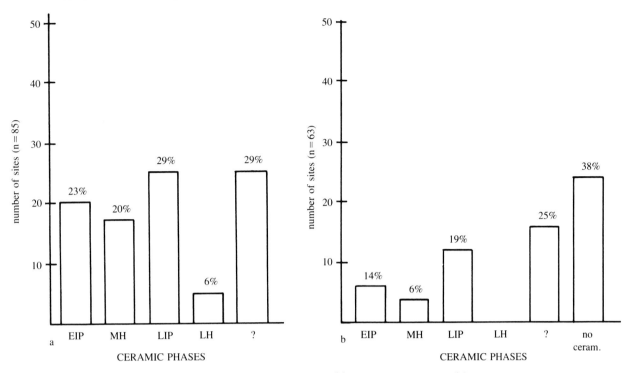

Fig. III.15. Chronological distribution of ceramics at pampa locales (a) and line center locales (b).

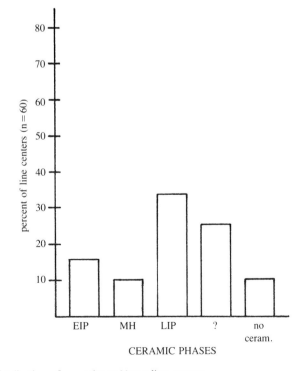

Fig. III.16. Chronological distribution of ceramics at Nazca line centers.

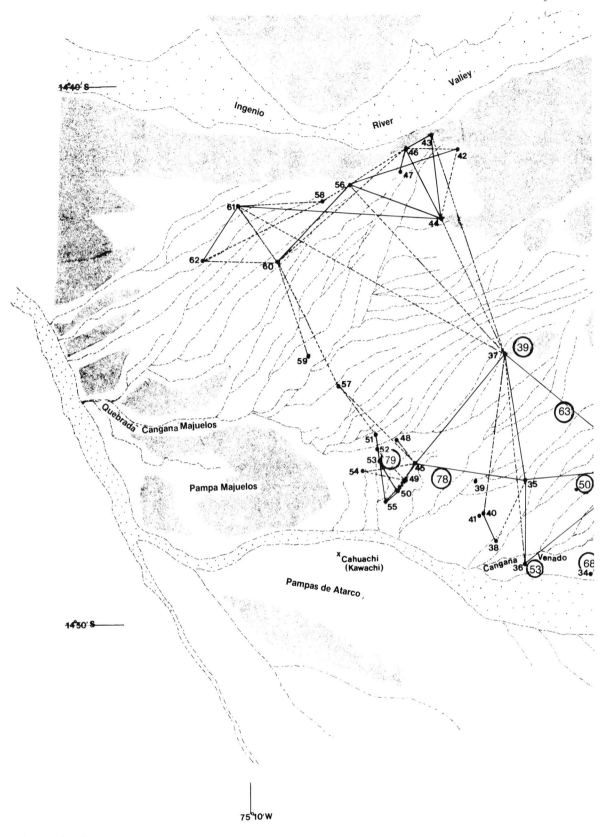

Fig. III.17. Line centers and Early Intermediate Period locales of the Nazca pampa.

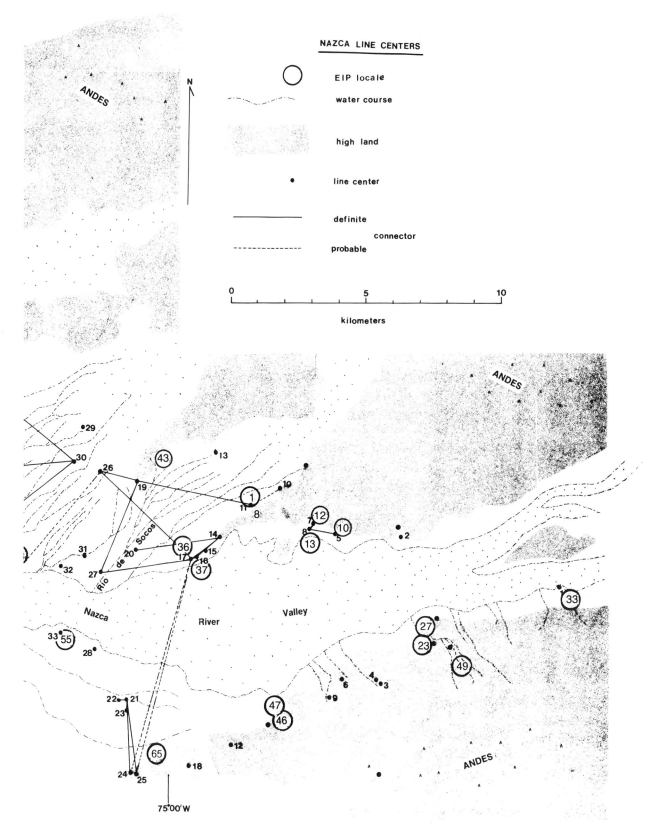

Fig. III.17 (continued).

centers, and with stone circles (Fig. III.21). The LIP presence in the Nazca region can be classed as Early, corresponding to the Carrizal epoch, and Late, which corresponds in part with the Poroma epoch. The major vessel forms of the Carrizal epoch include double handled bowls, round shouldered dishes, straight sided dishes, concave sided dishes, cumbrous bowls, and jars. Robinson (n.d.: 126–139) has described the salient decorative features of Carrizal pottery, which include the use of red, black, white, tan, red-violet and red brown, plus motifs of bird designs, double three-step designs, quadrangles with a short line emanating from each side, white triangles on a black background, "rick-rack" designs, interlocking opposed step designs, and interior rim decoration of a red band or a black-red-black band. The sample I recorded on the Nazca pampa (see Fig. III.22) included concave sided dishes, jars, and cumbrous bowls. Common designs on Carrizal pottery from the pampa include crosshatching and dots (Fig. III.22b), interlocking step design, and stepped Vs (Fig. III.22g), as well as disembodied feline heads (Fig. III.22h) and a two-headed "serpent" (Fig. III.22e). Black diamond patterns surrounded by white dots appear on a concave sided dish (Fig. III.22a) that was not as high relative to the width as those illustrated by Robinson.

The Poroma epoch spans the period of time prior to, during, and after the LH (Fig. III.23). Poroma is contemporaneous with Late Ica pottery (Ica 6–10) of the Ica Valley, which dates from 1350 to 1570 AD (Menzel 1976: 1). Although Menzel has defined the sub-epochs of Soniche, Tajaraca A, and Tajaraca B, pertaining to the LIP, LH, and Colonial periods in the Ica Valley, Robinson (n.d.: 160) had an insufficient sample by which he could separate all Poroma pottery of the Nazca area into sub-epochs relative to the LIP and LH. Wherever possible I have used Menzel's (1976) study of Late Ica ceramics to supplement Robinson's illustrations and identifications. One major problem in using the seriation from the Ica Valley to fill out the seriation from the Nazca Valley is that there are a number of vessel

Color Key to Ceramics from the Nazca Pampa

forms and design motifs that are unique to each area (Robinson n.d.: 140–153). Jars, round shouldered bowls, concave sided dishes, and cumbrous bowls are among the vessel forms found during the late LIP, although the round shouldered bowl was rare enough in Robinson's sample that he suggests it may have been an import, possibly from the Ica Valley. If this is the case, it is not surprising that no sherds from round shouldered vessels were identified in the pampa ceramic sample. Typical design motifs of the Poroma epoch include squares arranged in a diamond pattern (Fig. III.23 b and d) (Robinson n.d.: 183-1 and 7, 185-12), cross pattern (Robinson n.d.: 183-8, 185-1), or a triangle pattern (Robinson n.d.: 183-19, 185-6). The cross pattern was identified frequently on LIP ceramics from the pampa. Other designs present on vessels with designs specifically identified as part of the late LIP tradition may be construed as typical of the late LIP. These include diagonally cross-hatched triangles (Fig. III.23a), nested

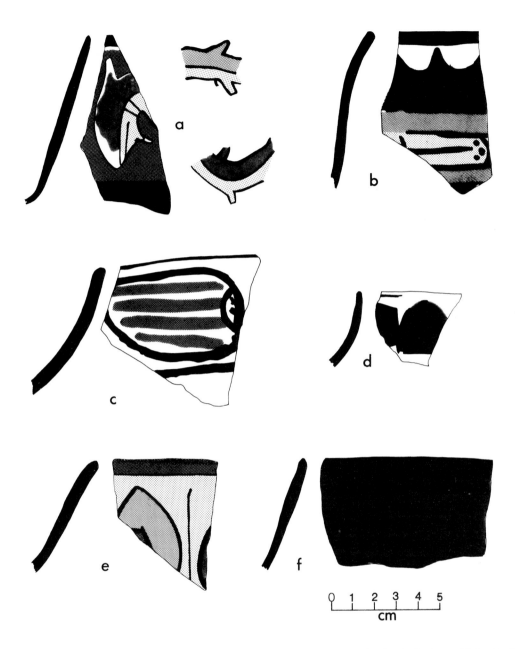

Fig. III.18.1. Early Intermediate Period ceramics from the Nazca pampa: (a) Nasca 3, locale 46; (b) Nasca 3C, locale 47; (c) Nasca 3, locale 10/line center 5; (d) Nasca 3C?, locale 80; (e) Nasca 3 or 4, locale 36/line center 17; (f) Nasca 3 or 4, near line center 34.

Vs with a diamond motif (Fig. III.23e) (Robinson n.d.: 185-12 and 16), and a crescent and dot motif (Fig. III.23f) (Robinson n.d.: 185-12). The crescent and dot element is also found with motifs associated with the LH (Robinson n.d.: 185-10 and 11), as well as a step-sided U element that is identified as "characteristic" of the Poroma epoch (see Robinson n.d.: 183-15, 185-5 and 12). Pendant half-step

pyramids and a semicircle on cumbrous bowls (Fig. III.23j) are also familiar motifs (Robinson n.d.: 183-15, 185-5 and 8).

There are several other motifs identified with Poroma that cannot be connected with either the LIP or LH (Fig. III.23). These include hanging squiggly lines (Fig. III.23h and i) (Robinson n.d.: 185-13 and 14) and Z designs, in addition to the stepped-V and cres-

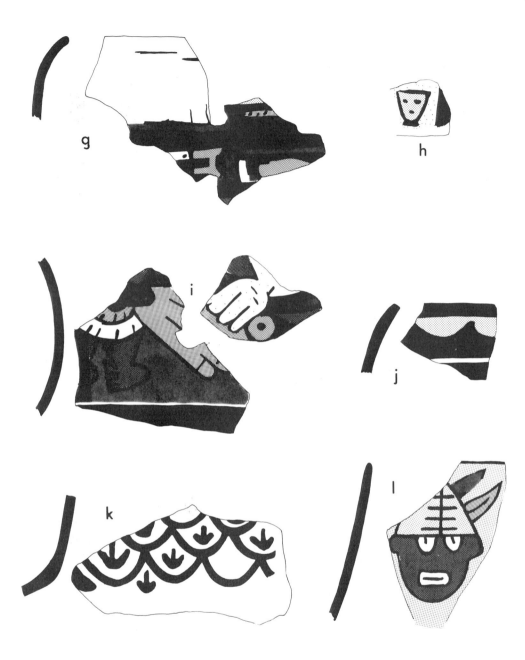

Fig. III.18.2. (g) Nasca 4, locale 36/line center 17; (h) Nasca 4, Cantalloc site, Nazca valley; (i) Nasca 4, locale 50 ("Mythical Bird" on left and "Occulate Being" on right); (j) Nasca 4 or 6, locale 31, near line center 16; (k) Nasca 4, locale 39/line center 37; (l) Nasca 4, locale 27.

cent and dot motif (Fig. III.23f) described above and a V pendant from the rim that surrounds or divides up stepped motifs (Robinson n.d.: 185-16, 17, and 18); all but the latter were identified on the pampa ceramics. A decorated jar neck is similar to examples illustrated by Robinson (n.d.: 183-1,2,3, and 4) that have both LIP and LH accompanying motifs.

Local developments in pottery during Inka rule do not reflect Inka presence at Nazca or Acari (Robinson n.d.: 161). While LH presence in the Nazca region is well documented by archaeological studies in the Nazca Valley, LH locales and ceramics on the pampas are largely restricted to two LH architectural complexes northwest of LC 44. At one of these complexes, Urton noted aryballoid vessel

Fig. III.18.3. (m) Nasca 5, Paredones site, Nazca valley; (n) Nasca 6, locale 39/line center 37; (o) Nasca 6, locale 39/line center 37; (p) Nasca 3, locale 68/line center 34; (q) Nasca, locale 55/line center 33.

sherds. The structures that I encountered with LH sherds were located close to the very wide line that zigzags across the pampa from the Socos to the Ingenio Valley, and perhaps farther (Aveni, personal communication). A distinctive LH sherd from a spouted vessel depicting long-beaked birds, Fig. III.24a) was noted along this wide line (see Pezzia 1968: 280–288), as well as other everted jar necks

(see Menzel 1978: figs. 589 and 590). A jar sherd decorated with rectangular elements was found at a locales very close to the Nazca Valley (Fig. III.24b), as well as other jar necks (Fig. III.24c and d) that compare to Ica 10 jars illustrated by Menzel (1978: nos. 262, 263, 589, and 590) and Pezzia (1968: 264, no. 1).

There is not enough published information on the ceramics of the Nazca region to discern

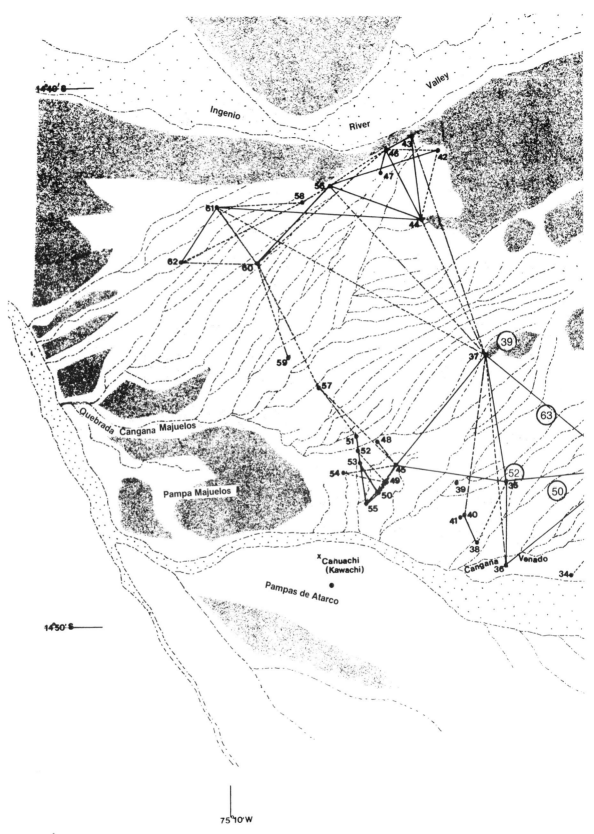

Fig. III.19. Line centers and Middle Horizon locales on the Nazca pampa.

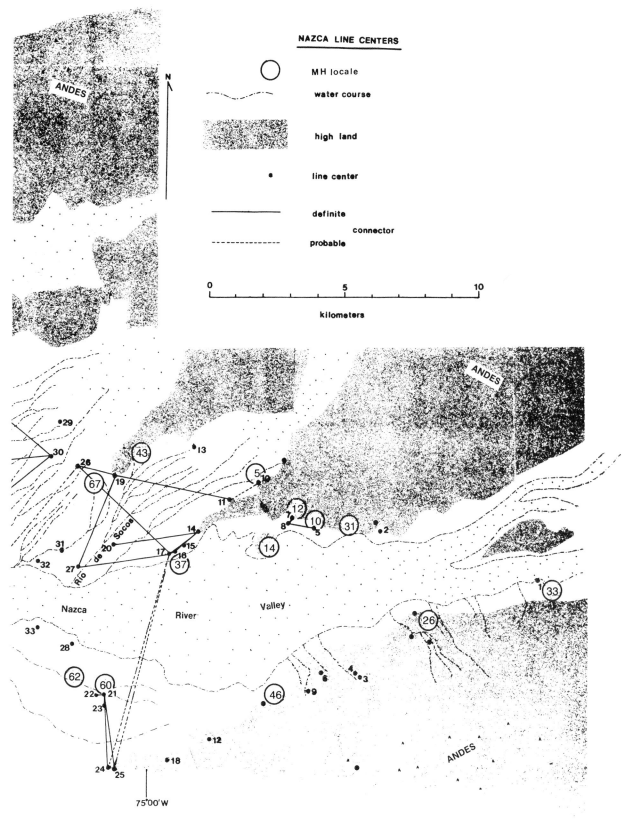

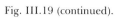

Fig. III.19 (continued).

Fig. III.20.  Middle Horizon ceramics from the Nazca pampa: (a) MH3, locale 2; (b) MH3, locale 81/line center 60; (c) MH4?, locale 19; (d) MH4?, near Soisongo site, Nazca valley; (e) MH4, locale 26; (f) MH4, near Soisongo site, Nazca valley; (g) MH4, locale 63.

the kinds of activities associated with ceramics found on the pampa. The use for which a tool such as a ceramic vessel is intended will determine its size, shape, material, etc. Certain aspects of morphology suggest probable functions and uses of the vessel, and this, in turn, provides information on activities, food and cooking preferences, and domestic unit size associated with certain kinds of vessels (Erickson, Read, and Burke 1972; Hally 1986). An analysis of the kind of the sherds found on the pampa might provide clues about how the geoglyphs were used. Detailed ceramic seriations plus data on *in situ* contexts of ceramics from excavated habitation areas are a necessity. Robinson (n.d.) provides some information on MH and LIP ceramics, but there is none on morphology or context. Thus, the dearth of background data available makes difficult any statements regarding the function of the geoglyphs based upon the kinds of ceramics found in association.

Nearly all lithics encountered during surveys are quartzite and chert which occur naturally in abundance on the pampa surface. These roughly formed flake tools, frequently with cortex (the original outer surface of a stone before it is worked) on them, are most often associated with stone circles, and on occasion with line centers. Crude flakes comprised the regularly spaced stone piles within a trapezoid in the far western pampa (near LC 53); this may in fact occur more frequently, as the stone piles in geoglyphs have not been examined on any consistent basis.

Large quartzite cores were associated with stone circles at Locale 40 and with stone alignment locale 27 (Fig. III.25). Hundreds of shattered quartzite cobbles were found in the saddle of the hills near Locale 40 (Fig. III.25i; see also Fig. III.25b and c from locale four nearby). Although the breaks could be natural, there is little—such as extremes in temperature or rolling down a steep slope—to explain them, and eolian erosion has worn many edges smooth, making it difficult to determine the nature of the fractures.

A small quantity of lithics made from nonlocal material was found. Fine obsidian flakes were found at six places (Locales 20, 27, 33, 74, and on the line connecting line centers 7 and 8 and beside the line connecting 30 to 35) (Fig. III.25m). There are no known obsidian sources in the immediate area, although there are outcrops in the mountainous Lucanas province which borders the Nazca area (Schreiber, personal communication, June 1984). The Tierras Blancas Valley, where three of the four locales with obsidian were situated, was and is a major access route to the highlands of Ayacucho and beyond. An Inka road probably ran through here, though it was not the first use of this route for access between the highlands and the coast. Other imported lithic materials found in the Tierras Blancas Valley at Locales 27 and 33 include basalt, a grayish-yellow quartzite, and jasper.

Comparison of lithics from the Nazca area with other lithics is not possible at present. The lithics encountered during surveys were surficial, and thus were exposed to sandblasting which has obliterated any traces of use-wear (see Vescelius and Lanning 1963). The only other lithics reported from the Nazca region were found on Bahía San Nicolás some 72 km away (Strong 1957); these are not comparable to anything found on the Nazca pampa.

*Geoglyphs and Line Centers*

A final aspect to consider in determining the age and function of the geoglyphs is the line centers and geoglyphs which form them. My discussion of geoglyphs and line centers will focus upon their location and distribution with regard to the prehistoric remains in the area.

The linear geoglyphs examined follow the general description given of them earlier (see Chapter II). There is nothing to distinguish the characteristics of a line that connects line centers with one that does not—nor was a particular alignment or dimension evident amongst center-connecting lines vs. non-connectors. Some lines have been preferred for an undefinable amount of time as footpaths, as evidenced by twisting trails that weave within the confines of the straight lines.

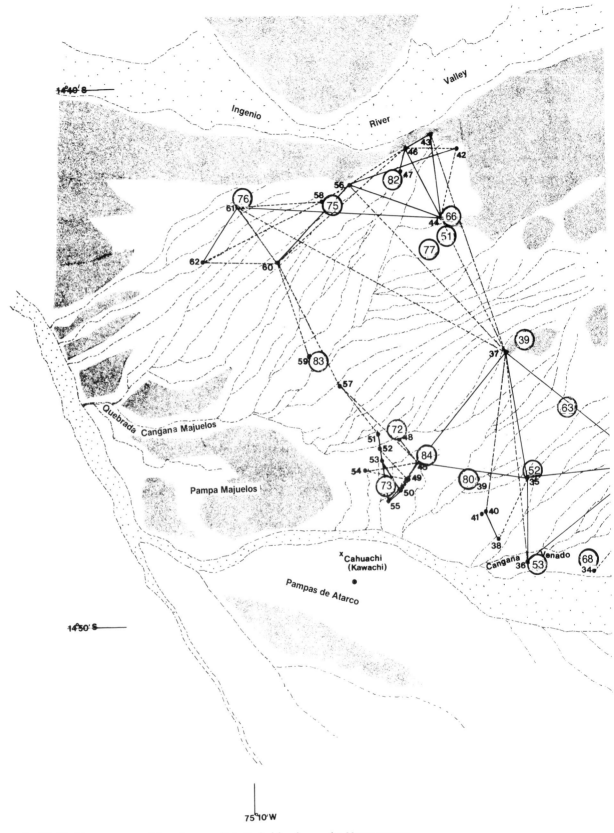

Fig. III.21. Line centers and Late Intermediate Period locales on the Nazca pampa.

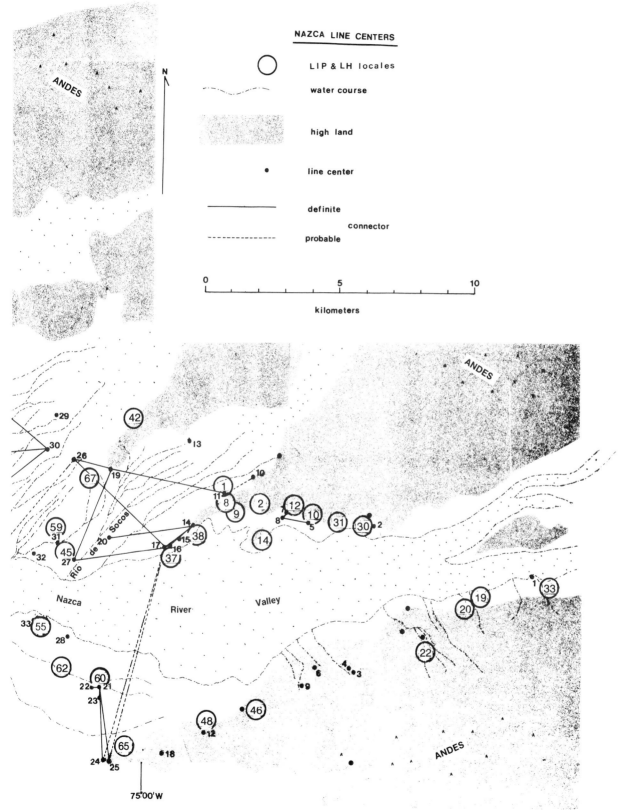

Fig. III.21 (continued).

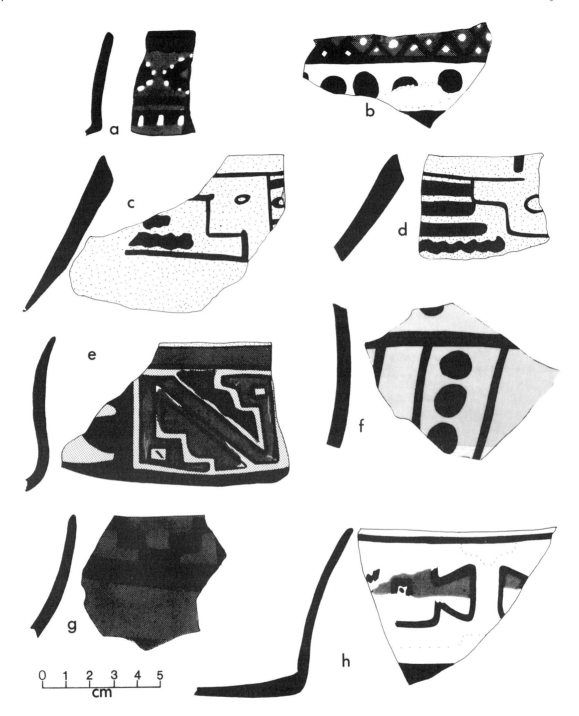

Fig. III.22. Carrizal Late Intermediate Period ceramics from the Nazca pampa: (a) locale 48; (b) locale 51; (c) locale 72/line center 50; (d) locale 72/line center 50; (e) north edge of Nazca valley across from Pacheco site; (f) locale 31; (g) locale 48; (h) locale 43 (possibly MH3 or 4).

There is a correlation between artifact density and line centers, as the quantity of artifacts, which in this case refers almost exclusively to ceramics, increases both on and off geoglyphs at line centers. However, the distribution of artifacts on lines and at line centers is imperfectly known for a variety of reasons. The extensive area examined in the study encompassed regions heavily and regularly frequented by tourists, as well as those fairly accessible to tourists and local inhabitants. *Huaqueros* have been systematically looting sites in the Nazca valley ever since archaeologists like Uhle and Tello showed an interest in the region. They claim to have found burials and intact Nasca vessels on the pampa (Hawkins 1969, 1974), although these claims are unsubstantiated. Nowadays the majority of looting occurs at the numerous sites within the valley, although it is not unusual to find the occasional looters' hole in stone circles on the pampa. Tourists have also left their mark on the pampa. Vehicle tracks are visible in many of the geoglyphs, particularly the animal figures in the northwestern corner of the pampa. Most of these tracks were made before the prohibition of vehicles on the pampa. Over the years, tourists have also carried away countless numbers of sherds as souvenirs. Most people are no doubt attracted to the colorful and fine Nasca pottery, although I have seen tourists walk away with attractive sherds of later ceramic phases, too. While the presence of tourists can be largely discounted on geoglyphs and line centers at any appreciable distance from the town of Nazca and major roads, human disturbance at some of the more remote locations cannot be entirely dismissed. Finally, Reiche and her colleagues have made a practice of collecting artifacts and sweeping geoglyphs to enhance the contrast between them and the surrounding pampa. It is impossible to estimate how much and what kinds of cultural material have been removed from context from geoglyphs or buried beneath them. Since it is also unknown which geoglyphs have been swept, it is difficult to make comparative assessments of the kinds and quantities of material associated with the geoglyphs throughout the research area.

Physically, line centers appear like a raised hub of a wheel surrounded by spokes, the spokes being the lines physically connected to the line centers. Although value judgments about function may be implied by speaking of lines radiating out from or converging upon centers, this is in fact not the case. It is not known how the constructors perceived the line centers, but the impression of Aveni and Urton (this volume) and myself is that movement by people walking along lines was intended in both directions. In this sense, it is convenient to think of line centers as terminals in much the same way as transportation terminals function as central locations from which traffic moves in both directions.

The sparse distribution of line centers on the Pampa de Atarco is difficult to assess. The pampa surface here is quite different from that of the northern pampas such as the Pampa Cinco Cruces and the Pampa del Calendario. The soil is very fine grained with a pale yellow color, and takes impressions easily. Near the foothills, such as Cerro Portachuelo in the southeast corner of the survey area, this very soft soil is overlain by dark shales. However, as one progresses away from the foothills, the surface becomes softer. Linear geoglyphs here are constructed differently from those north of the Nazca River. A shallow ditch runs along the edge of the line, with the contents piled in a low ridge outside the ditch. Because of the lack of contrasting color between the soil and shale, visibility of lines is quite poor at times. For this reason, the area was walked and viewed from several vantage points at different times of day. This area has been examined as thoroughly as the pampas north of the Nazca River, and I feel quite confident that the survey coverage is complete.

Line centers are not only foci of lines; the incidence of cultural remains is highest on or around line centers (85 percent of all line centers have cultural remains). These remains include stone circles, structures, and ceramic and lithic artifacts, in addition to geoglyphs (Fig. III.25). Thirty of the line centers are sit-

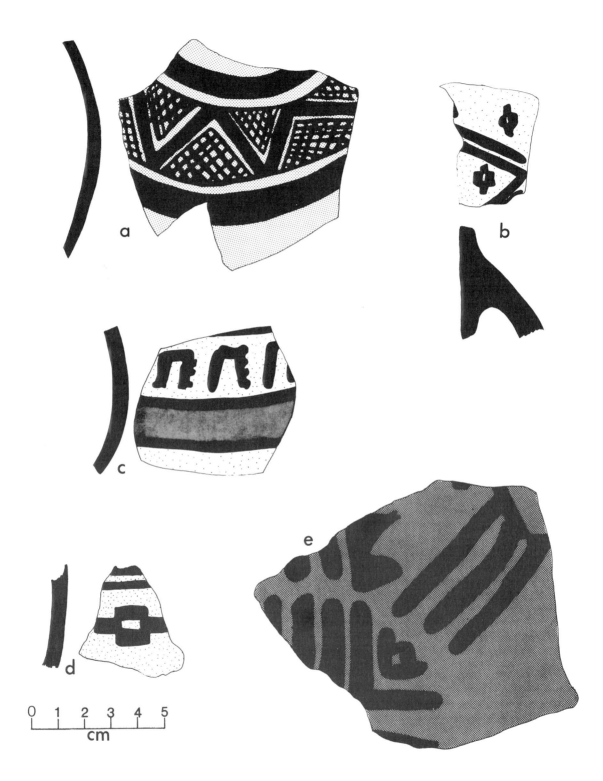

Fig. III.23.1.  Poroma Late Intermediate Period and Late Horizon ceramics from the Nazca pampa: (a) on line connecting centers No. 37 and 35; (b) locale 12/line center 7; (c) locale 51; (d) locale 52/line center 35; (e) on line from line center No. 30, near the Rio Nazca.

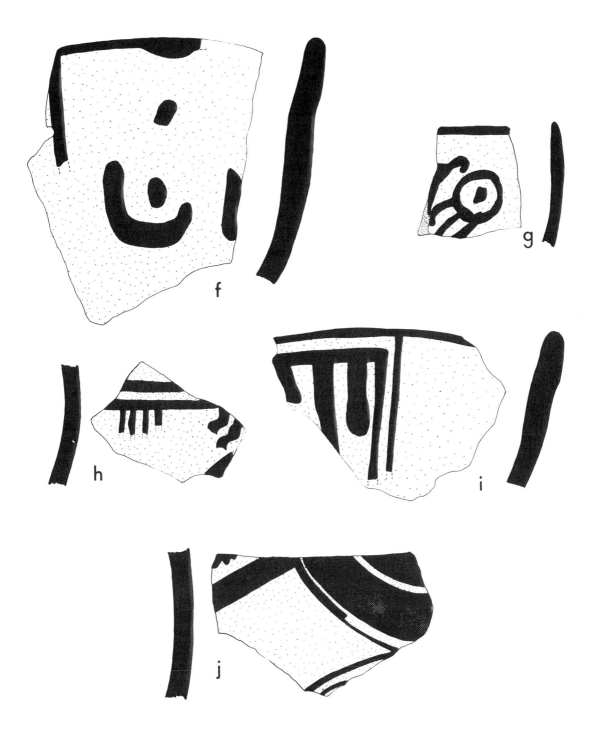

Fig. III.23.2.  (f) locale 14; (g) locale 51; (h) locale 52/line center 35; (i) locale 14; (j) locale 52; line center 35.

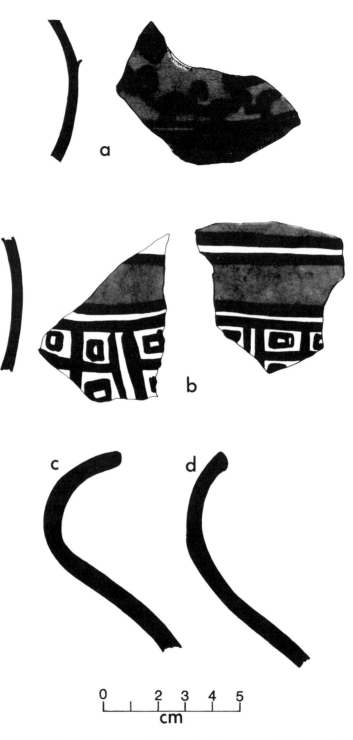

Fig. III.24. Late Horizon ceramics from the Nazca pampa: (a) Pampa Cinco Cruces, near wide line that connects the Ingenio valley with Nazca; (b) locale 10/line center 5; (c) locale 81/line center 60; (d) locale 81/line center 60.

uated within one kilometer of a river valley, although they are by no means limited to the river valleys. In fact, lines emanating from line centers often proceed away from the valley, strongly suggesting a non-riverine orientation or aspect to the geoglyphs and line centers. The focal location of line centers is upon projecting ridges extending from the Andean foothills that surround the Nazca pampa on three sides. Along the river valleys, line centers are situated on prominent hills, as are line centers on the pampa away from the mountains and river valleys.

DISCUSSION

*Prehistoric Uses of the Pampa*

The correlation of locales with line centers and geoglyphs on the pampa is a significant and unbiased observation, as survey transects were made through areas with no geoglyphs, line centers, geoglyphs, and modern roads (Fig. III.26). Such a high concurrence of locales with line centers and geoglyphs requires an examination of what governs the location of line centers and of geoglyphs. I have suggested here that line centers are visible from the ground over distances, and therefore functioned in some way to enhance or attract movement between them. Analogies have been made between the star-like appearance of line centers and *quipus*, as well as *ceques* (Aveni 1986 and Chap. 1, here). Both figured importantly in the sacred and secular aspects of Inka society, although both were in use prior to the Inka empire (see Conklin 1982). The artifacts and features found at line centers and geoglyphs can reflect the activities involved with the construction, maintenance, and use of the centers and the geoglyphs, provided there is contemporaneity and cultural continuity; the kinds of remains should reflect the use of the pampa, and the sacred or secular nature of the line center (if there is contemporaneity). Furthermore, relative and absolute ages for the geoglyphs can be hypothesized from the limited data at hand.

The vast majority of artifacts and features recorded on the pampa pertain to functional purposes. Most ceramics are plain or minimally decorated and thick walled, many with handles and constricted necks; no evidence of cooking was noted on any sherds. It is difficult to assess a chronological time within which these ceramics fall because of the lack of studies on local plain wares. Most of the identifiable pieces can be compared with LIP ceramics, although some vessels with handles are comparable to material noted at Cahuachi which may date to the EIP. The size and characteristics of many of these vessels suggest they were intended for water storage. While one is never more than 7.0 km from the Nazca or Ingenio Rivers, the absence of reliable water on the pampa necessitates storing water if any amount of time is to be spent there.

Vessel shape can be determined by the purpose it serves (Shepard 1956: 224; Hally 1986), and vice versa, and thus an analysis of the Nasca vessel shapes found on the Nazca pampa and elsewhere might provide some insight into the prehistoric activities on the pampa that left the Nasca sherds there. Determining prehistoric vessel use from shape is largely a function of context and contents; because this information is lacking for Nasca wares, this is not a very fruitful avenue of investigation. Less specific information on vessel use can be surmised from common sense: constricted neck vessels are not used for storing bulky items, liquids are stored in a way to minimize spillage and unintended evaporation (evaporation will keep liquids cooled), etc. None of the studies on Nasca ceramics includes any mention of the use to which Nasca vessels might have been put. It is evident from the polychrome Nasca ceramics that I recorded on the pampa that cups, bowls, and dishes are the predominant identifiable shapes.

A final means to determine the function of Nasca pottery is depictions of vessels on ceramics. In this way, contextual information is provided by the contemporary and identical culture, and little hypothesizing is involved (Clarkson 1985). To date, this has not proved to be a fruitful avenue of research.

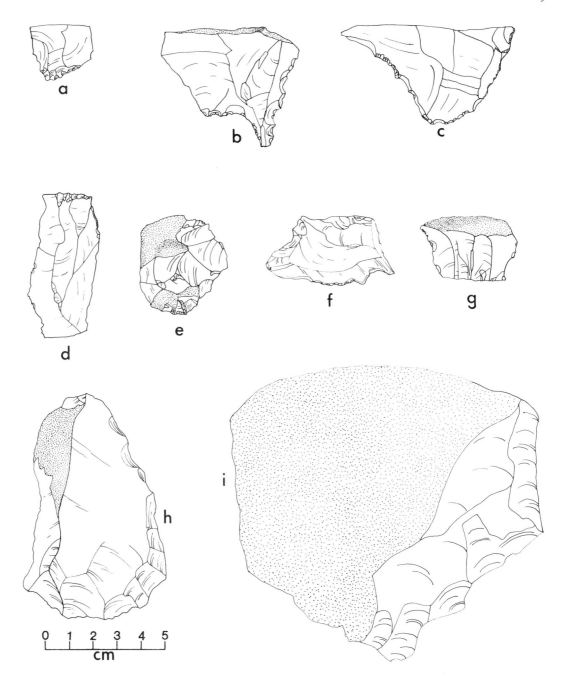

Fig. III.25.1. Lithics from the Nazca pampa: (a) utilized flake, grey-green chert, locale 27; (b) utilized flake, quartzite, locale 41; (c) utilized flake, quartzite, locale 41; (d) waste flake, basalt, locale 27; (e) waste flake, buff chert, locale 84/line center 46; (f) waste flake, basalt, locale 84/line center 46; (g) waste flake, quartzite, locale 84/line center 46; (h) waste flake, quartzite, locale 27; (i) waste flake, quartzite, locale 40.

Lithic artifacts are another indication of subsistence activities on the pampa. Finished or elaborate tools are rare, although flakes are, on occasion, abundant. The quantity of wind blasting that has obliterated or severely eroded the flaking and wear patterns makes it difficult to assess the uses to which the lithics had been put. It is hard to imagine that hunting on the pampa could have supported any but the most meager populations. The pattern of lithics and their distribution in the Nazca region is similar to that of Late Preceramic

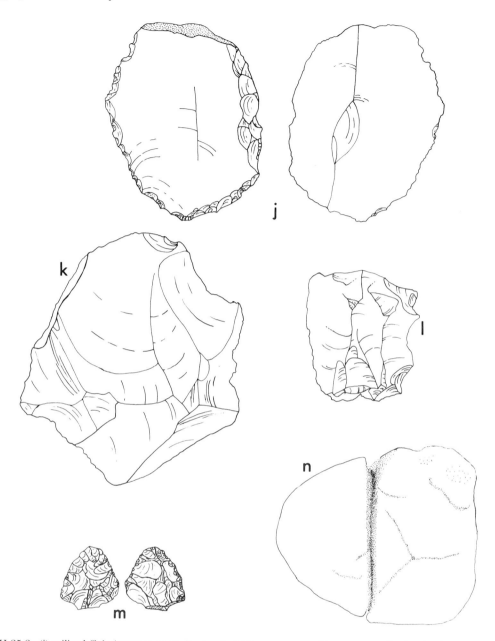

Fig. III.25.2.  (j) utilized flake/scraper, quartzite, locale 84/line center 46; (k) core, quartzite, locale 27; (l) core, basalt, locale 27; (m) biface, obsidian, locale 5; (n) grooved stone, quartzite, locale 36.

and Initial Period herders. With the exception of a few known lines in the western pampa comprised of piles of flaked stones, there is no direct association of lithics with geoglyphs or line centers.

Another piece of evidence that can be considered as indicative of the purpose of remains on the pampa comes from the numerous stone circles (Fig. III.27). To me, the most plausible explanation of their use is as bases to hold down shelter against the wind. Because

there is a fairly high correlation of stone circles with linear geoglyphs, it may be surmised that the people who used the stone circles also made use of the geoglyphs. The kinds of artifacts found with stone circles are plain pottery and crude flaked artifacts, in addition to occasional bits of shell and bone. The majority of bone fragments encountered were too tiny to identify. Several fragments from an exposed hearth were identified as immature camelid, but it was impossible to determine the

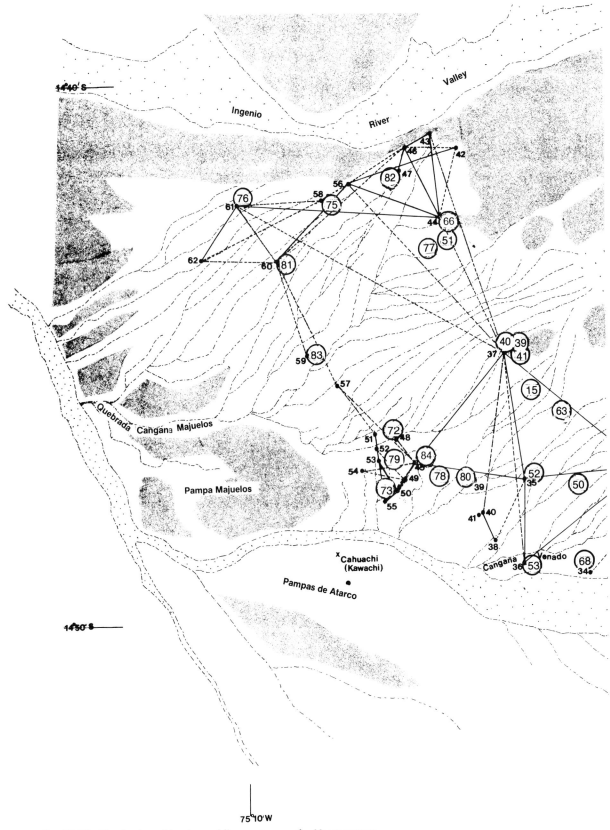

Fig. III.26. Distribution of locales and line centers on the Nazca pampa.

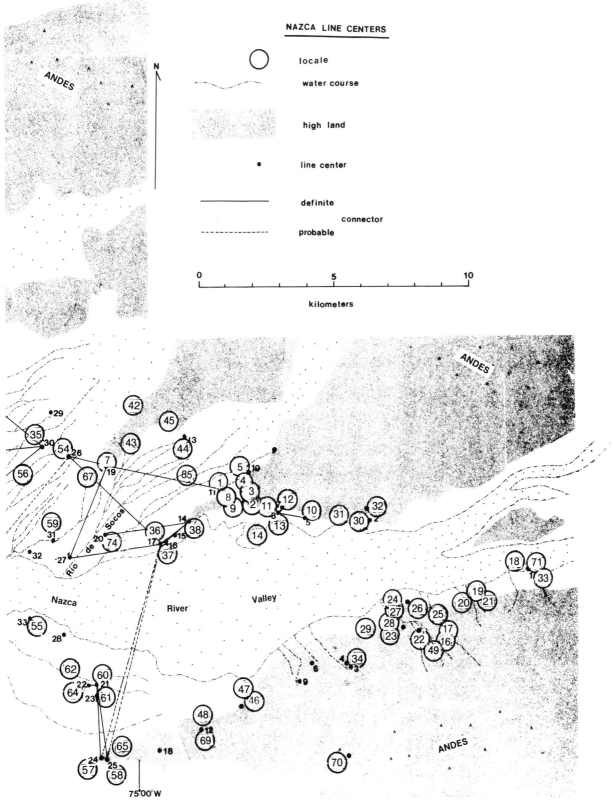

Fig. III.26 (continued).

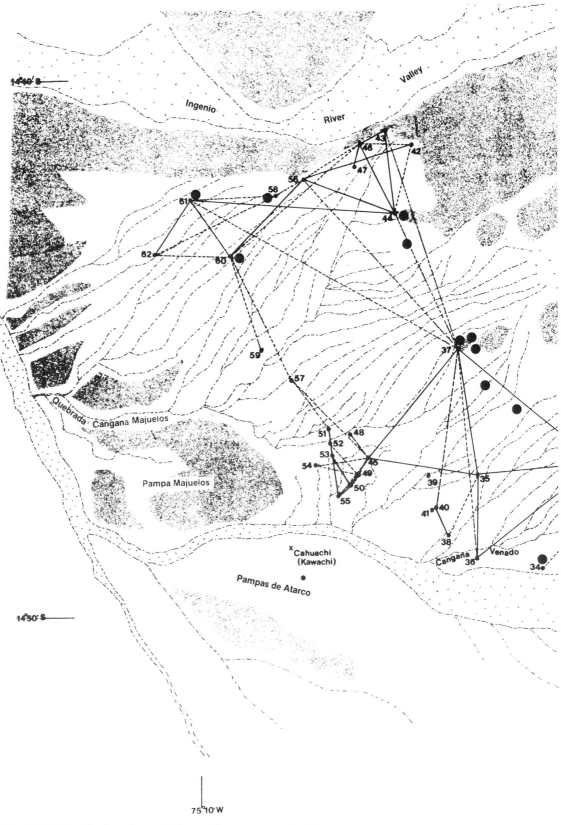

Fig. III.27. Distribution of stone circles and line centers on the Nazca pampa.

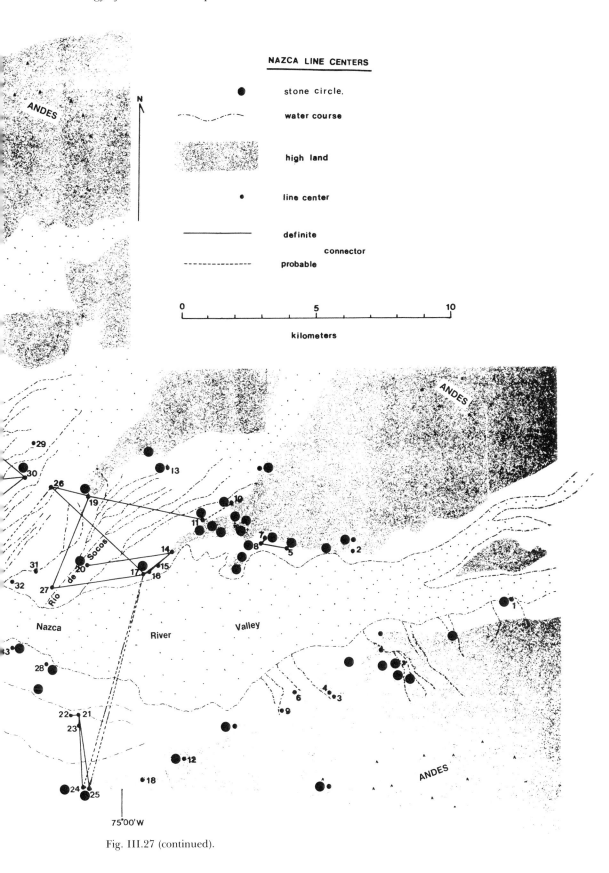

Fig. III.27 (continued).

age of the deposit. The quantity and distribution of these associated remains are extremely sparse. In fact, the majority of lithics and bone was found in locales near the limits of the extent of the geoglyphs on the eastern margin of the pampa. This kind of refuse scatter is not indicative of long term or permanent habitation sites, but rather brief intermittent temporary campsites or shelters. These patterns reflect hunters, herders, or travelers across the pampa.

In addition to evidence of utilitarian and subsistence remains on the pampa, other kinds of activities are evident in the deposition of fine polychrome ceramics, particularly Nasca. Very little is known about the context in which this pottery functioned, as the preponderance of excavations and looted cemeteries reveal nothing about its use in non-funerary context. On the pampa, Nasca ceramics are never found in funerary context, and despite the claims of some *huaqueros* that there were human burials associated with Nasca pottery (Hawkins 1969: 14), there is no other evidence that there were burials either above or below ground on the pampa. Nevertheless, the presence of fine polychrome Nasca pottery should be indicative of a kind of activity different than that implied by thick walled plain pottery. Only finely decorated ceramics are found in burials elsewhere, and the occasional inclusion of other exotic items, such as metals and textiles, indicates a high status for all the grave offerings.

The distribution of Nasca pottery is important in determining the prehistoric uses of the pampa. Although approximately one-quarter of the ceramics recorded and identified are Nasca sherds, this figure reflects a bias on my part in recording and identifying distinguishable pottery; some pottery has been sandblasted or deteriorated beyond recognition. However, it is somewhat significant that only eight line centers, or 13 percent, have identified EIP sherds at them. Seven of these line centers are situated within 1.0 km of the Nazca River, where the prehistoric settlements are concentrated; the exception is LC 48 which is 3.75 km from the river. Furthermore,

there are six documented sites (see Robinson, n.d.) with EIP components situated within 2.0 km of the seven line centers. The lack of Nasca sherds at the remaining line centers, most of which are not situated along or near the banks of the Nazca River, suggests that the EIP material at line centers is not contemporaneous with their construction.

The majority of the remainder of Nasca sherds found on the pampa are associated with or near to geoglyphs. Most of these geoglyphs are linear, although a group of several Nasca sherds was found in the "mouth" of a whale geoglyph and in an unidentified form near LC 17. In only one instance was a Nasca sherd seemingly unrelated to anything, and at two other locales there was evidence of there having been a campsite, one of which may have had linear geoglyphs (Locale 34). Locale 39, comprised of large quantitites of pure Nasca sherds, is the only significant Nasca deposit found on the pampa, although the locale is actually situated atop a prominent ridge projecting onto the pampa about 150 m above its surface. The dense clustering of the sherd deposit and the lack of evidence of looting suggests to me that these vessels were deliberately smashed at the peak of the ridge. Ritual activity of this sort has been postulated to explain the abundant quantity of smashed MH vessels recovered by Tello from Pacheco, and Silverman has suggested that pilgrims at Cahuachi did the same. Locale 39 is all the more significant because it is on a white cap of volcanic tuff that is visible from nearly all parts of the pampa.

While the survey area was unavoidably oriented toward linear geoglyphs, three figural geoglyphs in the survey area, plus a brief foray in the northwestern corner of the pampa where the majority of the figural geoglyphs are concentrated, allow a glimpse into the nature of archaeological remains associated with them. The only ceramics found with the three figural geoglyphs examined were Nasca sherds at two. On the other hand, the majority of ceramics found with linear geoglyphs and line centers date to the LIP. The archaeological survey done by Hawkins's

(1969, 1974) crew on the geoglyphs came to a totally diametric conclusion: he reports a majority of Nasca 3 and 4 ceramics. This pertains to the apogee of Nasca culture on the south coast. In addition, I noted much lower concentrations of sherds than that reported by Hawkins. Since his survey was conducted in the area of the densest concentration of figural geoglyphs, I believe his conclusions are applicable to figural geoglyphs. Thus, although there are discrepancies, my conclusions and those of Hawkins are not so different.

The question remains as to why the EIP inhabitants of the Nazca region were bringing fine polychrome pottery onto the pampa. The present distribution of this pottery does not help answer this question. Hawkins (1969: 14) notes that *huaqueros* told him of entire Nasca pots at the intersections and ends of lines, which would imply a religious or ceremonial aspect associated with the pottery. Although it is impossible to know what, if any, particular area of the pampa the *huaqueros* meant, I suspect that they referred largely to the famous northwestern corner of the pampa. This coincides with the figural geoglyphs, where Hawkins (1969; 1974) reports major percentages of Nasca pottery. The quantities of fine Nasca pottery at the white hilltop Locale 39 would seem to indicate a ritual association of the pottery and/or its distribution. However, the lack of evidence makes it impossible to confirm this assessment. There is practically no contextual information on Nasca ceramics from other archaeological sites. Strong (1957) excavated some Nasca architectural features at Cahuachi, but provides insufficient detail on the ceramics to discern the use of specific kinds of vessels. Lothrop (Lothrop and Mahler 1957: 7, 17) was the only researcher to discuss the possible uses of Nasca pottery he recovered from Chaviña, south of Nazca. He noted broken edges, scuffed bases, and mending by crack-lacing on most of the eighteen vessels he excavated from the cemetery. He concluded that "in spite of the complex symbolism with which some of them [effigy jars] are adorned, they cannot be regarded as ritual vessels" (Lo-throp and Mahler 1957: 17). While I would agree with Lothrop that the amount of use shown on the Chaviña pieces indicates that they were not made especially for interment, I do not believe that the vessels were necessarily utilitarian. If pottery is used regularly or repeatedly in ritual functions, it might display the same kind and amount of wear as utilitarian wares; furthermore, vessels used ritually or occasionally are more likely to last for longer periods of time than utilitarian ones. It is hard to imagine that the more complex polychrome convoluted pots found by Lothrop served only as utilitarian vessels (see Lothrop and Mahler 1957: pls. IV:c and II:b). Nevertheless, there is still no conclusive contextual evidence for the use of Nasca polychrome vessels. Analysis of the vessel itself—size, shape, etc., may provide some insight.

*Chronological Considerations of Nazca Geoglyphs*

The contrasting colors that distinguish the lighter, yellow colored geoglyphs from the remainder of the pampa have been a source of interest to various researchers. The dark color of the pampa is due to a varnish that forms on the surface, while the lighter colored stones, typically comprising the geoglyphs, represent unvarnished surfaces (cf. Chap. I, Fig. 3). Recent studies have indicated that the varnish is the result of microbial action on clays and on oxides and hydroxides of manganese- and iron-rich surfaces, plus other trace elements (Dorn and Oberlander 1981a, 1981b). The slow rates of formation and biogeochemical stability of these accretions make them suitable for dating geological formations, as well as artifacts and petroglyphs (Dorn and Whitley 1984; Dorn et al. 1986; Dorn n.d.). The most accurate and promising method of dating is accelerator mass spectrometry (Dorn, personal communication; Dorn et al. 1986: 830; Dorn et al. 1989). This offers the best hope for obtaining an absolute date for the geoglyphs, the results of which are forthcoming.

The ages of the linear and figural geoglyphs are theoretically assignable to three different combinations: figural preceding linear, linear preceding figural, and contemporaneous. Without any absolute techniques currently available for dating the lines or similarly dated phenomena from elsewhere, temporal assignations must make use of associated datable materials. Material overlying or superimposed upon a geoglyph may only indicate a maximum date of construction. Theoretically, this date could postdate the actual construction of the geoglyphs by more than one cultural period. The correlation of geoglyphs with sites and burials can narrow down the timeframe of construction of the geoglyphs, as at Pacheco, a Middle Horizon site in the Nazca Valley excavated by Julio Tello in 1927, where lines and burials may overlap at LC 33 (most of the burials have been looted; see also Fig. 14).

There are a tremendous number of overlapping geoglyph features, particularly in the northwestern corner of the pampa where there are both linear and figural geoglyphs. Because of the inaccessibility of this area, I have relied upon published airphotos for information on overlap of geoglyphs. They reveal a tendency toward figural geoglyphs underlying linear ones. I caution that the small number of examples make this only a preliminary conclusion. Since the destructive habit of sweeping the figural geoglyphs would tend to make them appear as if they overlaid the linear geoglyphs, some credence is lent to the apparent tendency of linear geoglyphs to be above figural geoglyphs.

Dating of the geoglyphs based on ceramic associations and common motifs of both the geoglyphs and ceramics agrees with the evidence of overlapping geoglyphs. Nasca ceramics show that the figural geoglyphs are a manifestation of the EIP. Hawkins's (1969, 1974) findings of Nasca ceramics in the environs of the figural geoglyphs, however flawed was his methodology, concur with the Nasca sherds I found on other parts of the pampa. The second line of evidence pointing to an affiliation between figural geoglyphs and Nasca culture is the similarity of subject matter on Nasca ceramics and figural geoglyphs—

specifically, the birds, fish, and a few of the animals. The birds and animals shared in common between the geoglyphs and ceramics include hummingbirds, herons, other water birds, condors or harpy eagles, fox (or some sort of canid), and lizards. While some of the figural geoglyphs may represent cultigens that are commonly portrayed on the MH oversized vessels from Pacheco with highland associations with Huari (Clarkson n.d. b: 50–53), EIP cultural ties with the sierra do not rule out the possibility that these cultigens were grown in the Nasca region prior to the MH. It should be noted that only MH sherds were found on the lines at LC 33, where Pacheco is situated. At Cantalloc, where a MH component has been documented (Robinson n.d.), numerous linear geoglyphs appear, and no EIP sherds are in direct association. Finally, many geoglyphs are situated near Soisongo across the Nazca valley from Pacheco. The Soisongo site has large MH and LIP components.

If the Nazca geoglyphs were made during the MH, it is difficult to explain the origin of the concept of making them, since they are not known from anywhere else in the Wari domain. There are comparable depictions, such as the petroglyphs inscribed on natural rock outcrops at Huari (Lumbreras 1974: 161). The most common form is a curvilinear dendritic configuration. A large rock outcrop at Huari measuring $14.0 \times 8.0$ m has a circular hole reported to be 0.54 m deep and 1.37 m in diameter (Fig. 28). Inscribed into the rock sloping toward this hole are manmade "canals" 6 to 30 cm wide (J. Sterner, personal communication). The configuration suggests water catchment channels and a cistern; the size indicates it was not meant to store any useful amount of water. Since water was not readily available in the Ayacucho basin for agricultural and other needs, a sacred or prophetical purpose may have been attached to the channel and cistern feature. Schreiber has also found rocks "carved with miniature channels, some of which seem to include terraced zones, almost like a three-dimensional map of an agricultural system." She also notes that they are found in the Carahuarazo Valley in Lucanas (adjacent to the Nazca region) near LIP and LH sites (Schreiber, personal communication).

Geoglyphs have been reported from Chile up through northern Peru (Wilson 1988), as well as in Bolivia (Morrison 1978). Some of these have been lost amidst the spread of modern cities and farmland; I am unable to comment on those I have never seen published or in person. The giant hillside figures in northern Chile are stylistically and thematically distinct from Nazca figural geoglyphs (see illustrations in Reinhard 1986). Long straight lines and radiating lines from hilltop "centers" on the Bolivian *altiplano* and in the Atacama Desert in Chile have been documented by Morrison (1978), who has demonstrated a degree of continuity in past and present Andean belief systems on the meaning of straight lines. There is no evidence that the geoglyphs in the Nazca area and other regions of South America are part of a singular cultural manifestation; indeed, the practice of making geoglyphs is widespread throughout the arid western regions of the Americas (see Davis 1981; Rogers 1966).

The distribution of the geoglyphs in South America *generally* coincides with the extent of the MH Tiwanaku-Wari culture. However, there is no concurrence of known MH sites with geoglyphs, except for Pacheco with LC 33 and Locale 55, mentioned above. It would be premature to conclude that the proximity (but *not* necessarily association) of geoglyphs to the beautiful and fine Nasca ceramics and Nasca sites implies that the geoglyphs dated to the EIP Nasca phase. Clearly, more needs to be understood about the MH in the Nazca region.

There is very little evidence to suggest any spatial or temporal correlation between linear geoglyphs and Nasca ceramics. Of the small quantity of Nasca sherds found during my surveys on the pampa away from the river valley, most were associated with two of three known figural geoglyphs outside the northwestern zone of figural geoglyphs. Contrary to Hawkins, the majority of ceramics associated with geoglyphs did not date to the EIP, but to the LIP. In addition, MH and LH ceramics have also been found on the pampa in greater numbers than any EIP ones. The dis-

Fig. III.28. Carved stone from Huari, Ayacucho. (Photograph by J. Sterner)

crepancy between my results and those of Hawkins should be explainable in terms of the two different areas surveyed. Both areas have linear geoglyphs, yet that surveyed by Hawkins has the vast majority of the figural geoglyphs. Although a high correlation of EIP ceramics with figural geoglyphs is based on a very small sample, it does reinforce the possibility that the broad divisions of geoglyphs into figural and linear are more than simply stylistic or thematic.

The combination of the association of Nasca ceramics with geoglyphs in the northwestern corner of the pampa and the congruency of some motifs in both ceramics and figural geoglyphs, plus the association of post-Nasca ceramics with linear geoglyphs, and a tendency for linear geoglyphs to overlie figural geoglyphs indicate that the two kinds of geoglyphs are products of two different cultural periods. Furthermore, the kinds of ceramic remains might indicate different functional uses. The ceramics thus far identified from the two areas can be classified only as to temporal affiliation. However, there is a large quantity of unidentified material from both Hawkins's (62–63 percent) and my surveys (29 percent). Thus, it may yet be discovered that the two geoglyph classes served functionally distinct purposes while being coeval or of different time periods. Until complete ceramic seriations and typologies of Nasca ceramics, including plain wares, are made available, it is impossible to discuss function based upon the ceramic evidence.

Pulling all these bits of data together does not point definitely to a specific culture group or groups as the constructors of the geoglyphs. Several trends appear evident: (1) lines and figures are separated in time and, to a certain degree, space; (2) figures predate lines; (3) figures date to the EIP; and (4) lines date to after the EIP, perhaps the MH or the LIP.

The identification and separation of the two separate phenomena are the most important factors to come out of the survey and analysis of the Nazca pampa. This information should

help frame future investigations into the region, as well as into the geoglyphs themselves. Determining the context of archaeological remains can help illuminate functions of artifacts and how they were integrated into prehistoric lifeways. With the addition of archaeological data in the environs of geoglyphs and line centers, the function of the Nazca geoglyphs remains elusive, in part because of the amount of looting and disturbance that has taken place in the vicinity of the lines on the pampa. In addition, published ceramic seriations devoted largely to fine decorated polychrome wares have been useless where the majority of the ceramic collections are undecorated sherds from utilitarian wares. Finally, incomplete survey of unique areas, such as those where figural and linear geoglyphs overlap in the northwestern corner of the pampa, results in an inadequate sample.

CONCLUDING REMARKS

Some general observations can be made concerning the function of the geoglyphs based on evidence presented here. The coincidence of stone circles with geoglyphs suggests use of the circles during and/or after construction of the geoglyphs. Post-construction uses may include ritual or functional walking. I have already pointed out that the lines can be followed and have been used as roads or paths when crossing the pampa, especially when visibility is obscured; many roads, including the Pan American Highway, follow segments of long linear geoglyphs. Ritual walking along straight, predetermined routes has been documented among the Inkas during the festival of Capac Hucha. A specific incident that took place around 1430 in Ocros (cited by Zuidema 1977a: 231) incorporated water origin and irrigation ritual into straight line walking. The presence of overlapping geoglyphs, particularly evident in the northwestern corner of the pampa where the figural and linear geoglyphs exist, raises an interesting and in many ways important question of why certain areas of the pampa look like a chalkboard used for many different lessons but never erased between each lesson. Was the act of construction as or more important than the recognizability of individual geoglyphs?

In spite of the specific problems associated with using ceramic remains to identify specific activities for which the geoglyphs were used, some factors are apparent. The majority of the ceramics noted on the pampa are thick undecorated sherds, suggesting some non-ritual, non-ceremonial activities in association with the geoglyphs. Although one is never more than about 7.0 km from the Nazca or Ingenio Valleys and water, it would have been convenient to have drinking water available on the pampa, particularly during construction of geoglyphs. Decorated sherds are generally found on the pampa close to river valleys; the types reflect the ceramics from sites and cemeteries at the edge of the river valley beside the pampa. Fine decorated Nasca sherds were found associated with two figural geoglyphs situated about 500 m from the Nazca Valley.

The archaeological evidence from the Nazca pampa indicates human presence and use for over two thousand years. All cultural phases represented in the river valley are reflected in the archaeological remains on the pampa. The range of remains found in valley sites is not found on the pampa, indicating, in part, specialized uses of the pampa; remains left exposed on the pampa may have not survived to the present, either because they were removed or have disintegrated. The presence of stone circles and cairns exclusively on the pampa provides further evidence that activities carried out there were different from those in the valleys. There is evidence of reuse of the geoglyphs, but it is not known if it conformed to their originally intended functions. The high correlation of line centers, geoglyphs, and locales indicates that the geoglyphs were a strong drawing factor.

This is not to say that the Nazca geoglyphs should be studied from the viewpoint of ar-

chaeology only. Single-minded approaches have been one of the greatest deterrents to serious investigation of the Nazca phenomenon for years. Archaeological investigations are an indispensable part of an examination of prehistoric phenomena, lifeways, and contexts, but investigations by scholars in adjoining and "separate" disciplines that have highlighted the range of possibilities inherent in Nazca geoglyphs reveal the complex fabric of Andean society as a whole. Many Andean concepts were recorded by the Spanish conquerors of the Inka civilization in the sixteenth century, yet many of these recorded ideas were crystallizations of one moment in time of processes that had been extant and evolving for hundreds and perhaps thousands of years. One has only to look at the similarity of complex iconography in early Valdivia ceramics of Ecuador (Damp 1982) which runs through all stages of cultural development in Andean South America to appreciate the tenacity of certain concepts and motifs. The association of the geoglyphs with water, ancestor homage, *quipus*, and *ceques* has been discussed by myself (Clarkson n.d. b) and others in this volume and elsewhere (Morrison 1978; Reinhard 1988); the significance of each of these is well documented among the Inkas, and archaeological evidence indicates that they also figured prominently among Chimú, Wari, Moche, and Chavín cultures, to name but a few. Thus, a key to understanding the Nazca geoglyphs is to view and study them through the broader perspective of Andean (or northwestern South American) lifeways as evidenced by both archaeological remains and conceptual beliefs.

## ACKNOWLEDGMENTS

The author gratefully acknowledges the assistance of many people and institutions who made this research possible, particularly Jonathan Damp, Carlos Guzman Ladron de Guevara of the Instituto Nacional de Cultura, Alejandro Pezzia Assereto of the Museo Regional de Ica, Josue Lancho of the Instituto Nacional de Cultura in Nazca, the Izaak Walton Killam Foundation, the Wenner-Gren Foundation, and the University of Calgary Dissertation Fellowship Fund. Further assistance was rendered by Duccio Bonavia, Eduardo Herrán, Bill Isbell, Margaret Kennedy, Pat Knobloch, Karen McCullough, Donald Proulx, Katharina Schreiber, Izumi Shimada, and Judy Sterner. All photos are by the author unless otherwise noted.

## IV. Andean Social Organization and the Maintenance of the Nazca Lines

**Gary Urton**

## INTRODUCTION

Since the "rediscovery" of the Nazca lines over half a century ago, there has been a remarkable amount of speculation concerning why and how the lines were made and how they may have been used. However, one point that comes through clearly in Aveni's summary and synthesis of several of the major studies of the lines (Chap. I here) is that rarely—if ever—have hypotheses concerning the priorities, interests, and principles of organization of the societies which inhabited the river valleys bordering the Nazca pampa provided points of departure for studies of the lines. In the majority of cases, hypotheses concerning the lines have been formulated on the basis of presumptions about the importance, or the necessity, of certain forms of technology (such as astronomy, calendrics, or irrigation) for the survival of people in this arid environment. Whether the hypotheses have focused on one or another kind of technology, or on ritual activities (such as running), there has been little attempt to try to situate these explanations in the context of certain well-documented forms of social, political, economic, and religious organization in the Andes (for a notable exception, see Isbell 1978). As a consequence, most of the hypotheses about the Nazca lines have tended to reflect Western scientific interests and priorities rather than those of Andean societies, as the latter can be understood from ethnographic, ethnohistorical, and archaeological materials.

In this study, I will attempt to formulate a line of investigation on the geoglyphs that begins with such questions as the following: How are we to understand how the people who lived in the river valleys bordering the pampa in Inka and perhaps earlier times thought about, used, and interacted with the geoglyphs on the Nazca pampa? And, how might the forms of social organization, as well as the political, economic, and ritual institutions and practices of the societies in the river valleys provide us with Andean perspectives for interpreting the construction and maintenance of the lines? Therefore, the purpose of this

article is to attempt to formulate a hypothesis about social interactions in the context—or the space—of the Nazca lines whose terms are based on local (Nazca) interests and priorities and whose principles are drawn from Andean forms of organization and practice.

As I will make frequent use of ethnographic analogies drawn from contemporary Andean societies in the interpretation of the ethnohistorical and archaeological data presented here, I should begin with a few comments on the appropriateness, and the limitations, of this type of analysis. We will find throughout this study that certain forms of social organization—especially *ayllus* (groupings based on shared landholdings, kinship, and ceremonial and public labor obligations) and moieties—are found quite commonly as the basic units of social organization in Andean communities both today and during colonial times throughout much of Peru. However, it cannot be assumed that the *ayllus* and moieties of contemporary communities are the same things they were three or four centuries ago. The relevance of a comparison between two communities which are organized by *ayllus* and moieties must be demonstrated on the basis of similarities in the areas of: modes of recruitment, types of communal action for which the groups are mobilized, and similarities in the redistribution of resources among the groups through time. If the two communities are similar with respect to these (and other) forms of organization, then I think that we are warranted in drawing analogies between the two as the bases for formulating hypotheses with respect to certain features that might remain obscure in one case but for which we have data from the other. For instance, this approach is particularly useful in trying to understand the social practices—rather than the structures—that may have been a part of the organization of activities among local groups in the past.

In line with the above comments, the argument will begin with the development of a model of the social and ritual practices of multiple *ayllu* groupings in a contemporary Andean community. The model will be based on material collected during eighteen months of ethnographic fieldwork which I carried out over the period from 1981 to 1984 in the community of Pacariqtambo (Department of Cuzco) in the southern Peruvian highlands. These data will concern the organization of the ten *ayllus* in Pacariqtambo and of the ritual practices whereby these groups divide the churchyard and plaza of the community into rectangular strips and sweep them clean of debris on the occasion of annual religious festivals. After developing the model of the division and maintenance of strips of ritual territory on the basis of contemporary Andean ritual practices and forms of social organization, I will then turn to a discussion of ethnohistorical and archaeological data from the south coast of Peru which attest to social groupings and public labor practices from late pre-Hispanic and early colonial times that seem to be similar in many respects to those described from Pacariqtambo. The final section of this study will examine the relevance of the "ritual maintenance" model for interpreting some of the institutions and practices that may account for how and why the Nazca lines were maintained over time.

Before beginning with the discussion of the ethnographic material, I want to make two observations on the actual appearance of the ground within the borders of the geoglyphs on the Nazca pampa. These observations will help establish what is, I think, an important but generally overlooked feature of the Nazca lines; that is, that the lines are dynamic features. That the Nazca geoglyphs are continually changing (in ways to be defined below), and that the people who used or interacted with them were aware of—and actively manipulated—this characteristic of the lines, are two of the central premises on which this study is based.

The first point of clarification concerning the dynamic nature of the lines is derived from the observation that while the general outlines of the geoglyphs at Nazca are exceptionally long-lasting—having endured for centuries—nonetheless, over time, small pebbles and dust blow into these cleared spaces. This has the effect of slowly diminishing the

contrast between the lighter-colored surfaces within the borders of the lines and the darker earth of the surface of the pampa outside the borders (see Reiche 1968: 40,44). That such a slow transformation of the cultural features on the pampa does, indeed, take place can be realized by a comparison of an ancient geoglyph with one made in recent times. Fig. 1 shows the typical light/dark contrast that one sees between the cleared space within an ancient (undisturbed) Nazca geoglyph and the surrounding pampa. Fig. 2 shows the striking visual contrast that is produced by a newly made geoglyph.[1] What one actually sees across the broad stretch of pampa today is a range of contrasts between the extremes illustrated in Figures IV.1 and 2.

The point that should be stressed from the observations and comparison made above is that, due to the slow deposition of wind-borne dust and pebbles within the lines, the light/dark contrast between the ground inside the borders of the geoglyphs and that outside gradually diminishes through time. As a result of these dynamic forces and processes of change, if—for whatever reason—the preservation of the lines on the pampa was important to pre-Hispanic peoples in the Nazca area, then they may well have undertaken maintenance work, in one form or another, on the lines. This could have involved actually sweeping the lines—and other cleared spaces—to remove the dust and pebbles (see the photograph of Maria Reiche sweeping the lines, in Reiche 1980: 40). On the other hand, such direct, or purposeful, means of cleaning the lines need not have been the only ways of maintaining them; that is, since walking on a line disturbs the surface and reexposes the lighter-colored subsoil which may be covered over with dust, any movement along a line— i.e., walking, running, or dancing on it—has the effect of maintaining, or "preserving," the line by renewing the light/dark contrast. I will

---

1. The geoglyph illustrated in Fig. 2 was constructed as an experiment on a remote part of the pampa by the members of an Earthwatch group that Aveni and I led in Nazca in 1983. The geoglyph was covered over after the experiment was completed and the photographs of it were taken. For details of this experiment, see Chap. I, pp. 23–25, this volume.

Fig. IV.1. Photograph of a relatively undisturbed Nazca line showing minimal light/dark contrast between the ground inside and outside the line.

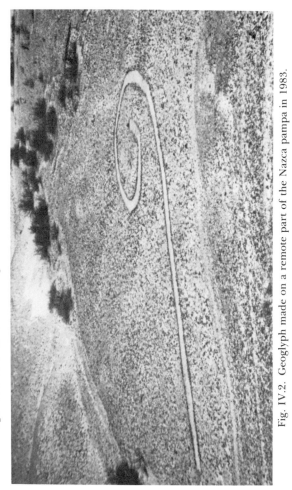

Fig. IV.2. Geoglyph made on a remote part of the Nazca pampa in 1983.

Fig. IV.3. Narrow line with footpath passing through the center.

Fig. IV.4. Wide line with multiple footpaths.

discuss later some of the activities whereby the people living in the river valleys bordering the pampa may have gone up onto the pampa and walked on the lines.

The second point of clarification that I want to make concerning the appearance of the lines is directly connected with the first; that is, having walked some 30–40 miles of lines and geometry during several months of research on and around the Nazca pampa, I do

not recall seeing one of these cleared spaces which did not have at least one fairly well-defined footpath passing through it; "wide" lines (i.e., those over some two meters wide) and geometrical figures often have several footpaths passing through them (see Figs. IV.3 and 4).

In discussing the footpaths, it is necessary to consider the question of whether or not they might be the result of modern foot-traffic on the pampa and, therefore, might have nothing to do with pre-Hispanic activities. It is undeniable that there has been, and continues to be, occasional traffic across the Nazca pampa. As far as I am aware, there are three main sources of modern foot-traffic: first, tourists who stop along the Pan American Highway and walk lines near the highway; second, people who are engaged in research on the lines; and third, local people who live in the Nazca or Ingenio Valley who—for one reason or another—may at times choose to walk across the pampa rather than catch a ride along the Pan American Highway. While it is clear that there are at least these three sources of traffic on the pampa, I do not think that they can account for the quantity of footpaths that one finds, nor for the ubiquity of footpaths on lines in the very remote parts of the pampa. For instance, in the central and western parts of the pampa—i.e., in those areas which are far removed from the Pan American Highway and from the northeastern corner of the pampa, where most of the animal figures are located—one finds relatively deep (one to two inches below the desert surface) and undisturbed footpaths. It is not uncommon to find sherd scatters on the surfaces of these lines as well (see Clarkson, Chap. 3 here). From these observations, I conclude that in the past, people traveled (i.e., walked, ran, danced, or in some other way moved) along the geoglyphs on the Nazca pampa in sufficient numbers—or a sufficient number of times—to produce well-worn footpaths.

Based on the two observations described above, as well as other data to be discussed later, the central argument that I make here is that a dialectical interaction went on for some time in the Nazca area during pre-Hispanic (and perhaps early colonial) times between the geoglyphs on the surface of the pampa and the people who lived in the river valleys bordering the pampa. As I will argue below, the pampa was the place where the social groups in the area interacted with each other on ritual and ceremonial occasions; through these interactions, the geoglyphs were continually "preserved." Therefore, the lines are viewed

here as social constructions and the maintenance of the lines (i.e., the renewal of the light/dark contrast) as a product of social interactions.

## RITUAL SWEEPING AND THE DIVISION OF PUBLIC SPACE IN PACARIQTAMBO

The modern-day community of Pacariqtambo (Province of Paruro, Department of Cuzco, Peru), has a population of some 850 people, about one-third of whom are monolingual Quechua-speakers, while the remainder are bilingual Quechua/Spanish-speakers. The community is located at an altitude of 3585 m above sea level, about 40 km directly south of Cuzco. The lands controlled by this primarily agricultural community range within altitudinal extremes from 2500 m up to 4300 m (for more complete descriptions of the community, see Urton 1984, 1985, 1986, n.d. a and b).

The principal socio-political and ceremonial groups in Pacariqtambo are called *ayllus*. All adult members of the community belong to one or another of ten of these groupings. The ten *ayllus* are divided into moieties, each composed of five *ayllus*. The moieties are called *Hanansayaq* ("of the upper part") and *Hurinsayaq* ("of the lower part"). It is important to stress at the beginning of this discussion that *ayllus* and moieties were common forms of organization in the socio-political systems of both the Andean highlands (Zuidema 1964) and the coast in pre-Hispanic times (Netherly 1984; Rostworowski 1977, 1983). As I will document later, there is also ethnohistorical evidence which confirms that the people living in the river valleys bordering the Nazca pampa were grouped into *ayllus* and moieties at the time of Spanish contact.

The basis of *ayllu* membership in present-day Pacariqtambo is landholding; that is, all the members of an *ayllu* have usufruct rights over parcels of land which are considered to be the common property of that *ayllu*. In addition, the *ayllus* are the principal groups for undertaking communal labor projects (*faenas*).

These involve activities like cleaning and repairing public buildings, such as the town hall,
the cemetery, the church, and the adobe walls
around the church (Urton 1984). The *ayllus*
are also each responsible for celebrating a festival, most of which are Catholic saints' days
that fall within the period from the end of
one agricultural season through the beginning
stages of the next (i.e., from June through
September). The activities undertaken by the
*ayllus* during these festivals include preparing
food and drink, and building altars for the
adoration of the saints, as well as sweeping the
public plazas clean of debris. As I will attempt
to show here that the spatial divisions and ritual activities that are undertaken by the *ayllus*
during the sweeping of the plazas in Pacariqtambo are relevant for a consideration of similar practices that may have gone on in early
colonial and pre-Hispanic times in the ritual
divisions of territory during the performance
of public labor service, I will describe these
activities in some detail.

One of the principal events during any one
of the *ayllu*-sponsored festivals in Pacariqtambo is the procession of the image of the
saint through the churchyard and the plaza at
the center of the community. The churchyard, which lies to the south of the church, is
surrounded by a two to three meter high
adobe wall. The large central plaza lies to the
west of and at a somewhat lower elevation
than the small, enclosed churchyard. The image of the saint whose day is being celebrated
during any one of the festivals is first carried
from the church and through the churchyard;
the procession then makes a counter-clockwise
circuit of the plaza, and the saint is then returned to the church.

During this procession, the saint is accompanied by a large group of devotees (from 50–
100 people), all of whom are expected to walk
barefooted as a sign of respect. Another sign
of respect is the cleaning of the public spaces
through which the saint will pass; that is, the
churchyard and plaza are transformed into sacred spaces at the time of religious celebrations, and therefore they must be cleaned and
made presentable for the saints. The cleaning

of the churchyard and plaza is the duty of the
*ayllus*, all but two of which are assigned rectangular strips of territory, called *chhiutas*
("stretches, extensions").[2] The *chhiuta* divisions are illustrated in Fig. IV.5.

As is evident in Fig. IV.5, there are nine
*chhiuta* divisions (recall that there are ten *ayllus*
in Pacariqtambo). Of the nine *chhiutas*, eight
are the responsibility of the eight *ayllus* of Pacariqtambo (four per moiety) which are considered to the oldest, or the "original" *ayllus* of

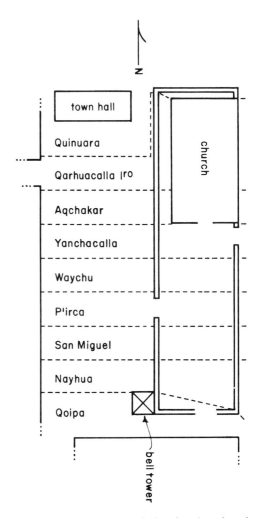

Fig. IV.5. The *chhiutas* of the churchyard and
plaza in Pacariqtambo.

2. In an earlier study (Urton 1984), I referred to these strips of
territory as *chutas*. This spelling of the term is the same as that
given in Cusihuamán's dictionary of Cuzco Quechua (1976: 40).
However, a number of people in Pacariqtambo who looked over
my 1984 publication informed me that I had misspelled the
term; the proper spelling, I was told, is "*chhiuta*."

the community. The ninth *chhiuta*, that assigned to "Qoipa" in Fig. IV.5, is the responsibility of the residents of a small village which is located a short distance to the south of Pacariqtambo and which has the obligation to perform ritual labor service in Pacariqtambo.

Early in the morning on the day of one of the religious festivals, at least one member of each one of the nine groups goes to the center of town and sweeps up the debris within his *chhiuta*, loads it into a carrying cloth, and dumps it off the plaza grounds. The lines of division between the *chhiutas* are not visible on the grounds of the churchyard and plaza. Rather, the dividing lines are negotiated boundaries between the rectangular strips of territory which must be reestablished by the *ayllu* representatives of contiguous *chhiutas* at the beginning of each festival. The method of delineating the boundary lines is important for our later discussions; therefore, I describe it in some detail.

Fig. IV.6 is a photo-mosaic taken from approximately the point indicated by the name "Waychu" in Fig. IV.5. The mosaic shows the grounds of the plaza and the western face of the west wall enclosing the churchyard. The church is at the left of center, the bell tower at the extreme right. A group of men belonging to one of the *ayllus* can be seen building an altar in the lower right-hand portion of the mosaic. Surrounding the churchyard is an approximately two meter high adobe wall which is regularly broken by arched windows and which shows variations in a number of ornamental and structural features along its length. These include the presence or absence of whitewash and of roofing tiles on the wall. For example, the section of wall to the far left in Figure 6 is not covered with roofing tiles.

The adobe walls surrounding the churchyard are maintained in annual work parties (*faenas*) which are carried out by the nine groups that have the responsibility for maintaining the *chhiutas*. The walls are divided into stretches which are also called *chhiutas*, or *curawa surcos* ("rows [ridges] of the priest"). The approximate dividing lines between the wall

*chhiutas* can be seen in Fig. IV.6 as well as in the drawing in Fig. IV.5. The maintenance (e.g., the repainting, reroofing, etc.) of the sections of walls is the responsibility of the nine groups which are assigned the duty of sweeping the grounds of the churchyard and plaza. The differences in the physical appearance of the various sections of the walls around the churchyard are the result of the differential maintenance of them by the *ayllus* over the past several years. Variations in the physical features along the churchyard wall provide the information used in establishing the *chhiuta* divisions on the grounds of the plaza. (For the sake of clarity, I will discuss only the *chhiuta* divisions that are made in the plaza. However, the reader should be aware that the division of the churchyard grounds is made by a similar process to that which I will describe for the plaza, although the east wall of the churchyard is observed in making those divisions.)

The boundaries of a particular *chhiuta* on the grounds of the plaza coincide with and are determined by lines of sight extended from the boundaries between the various wall segments along the west wall of the churchyard. At the time of a festival, when the representatives of two *ayllus* with contiguous *chhiutas* arrive at the plaza to sweep their strips, they begin by reestablishing the boundary line between their respective *chhiutas*. This they do by negotiating the extension across the plaza grounds of the boundary as it is indicated by discontinuities in the physical characteristics of the wall (as described earlier) and by recounting—or mutually "reenumerating"—the windows within their respective wall segments (each *chhiuta* contains a certain number of windows). In some cases, the boundary line between two *chhiutas* may actually pass through a window, dividing it between two *ayllus/chhiutas*. The *ayllu* representatives of contiguous *chhiutas* stand in the plaza and, looking at the adobe wall above the plaza, negotiate their mutual boundary. Having agreed upon a boundary, they then set about sweeping their respective strips of ritual territory. Thus, the boundary lines on the plaza grounds between

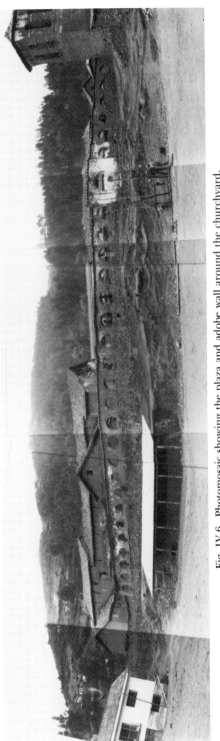

Fig. IV.6. Photomosaic showing the plaza and adobe wall around the churchyard.

the *chhiutas* are ephemeral and negotiable; they require acts of social confrontation and cooperation among the representatives of the *ayllus* for their definition. The flexible and negotiable nature of the *chhiutas* renders them an active, dynamic element in the reproduction and reformulation of relations among the *ayllus* over time (cf. Urton 1984: 37–39).

This description of the division and cleaning of the plaza *chhiutas* in Pacariqtambo lays the groundwork for a model of—and for—some of the practices which may be associated with the reproduction and maintenance of strips of ritual territory elsewhere in the Andes. To my knowledge, there are no other examples of the ritual sweeping of plazas in the ethnographic literature on contemporary highland communities that are similar to the example described above (although see the discussion of the cleaning of the plaza at the festival in Yauca in Silverman, this volume). On the other hand, there are a number of descriptions from highland Andean communities of the division of public buildings and communal work projects into sections and of the assignment of the responsibility for maintaining these sections to *ayllus*. Examples are reported for the construction and maintenance of cemetery walls (Ossio 1981: 195–196) and irrigation canals (Gelles n.d. 164–165; Sherbondy 1982: 21–24; Wachtel 1976: 94–98).[3] There are also ethnohistorical data from the early colonial period which attest to the use of the term *"chhiuta"* (or *chuta*, *chota*) for divisions among *ayllus* during games and ritual contests (e.g., Avila 1966 [1608]: 143–145) and for the division of roads—and perhaps for their maintenance—into sections or strips (Callapiña et al. 1974 [1542?]: 37). The last reference concerns testimony recorded in Cuzco from natives of Pacariqtambo in which it is stated that during Inka times, the royal roads were divided into sections, called *chotas*.[4]

The *chotas* would probably have been maintained by local *ayllus* working in corvée labor for the state (cf. Murra 1980; Urton 1984; and the discussion of *mit'a*, below).

To summarize, we have found in the ethnographic data from Pacariqtambo a contemporary example of a process whereby social groups divide among themselves the responsibility for maintaining the buildings and communal spaces which form the settings for their annual ritual activities. The activities call for cooperation among the members of the *ayllus* in providing the labor and materials (roofing tiles, adobe blocks, paint, and so on) necessary for repairing their wall segments. The maintenance activities also entail moments of confrontation and potential conflict between members of *ayllus* having contiguous *chhiutas* as representatives from these groups negotiate their mutual boundaries. What is "maintained" in these periodic episodes of cooperation and confrontation is not only physical structures but also the relations within and among the social groups in the community. In short, at the same time that *chhiuta* labor addresses the inevitable deterioration of physical structures and the tendency for what is clean to become dirty, it simultaneously represents a form of ritual practice for the maintenance and reproduction of a strong and flexible social organization.

With the example of Pacariqtambo serving as a model, I will turn now to a discussion of various forms of socio-political and communal labor organization in the Andes along the south coast of Peru during early colonial times. I begin with the description of an archaeological site south of Nazca; this is Quebrada de la Vaca which incorporates a building that exhibits some of the same elements found today in the plaza/*chhiuta* complex in Pacariqtambo.

3. For interesting comparative material from Bali on the responsibilities of social and irrigation groups in maintaining corporate property (especially irrigation canals and temples), see Liefrinck 1969: 23–28 and Goris 1969: 86–87.
4. This information is of particular interest in light of the modern-day practice in Pacariqtambo whereby every year, just before the harvest, the *ayllus* clean and repair the truck road which connects the community with the main farm-to-market road between Cuzco and Paruro. The branch road to Pacariqtambo is divided into 10 sections, called *chhiutas*, each of which is assigned to one of the 10 *ayllus*.

QUEBRADA DE LA VACA: PLAZA DIVISIONS
IN AN ARCHAEOLOGICAL CONTEXT

The archaeological site of Quebrada de la Vaca is located at the head of a shallow, elongated cove on the south coast of Peru, about 150 km south of Nazca and nine km north of the modern fishing village of Chala. Fishermen from Chala often go in small boats to the rocky shoreline at the mouth of the cove to dive for shellfish. The narrow beach at the head of the cove, sheltered as it is from the strong southerly winds and the northward-flowing current, would have provided an excellent location for shellfish collecting and on- and offshore fishing in pre-Hispanic times (as it does today).

It may be helpful in understanding my interest in Quebrada de la Vaca to describe briefly the situation in which I first visited the site. In early October 1982, after completing thirteen months of fieldwork in Pacariqtambo, I traveled from the highlands to the coast to undertake two months of fieldwork in fishing villages on the south coast of Peru. The majority of that time (five weeks) was spent in Chala. During that time, I visited Quebrada de la Vaca on three occasions, making site plans and taking measurements of buildings at the site. This juxtaposition of fieldwork in Pacariqtambo and the area of Chala and Quebrada de la Vaca was made all the more meaningful by encountering in the ruins at Quebrada de la Vaca a structure which would not, I suspect, have appeared totally unfamiliar to the people in Pacariqtambo, I will discuss this structure after a description of the archaeological setting within which it is situated.

The ruins at the head of the cove at Quebrada de la Vaca are extensive and relatively well preserved. Two separate building units, each constructed of large fieldstones and water-polished cobbles, are located near the corners of the cove. Below the two sites there are two (usually dry) stream beds that enter the area at the head of the cove through narrow canyons that come down from the northeast. A walk of one-half to one kilometer inland along either one of these canyons brings one

to the well-preserved remains of the Inka road which connected Quebrada de la Vaca with the *lomas* (fog vegetation) at Atiquipa—and eventually with Nazca—to the north, and with the site of Quebrada Honda, about one kilometer to the south.

A number of site surveys and test trenches have been made at Quebrada de la Vaca. The site was first described in 1955 by Victor von Hagen. In his description, which was based on the fieldwork carried out by Fritz Riddell and Dorothy Menzel in 1954, von Hagen mentions that the site contained bronze and copper implements, mummies, and over 270 underground storage chambers. He suggested that the site may have served as a fish distribution center for the Inka (von Hagen 1955: 243–244, 249–250). A team of Japanese archaeologists excavated briefly at the site and concluded that it may have served a more militaristic function (Izumi 1971).

As for the chronology of the occupation of Quebrada de la Vaca, one finds a range of suggestions in the published reports. Lumbreras maintains that the site ". . . is undoubtedly Inca, although it shows no evidence of the Cuzco style except that most of the buildings are of the *chulpa* style" (1981: 229). Engel also noted the absence of Cuzquenian motifs on the pottery at Quebrada de la Vaca; the patterns, he states, are more typical of pottery made to the south, around Arequipa (1981: 27). At the nearby site of Quebrada Honda, Engel found two spatially segregated pottery styles: first, an Arequipan style, called *Churrajon*, which he dated between late Nazca (ca. AD 200) and Inka, and second, an *Inka* style (1973: 278). In the three days which I spent at the site, I noted many sherds of undecorated, utilitarian ware, but no typical Inka (Cuzquenian) style pottery. From her work in 1954, Dorothy Menzel concluded that

> So far as we could determine the site was occupied only during the later Inca occupation . . . and into the early Colonial period (not later than 1571, when the Spaniards consolidated their administration under Viceroy Toledo). I was unable to discover any changes in the artifacts of native tradition, but the presence of occasional

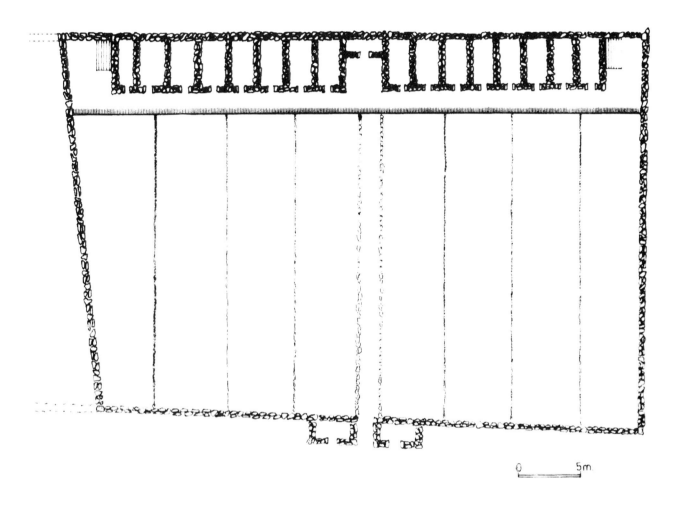

Fig. IV.7. The plaza/chamber complex at Quebrada de la Vaca (cf. Chap. II Fig. 20).

Spanish glass beads indicated the dating for the Colonial period (from a letter to the author, 8 April 1985).

The architectural complex at Quebrada de la Vaca is located some 20–30 m to the northeast of the unit of buildings on the south side of the cove. The structure in question is an unroofed, trapezoidal compound with walls enclosing a plaza and a rectangular building which is subdivided into seventeen roofed chambers. The outer wall of the complex encloses an area measuring approximately 45 m × 30 m. This enclosed, chamber-and-plaza complex, shown in Fig. IV.7, is described by Engel as follows:

Inside the walled area, the floor had been leveled and paved and subdivided into eight equal rectangular spaces delineated by planted stone blocks. This was divided into two groups by an alley giving access to a structure standing in the rear. This structure stands on a terrace surrounded by a contention wall of stones. Two staircases, one at each end, give access to the roof and to the inside, which is subdivided into seventeen chambers—all of them with a frontal door. The ninth chamber is the central one. Its frontal door opens to a central passage, with one narrow room on each side, each one subdivided into two small rooms. These frontal accesses are small and narrow. When the roof was covered with stone slabs, the engineers maintained a narrow and elongated opening above each chamber. The slabs forming the roof had been plastered with crude clay (Engel 1981: 26–27).

I would elaborate on Engel's description by emphasizing that the lines in the plaza—which are composed of water-polished cobbles, not "stone blocks"—are perfectly straight and very carefully laid out.[5]

A comparison of Fig. IV.5 with Fig. IV.7 will readily establish the structural similarity that I am interested in discussing between the division of the plaza at Quebrada de la Vaca and the *chhiuta* divisions of the plazas in Pacariqtambo.[6] The similarities between the two—one embedded in stone, the other an ephemeral product of ritual practices—are striking. Both plazas are divided into a total of nine strips by a process of combining eight units of essentially the same character (i.e., the eight wide strips [2 × 4] at Quebrada de la Vaca, and the eight "original" *ayllus* [four of the upper moiety and four of the lower] in Pacariqtambo) with a ninth unit of a different form, or character (i.e., the central pathway at Quebrada de la Vaca, and the "outsider," annex group in Pacariqtambo). In both cases, the divisions of the plazas are juxtaposed with a

wall which contains a number of openings (niches or windows); the strips in the plazas at the two sites are associated with at least one opening in the walls.

These similarities are compelling but whether or not they are meaningful depends, I think, on the degree to which they involve comparisons that go beyond a formal level; that is, are the two examples similar solely on the level of a coincidence in their structural features (particularly when these are represented in two-dimensional drawings), or can an analogy between them be made in terms of the processes by which they are (or were) constructed? I think that there are sufficient data to support an argument that the latter is the case. In order to explicate the analogy, we should take into consideration similarities in the socio-political institutions and the modes of apportioning communal labor responsibilities that are shared by the societies in question.

In the case of Pacariqtambo, the social organization of this modern-day community is the product of a long history of the transformation of "traditional" Andean institutions—such as *ayllus* and moieties—under the influence not only of Spanish colonial administrative procedures and practices, but also of recent social, political, and economic forces (see Urton n.d. a). Therefore, although the Pacariqtambo side of the analogy is by no stretch of the imagination a "pristine" Andean situation, communal labor is apportioned among the *ayllus* according to principles of reciprocity and rotation that have a long history in the Andes. These forms of apportionment appear in the early colonial documents under the rubric of the *mit'a* (see below). This observation notwithstanding, however, the analogy that I wish to draw between Pacariqtambo and Quebrada de la Vaca is relevant only when seen in the context of a number of fundamental changes in Pacariqtambo with respect to the *ayllus*—and other institutions—over the past four centuries. I will consider the implications of some of these transformations, particularly as they help us to understand differences between the two examples of divided plazas (such as that between fixed and ephem-

5. The widths of the plaza strips at Quebrada de la Vaca, going from right-to-left across the center of the plaza, are as follows: 5.32 m, 5.24 m, 5.24 m, 5.38 m—central pathway = 1.26 m—5.81 m, 5.36 m, 5.43 m, and 5.60 m.
6. For another example of coastal Peruvian archaeological ruins exhibiting divisions similar to those of the plaza at Quebrada de la Vaca, see Hyslop's plans of Inkawasi, in the Cañete valley (1985: Fig. 44 and 75).

eral boundaries in the division of ritual space) after a consideration of the forms of socio-political organization that were present in the area of Quebrada de la Vaca at the time of Spanish contact (i.e., near the end of the occupation of the site).

## THE PLAZA AT QUEBRADA DE LA VACA IN ITS ETHNOHISTORICAL CONTEXT

Shortly after their entry into Peru in 1532, the Spanish began the process of consolidating the territory which they had conquered by imposing forms of organization and bureaucratic procedures that were designed to control the native populations and turn their labor and resources to the benefit of the Spanish crown. One of the principal institutions for the consolidation of power and the distribution of the spoils of the Conquest among the followers of Pizarro was the *encomienda* system. *Encomiendas* were royal grants of trust over groups of indigenous peoples. The *encomendero* served the Crown's military and political interests and had the responsibility for seeing to the material and spiritual needs of the Indians who were entrusted to him. In return, the *encomendero* had the right to demand tribute and labor service from them (Stern 1982: 27–28). At the end of the 1540s, the *licenciado* Pedro de la Gasca ordered a series of "visits" (*visitas*) to the *encomiendas* for the purpose of establishing standardized forms and levels of taxation in the tribute that was being collected by the *encomenderos*. One such "visit" was to the *encomienda* of don Hernando Alvarez de Carmona. The territory covered by this visit centered on the area of Atico and Caravelí, which are located in the next major river valley to the south of Chala (Chala is mentioned by name in the document, but there is no reference to Quebrada de la Vaca; Galdos Rodriguez 1975–76 [1549]: 78).

The Indians who were included in the *encomienda* of Alvarez de Carmona were under the authority of dual indigenous officials, called *curacas principales*. The men who occupied these positions in 1549 were Chincha Pulca

(whose *curaca*ship was centered in Atico) and Guaman Cagia (of the Aymaraes ethnic group). As Galdos Rodriguez concludes, the two *curacas principales* were joint headmen over all the Indians within this *encomienda*, irrespective of their particular local or ethnic affiliation. The point that I wish to stress here with respect to the data recorded in the visit to Atico and Caravelí is that dual political authorities formed a central element in the organization of polities in the area of Chala in 1549.

During the two decades following the initial series of visits ordered by Pedro de la Gasca, it became increasingly clear to the Spanish vice-royalty in Lima that as long as the indigenous populations continued to live in their traditional pattern of dispersed settlements, their pacification, education, and exploitation would be difficult undertakings. Therefore, beginning in 1571 the fifth viceroy of Peru, Francisco de Toledo (1569–1581), instituted a program of "reducing" the dispersed populations into centralized towns, called *reducciones*. The new towns were grouped together into administrative provinces called *corregimientos* (see Gade and Escobar 1982).

Soon after the formation of the *reducciones* and *corregimientos*, a new round of visits was undertaken by Spanish officials for the purposes of assigning land to the inhabitants and taking censuses in order to determine the appropriate level of tribute to be levied against the populace of each *reduccion*. In many cases, "revisits" (*revisitas*) were later made to these towns when, for example, epidemics reduced the population to a level that made the tribute obligation unbearable to the remaining population.

In the last decade of the sixteenth century, following a "great illness" that spread through the towns along the south coast of Peru, a number of *revisitas* were ordered to count the remaining populations. One such *revisita*, referred to as the *Visita de Acarí* (1973 [1593]), provides information on the *ayllu* composition of a number of towns from Camaná up to Acarí, the latter of which is located some 90 km south of Nazca and 40 km north of Que-

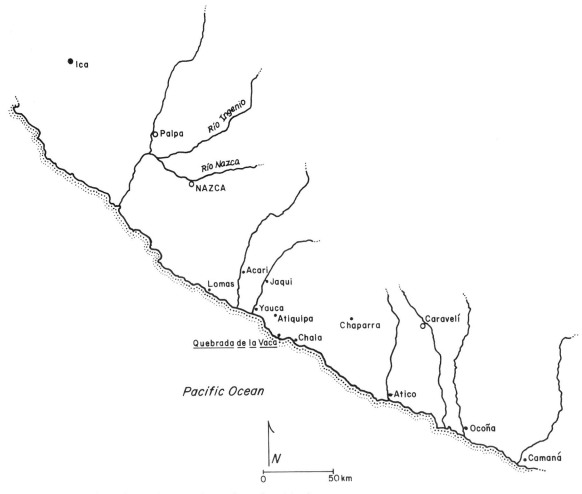

Fig. IV.8. Toponyms along the south coast of Peru from the *Visita de Acarí.*

brada de la Vaca (see Fig. IV.8). The *visita* of Acarí provides a household-by-household count, in 1593, of the people in the towns of Acarí, Xaqui, Atiquipa, Chaparra, Molle-guaca, Atico, Caravelí, Ocoña, Tirita, and Aco-pana. Although neither is mentioned by name in this document, Chala and the site of Que-brada de la Vaca are located near the center of the territory covered by the *visita of Acarí*. The towns in this area were under the jurisdiction of the *corregidor* Gaspar Rodriguez de los Ríos who lived in Camaná. The inhabitants of these towns were included within the *encomienda* of Pedro de Melgar; the two principal indige-nous officials, called *caciques principales*, were Felipe de Guzman and Alonso Satuni. Felipe de Guzman was the *cacique principal* of a group of *ayllus* that formed the upper "moiety"— referred to in the document by the term *par-*

*cialidad* (see below)—of *Hanansaya;* Alonso Sa-tuni was the headman of the *ayllus* that made up the lower moiety, or *parcialidad,* called *Hu-rinsaya* (*Visita de Acarí* 1973: 135, 136, 137, 158). Each *ayllu* within the two *parcialidades* had its own headman.

Some of the *ayllus* in Acarí in 1593 were made up of local people, while others were composed of *mitimaes;* the latter were groups of people who had been moved from distant places into the area during Inka times. This policy of resettlement was maintained by the Inkas for a variety of socio-economic and po-litico-military reasons; for example, craftsmen were moved to places where their skills were needed, and rebellious groups were removed from their home territories (Caillavet 1985; Salomon 1978; Vitale 1981). The *mitimaes* who were living in the area of Acarí at this time had been sent there from the highlands (especially from around Cuzco), as well as from other towns along the coast, including Nazca, Ica, and Chincha (*Visita de Acarí*, 1973: 186–187). (The earlier *Visita* to Atico and Caravelí states that there were no *mitimaes* in the area at that time; Galdos Rodriguez 1975–76: 76.) The total population in the ten towns of the *repartimiento* of Acarí in 1593 was 1253 people; however,

> The majority of Indians of this *repartimiento* are highland *mitimaes* and *mitimaes* from Ica, Chincha and Nasca and other places, so that in the said *repartimiento* there do not reside, nor did there reside, more than some 160 [tribute-paying] Indians; and at present the said residents are those who have paid and suffered the tax of clothing and wheat (*Visita de Acarí* 1973: 190).

Clearly, the burden of taxation would have fallen heavily on the shoulders of the tribute-paying residents in these towns.[7] It is of particular interest in the context of this study to note the presence of an *ayllo Nasca*, and of *mitimaes* from Nazca[8]—who are described in the document as belonging to *ayllo Chauiña*—in the area of Acarí in the 1590s. I will return later to a discussion of the implications for this study of the presence of these people in the region of Chala and Quebrada de la Vaca (Chauiña [Chaviña] is located only 20 km north of Quebrada de la Vaca). But first, I will consider the relevance of the forms of socio-political organization that are represented at this time in the area of Acarí (i.e., multiple *ayllus* grouped into moieties) for interpreting the divided plaza and chamber complex at Quebrada de la Vaca.

Although there are few (if any) coastal Pe-

ruvian communities today that retain *ayllu* and moiety organizations, María Rostworowski de Diez Canseco has shown that the division of populations into *ayllus,* and the grouping of these into dual moieties—with each moiety under the authority of a *cacique principal*—were common features of the pre-Hispanic social organizations in south coastal river valleys at the time of Spanish contact (Rostworowski 1983: 114–118; cf. Barriga 1939: 384–402; Castro and Ortega y Morejón 1968 [1558]: 479; and Galdos Rodriguez 1975–76 [1549]). While, as Rostworowski has argued, dual organization was historically as common a feature of coastal political organizations as it was in the highlands, two other features that appear with some regularity in the colonial documents from the south and central coasts—the decimal organization of social groups and the imposition of public labor requirements on these groups—appear to have been the products of a general reorganization of coastal polities that was carried out at the time of the Inka conquests (Rostworowski 1983: 116, 129; cf. Hyslop 1985: 8–13; Netherly n.d., 1984). Although there is no evidence in the documents available to me that would confirm that the social groups in and around Quebrada de la Vaca were organized in decimal groupings, there is evidence that the *ayllus* and moieties were responsible for carrying out public labor projects as a part of the local tribute obligations under both the Inka and colonial Spanish regimes.

The public labor projects undertaken in Inka times would have included such tasks as fishing, weaving, collecting salt, repairing roads, and manning way stations (*tambos*) along the roads. In addition, the production, storage, and transportation to Cuzco of agricultural produce were important elements of the tribute obligations. According to testimony in the *Visita de Atico y Caravelí* (1549), the Indians along the coast—in the vicinity of Chala—"said . . . that it was their custom to plant the fields of the Inca that were in their territory in maize, and that in one year they harvested and carried to Cuzco 100 loads [*cargas*] and in other years 50 and the rest they

---

7. The outcome of the review undertaken in the *Visita de Acarí* was the reclassification of many of the *mitimaes* as tribute-payers, thus bringing the total to 334 (which was still down considerably from a high of 625 at the time of the Viceroy Toledo). In addition, the level of taxation was decreased from 2,111 pesos per year to 1,650 pesos per year (*Visita de Acarí* 1973: 197–205).
8. In the standard orthography used by archaeologists today, Nasca refers to the archaeological culture, while Nazca is used for the town and the geographical area. However, in many of the colonial documents, the latter is also spelled Nasca.

placed in a deposit for when [the Inca] sent for it" (Galdos Rodriguez 1975–76: 77).

It is of special significance to note at this point that from the survey and excavations undertaken by Menzel and Riddell at Quebrada de la Vaca in 1954, it appears that the 17 chambers of the plaza/chamber complex were used for the storage of agricultural produce (D. Menzel, personal communication, 1985; F. Riddell, personal communication, 1986). My inference from this evidence, as well as from the observations that the plaza/chamber complex at Quebrada de la Vaca is set apart from the dwellings at the site and that the strips in the plaza are very carefully and precisely laid out in straight lines (see Note 5), is that this structure may have been a state storage facility for the deposit of agricultural produce to be used for the payment of tribute. I would further hypothesize that it may have been used by the *ayllus* in the area for ritual activities celebrating the harvest and storage of the crops in the Inka's fields.

The performance of communal agricultural labor in the production of crops for tribute was undertaken in the area of Quebrada de la Vaca during early colonial times as well. This took the form of the production of wheat—a Spanish-introduced crop—by the *ayllus* for the payment of tribute to the Spanish. We read in the *Visita of Acarí* that ". . . the Indians of this *repartimiento* have no communal property nor income nor anything else other than the wheat which the said Indians plant for the community each year in order to pay their *encomendero*" (*Visita de Acarí* 1973 [1593]: 191, 193).

Although the document from Acarí does not state this, the work in the communal wheat fields during the colonial period would no doubt have been undertaken by the *ayllus* in the *mit'a* (rotating corvée labor) system under the overall direction of the *caciques principales* of the moieties (see Gonzalez de San Segundo 1982: 649, 655, 658, on the ordinances from 1566 requiring the *curacas* to oversee the production and collection of tribute; and cf. Platt 1982: 33, 38, on the commercialization of communal grain products by the *curacas* in

Bolivia). In the immediate area of Quebrada de la Vaca, the trapezoidal plaza could have served as a storage facility for the wheat; half of the chambers would have been used by the *ayllus* of the upper moiety, the other half by those of the lower moiety. The evenly divided strips in front of the chambers could have served for the cleaning and drying of the wheat or for other communal/agricultural activities. Presumably, the *ayllus* would have also been responsible for the maintenance of the plaza/chamber complex itself. In this work, their interactions may have produced episodes of cooperation and confrontation similar to those in modern-day Pacariqtambo during the sweeping of the *chhiutas*.

Therefore, I believe that the trapezoidal plaza at Quebrada de la Vaca was a public complex which was the setting for communal activities carried out by the *ayllus* within the area during pre-Hispanic and early colonial times. The division of the plaza grounds into two equal parts, each subdivided into four narrow, rectangular strips, could reflect levels of social differentiation among the *ayllus* which regularly assembled at the site. In the assignment of the plaza strips to the *ayllus* for the performance of public labor, both the division of the plaza and the activities that occurred within (and between) these divisions may have been similar in some respects to the *chhiuta* divisions—and the reproduction of social groups—that are affected today during festivals in the plazas in Pacariqtambo.

One point which remains for our consideration in this comparison between the plazas at Quebrada de la Vaca and Pacariqtambo is that in at least one respect, the two are quite dissimilar: while one contains a division of territory permanently embedded in stone, the other is the product of a process of dividing ritual space which is reproduced briefly on the occasion of community-wide religious celebrations. The difference between the two examples with respect to this characteristic—that is, fixed vs. ephemeral boundaries—is fundamental and calls for an explanation. I suggest that the best place to turn is to the larger sociopolitical contexts within which the two plazas and their respective ritual and communal activities were/are situated. In the case of Quebrada de la Vaca, the site was—probably from its inception—a provincial installation within the large, well-organized and tightly regulated Inka empire. As Murra has noted with respect to the Inka bureaucratic organization in census taking and in the control of the movement of people within the empire, "the bureaucratic tendency is always to freeze the situation, keep it quantitative, controllable and undisturbed" (Murra 1980: 110). What we find today in the plaza at Quebrada de la Vaca are the remains of such a "frozen" and "undisturbed" setting for the performance of *mit'a* labor obligations by the social groups within the area in the fulfillment of their tribute service to the Inka state. Finally, if the site of Quebrada de la Vaca continued to be occupied into the early colonial period, as the archaeological record indicates, there is no reason to suppose that the Spanish would have destroyed or substantially altered a facility whose utilization (the storage of produce for tribute) worked to their advantage.

In modern-day Pacariqtambo, on the other hand, there exists no external mandate or force for fixing permanent boundary markers between the *chhiutas* in the plazas (not to mention the fact that trucks passing through the lower plaza would run over any fixed markers!). But, as I have tried to show elsewhere (Urton 1984), flexibility, rather than permance and rigidity of structures, is a fundamental feature of the *chhiuta* divisions in Pacariqtambo. The boundary lines between the plaza *chhiutas* are renegotiated on the occasion of each community festival; this dynamic process of renegotiation is central to the reformulation and representation of status and hierarchical relations among the *ayllus* today. As the fortunes of the *ayllus* have waxed and waned with respect to each other over time, the resulting transformations have become elements, or new sets of conditions, that are taken into account in future negotiations of public responsibilities.

In contrast to the pre-Hispanic and colonial contexts, in which centralized bureaucracies

attempted, with varying degrees of success, to oversee and control the relations of production within Andean communities, the current situation in communities like Pacariqtambo is relatively more fluid; if anything, the external forces which most directly affect communities today—forces such as markets, wage labor, national systems of communication, and so forth—promote flexibility and change rather than rigidity and adherence to tradition. The modern-day practice of dividing public space and labor projects into *chhiutas* whose limits are negotiable and flexible is one of the means for accommodating change; it is this very flexibility which distinguishes modern structures and practices for the division of space, time, and labor from pre-Hispanic and early colonial ones.

Before leaving Quebrada de la Vaca and the question of late pre-Hispanic structures and practices for the division of public space and labor obligations, it is relevant to discuss briefly a study by Nathan Wachtel of the Inka organization of *mitimaes* in the Cochabamba Valley in what is now central Bolivia (Wachtel 1982). In this study, Wachtel analyzes early colonial documents which detail a massive movement of *mitimaes* and *mittayocs*[9] into the Cochabamba Valley. This program of resettlement was carried out under the direction of the Inka king, Huayna Capac, during the decade or so immediately preceding the Spanish conquest. According to the ethnohistorical documents, Huayna Capac had some 14,000 Indians belonging to various ethnic groups moved into the Cochabamba Valley in order to work the fertile lands of the valley to produce a surplus that could be used by the Inka state. As the different ethnic groups were brought into the valley, they were assigned to land within rectangular strips of territory called *suyos* or *urcos* (Wachtel 1982: 205–206; cf. Espinoza Soriano 1981: 302–308 on the Inka resettlement of *mitimaes* in five "sections,"

---

9. The *mitimaes* were ethnic groups that took up permanent residence in the Cochabamba valley and that were responsible for servicing the granaries. The *mittayocs* did the agricultural work; they were regularly replaced according to the rotating labor obligations (*mit'a*) imposed on ethnic groups by the Inkas (Wachtel 1982: 213).

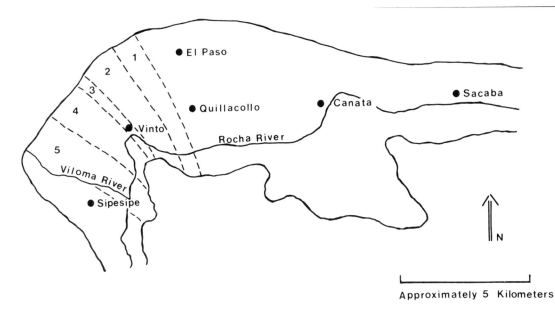

Fig. IV.9. The *suyus* in the Cochabamba Valley. (From Wachtel 1982: fig. 81).

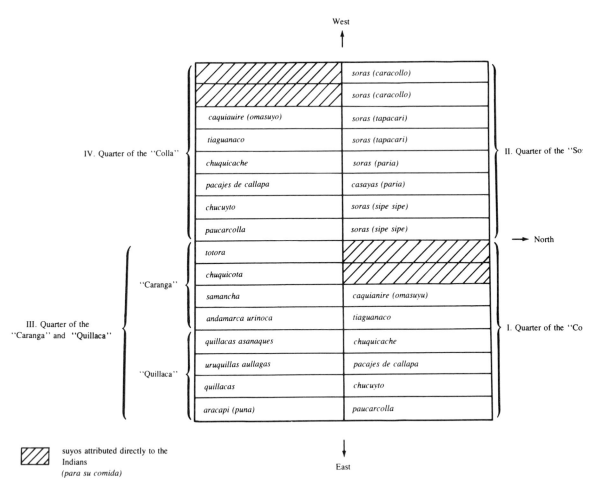

Fig. IV.10. The disposition of *suyus* and ethnic groups in the *chacara* of Colchacolla. (From Wachtel 1982: fig. 8.2).

called *moyas*, of the state lands in the valley of Abancay). Five of the major *suyo* divisions within the Cochabamba valley are shown in Fig. IV.9. Wachtel describes the conformation of the *suyos* as follows[10]: ". . . these 'plots' [*suyos*] were indeed long and narrow strips running crosswise through the valley . . . from end to end. All these strips were of equal width (44 *brazadas*) but unequal length (2–4, even 5 km.), depending on the conformation of the valley" (Wachtel 1982: 206).

Wachtel examined the organization and arrangement of ethnic groups within one of these large rectangular strips; this was the *suyo* called *Colchacolla* (#2, Fig. 9). This *suyo* was divided into 16 subunits—also called *suyos*—each of which was further subdivided into dual "half-*suyos*," producing a total of 32 *suyos* in all (Fig. IV.10). These narrow strips of land were assigned to various groups in a way that produced an overall ethnic quadripartitioning of the *suyo* of Colchacolla; each quarter was composed of eight sub-*suyos* ($16 \times 2 = 8 \times 4 = 32$).

In concluding this section, I would summarize by pointing out that what we have found in these archaeological and ethnohistorical data is further evidence for the division of public territory into narrow, elongated strips and the assignment of the responsibility for public labor activities (*mit'a*) within the strips to different *ayllus* and/or ethnic groups. Through the data from Quebrada de la Vaca and the Cochabamba Valley, these processes have been placed "historically" (i.e., according to post-Conquest historical traditions recorded by the Spanish) during the period of the Inka expansion just prior to the European invasion.

It is also relevant to point out that in the comparison of the divisions of the plazas at Quebrada de la Vaca and Pacariqtambo we have found two different expressions—widely separated from each other in space and time—of the division of public territory by straight

lines which is similar to that which underlay the far more complex and highly elaborated *ceque* system of the city of Cuzco during Inca times. Zuidema has described and analyzed the *ceque* system in terms of its formulation through, and its articulation of, Inkaic mythology, calendrics, and social and ritual organization (Zuidema 1964, 1982a). My purpose in raising this issue is not to argue that these examples can be linked by direct, historical connections, but rather to suggest that each in its own time, place, and historical circumstances appears to represent an example of one of the ways that Andean societies—organized around *ayllus* and moieties—construct public, social spaces and divide up the responsibilities for their maintenance. Similar forms of organization and practice have produced comparable structures, not the reverse. I now turn to Nazca in an attempt to relate the forms of organization derived from the foregoing to the ethnohistorical and archaeological records from the area of the Nazca pampa during early colonial and late pre-Hispanic times.

## SOCIAL ORGANIZATION IN THE RIO GRANDE DE NAZCA AND THE MAINTENANCE OF THE NAZCA LINES

The previous discussions of Pacariqtambo and Quebrada de la Vaca have provided the essential context for constructing an argument—based on Andean institutions and practices—for understanding some of the processes whereby the Nazca lines may have been maintained over time. What follows is an attempt to sketch some of the principal features of the social history of the Nazca and Ingenio Valleys during the early colonial period and to consider the implications of the socio-political organizations in these two river valleys for understanding the maintenance of the lines.

It is important to begin by pointing out that, at least to my knowledge, none of the documents from the early colonial period "visits" or "revisits" to the *reducciones* in the area of the Río Grande de Nazca (here taken to be the river valleys of the Santa Cruz, Río Grande,

---

10. Wachtel also points out the similarity between the pre-Hispanic mode of land division by *suyos* and the land divisions in narrow strips, called *tsvis*, which are made today by the Uru Indians of Bolivia (1982: 206).

Palpa, Ingenio, Nazca, and Las Trancas) has been published. Therefore, in constructing a reasonable hypothesis for the social and political organizations within the two river valleys bordering the Nazca pampa at the time of Spanish contact, we must work both from more indirect information provided in the ethnohistorical documents recorded in Nazca as well as on the basis of analogies drawn from other contemporary polities along the south coast. The information provided by the *Visita* of Acarí is of special interest in this regard.

The *Visita* of Acarí (1593) states that there were two *ayllus* along the south coast, in the general area of Quebrada de la Vaca, which were composed of *mitimaes* drawn from the Nazca valley; these were the groups called *Ayllo Nasca* and *Ayllo Chauiña* (Chaviña), both of which belonged to the lower moiety of the *repartimiento* of Acarí (1973 [1593]: 186–187, 190). Secondly, a careful reading of the document shows that there were many people living in Nazca at this time who actually belonged to *ayllus* of the towns along the south coast. Thirteen men from *ayllus* of the upper moiety (*Hanansaya*) of Acarí were living in Nazca, having married women there; seven men of *ayllus* of the lower moiety (*Hurinsaya*) of Acarí were married and living in Nazca in 1593. In all, more than 80 men and women maintained connections of one kind or another (e.g., marriage, *mitimae* status, etc.) with Nazca and the towns along the south coast. Given the large number of people who had ties with both of these areas at the end of the sixteenth century, it is reasonable to suppose that similar contacts and interchanges would have been maintained in pre-Hispanic times as well. In fact, it appears from the archaeological records in Nazca and Acarí that these two areas formed part of a single interaction sphere as far back as middle to late Nasca times (ca. AD 100–500; see Lothrop and Mahler 1957: 3, 47). This is an important point to bear in mind because it suggests that what has previously been established concerning the imposition of tribute by the Inkas in the form of *mit'a* obligations, and other such features of the pre-Hispanic organizations in

the area of Quebrada de la Vaca, probably obtained in the Nazca and Ingenio valleys as well. I shall return to this topic after establishing some of the principal characteristics of the social organization of the Nazca area during early colonial times.

During the first two decades following the arrival of the Spanish, a number of transformations took place in the Nazca and Ingenio river valleys. One was the sale of virtually the entire valley of the Ingenio River (the valley bordering the Nazca pampa on the north) to a Spaniard, Pedro Suarez. This information comes from a compilation of documents made in 1648 in which the Jesuits were trying to establish the legitimacy of their claim to the lands of hacienda San Jose, which is located within the Ingenio Valley, just off the northeastern edge of the Nazca pampa. In the document ("Memoria . . .", 1648), the Ingenio is referred to as the *"valle de Collao de Lucanas"*[11]; *Collao* was the pre-Hispanic name of the Ingenio. The relevant part of the summary of the documents compiled by the Jesuits in 1648 is given below (for the Spanish text, see Appendix IIIA):

> The *curacas* of Nasca–Don Francisco Ylimanga sold all the valley of Collao (which today is called Ingenio) from the origin of the water to Tambo Viejo to Pedro Suarez the elder, by deed, in the Tambo of Ica before Francisco de Talavera, the royal scribe, on 19 July of 1546 [ . . . ]. Pedro Suarez sold and transferred all the said valley to the overseer Garcia de Salcedo in the City of the Kings [Lima] on 15 March of 1549 before Alonso Valencia, public scribe of his majesty and of [..?..]. Don Garcia Nasca and Don Alonso Limanga *caciques*, sons of those named above, ratified the two earlier sales . . . in 1556 . . . ("Memoria. . .", 1648).

I suspect that an error was made in the first line of this document. At the end of the citation, it is stated that the *caciques* Don Garcia Nasca and Don Alonso Limanga were "sons of those named above"; therefore, the first line should probably read: *"Los Curacas de la Nasca*

---

11. Lucanas is located about 150 km east of Nazca.

*[Don Garcia Nasca y] Don Francisco Limanga. . . .*" The references to dual *caciques principales,* or *curacas,* indicates that there was an organization of groups into moieties in the Nazca area from the mid-sixteenth to the mid-seventeenth centuries. In fact, from an examination of a number of ethnohistorical documents recorded in Nazca during this time, it is clear that there were two hereditary lines of *curacas;* one *curaca*—*cacique principal*—was of the *Nasca* (or *Nanasca*) family; the other was of the *Ylimanga* (or *Limanga*) family. The two *caciques principales* were probably localized within the two river valleys on either side of the Nazca pampa; the Nazca Valley itself may have been the home of the *caciques* of the Nasca line, while the Ingenio (Collao) Valley was the home of the Ylimanga *caciques* (cf., "Autos", *Tit. Prop.* . . ., 1635: 85; 1644: 22). From these and other documents in the *Archivo General de la Nación* in Lima, we may reconstruct the succession of *caciques principales* in the line of the Nasca family from the mid-1540s through the mid-1640s as follows (Fig. IV.11):

In addition to moieties with dual *caciques principales,* there are also references in the ethnohistorical documents to four sub-groups, called *"parcialidades";* these were named *Nasca, Cantad, Poromas,* and *Collao.* The best description available to me of the *parcialidades* is contained in the last will and testament of the Garcia Nasca who was *cacique principal* during the mid-1560s and who died in Lima in 1569.

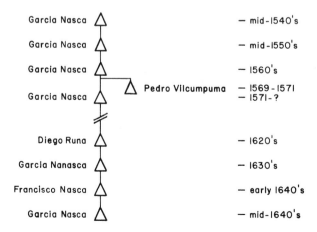

Fig. IV.11. The genealogy of the *caciques principales* of the Nasca line from the 1540s–1640s.

On 4 November 1569, the last will and testament of Garcia Nasca was presented to one of the *alcaldes* of Lima, Francisco de Zarate. Relevant portions of the will are translated below (see Appendix IIIB for the Spanish text):

> Item—I order that after paying all my debts, bequests, religious works, suits and legacies, that my large vineyard be divided into three parts and two of these I order to be given to my Indians so that from them they can pay the said 200 pesos [of tribute?] and all of that which is produced from the said 200 pesos mentioned above. The aforementioned two parts of the said vineyard and estate I order should go to the aforesaid Indians of my *parcialidad* [i.e., the *parcialidad* of Nasca?] . . . [and] taking out the 200 pesos, they should take out 500 pesos in currency for the poor people of the three *parcialidades* of Indians which are those of *Cantad, Poromas* and *Collao* and if it should appear to my executors that it is best to help with the tribute of the aforesaid three *parcialidades* I instruct that it be paid and then taking out the 500 pesos I freely leave the said two parts of the said vineyard, and that which they produce, to the said Indians of mine that they should divide it as declared above with the condition that ordinarily the Indians of my *parcialidad* provide 12 [men] for their *mitas* so that the profits of the said vineyard will pay them for their work . . . ("Testimonio. . .", 1569: 5r-6v).

This document helps us to establish two of the central features—aside from moieties—of the social organization in the Nazca and Ingenio Valleys during the first few decades following the Spanish conquest. These included, first, a division of the population into multiple *"parcialidades,"* and second, the assignment of rotating labor obligations (*mit'a*) to the members of these groups. I will consider each of these points in turn.

In an important study of the uses of the Spanish term *parcialidad* ("part") in the ethnohistorical documents from Peru, María Rostworowski has shown that the Spanish often confused this term with the *"ayllu";* however, the two should actually be used for different types or levels of social groupings. *Ayllu* referred (as it still does today in many highland communities), to groupings based on land

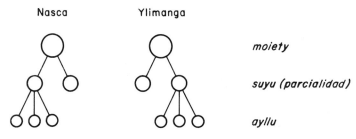

Fig. IV.12. Socio-political divisions in the Nazca and Ingenio valleys.

ownership, the sponsorship of festivals, the performance of communal labor, and (in some cases) kin-based groups (Rostworowski 1981: 42). *"Parcialidad,"* on the other hand, should be used for higher, or more inclusive levels of organization in which, for instance, several *ayllus* were grouped together into larger socio-political units. An example of the latter would be the grouping of several *ayllus* into moieties. In the *Visita of Acarí*, for instance, the two moieties (*Hanansaya* and *Hurinsaya*) are consistently referred to as *"parcialidades"* (1973 [1593]: 195). However, moieties were only one form or level of *"parcialidad"*; these could also take the form of intermediate levels of social grouping between *ayllus* and moieties. For example, in the organization of socio-political groupings in the Inka capital city of Cuzco, several *ayllus* were first grouped together into *suyus* ("sections," or quarters); two of the four *suyus* of Cuzco went together to form the upper moiety, the other two made up the lower moiety (Zuidema 1964; and cf. Zuidema 1982b on two-, three- and six-part divisions in Inka social organization). In the latter example, the Spanish term *"parcialidad"* could be used equally for the four *suyus* and the two moieties. As Rostworowski has argued: "The *suyu* or *parcialidad* had the function of being a part within a whole, naturally not only could it indicate a dual division, but also a tripartition or a quadripartition" (Rostworowski 1981: 43).

In the ethnohistorical documents recorded in Nazca, *"parcialidad"* appears to refer to the four groups Nasca, Cantad, Poromas, and Collao. At the same time, we have seen that a moiety system—headed by dual *caciques principales*—was an element in the political orga-

nization in the Nazca-Ingenio area. Therefore, it was probably the case (as in Inka Cuzco) that there were at least three levels of socio-political organization in this region during late pre-Hispanic and early colonial times: moieties, *suyus* (or *"parcialidades"*) and *ayllus*. The four *parcialidades* alluded to in the last will and testament of Garcia Nasca in 1569 probably represented an intermediate level of socio-political grouping similar to the *suyus* of Inca Cuzco; each *suyu*, or *parcialidad*, would have been composed of several *ayllus* (see Fig. IV.12).

We can go one step beyond the hypothetical reconstruction of the pre-Hispanic socio-political organization of the Nazca and Ingenio Valleys shown in Fig. IV.12 by suggesting that each river valley within the Río Grande de Nazca drainage may have been the site of at least one *parcialidad;* that is: *Collao*, as we have seen, was the name of the Ingenio River valley during pre-Hispanic and early colonial times; *Nasca* would have been located at, or near to, the site of the modern-day town of Nazca (perhaps at the site on the southern side of the valley which is known today as *Paredones*); *Cantad* (or *Cantao*) is a well-known toponym in the Nazca Valley (it refers to an area some two to three kilometers west—up-river—from Nazca); and *Poromas* is the name of a stretch along the Las Trancas River valley, located 10–15 km south of the Nazca Valley. These data permit us to suggest, first, that in the Río Grande de Nazca there were probably more than the four *parcialidades* identified in the last will and testament of Garcia Nasca; that (as we saw explicitly in the case of the Nazca Valley) each river valley may have had at least two *parcialidades*—one upriver, the other downriver; and finally, that each *parcialidad* would have been composed of multiple *ayllus*.

As I have already suggested that the Nazca pampa may have been the geographical division between a north/south pair of moieties, I would propose that this first pair was cross-cut by a second, which grouped the *parcialidades* and *ayllus* of the upper valleys apart from those in the lower valleys (for a similar example of cross-cutting dual divisions—right bank/left bank; upriver/downriver—see Rostworowski 1978b: 156). I would hypothesize that the schematic representation of the socio-political organization of the Nazca and Ingenio River valleys which is depicted in Figure 12 can be expanded and translated to the topography of this region as shown in Fig. IV.13.

There is one important implication of the construction arrived at in Figure 13 for our study of the Nazca lines. Throughout this paper, the central theme which has emerged has been an association between multiple *ayllus* and the division of territory into rectangular strips. If this association does, in fact, represent a typical Andean pattern for the apportionment of space and resources among multiple *ayllus*, then we should consider the implications of this for an investigation of the lines and other configurations of cleared spaces on the Nazca pampa. That is, if the

river valleys bordering the pampa were, indeed, the sites of multiple groupings of *ayllus* divided into upriver and downriver moieties, then might not the complex organization and division of space and resources emerging from the coordinated activities among these *ayllus* have in some way been related to the construction, use, and/or the maintenance of the cleared strips on the Nazca pampa? Unfortunately, there is very little archaeological or ethnohistorical evidence from Nazca that would allow us to test this hypothesis directly, but a number of indirect lines of evidence make it appear not altogether unreasonable to propose that there may have been some connection between the social groups in the valleys and the cultural remains on the Nazca pampa. Two of these lines of evidence concern the irrigation systems in the Nazca and Ingenio Valleys and the network of roads passing through the area; both of these topics will involve us in further discussions of the *mit'a* (rotating labor obligations). Before turning to these examples, however, it is interesting to note that irrigation and roads were two of the things which most impressed one of the earliest European visitors to this area, Pedro Cieza de Leon. Writing in 1551, Cieza noted that:

> From this valley of Ica [which is located to the northwest of Nazca] one walks until one sees the beautiful valleys and rivers of Nasca. These valleys were in times past heavily populated and the rivers irrigated the fields of the valleys in an orderly and prescribed manner. The past wars [between Pizarro and Almagro] consumed with their cruelty (as is well known) all of these poor Indians. . . . In the principal valley of these of Nasca (which by another name is called Caxamalca), there were large buildings with many [storage] deposits, which were ordered to be built by the Inkas. And of the natives I have nothing more to say than that they say that their ancestors were very brave compared to themselves and were esteemed by the kings of Cuzco. . . . Through all these valleys and through those which I had been there passed the beautiful and grand road of the Inkas, and through some parts of the sand dunes can be seen marks [señales] by which one finds the road which

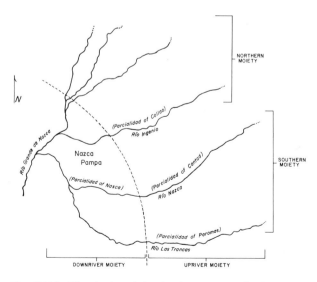

Fig. IV.13. The dual moieties in the Río Grande de Nazca drainage.

passes through there. From these valleys of
Nasca one goes until arriving at Hacari [Acarí],
and further along are Ocoña and Camaná and
Quilca, in which there are large rivers (Cieza de
Leon 1973 [1551]: 185; my translation).

## MIT'A: IRRIGATION AND ROADS

In the earlier section on Quebrada de la
Vaca, I discussed some of the general features
of the Inka institution of the *mit'a* whereby
local groups performed labor service in the
fulfillment of their tribute obligations to the
state. The *mit'a* institution was grounded in
the two principles of turn-taking and reciprocity; these principles, working together in a variety of contexts, produced multiple temporal
and spatial subdivisions. Two examples of the
application of the institution of *mit'a* in different contexts will help clarify the multi-dimen-
sionality of this form of labor organization.
The first example emphasizes the division of
space.

According to Bernabé Cobo (ca. 1653), the
following practices were observed by the *ayllus*
during their performance of *mit'a* in the fields
of the Inka:

> . . . the *Hilacatas* [Aymara: "heads of ayllus"] and
> decurions in charge of ten subjects worked all
> day, as did the commoner Indians who had no
> official position. These divided among them-
> selves the work they had to do by lines [*rayas*],
> each section of work or division of which was
> called a *suyu;* after thus partitioning the task,
> each one placed into his section his children and
> wives and all the people of his house to help him;
> and the one who had the most workers finished
> his part and *suyu* first. (Cobo 1956 [ca. 1653]: bk.
> 12, chap. 28)

This process of dividing up the land by
lines, and of assigning each *ayllu* to a *"suyu"* of
territory, was probably the form in which agricultural labor would have been performed
in polities all along the south coast. For instance, the *mit'a* labor discussed earlier in the
area of Quebrada de la Vaca would have been
undertaken according to these principles of
land division. But beyond the divisions of the

agricultural lands, the plaza/chamber complex
at Quebrada de la Vaca represents a concrete
expression of the division of space into strips
(*suyus*) by the delineation of straight lines
(*rayas*). In addition, when Garcia Nasca testi-
fied that the Indians of his *parcialidad* provided 12 mit'as for work in his vineyard (see
above), this probably would have involved the
division of the vineyard into 12 strips of land.
The method described by Cobo for dividing
territory into strips is also reminiscent of the
division of the plazas in Pacariqtambo into
*"chhiutas"* (also cf. Urton 1984 and n.d.a for
discussions of *chhiutas* in a communal agricultural setting).[12]

The second example of *mit'a*—emphasizing
the temporal dimension of these practices—
comes from a modern application of the term,
although we will see that a similar use of
the institution is also described in documents
from the colonial period. In a study of the
organization and coordination of agricultural
activities in contemporary Andean communities, Enrique Mayer has discussed the variety
of controls which are placed on the distribution of water for irrigation. The more strin-
gent examples of communal controls are
termed *mitas de agua* ("turns of water"). As
Mayer concludes from a comparison of the
various methods found in different communities:

> *Mitas* can be assigned to individuals, or groups of
> individuals, who then have water during the
> whole day to irrigate all of their fields. . . . Or
> *mitas* can be assigned to the canals. In this case
> the order of irrigation can be from the last field
> at the tail end of the canal to the first, or it can be

---

12. For interesting comparative material on land divisions in
East Africa, see the article by Shipton, entitled, "Strips and
Patches: A Demographic Dimension in some African Land-
Holding and Political systems" (1984). Shipton did a comparative study of the distribution of locality-based and descent-based
systems of political organization and land rights in non-irriga-
tion farming systems in East Africa. He found that locality-
based landholding systems are found in the context of chiefdoms and sub-chiefdoms with "fields laid out in patches, their
placement having little or no correspondence with the genealogical positions of the holders." Descent-based systems, on the
other hand, are found in societies with segmentary lineages in
which "fields are laid out in parallel strips extending from
homesteads, their placement reflecting genealogical positions
of holders" (Shipton 1984: 615–6).

from the first to the last, or other variations, each one with particular advantages and disadvantages to individual farmers or to groups (Mayer 1983: 37).

We have ethnohistorical data on the institution of *"mitas de aguas"* in the Nazca and Ingenio Valleys in late colonial times. One document concerns a dispute over water rights among the hacienda owners in the Ingenio Valley during the eighteenth century. This dispute arose from charges brought by the hacienda owners in the lower part of the Ingenio Valley—in the area adjacent to the Nazca pampa—against those in the upper valley. The latter, it was charged, were using all the water in the river, leaving little or none for the irrigation of the fields lower down in the valley. The following solution was proposed by the hacienda owners of the lower Ingenio:

. . . so that there will be a sufficient amount of water to reach our haciendas, the hacienda owners higher up must be compelled to recognize the allotment of the said water; thus, there should be approved and set aside customary days for turns ["*dias comunes de mitas*"] both for the haciendas above and for those lower down, which is a distance of three leagues . . . and the *mitas* that you [the judge] assign should run without confusing anyone, as is done, and as has been done, in all these valleys of Nasca ("Repartimiento. . .", 1772).

This dispute was resolved in the manner proposed by the hacienda owners of the lower valley by establishing a pattern of turn-taking in the use of the water among the five large haciendas within the Ingenio Valley. The turn-taking went from the lower end of the valley to the upper end (see Netherly 1984 and Sherbondy n.d.: 59, n. 13 for discussions of "tail-to-head," as opposed to "head-to-tail," forms of irrigation). The five haciendas were assigned turns which were roughly proportionate to the size of their landholdings. Beginning at the lower end of the Ingenio Valley, the following *"mit'as"*—units of 24-hour periods—were assigned to the five haciendas in question: 14, 8, 6, 12, and 6 days. After

each hacienda had its turn, the cycle began again and was repeated for as long as the water lasted. It is of particular interest to note that the counting of days in this cycle excluded Sundays; these days were set aside for the Indians in the valley to irrigate their lands: ". . . there should be left for the Indians the Sunday of each week for them to enjoy the benefit of the said water for their turns so that they may irrigate their fields" ("Repartimiento. . .", 1772: 4).

The point that I want to stress is that the apportionment of irrigation water in the Ingenio Valley—and in the other valleys of the Río Grande de Nazca—would have been as essential a part of the organization of pre-Hispanic agriculture in this arid land as it was in post-Hispanic times. The methods employed in the apportionment during pre-Hispanic times would no doubt have been based on a *mit'a*-like turn-taking among the *ayllus* of the upper and lower *parcialidades* within each river valley. As we have seen above that the implementation of *mit'a* produced both spatial and temporal divisions, I would propose that such an institution, applied to the organization of irrigation in the valleys of the Río Grande de Nazca, may have resulted in the partition of agricultural lands into strips, each defined by a major canal system irrigating the lands of a particular *ayllu*.

An excellent analogy for the types of land divisions that would have emerged from a situation such as that outlined above is found in a recent study by Patricia Netherly, "The Management of Late Andean Irrigation Systems on the North Coast of Peru" (1984). Netherly has shown that the basic socio-political grouping among north coastal polities in late pre-Hispanic, early colonial times was the *"parcialidad."* Along the north coast (as opposed to the central and south coasts), *parcialidades* combined economic and religious functions, and they provided a social as well as an ethnic identity for their members. At the lowest level of integration, the *parcialidades* were grouped by economic activities; these included farmers, fishermen, and artisans. Furthermore: ". . . each of these units was usually subdivided into two subgroups or moieties, one of which outranked the other, and each of which was led by a lord whose hierarchical position was determined by that of the moiety he headed" (Netherly 1984: 231).

The subdivisions of the *parcialidades* resulted in dual, quadripartite, and eight-part hierarchies of socio-economic groupings and political officials (Netherly 1984: 230–231, 234; cf. Rostworowski 1978b: 53, 58). Of particular interest for the study of the Nazca area is Netherly's argument that the organization of *parcialidades* on the north coast was directed, in one of its aspects, at the recruitment of labor for the construction and maintenance of irrigation canals.

At all levels of organization there was an intimate correlation between rights to water and land, and the bounded corporate groups of *parcialidades*. In the Spanish colonial documents of the sixteenth century particular groups claim

rights in a particular canal because it watered their lands and, conversely, assert claims to particular lands because they are watered by their canal (Netherly 1984: 239).

An example of the relationship between *parcialidades* and irrigation canals on the north coast is illustrated in Fig. IV.14. The drawing is a reproduction of a sketch map which was made in 1567 as part of the litigation over water rights along the Taymi canal, which was diverted from the large canal known as the Río de Lambayeque (which itself was diverted from the Chancay river; see Shimada 1982: 155, Fig. 7).

The right portion of Fig. IV.14 shows the distribution of twelve *parcialidades* along the Taymi canal. The twelve *parcialidades* occupied strips or narrow wedges of territory; each strip of land was irrigated by a sub-canal diverted from the Taymi canal. The mainte-

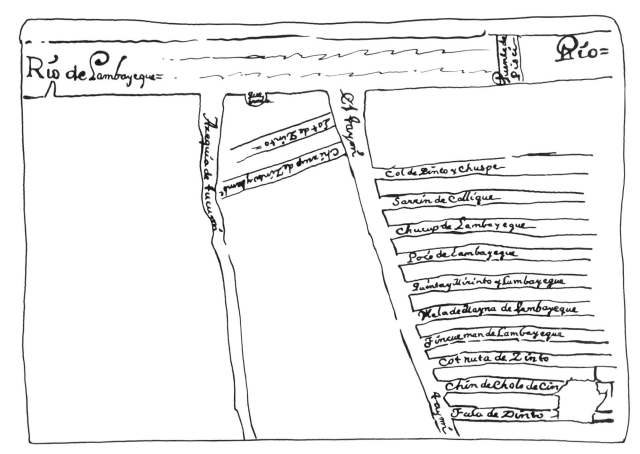

Fig. IV.14. The *Parcialidades* along the Taymi Canal, North Coast of Peru (from Netherly 1984: fig. 4).

nance of the Taymi and the sub-canals was apportioned in the following way:

> The users of the twelfth canal, the one farthest from the intake, cleaned the Taymi from the intake of their canal to the intake of the eleventh canal. The users of the eleventh canal cleaned the Taymi from the mouth of their canal to that of the tenth canal and so successively until the intake of the first canal was reached, from which point all the users were responsible for cleaning the Taymi to [its] main intake (Netherly 1984: 243).

Although we do not have good ethnohistorical data from the Nazca area for the early colonial period from which to reconstruct patterns of the division of irrigated land and the maintenance of canals, it is probable that they would have been similar to those illustrated in Figure 14 and described in the above quotation (cf. Wachtel 1976: 102 and Fig. 4, for similar examples of the division of irrigated lands—and other resource zones—among multiple *ayllus*). These land divisions would have constituted another form of the division of territory in the valleys bordering the Nazca pampa into strips, or wedges (the first example involved the division of the state agricultural lands into *suyus* during the performance of *mit'a* labor). These data allow us to assert with some confidence that the division of space into strips may have been a fairly common pattern emerging from the agricultural and labor practices among the *ayllus* within the valleys of the Río Grande de Nazca.

Two problems remain at this point in establishing a connection between the strips within the river valleys and those on the pampa: In the first place, the lines on the pampa are (with a few exceptions) not laid out in parallel lines; rather, they are organized into a network of radial centers (see Aveni, Chap. II, this volume). Can we compare forms as radically different as parallel and radial systems? Secondly, the river valleys are not the pampa; how, if at all, might the structures and activities of one zone have been coordinated or brought into contact with those in the other?

These questions cannot be answered in a completely satisfactory way. However, there are certain lines of evidence, and other examples of similar quandaries, from elsewhere in the Andes that provide perspectives from which to resolve these problems partially.

## PARALLEL AND RADIAL SYSTEMS OF SPATIAL DIVISION

Jeanette Sherbondy has made a number of observations concerning the organization of the irrigation canals in the Cuzco Valley that are relevant to the problem of parallel strips contrasted with radial centers. In the first place, Sherbondy argues that throughout the Inka empire the *ayllus*—not the state—owned canal systems and the rights to water (cf. Mayer 1983: 23). These claims were grounded in the principle that it was the ancestors of the *ayllus* who originally distributed the rights to both land and water (Sherbondy n.d.: 22). In the case of Inka Cuzco, the owners and users of the canals were the members of: (a) the *ayllus*, (b) the *panacas* ("royal *ayllus*"), and (c) private individuals of the nobility. In the application of these principles of the ownership and use of the irrigation canals to the formal organization of the Valley of Cuzco, which was realized in the *ceque* system (the system of 41 lines that radiated from the Temple of the Sun in the center of the city), Sherbondy concluded that

> . . .the intention of the radial organization of space in Cuzco was to assign discrete canal systems and irrigation districts to specific *panacas* and *ayllus* in an ideal pattern of radial divisions of land into sectors of a circle based on a central point in Cuzco . . . [T]he ideal intention was to also use *ceques* as boundary lines for the lands of each *panaca* and *ayllu* . . . (Sherbondy 1982: 80).

Sherbondy goes on to draw a distinction between two forms of spatial division that were made in various contexts throughout the Inka empire: one form was based on radial systems, the other on grids. A radial distribution and representation of space was a conceptual scheme that was particularly well suited to elites who viewed local and imperial organizations from a central point. A grid system, on the other hand, was a more practical conceptual scheme for the individual landholder in locating the position of his landholdings within a particular area. As Sherbondy concludes: "radial distribution is a useful method for the elite; grid distribution for the lower classes" (n.d.: 95–97; cf. Zuidema 1973b). Although Sherbondy specifically opposes radial systems with those based on the grid, I think that the parallel line systems that we have analyzed in this paper—e.g., the *chhiutas* in Pacariqtambo, the *"suyus"* in Quebrada de la Vaca, and the strips of landholdings along irrigation canals—are conceptually similar to grids and may, therefore, be considered a sub-category of grid systems in their contrast to radial systems. What is important to recognize in these data is that both schemes—radial and grid—can be maintained simultaneously by different groups within the same territory. The two viewpoints represent different, but complementary, conceptual schemes for political and social action by the members of hierarchically distinct groups within a state structure.

A similar kind of resolution to the radial/grid problem is found in Javier Albó's study of the organization of territorial and political groups in the Bolivian community of Jesús de Machaca (Dept. of La Paz; Albó 1972). In ideal, conceptual terms, Jesús de Machaca is considered to be organized on a radial plan with the community at the center. The territory ("sector") controlled by Jesús de Machaca is divided into two moieties (*parcialidades*), each of which is subdivided into six *Comunidades*, or *ayllus*.

In contrast to this ideal representation of the structure of the community is the realization that Jesús de Machaca is not actually (i.e., geographically) situated at the center of the sector of land which it controls, nor are the *ayllus* actually organized around the central community in a perfectly radial pattern. Rather, the community is the center of a radial system from a purely conceptual political, ritual, and administrative point of view. Jesús de

Machaca is the place of residence of the principal bureaucratic officials of the region. In addition, each one of the *ayllus* maintains a house in the central community from which it celebrates festivals and carries on its bureaucratic affairs with the central administration (Albó 1972: 792–793). The central community is also the point of orientation and articulation of a number of agricultural and ritual cycles of rotation (*mit'a*; Albó 1972: 782–786).

In addition to these radial, and what can only be termed "non-radial," representations of the structure of Jesús de Machaca, Albó discusses others, such as a conceptual scheme, modeled on body parts, which may represent two pumas laid out face-to-face across the landscape (1972: 788–790). For our purposes, what is of interest is Albó's summary of these various, apparently contradictory representations of the community:

> . . . in [Jesús de] Machaca there are simultaneously in force a number of structural forms which at times are in contradiction. Theoretically, each structure performs a distinct function. But in practice, there is no lack of ambiguities and superpositions. Moreover, each one of these structures has been more or less transformed and reinterpreted in functioning with the others . . . without there having emerged a full integration (1972: 775; my translation).

These data and comments from Albó and Sherbondy permit the following hypotheses with respect to the contrast between radial and parallel line systems within the Nazca region. The two conceptual schemes may reflect hierarchically distinct representations of the division and organization of space, resources, and manpower in the Nazca area. The parallel line (and grid) systems of land and water division would have developed among the *ayllus* and *parcialidades* in the organization of irrigation agriculture within each river valley. The relations and interactions among the groups within each valley would have been overseen by local elites. In their coordination of activities among the various groups throughout the Río Grande de Nazca drainage, the elites may have conceptualized the regional organization from a hierarchical, centralized point of view; thus, a radial system of representation would have accommodated this regional perspective.

Therefore, the radial line systems on the Nazca pampa could have been produced and maintained in the context of the coordination and representation of regional hierarchical relations—that is, among the moieties, *parcialidades*, and *ayllus* that occupied the numerous river valleys of the Río Grande de Nazca drainage. The maintenance of these lines and radial line centers—much like the maintenance of the plaza *chhiutas* by the *ayllus* in Pacariqtambo today—would have constituted one of the major settings and forms of interaction for the reconstitution and reproduction of regional relations among the various social and political groups within the area under the direction of the local elites. Ritual or ceremonial activities (perhaps including confrontations in the form of ritual battles) may have formed part of the interactions among the various groups via the interconnected network of radial line centers on the pampa.

The two schemes outlined above would have been maintained simultaneously but in different settings and for different purposes. The contradictions in the formal structures that would have emerged from these two modes, or styles, of interaction may have been resolved in some manner unknown to us. Or, on the other hand, they may have remained unresolved and thereby constituted sources of tension between the elites and the commoners of the local *ayllus* which drove these societies to new levels of conflict and/or integration. However, what should not be lost sight of in this attempt to account for the differences between the two conceptual schemes is that in the river valleys and on the pampa, both the basic mode of dividing up territory—that is, by making narrow strips—as well as the type of groupings that produced and maintained the strips—the *ayllus*—was the same; what differed was the ways in which the strips were organized and the nature of the relations and forms of interaction among the *ayllus* within these different settings.

## MIT'A LABOR AND THE MAINTENANCE OF THE ROAD ACROSS THE PAMPA

Two common forms of *mit'a* obligations which were imposed by the Inka state on local groups were the maintenance of roads and the manning of *tambos* ("way stations") along the roads (cf. Cobo 1956 [1653]: bk. 12, chaps. 31, 32; González de San Segundo 1982: 659; Murra 1980 [1955]: 103–106). Cobo tells us that the repair of the roads was the responsibility of the inhabitants of the regions through which they passed; each province, town, and, in some cases, lineage was assigned a stretch of road (Cobo 1956 [1653]: bk. 12, chap. 31; cf. Garcilaso 1966 [1609]: bk. 3, chap. 8; Murra 1980: 104). In one early account, these stretches of road are referred to as *"chotas"* (Callapiña et al. 1974 [1542?]: 37; cf. Urton 1984: 35–37).

The Nazca area was an important link in the Inka road system because it was one of the places from which a trunk road connected the main coastal and highland routes (Hyslop 1985: 245, 266). Ethnohistorical documents written in Nazca allow us to establish the existence of three segments of roads in this region: one stretch connected the Ingenio Valley with Ica, to the northwest (*"Fund. del Convento. . ."*, 1774; f. 139; and cf. Cieza de Leon 1973 [1551]: 185); another stretch went eastward up the Ingenio (Collao) River valley to the province of Lucanas (*"Titulos. . ."* 1620: f. 231; and *"El Maestro. . ."*, 1677); and a third went from Usaca, at the conjunction of the Nazca and Las Trancas Rivers, to the south coast (*"Testimonio. . ."*, 1665: f. 6–6v.). This last stretch of road would probably have been the route used for travel between the Río Grande de Nazca and the area of Acarí and Quebrada de la Vaca.

Fig. IV.15 is a schematic representation of the area of the Río Grande de Nazca showing the three segments of roads described above. These roads would have formed the principal routes for the movement of people within and through this area. The segment of road which is of most immediate interest is the hypothetical stretch shown as a dotted line crossing the

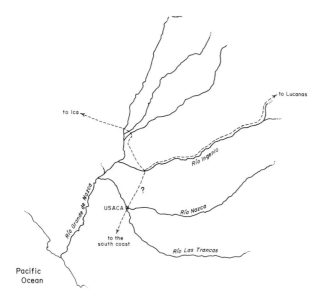

Fig. IV.15. The Inca roads passing through the Río Grande de
Nazca drainage.

pampa of Nazca, linking the Ingenio with the
Nazca Valley and, eventually, with Usaca.
Given the location of the segments of road
described in the ethnohistorical documents, it
seems reasonable to suppose that there would
have had to have been at least one road passing across the pampa. I would point out that
the road shown entering Fig. IV.15 from the
upper left and passing across the pampa (and
continuing on through Usaca) is only a few
kilometers to the west of the modern-day
route of the Pan American Highway. The Pan
American cuts inland to Nazca between Pisco
and Lomas, primarily because along this long
stretch of coastal desert, few (if any) of the
rivers carry water all the way to the coast.
Therefore, the safest route (in terms of the
provisioning of water) along this stretch of
coast is to cut inland to the Río Grande de
Nazca and then to return to the coast farther
north and south.

Given that it was common practice in Inka
times to require local populations to maintain
the royal roads within their home territory, we
may assume that the socio-political groups
that occupied the valleys of the Río Grande de
Nazca would have been required to maintain
the stretch of road which crossed the pampa
(as well as the other roads in the area). The
road across the pampa may well have been

divided into segments (*chota*, *chhiuta*), each one
of which would have been the responsibility of
a different group, working in *mit'a* rotation.
The *mit'a* labor on the roads represents one
context in which we can be reasonably certain
that the *ayllus* within the river valleys would
have been required to go onto the pampa. In
their movement onto, and across, the pampa
from their dispersed locations along the river
valleys, these groups may well have taken different routes to and from the work sites; thus,
each *ayllu* may have had—as a part of its "corporate property"—one or more of the radial
line centers near its home territory. As Aveni
has shown in his description and analysis of
the distribution of the radial line centers on
the Nazca pampa (Chap. II, Fig. II.1b), most
of the centers are located along the edges of
the pampa, overlooking the Ingenio and
Nazca River valleys.

My summation of the above, hypothetical
scenario is that the maintenance of the road(s)
which crossed the pampa would have constituted one of the occasions for the people of
the *ayllus* in the river valleys to use, or to "interact with," the complex of radial line centers
on the pampa. But these uses of the lines for
travel to and from public labor tasks on the
pampa—or in a river valley on the opposite
side of the pampa—could well have been sup-
plemented by other occasions for carrying out
activities on the pampa; these may have included more ritualistic interactions within,
and among, the *ayllus* or simply between people and the pampa itself (i.e., sitting alone in
an empty corner of the pampa).

Therefore, one part of my argument concerning interactions between social groups
and the Nazca pampa is that during Inka
times, road maintenance would have been carried out on the pampa according to some of
the same principles of spatial and labor division which have been discussed throughout
this paper (e.g., *chhiuta*, *suyu*, *mit'a*, etc.).
Through the performance of *mit'a* labor, as
well as other forms of ritual encounters on the
pampa, the social groups would have maintained and reproduced these narrow strips of
cleared space by renewing the contrast be-

tween the lighter soil inside the lines and the darker stones and pebbles on the surface of the pampa. As the site of this activity, the pampa would have represented one of the central places in the Nazca area where the hierarchical relations among the *ayllus* and the various groupings of *ayllus* (i.e., the *parcialidades* and moieties) would have been maintained, reformulated, and reproduced over time.

CONCLUSIONS

Given the size and overall complexity of the cultural remains on the pampa at Nazca, we may find that no single explanation—no matter how general and all-embracing its terms—can adequately account for why the Nazca lines were constructed or for how and why they were used. I have attempted here to provide descriptions of a number of institutions and practices that appear commonly in Andean communities from contemporary to early colonial times as a way of establishing a broad context within which to situate an interpretation of the maintenance of the cultural remains—especially the radial line centers—on the Nazca pampa. It will be noted that I have not discussed the actual construction of the lines in this article. The most direct ethnographic and ethnohistorical data available to me concern the maintenance of public structures or spaces (e.g., community buildings, plazas, etc.); therefore, I have chosen to focus on those features of the interactions between social groups and cultural remains. My assumption, however, is that the basic types of groupings and processes of social and ritual interaction that accounted for the maintenance of the lines were probably similar to those that accounted for their original construction as well (see Silverman, Chap. V this volume).

To summarize, we have found that one of the principal groupings for political, social, economic, and ritual action in communities over much of the Andes is the *ayllu*. In those situations in which communities are divided into multiple *ayllus*, and where these are, in turn, grouped into moieties, the groups commonly distribute rights to resources and responsibilities for public works according to certain well-defined principles and practices; these include turn-taking (*mit'a*) and the division of territory into narrow strips (*chhiuta, suyu*, etc.). These forms of temporal and spatial organization appear throughout the ethnographic and ethnohistorical literature from diverse places and times in the Andes. I think that if we are to understand the Nazca lines, we must see them as products, or constructions, of some of these same Andean forms of organization and practice. In short, if the inhabitants in the river valleys bordering the Nazca pampa were, in fact, organized into the complex socio-political and ritual groupings that I have suggested, then it seems reasonable to suppose that at some point in the pre-Hispanic past in the Nazca area the complex cultural remains on the Nazca pampa may have been a practical or symbolic (or both) focus of working out the problems of the distribution of space and resources among the multiple *ayllu* groupings in the river valleys.

My argument here has been based on the notion that local-level concerns were the driving forces behind the social and ritual interactions through which the lines were maintained. However, the types of spatial and temporal divisions that I have emphasized were, after all, common throughout the Andes; therefore, it is possible that the interactions that went on on the Nazca pampa were not limited to local groups. For instance, Silverman (this volume) has made a strong case for the existence of a pilgrimage tradition centering on Cahuachi (which is located across the Nazca River from the pampa) during pre-Inkaic times. It seems entirely possible that groups from outside the Nazca area (i.e., outside the Río Grande de Nazca drainage) could have gathered at the pampa on certain ritual occasions.

But whether the visitors to the pampa were locals, foreigners, or both, I think that the forms of organization and obligation that would have brought them to the pampa in the first place—and the ways they would have in-

teracted with each other once there—would
have been grounded in some of the same principles and practices of the division of space and
time that have appeared throughout this study.
These divisions (*mit'a, suyu, chhiuta,* etc.) were
reproduced in the renewal of the light/dark
contrast between the geoglyphs and the surface of the pampa; such "renewals" would have
constituted the ritual reproduction of the *ayllus*
themselves in the sacred, communal space between the Nazca and Ingenio River valleys.

### ACKNOWLEDGMENTS

I would like to thank the following people
for their helpful comments and suggestions
on earlier drafts of this paper: Anthony
Aveni, Julia Meyerson, Patricia Netherly, Helaine Silverman, and Tom Zuidema. I alone,
of course, am responsible for the arguments,
opinions and errors contained in the article. I
would also like to express special thanks to Dr.
Hugo Ludeña of the Instituto Nacional de
Cultura in Lima for his support and help
throughout the long period during which
fieldwork for this project was carried out in
Nazca. Financial support for fieldwork in Pacariqtambo in 1981–82 was provided in the
form of a post-doctoral research grant from
the National Science Foundation (BNS-
8106254). Return visits to the community in
the summers of 1983 and 1984 were made
possible by grants from the Research Council
of Colgate University (1983) and the John Ben
Snow Memorial Trust and the Native American Studies program of Colgate University
(1984). The fieldwork in Nazca over the period from 1981–83 was made possible by
grants made jointly to Anthony Aveni and myself by the National Science Foundation, the
National Geographic Society, the Wenner-
Gren Foundation for Anthropological Research, and Earthwatch. I received support
for fieldwork in Chala and Quebrada de la
Vaca from the Research Council of Colgate
University. The support of all these organizations is greatly appreciated. Finally, I want to
express my thanks to my wife, Julia Meyerson,
with whom I spent many wonderful days
walking the Nazca lines.

*V. The Early Nasca Pilgrimage Center of Cahuachi and the Nazca Lines: Anthropological and Archaeological Perspectives*

**Helaine Silverman**

## INTRODUCTION

Eliade (1959: 20) has argued that there is "an opposition between space that is sacred— the only *real* and *real-ly* existing space- and all other space, the formless expanse surrounding it" (his emphasis). He envisions a sacred place as a "break in the homogeneity of space" (ibid: 37) and conceives of the religious Center [sic] as "precisely the place where a break in plane occurs, where space becomes sacred, hence pre-eminently real . . . an irruption of the sacred into the world" (ibid: 45). Here I argue that the archaeological site of Cahuachi, in the Nazca Valley on the south coast of Peru (Fig. V.1), is such a sacred locus and that the geoglyph-marked plains that face it to the north and south are functionally and symbolically associated with it.

## CAHUACHI AS A NON-DOMESTIC SITE

Cahuachi (Figs. V.2–4) is the largest known site of the Nasca[1] culture which flourished on the south coast of Peru in the Early Intermediate Period, ca. AD 1–750. Cahuachi has been canonized in the major archaeological literature as a city or urban settlement (Rowe 1963; Lanning 1967; Lumbreras 1974, 1981; Matos 1980). My recent excavations and survey at Cahuachi were designed to test that interpretation since much of our understanding of the development of complex society in the Central Andes rests on the premise that there was an early urban tradition in southern Peru and the corollary association of urbanism with state-level society. Because so little is known about Nasca culture beyond its exquisite ceramic and textile art, iconography, and chronology,[2] I believed that excavation of habitation remains at the major site would provide much and needed new information on daily Nasca life and Nasca sociopolitical organization.

1. See Aveni, Chap. 1, note 2 for an explanation of Nazca-Nasca.
2. Examples of this research are Seler (1923), Yacovleff (1932a,b, 1933), Sawyer (1961, 1966, 1979), Zuidema (1972), Proulx (1968, 1983, 1986), Wegner (ms.), Silverman (1977), Roark (1965), Dwyer (1971, 1979), Blasco and Ramos (1980), Ramos and Blasco (1977), and Townsend (1985), inter alia.

Surprisingly, the new fieldwork at Cahuachi yielded no evidence in support of Cahuachi's alleged urban nature (see Silverman 1986). Excavation within Cahuachi's large, central enclosure formed by the Unit 16 wall (Fig. V.5) did not produce a dense agglutination of habitation remains as was expected based on the similarity of layout between Cahuachi's central zone and the contemporary Nasca site of Tambo Viejo in Acarí (Figs. V.6, 7), where some 8000 rooms fill two walled areas. Instead, alongside Cahuachi's major wall, Unit 16, only two thin *apisonados* or earth surfaces compacted by foot-traffic were revealed. These were almost devoid of cultural remains with scant material remains in the strata above them and sterile soil beneath them at only some 60 cm. below the surface (Fig. V.8). The Unit 16 wall, which appeared to be a defensive fortification as depicted on Strong's (1957: Fig. 4) map of the site, turned out to be only 40 cm. high although 1m wide (Fig. V. 9a,b). Twenty-three test pits scattered across the open spaces (Fig. V.10) likewise produced few if any domestic remains. In other words, in the 125 hectares of open or unconstructed space at the site—corresponding to almost 85 percent of Cahuachi's total area—no evidence of a large, residential, domestic occupation was found.

Yet many of these open areas are patterned. The shape and actual disposition of hills on the river terrace on which Cahuachi is built create many open spaces between the hills, thereby forming a characteristic three-sided enclosure. Where such a delimitation of space did not occur naturally, it was added with low adobe walls. Some of the man-made enclosures are four-sided. In late Nasca and post-Nasca times many of these served as cemetery areas, but during the apogee of Cahuachi in epoch 3 of the Early Intermediate Period they appear to have been devoid of structures or to have had temporary ones as indicated by post-holes found in the *apisonado* of the Unit 16 wall and in an *apisonado* just beneath it (Fig. V.9a,b).

I suggest that the human addition of walls of delineation—where such were not provided

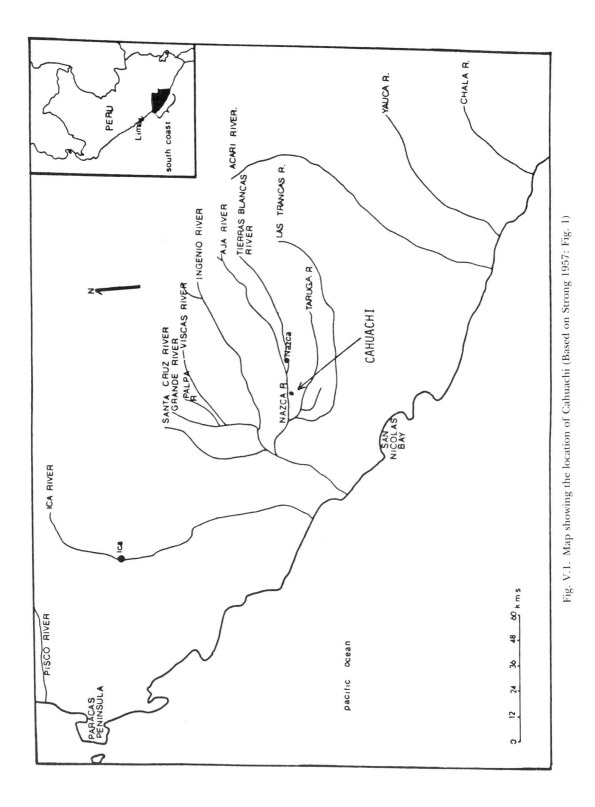

Fig. V.1. Map showing the location of Cahuachi (Based on Strong 1957: Fig. 1)

by nature—did more than create enclosed areas of space as such; it served to distinguish and create an artificial, cultural province from the unmodified expanse outside its border. For instance, as vividly seen in an aerial photograph of the site (Fig. V.11), Cahuachi's major wall, Unit 16, both creates a 20,000 sq. m enclosure of empty space and circumscribes a large area of natural hills by continuing westward along the back of several natural hills and then heading northward. I contend that the purpose of this major architectural feature was to convert natural space into cultural space, untamed space into man-made, human, and controllable space, profane space into sacred space. In so arguing, my position differs somewhat from Eliade's (1959). He sees religious space as a given. I see it, at least in part and sometimes, as created.

The remaining 15 percent of the site consists of lightly modified hills, the semi-artificial mounds which are Cahuachi's monumental architecture (Silverman 1985b, 1986: Chap. 16). Interestingly, these have a naturally truncated form by virtue of the manner in which their caliche strata erode and it can be suggested that these hills were *huacas* or sacred features even before their modification by man.

Analysis of William Duncan Strong's[3] open cuts at Cahuachi and profiles of these revealed that the mounds on which these trenches had been excavated thirty years ago are not habitational as Strong (1957) and others after him have claimed (e.g., Matos 1980: 488), but

rather platform mounds created with construction fill contained by thick adobe walls (Silverman 1985a: Figs. 3, 4, 5). Both by the remains of ritual paraphernalia found on some of these mounds, such as Strong's Great Temple (Strong 1957: 31), and the lack of associated domestic architecture and material on virtually all[4] it can convincingly be argued that Cahuachi's more than forty semi-artificial mounds of varying size and form[5] correspond to ceremonial rather than domestic construction. Indeed, an intact temple precinct was discovered on one small mound, Unit 19, on the western side of the central area of the site (Silverman 1986: Chap. 7).

Cahuachi's mounds, because they were elaborated over the existing topography, became scattered sacred points on a profane landscape. The area around them had to be brought into the cultural realm through the act of enclosure (*kancha*: see Isbell and Fairchild ms.) and that area was made sacred by the nature of activities performed there. Thus, Cahuachi became a Center in Eliade's sense of the word.

There is no other Nasca site known that is comparable to Cahuachi in terms of size, form, layout or material culture. Although local-level and social group-specific religious activities undoubtedly were carried out in the domestic settlements, Nasca religion and its associated ceremonialism were most fully played out at Cahuachi. Just as Chavín de Huantar was the principal cult center of that religious tradition during the Early Horizon,

3. In 1952–53 Strong led the Columbia University Expedition to the south coast of Peru during which time excavations were conducted at Cahuachi. Strong's concern was to determine stratigraphically the temporal relationship of Paracas and Nasca since at that time the two cultures were still floating in a sea of stylistic speculation. To settle the issue, Strong excavated a series of deep trenches in several of the mounds at Cahuachi. One mound, the "Great Temple," was interpreted as a ceremonial structure. The others were interpreted as habitation mounds. Excavations at Cahuachi prior to Strong's had been solely directed at the excavation of tombs for the sake of obtaining interesting and valuable archaeological specimens (e.g. Farabee in Mason 1926; Tello 1917) or provenienced pottery with which to order chronologically the complex Nasca style (Kroeber 1956, ms., Doering 1958). While Strong's concern was chronological, he nevertheless was interested in the cultural correlates of the Nasca style as can be readily seen in his preliminary report (cf. Strong 1957).

4. Only a handful of mounds at Cahuachi have internal room divisions on their terraced north faces. These include Units QQ, 11, 19, and CC whose locations can be seen on Figs. V.2–4. Units 11, 19 and QQ, in particular, have abundant cultural material on their surfaces and it is possible that they fulfilled some kind of restricted domestic as well as specialized ritual function. Further excavation on Unit 19 and new excavations at Cahuachi are necessary to elucidate fully the function and nature of this architecture. G. Orefici has undertaken this task.
5. The variation in size and form of Cahuachi's mounds is due to the fact that these are semi-artificial constructions built over the natural hills. A large natural hill would produce a large mound, even if this was modified with only a small amount of adobe. Some mounds, such as Units A and HH might have rather amorphous shapes whereas other mounds, based on underlying natural topography, could be high, truncated pyramids (e.g., Units 1 and K) or long, low, platform mounds (e.g., Units 5, 6, 18, 19).

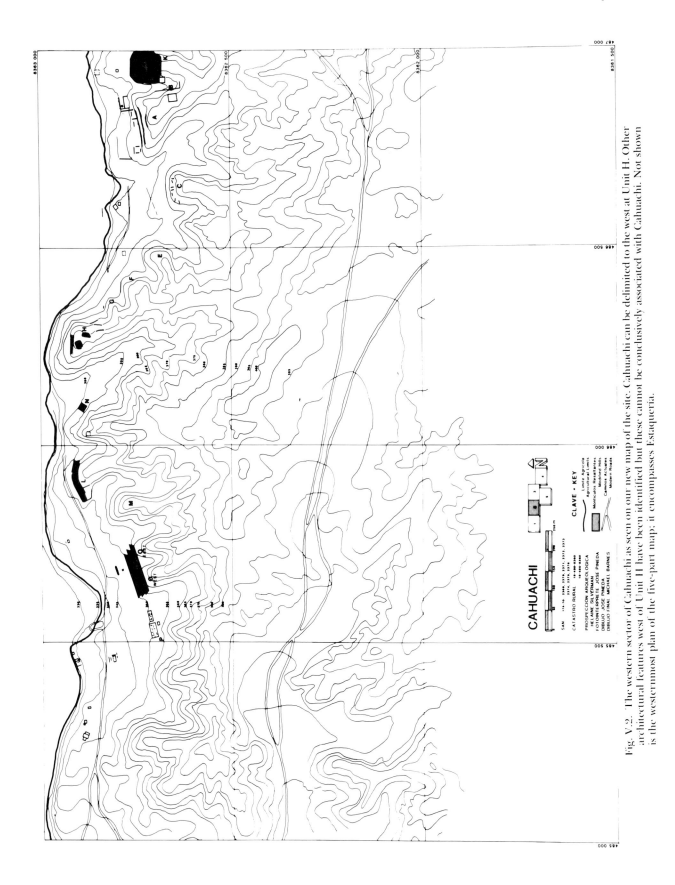

Fig. V.2. The western sector of Cahuachi as seen on our new map of the site. Cahuachi can be delimited to the west at Unit H. Other architectural features west of Unit H have been identified but these cannot be conclusively associated with Cahuachi. Not shown is the westernmost plan of the five-part map; it encompasses Estaquería.

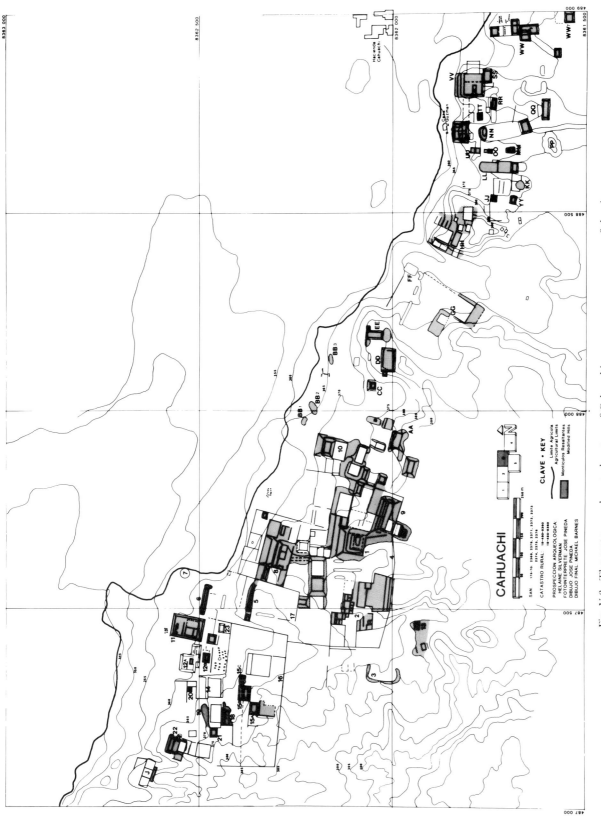

Fig. V.3. The eastern and central sectors of Cahuachi as seen on our new map of the site.

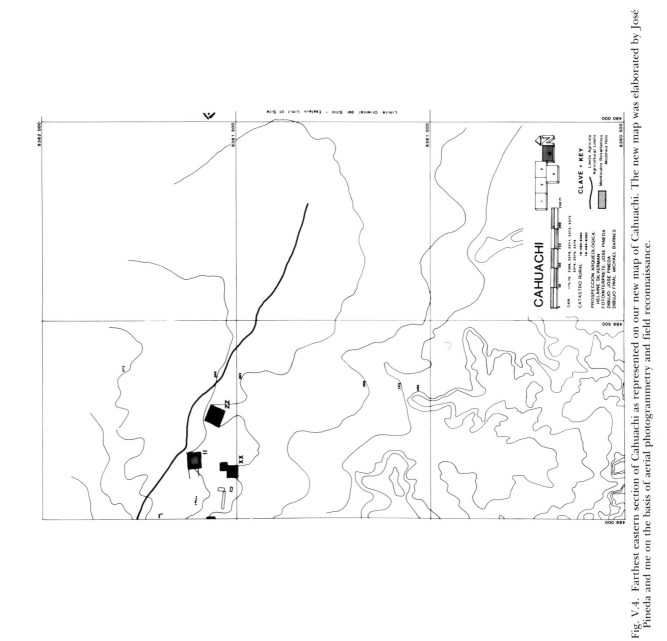

Fig. V.4. Farthest eastern section of Cahuachi as represented on our new map of Cahuachi. The new map was elaborated by José Pineda and me on the basis of aerial photogrammetry and field reconnaissance.

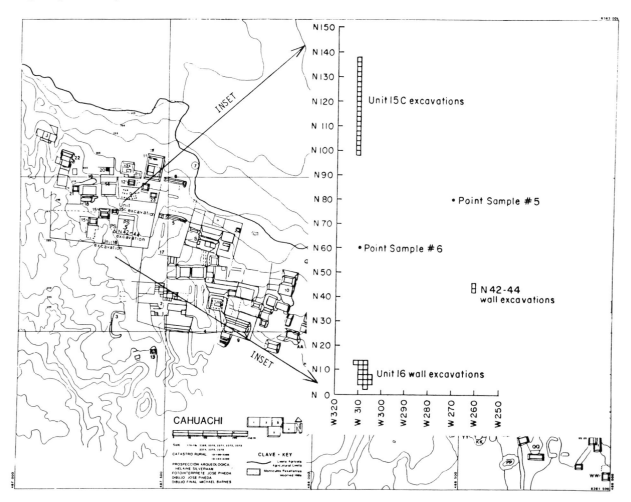

Fig. V.5. Location of the Unit 16 wall and corresponding excavations. See Silverman (1988: Fig. 9).

so too Cahuachi was the global repository and stage for the Nasca religious tradition for a brief time—Nasca 3—during the Early Intermediate Period on the south coast of Peru.

On the basis of the data briefly outlined above I contend that rather than being a major habitation site, Cahuachi was the great, early Nasca ceremonial center (Silverman 1986).

## CEREMONIAL CENTER VS. URBAN CENTER

I have set up the dichotomy urban center-ceremonial center, yet many archaeologists have correctly suggested that the latter can fulfill the functions of the former without the presence of a dense, heterogeneous residential population (e.g., Hammond 1974: 329 cited in Becker 1979:18; Rowe 1963: 20; Lan-

ning 1967:118–119; Wheatley 1971: 225–226 inter alia). It is this overlap of functions that situates many ceremonial centers in the socio-political context of complex society.

Nevertheless, it is important to distinguish between the two settlement patterns because they represent different organizational configurations with distinct historical trajectories. In arguing that Cahuachi is a ceremonial center I am pointing out that, while the sacred and profane worlds were never separated in pre-modern times and non-Western cultures, still at Cahuachi early Nasca society visibly emphasized ceremonialism. Whatever other activities may have taken place at Cahuachi—political, economic, social—these were all clothed in ritual.

It is also important to consider the demographic basis of ceremonial centers rather

Fig. V.6. Aerial photograph of Tambo Viejo in the Acarí Valley.

than lumping them together with ceremonial cities (cf. Wheatley 1971) because this, too, has a bearing on the level of sociopolitical integration of the particular society. The ceremonial center concept entered modern archaeological thought with J.E.S. Thompson's (1954) faulty reconstruction of the great lowland Maya sites as *empty* ceremonial centers, inhabited by a small residential corps of elite priests supported willingly by a docile farming populace in the hinterland. Thirty years of subsequent research into the nature of Classic Maya civilization have proven that these jungle sites were neither empty nor built by a homogeneous population (Becker 1979; Schele and Miller 1986). In the case of Cahuachi, however, we have a ceremonial center that could be bustling with activity or virtually depopulated depending on the day. This is the paradox of pilgrimage to a ceremonial center rather than to a ceremonial city.

## CAHUACHI AS A PILGRIMAGE CENTER

Morinis and Crumrine (n.d.: 15) have described the pilgrimage center as "geographi-cally and socially separate from the home community" and note that "the sacred place participates in the sacred/profane opposition by representing the sacred within the profane sphere. The shrine is usually remote from the homes of pilgrims, and is bounded off by ecclesiastical architecture" (ibid:18). In a similar vein Eliade (1959: 39) argues that "holy sites and sanctuaries are believed to be situated at the center of the world" and that the center is an absolute fixed point and *axis mundi*.

Cahuachi conforms to these expectations. It is characterized by ceremonial rather than domestic architecture and is located in a narrow, agriculturally problematic part of the Nazca River (Silverman 1986: Chap. 2), separated from the valleys to the north and south of its by the pampas of Atarco and Nazca.

Furthermore, Cahuachi is associated with what must have been seen as a magical source of water. The immediate Cahuachi locale is legitimately renowned as a place *"donde aflora el agua"* ("where water emerges"; a great quantity of such water is not implied nor does it exist). This physical property is due to the meeting of water table and ground surface at

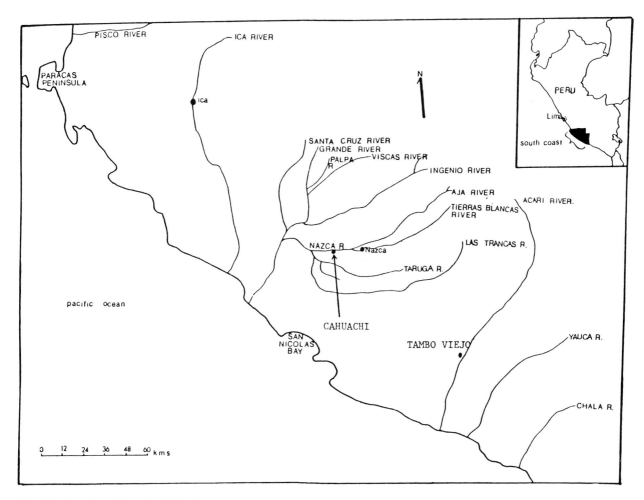

Fig. V.7. Location of Tambo Viejo with respect to Cahuachi.

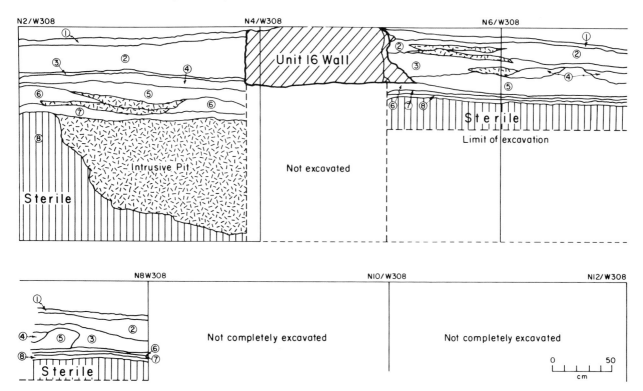

Fig. V.8. Profiles of the excavated area immediately south and north of the Unit 16 wall.

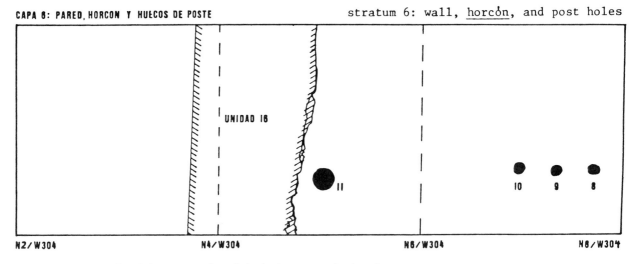

Fig. V.9a. Unit 16 wall and the pattern of postholes in the stratum 6 *apisonado*.

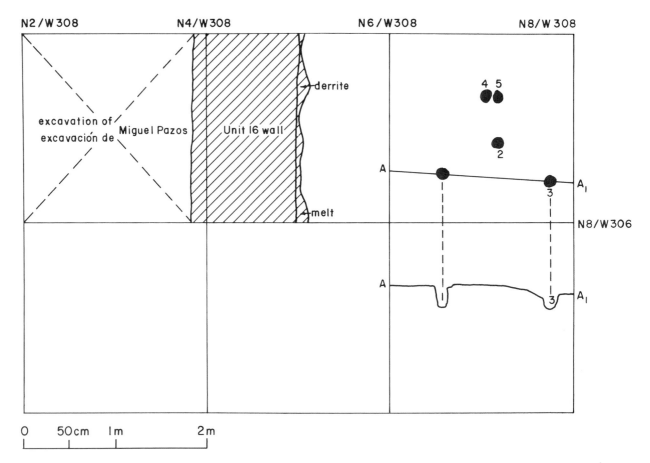

Fig. V.9b. Unit 16 wall and the pattern of postholes in the stratum 8 *apisonado*.

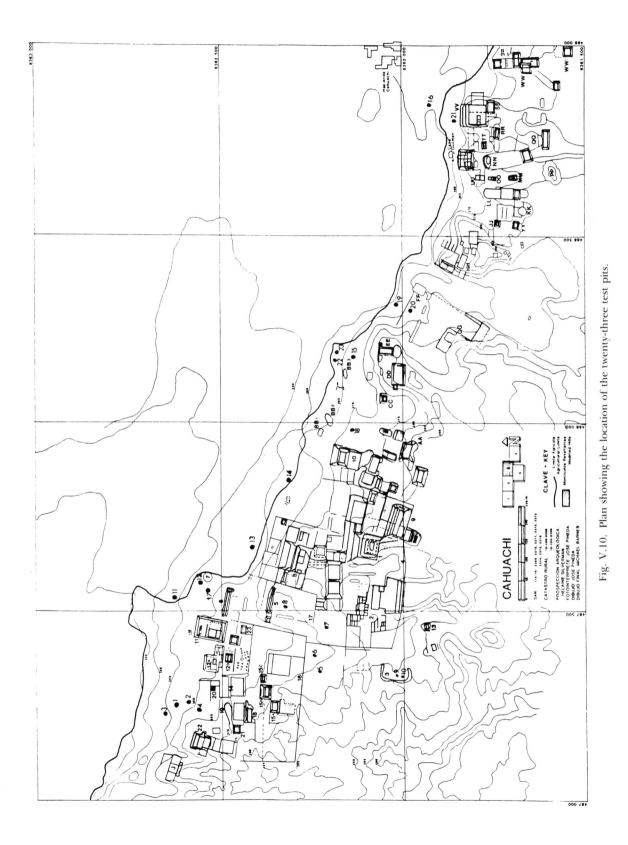

Fig. V.10. Plan showing the location of the twenty-three test pits.

Fig. V.11. Strong's aerial photograph of Cahuachi taken in 1952.

this point (ibid: Chap. 2). No matter how dry the Nazca River proper is, there is always water in several springs above the river at Cahuachi (personal observation; Sr. Josue Lancho, personal communication). Cahuachi manifests an Eliadian *axis mundi* nature in its connection to the underworld via this subsurface water which emerges to the surface here. Indeed, it is conceivable that a connection between Cerro Blanco, Nazca's sacred mountain and reputed source of the underground aquifer (cf. Urton 1984; Reinhard 1985), and the springs at Cahuachi was actually perceived in Nasca times.

The interpretation of Cahuachi as a pilgrimage center also rests on comparison of Cahuachi's material remains to those found at other Andean ceremonial centers known or believed to have had a pilgrimage function (Silverman 1986: Chap. 14) though here it is important to point out that unlike many of these, such as Pachacamac, where "the fortunes of the shrine were intimately connected with the economic and political fortunes of the local populace, and both seem to have been connected with the development and florescence of the widespread commercial network established . . ." (Hammond 1984: 1), at Cahuachi we do not see the development of such an economic function and this in turn explains the lack of a large, permanent, heterogeneous population at the site. The pilgrimage function of Cahuachi can also be argued on the basis of an ethnographic analogy to a modern-day Catholic pilgrimage shrine in the Ica Valley some 190 km north of Nazca, the sanctuary of the Virgin of the Rosary of Yauca (Fig. V.12). The data on Yauca are particularly relevant to this consideration of Cahuachi as a pilgrimage center.

I first became aware of the Yauca sanctuary at a *fiesta* in late July 1984 at Cahuachi, when the women who were cooking began to inquire of each other if they had made a *promesa* ("promise," a vow to a patron saint). When I inquired "promise for what?", they told me about the miraculous Virgin whose cult was celebrated the first Sunday in October every year at Yauca. It was not, however, until my

colleague, Miguel Pazos, and I visited his aunt and uncle in Ica that the possible value of visiting the shrine became clear. That night at dinner, Dr. and Mrs. Rejas began to talk about the shrine whose *fiesta* was approaching and how it was a pity that the sanctuary was used just once a year save for an occasional mass. Inasmuch as it was starting to appear that Cahuachi might also have been used periodically rather than continuously and that, like Yauca, it lacked a dense, residential supporting population, we resolved to go to Yauca to look around and perhaps get some ideas.

The sanctuary of the Virgen del Rosario de Yauca is located about 30 km east of Ica city, in the middle of a desolate, sandy plain in a side-branch of the Ica Valley that is undergoing drastic dessication. The Yauca Valley is the natural communication route to the adjacent highlands of Huancavelica.

Williams (1980) and Pazos (Williams and Pazos 1974) mention several prehispanic sites in this valley, among which is Chokoltaja, a Nasca 3–4 habitation site similar in layout and geographical setting to another early Nasca settlement along the middle reaches of the Aja River in Nazca (Silverman n.d. c 1983; Silverman and Pazos n.d.). Local informants speak of the Yauca area's *huacas* or natural shrines.

Like Cahuachi, Yauca is reached by crossing a bleak, barren plain (see Fig. V.26 in which the approximate route of pilgrimage is traced).

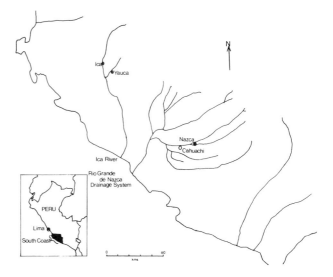

Fig. V.12. Map showing the location of the Yauca sanctuary.

In the case of Cahuachi, if coming from the north one crosses the Pampa de Nazca and from the south the Pampa de Atarco to arrive at the site. At both shrines the wind frequently blows fiercely. And, as we shall see, both places have plazas that are kept ritually and naturally clean.

The cult of the Virgin of Yauca could be classified as a fourth-order shrine. It is not international like the Virgin of Guadalupe nor national like Señor de los Milagros whose church is in Lima. It is regional but not on a par with Señor de Luren, also in Ica. It is not, however, a local shrine (cf. Sallnow 1982).

The Virgin miraculously appeared on 3 October 1701. Her appearance conforms to the shepherds' cycle tradition defined by Turner and Turner (1978: 41–42) which itself suggests prehispanic origins (the connection with the earth or striking natural features that in Peru would be called *huacas*). It is likely that there was a prehispanic shrine in the Yauca area and that landowner Don Nicolas Ortega witnessed the appearance of the Virgin precisely where his Indian peons were working in the field because surely he saw them performing some prehispanic or syncretic rite associated with the place.

Visited weeks before its festival, the Yauca shrine is a lonely spot indeed. Its austere white church (Fig. V.13) is closed because there is no priest in residence. The buildings around the large (ca. 10,000 m$^2$) plaza are abandoned and in varying degrees of disrepair (Fig. V.14). The plaza itself is empty save for the presence of two posts which visibly serve to tie up the burros of the muleteers who traffic between the Huancavelica highlands and Ica; abundant burro excrement surrounded these hitching posts (Fig. V.15). The muleteers stop here because there is a well at which they can get water. The plaza surface is a broken *apisonado* with little evidence of the activities that take place yearly (Fig. V.16). Some corn husks, a bit of broken glass, broken china (Fig. V.17), a fragment of rope, bits of textile, and some loose canes were observed in the plaza at this time. Behind the abandoned houses surrounding the plaza there was a greater concentration of refuse. It was noted during this visit that the place has a strong echo when the air does not blow. Interestingly, the same feature was observed at Cahuachi between Units 12 and 13 during a similar, quiet day.

The sanctuary at Yauca was revisited ten days before the festival to observe the "sweeping of the plaza." When we returned to Yauca for the sweeping, we inquired of those at the shrine what would be swept since we had noted weeks earlier that the plaza was basically clean. Informants there and in Ica contradicted us, saying "no, it's really dirty." This seems to be a shared perception. The faithful thus came with their new brooms, carrying shawls and plastic sacks and enthusiastically swept the plaza, removing the loose dirt and burro excrement and the few other surface remains we had already noted. This dirt was thrown out behind the plaza in the plain through which the dry Yauca River runs. It is the wind that blows the refuse up against the backs of the plaza houses, catching it there; the rest of the dirt is carried away by the wind in other directions or washed away by the river when it occasionally floods.

Following the brief sweeping, the shrine was again deserted.

What a change presented itself to us the next week when we returned to the sanctuary for the celebration of the festival of the Virgin. By late Friday afternoon the sanctuary was filling up with pilgrims. Many of the faithful, who had made a promise to the Virgin, had crossed the dry Yauca plain on foot on a six to eight hour trek from Ica under the hot, spring sun (Fig. V.18). As is the case with Christian pilgrimage in general, they pass a series of smaller religious way-stations en route to the shrine (Turner and Turner 1978: 23). In Yauca these are natural and man-made stops: a special *huarango* tree, a little, dry river that charges during the summer when it rains in the highlands, and several crosses. Most pilgrims arrived by public transportation (a service provided by the municipality), in private cars, or by truck (both privately owned business trucks which earn extra money carrying pilgrims and trucks from the various agrarian

Fig. V.13. The plaza of the sanctuary of the Virgin of the Rosary of Yauca is empty and abandoned prior to the fiesta.

Fig. V.14. The buildings lining the plaza of the Yauca sanctuary are in varying states of disrepair.

Fig. V.15. In the plaza there are some hitching posts for the muleteers who obtain water for their animals and themselves at the Yauca sanctuary. Note the abundant burro excrement surrounding the posts.

Fig. V.16. The plaza surface at Yauca is a broken *apisonado*. There is some garbage littering the surface of the plaza but not much.

cooperatives which transport their members to the shrine). By Saturday there were thousands of persons camping outside the plaza area, on the terrace of the church itself (Fig. V.19), sleeping in the cars and trucks, or being lodged in the otherwise abandoned houses lining the plaza which, during the festival, service the pilgrims of the distinct *cofradías*, each *cofradía* having a house on the plaza. Certain families have houses on the plaza as well.

The plaza itself was transformed into a great market, close-packed with kiosks selling food, alcoholic beverages (beer and moonshine) and soft-drinks (Fig. V.20). Among the ephemeral reed structures that served as restaurants circulated the pedestrian hawkers of cold drinks, ice pops, and sweet bean paste from Chincha in its enticing, white gum-sealed gourd containers. On the main staircase of the church and on the terrace on which the church rests, many vendors of religious paraphernalia such as candles, images, orations, and amulets were observed. The candle makers told me that they are a guild and travel from shrine to shrine all over Peru selling their wares during the particular saints' days.

It was only on Sunday, at the moment of removing the Virgin and her four little assistant Virgins (altar Virgins for the four altars in the four corners of the plaza) from the Church, that a partial cessation in secular activity could be noted when many (but by no means all nor even the majority) of the public

Fig. V.17. Some broken china and bits of vegetal fiber on the *apisonado* of the Yauca plaza.

Fig. V.18. Pilgrims trek across the hot plain to Yauca carrying the altar virgins.

Fig. V.19. The empty church springs to life as thousands of pilgrims mill about on its steps and terraces, some going into the church to worship and others eating, sleeping, or buying religious paraphernalia.

Fig. V.20. The empty plaza itself is suddenly booming with activity as a temporary market town springs up there.

lined up behind the priests and litters to form the procession.

After the procession, the throng of pilgrims quickly abandoned the site.

We returned the next day, Monday, to watch the process of abandonment of the ceremonial center, and especially to note the material condition of the site, once abandoned. The shrine was filthy. We saw the refuse, left by the thousands of pilgrims, littering the site surface: food remains, toppled hearths, broken glasses and plates, lots of plastic bags and paper blowing about (Fig. V.21). Once the kiosk owners had rolled up and taken down the mat walls of their stands, there was virtually no trace of the Brigadoon city that had existed the day before (Fig. V.22). The "city"

had been dismembered almost as quickly as it had been installed. We asked various vendors if they were going to clean up the mess or leave the shrine in this littered condition. All answered that they would not clean it now nor did they ever clean "because the wind carries away all the filth in a short while. Here the air blows hard". Indeed, three months later when I returned to the site, it was almost as devoid of surface refuse as it had been several weeks before the sweeping.

This pattern of material remains corresponds quite closely to the situation encountered in the three- and four-sided enclosures of Cahuachi which are interpreted as plazas where the pilgrims to the ceremonial center congregated. Cahuachi's plazas were demonstrated, through surface collections and exca-

Fig. V.21. By Monday, following the Sunday procession, the shrine is being abandoned. The pilgrims have left and the plaza kiosks are being taken down. Note the filthy state of the plaza.

Fig. V.22. The Brigadoon city disappears as the temporary kiosk structures are rolled up and taken away. All that will remain are some postholes till the windborne sand fills these.

vations, to be essentially clean save for pockets of trapped garbage. The refuse that accumulated at Yauca either blew away or was carried off the plaza premises to be disposed of elsewhere. At Cahuachi, the lack of stratified kitchen middens has been noted by various researchers, and I suggest that Cahuachi was being kept clean by wind and man. The refuse that accumulated during the cyclical use of Cahuachi both blew away and was removed by dumping it near or in the Nazca River valley bottom, to be carried away by periodic and sometimes intense floods or recycled in the construction fill with which Cahuachi's monumental architecture was built. Whereas at Yauca the infrequent use of the site served to permit the wind to maintain the plaza clean and sweeping was more a perfunctory ritual gesture than hygienic act, at Cahuachi, where the use of the shrine(s) was frequent and intense, wind alone was not a sufficient cleaning agency and sweeping may have been necessary to maintain the ritual purity of the zone (cf. Douglas 1966: Chaps. 1,2) as well as a certain level of sanitation.

## CHHIUTAS AND SOCIAL HIERARCHY

It is in this context of sweeping and clean plazas that Urton's (1984) work on *chhiutas* becomes tremendously important for our cultural reconstruction of Cahuachi and early Nasca society. Urton has observed, in Pacariq-

tambo, Cuzco, a custom of sweeping the plaza of the church prior to a religious ceremony. The plaza is swept in a pattern called *chhiutas*. Sweeping is done with a natural broom (*chachakoma*) and the dirt is removed with old sacks.

*Chhiutas* are rectangular strips of space in the church plaza. The plaza is divided into *chhiutas* of differing sizes: big *ayllus* (social groups: cf. Zuidema 1965; Isbell 1977: 91 inter alia) have big *chhiutas* to sweep and small *ayllus* have narrower *chhiutas* to sweep. The task of sweeping the plaza is coordinated by and is the responsibility of the distinct *ayllus*.

Urton notes that any physical space involved in or created by communal labor can be divided into *chhiutas*. He mentions communal agricultural work performed in *chhiutas* and the use of the word to refer to the division of a church wall into segments of space. This would be analogous to the segmentary sections of wall construction that archaeologists recognize and interpret as reflecting the existence of distinct *mit'a* work groups (Moseley 1975). Urton indicates that *mit'a* (temporal) and *chhiutas* (spatial) are integrally interrelated aspects of the same phenomenon: communal obligations for work.

On the general level I would say that the *chutas* represent at the same time a principle of social interaction and a division of space that has its roots in social structure (moieties and *ayllus*), principles of organization (hierarchy, complementarity, and alternation), and work practices (*ayni* and *mit'a*) of the prehispanic Andes. (Urton 1984: 52; my translation)

It was the existence of visually recognizable segments of church wall that enabled the *ayllu* leaders of Pacariqtambo to lay out the *chhiutas* in the plaza for their social groups to sweep. There was no permanent, physical mark on the ground to guide them. Urton points out that the *chhiutas* "do not have predetermined lengths or widths, rather they are established by means of processes in which orientations and measurements are taken whose criteria are ultimately social, flexible, and elastic, and not standardized" (ibid: 34; my translation).

*Chhiutas* are momentary objects or ephemeral units of social territory that are established during communal work projects (ibid: 8) and are also intimately related to the maintenance of public constructions (ibid: 38). The *chhiutas* only come into existence when communal work is undertaken. Similarly but not identically, by comparison and contrast, it can be noted that the *ayllus* always exist but are dormant, only manifesting themselves when thrown into opposition (structural and real) with other social groups as when communal work or other super-group activities take place.

Because communal work is precisely that, involving the participation of more than one group, it does not matter if that work is achieved through mechanical solidarity with each group doing the same task—albeit on a larger or smaller scale—and separately from the other groups. In point of fact, the groups are ultimately working together (whatever the basis of the leadership of the project may be) and as such "the practice of communal work, organized around the *ayllu* and directed at correcting the physical disorder and natural erosion [of a structure] provides the context to repair social disorder and the structural changes in the social organization" (ibid: 328; my translation).

It is this aspect of Urton's argument that is the most provocative. If we abandon Urton's fluid yet homeostatic model which seeks to repair social structural change, we can interpret these periods of communal work as ritual per-

formances and see them as liminal, unstable situations in which the opportunity for change in social structure is presented, though it need not automatically provoke an alternative response nor can the direction of change be predicted.[6]

The liminal periods are, therefore, very dynamic. It is during them (be they overtly for the purpose of work or manifestly for religious celebration) that the changes in social hierarchy Urton is unable to account for can take place. Indeed, Urton says (ibid: 39; my translation): "The flexibility and elasticity inherent in the *chutas* permit the maintenance and restructuring of inter-*ayllu* relationships by means of confrontations and cooperation along the borders of the *chutas*." I suggest that this is precisely what happened at Cahuachi: Cahuachi, in addition to overtly religious functions, was the sociopolitical forum of early Nasca society. It was at Cahuachi where early Nasca social hierarchy was manifested, tested, and worked out. This is the major political concomitant of the ceremonial center.

Urton's discussion of *chhiutas* thus provides us with the possibility of inferring the social

---

6. Here I see an interesting analogy between energy models of the behavior of human societies (Adams 1975, 1978; Allen 1981) and the processual symbolic analysis practiced by Turner (1967, 1974, 1979). The instability that occurs at a critical distance as one moves away from equilibrium could be considered the *limen*, a threshold (energetic or social depending on the vocabulary of one's paradigm). It is at this threshold where "the least fluctuation can cause the system to leave its uniform, stationary state" (Allen 1981: 27). This is the flexibility, elasticity, and "social disorder" discussed by Urton (1984). When the fluctuation occurs (as it will in ritual performance when the liminal condition is entered), that fluctuation is amplified and the system (social, energetic) is driven or metamorphoses into a new state or social configuration. This is what I mean by the "opportunity for change in social structure." What is of great value in the energy model approach to complex systems (social and physical) is the role that is given to stochastic or unpredictable random events and the manner in which they come into play. These are the unpredictable variations in human behavior that occur in ritual performance. Allen's outstanding contribution is the concept of "bifurcation point." Liminality is a kind of bifurcation point. Stochastic events become very important when the

system is near to points at which a new organization may emerge. These points are called bifurcation points. . . . Complex systems can have, of course, a whole series of bifurcation points. . . . Between two bifurcation points, the system follows deterministic laws . . . but near the points of bifurcation it is the fluctuations which play an essential role in determining the branch that the system chooses. (Allen 1981: 29)

organization involved in the ritual maintenance of Cahuachi. Just as large *ayllus* swept large *chhiutas* and small *ayllus* swept small *chhiutas*, it can be argued that at Cahuachi large pyramids were built by large *ayllus* and small ones by the smaller *ayllus* which did not dispose of as much human energy. The size of a mound at Cahuachi, therefore, could correlate with the demographic base available for its construction and thus be an indication of the effective social power of the *curaca* (leader) of each *ayllu* or multi-*ayllu* social group.

Given that Cahuachi did not have the sufficiently large residential population with which to build all of its mounds in the brief apogee period during which such construction was undertaken (end of Nasca 2 through Nasca 3 and declining sharply in Nasca 4), it can be argued that the site's public architecture was largely erected during pilgrimage episodes to the site when the necessary labor was at hand.

CAHUACHI'S MULTIPLICITY OF MOUNDS

In any discussion of Cahuachi, the single most important characteristic of the site must be considered to be the presence of multiple mounds (see Figs. V.2, 3, 4; see Fig. V.27a, b for a low-altitude view of some of these mounds) rather than a monolithic architectural religious focus. This is what makes Cahuachi Cahuachi. This is the paramount, the distinguishing feature, and it must be explained if we are to understand the site and early Nasca society.

I have previously and but casually indicated that the existence of so many mounds at Cahuachi contrasts with the situation at other contemporary ceremonial centers, such as Moche, and have suggested a model of site organization based on Jimenez Borja and Bueno's model of provincial temples at Pachacamac (Silverman 1985a: 92–93). I would here like to consider in greater depth the significance of multiple mounds at Cahuachi.

Analyzed within the anthropological, ethnohistorical, and archaeological context of Andean societies, three explanations of Cahua-

chi's many mounds are possible. These three are not necessarily mutually exclusive. They are:

1. the mounds are the result of a macrosocial group's repetitive, cyclical worship at the site, this devotion being manifested by the diachronic construction of sequential mounds (e.g., "a multitude of ceremonial hearths, all apparently serving the same function" at Huaricoto: cf. Burger and Salazar-Burger 1985: 116–117)
2. the many mounds correspond to many, less inclusive social groups, each group building and synchronically worshipping at the appropriate *huaca* in accordance with a ritual calendar of socio-ritual obligations (e.g., Zuidema's [e.g., 1964] *ceque* system of Cuzco or, in a sense, the provincial temples of Pachacamac [Jimenez Borja and Bueno 1970])
3. the various mounds are functionally different and also reflect a social hierarchy at the site (for Cahuachi this has been specifically proposed by Pezzia [1969: 120] and Anonymous [1953])

Let us test Cahuachi against these expectations.

*Synchrony or diachrony*

There are some diachronic differences among the many mounds. Although excavation oriented to the standing architecture of Cahuachi was conducted at only one small mound (Unit 19) and surface collection on others was not systematically undertaken (nor do all mounds have much surface material), it is my conclusion from the construction techniques of the many mounds, sherds seen on the surface of the individual mounds, and the material from Strong's cuts at Cahuachi and my own excavations on Units 15C and 19 that the mounds of Cahuachi date, in large part, to epochs 2 and especially 3 of the Early Intermediate Period (Fig. V.28). However, not all mounds began to be built at the same time and some construction on existing mounds continued into epoch 4 (e.g., the Room of the Posts on Unit 19) with very late use in Nasca 5 (as seen in Room 1 on Unit 19). The Great Temple was started at the very end of Nasca 2 (Silverman 1977) whereas Room 1 on Unit 19 and perhaps that whole mound may not have begun till Nasca 3C times. But we are basically talking about a site whose apogee occurred within epochs 2 (e.g., Unit 7) and especially 3 of the Early Intermediate Period. If we use public construction activity as the indicator of site use and apogee (as is done in the Maya lowlands) then the site is relatively short-lived.

Although the volume of architecture at the site is great, the mounds are many. It can be argued that there is no temporal-demographic problem in positing simultaneous mound construction and synchronic use of the mounds rather than a one-by-one sequential growth of the site. Other arguments in favor of overall contemporaneity within the site are the basic shared techniques of mound construction, the pervasive mound-and-plaza pattern found across the site, and the existence of specific, shared details of construction (such as eastern access stairways made of adobe steps topped with *huarango* post corners as in Units VV and 15C) between distant mounds.

*Functional differences*

Although there are features of the individual mounds which make them recognizable as Cahuachi, the almost eccentric differences among them argue for construction by different social groups with differing requirements. This, of course, relates to the issue of functional differences and hierarchy of architecture at the site.

Unit 1 is connected to Units 9, 8, and 2 and all are enclosed by the Unit 4 wall. It is tempting to interpret this area as one architectural complex, a kind of acropolis. With its centrality and height above the plain, this complex is visibly the most important one at the site. It is possible that as such it was the result and focus of pan-Nasca or macro-ethnic group attention.

Indeed, this grouping could be considered a "palace" as this term is used by Schele and Miller (1986: 133–134) although architecturally there are differences of access and design that contrast greatly with the truly self-contained and interconnected elements of the lowland Maya palaces (cf. Schele and Miller 1986: Figs. III.1a, b, 2a, b, 3).

The function of the Unit 4 complex, however, may have been similar to the Maya palaces at the various lowland city-states. These were the settings for dramatic rituals as well as the administrative hub for the cities (this would be in the sense of Uphill's [1972] study of the Egyptian palace as a ruling machine). As such they were places where visiting nobles were received, rulers installed, tribute presented, and captives displayed and dispensed (Schele and Miller 1986: 134). They were also the residences of the elite and Schele and Miller (ibid: 133–134) note the existence of private interior galleries and rooms. Interestingly, however, they suggest that the real domestic locus of the elite may have been in the smaller "house mounds" surrounding the massive palatial compounds.

The residential nature of the Unit 4 complex is doubtful because private roomed areas are absent save the little area of small, agglutinated rooms atop the north face of Unit 2 whose function is unknown but which spatially and superficially resemble storerooms. Only a handful of mounds elsewhere at the site have compartmentalized architecture which could prove to be domestic, though one such mound which was investigated, Unit 19, does not appear to conform to a residential locus—despite its rooms and *apisonados*—because the appropriate domestic artifacts are missing. This, however, may be a problem of interpretation since Topic (1977, 1982) has argued strongly for an elite residential character to Huaca de la Luna.

The other mounds of Cahuachi do not form an "acropolis" but are individual, either composed of one hill or several component parts that are easily delimited one from the other and not usually connected. Some of these, however, are fairly impressive, for instance,

Units VV and WW. Other mounds are small and very simple, for instance, Units OO or MM. Others fall between these extremes. This diversity conforms to my suggestion that those social groups with more resources built larger and more complex mounds whereas those with less resources (basically labor) built smaller mounds.

Despite the differences noted above, I do not see pervasive functional differentiation in the many mounds with the exception of Units 2, 7, and 12B (cf. below) and Orefici's (personal communication, 1988) possible evidence for ceramic production on Unit 10. Only a few mounds have superficial room divisions and only a few have possible storage facilities. Few appear to be physically appropriate as domestic loci for large numbers of people nor, on Unit 19, was there sufficient refuse of ordinary, domestic life with which to posit a large domestic population; this is precisely the conclusion of Peter Harrison about the Central Acropolis at Tikal (cited in Schele and Miller 1986: 145).

On the other hand, such architectural areas as the small one at the base of Unit 12B may have played a limited residential role. And, if domestic architecture was made of perishable materials and interspersed between the mounds, then time, looting, and modern scavenging may have destroyed the surface and much of the sub-surface evidence of it.

Of all the mounds, it is Units 2 and 12B which physically differ the most from the others. Unit 2 has a distinctive step-fret shaped terrace and is associated with abundant ritual paraphernalia. Unit 12B is a small, solid adobe mound whose platform surface contains three or four rows of aligned, adobe-lined cylindrical shafts (Fig. V.23). Their purpose is unknown but they could have been storage facilities for ritual paraphernalia, an *ushnu*-like offering conduit, or both. Miguel Pazos recovered the hindlimb of a llama from one shaft and parts of a large storage vessel from another. Both mounds may be pan-Nasca temples. Strong (1957) appears to have found a textile production area on Unit 7.

The visible differences among the other

mounds are largely due to the nature of the hill upon which they were elaborated. Save in the cases of Units 2 and 12B, no mound was so artificially modified that a deliberate physical layout appropriate to differential functions can be detected.

### The Pachacamac Model

I still favor a "provincial temples" kind of model as the explanation of Cahuachi's unique spatial organization (Silverman 1985a) but would substitute the word *"ayllu"* for provincial. Cahuachi both shares and departs significantly from the following description of Pachacamac's provincial temples which are characterized by a monotonous

repetition of the same pattern of construction, with distinct dimensions. Around them are enclosed empty fields, apparently parcels of land ready to be turned over to the new coastal provinces that requested permission to have a temple in the city. (Jimenez Borja and Bueno 1970:16; my translation)

From each coastal canton probably departed, according to the proper schedule, the local chief

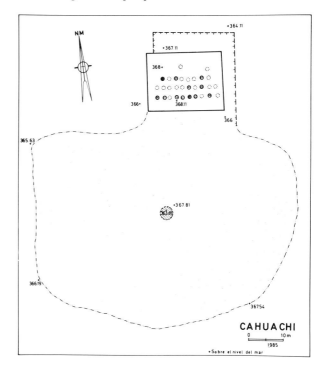

Fig. V.23. Plan of Unit 12B showing the regular rows of cylindrical depressions.

accompanied by a cortege of servant helpers with offerings which were stored in the storage houses as Estete and Hernando Pizarro called them. These houses were, in a certain way, provincial temples. . . . In Pachacamac they exist in a varity of classes, most of them quite similar. They consist of a great front patio or atrium and then a building in the form of a truncated pyramid at whose summit are a few sacred chambers. Behind all this are enormous storage facilities. Each of these provincial temples received offerings from a particular community. (ibid: 22; my translation)

At Cahuachi there is not the degree of architectural standardization as Pachacamac, yet there is overall unity of spatial organization and architectural design at the site despite differences in the dimensions of the different mounds. Around these mounds, as we have seen, are plazas. Unlike those at Pachacamac, however, these were not destined to be filled in with more architecture.

In significant contrast to Pachacamac, large-scale storage facilities are missing from Cahuachi. The material goods brought in to Cahuachi were rapidly consumed, not stored at the site. I believe that the major offerings brought to Cahuachi were food and fine pottery, of which the latter was produced for and ritually, as well as accidentally, broken during the course of celebrations at the site. My interpretation has been influenced by well-known cases of ancient Central Andean practice (e.g., Middle Horizon ceramic offerings at Conchopata, Pacheco, Ayapata and elsewhere: cf. Menzel 1964; Ravines 1968), as well as Norman and Dorothea Whitten's (Whitten and Whitten 1978, N. Whitten 1985 inter alia) and Elizabeth Reeve's (1985) ethnographic work among the lowland Canelos Quichua of Ecuador.[7] Wobst's (1977) analysis of the social

concomitants of style and stylistic behavior is also relevant to any consideration of why there is so much decorated ware at Cahuachi.[8]

_____

(the serving bowl for *asua*), 10 *purus* (anthropomorphic serving vessels), 2 *cornetas* (trumpets), 5 *callanas* (eating bowls), and one or more *usisa purus* (flower vases for the church). On the third day of the *jista*

> As the fervor builds, suddenly the *chayuj* calls "stop," ordering all the ceramics to be broken. The guest male *jisteros* are handed ceramics by the host female *jisteros* and selecting a suitable part of the roof, preferably in the southwest, one by one the men hurl the ceramics up against the roof, attempting to pierce the woven palm thatch with sherds which will remain there as a reminder that the *jista* took place and ended in that house. They break the *purus*, *mucahuas* full of *asua* and the remaining *cornetas*. As they throw the ceramics the men yell "end the *fiesta*" ("*Jista tucurin*"). Once all the ceramics are broken in the *huarmi jista huasi*, all go to the *cari jista huasi* where the ceramics are broken in the same way. Following this the men again begin to drum, their drums sounding now only heavy thuds from the *asua* soaked skins, while the women dance on a house floor now turned to *asua* mud mixed with ceramic sherds. Any remaining ceramics are used to continue serving till all of the *asua* has been drunk. (Reeve 1985: 170–171)

This situation is, of course, different from Middle Horizon patterns of ritual pottery smashing (e.g., Pacheco, Conchopata, Ayapata: cf. Menzel 1964; Ravines 1968; Cook n.d.). It is also different from the pattern I observed in the Room of the Posts on Unit 19 at Cahuachi where 16 whole pots and hundreds of sherds in the Nasca 8 style were left as offerings in the deliberately interred temple room, but where the sherds cannot be put back together again as whole vessels. Nevertheless, it serves to illustrate a possibly ancient, underlying pan-Andean custom of ritually breaking pottery. Reeve (1985: 174–176) analyzes and interprets the *jista* in the context of and as an Andean ritual. (Unfortunately, she does not tell us what happens to all the sherds. Are they left in the mud to become hardened into an *apisonado* or is the floor eventually cleaned? At Cahuachi sherds were rarely found worked into floors of any kind. The sherd found in the floor of the Room of the Posts is one of those rare instances.)

I suggest that there is so much broken fineware at Cahuachi that it cannot result solely from accidental breakage. Rather, I contend that pottery was made especially to be taken to the ceremonial center; it was used there (including in burial) and some broke accidentally; some was also deliberately broken as part of the activities occurring at the site; and some pots were surely taken out of the site again.

At the same time, the abundance of bowls at Cahuachi is notable (Silverman 1986: Chap. 9) and perhaps significant. Morris and Thompson (1985: 74), writing of Huánuco Pampa, have suggested that the Inka state provided the pottery that symbolized Inka power and control. They have furthermore noted a preponderant clustering of certain forms with certain architectural areas such as wide-mouth vessels in the storage zone (ibid: 77) and plates but not cooking pots in a walled, barrack-like compound (ibid: 79). While Cahuachi has not been sufficiently sampled to reveal the existence of these kinds of correspondences, it can be suggested that the high quantity of ceramic vessels not appropriate for storage nor indicative of cooking is suggestive of the kinds of activities that occurred at the site: these vessels, especially bowls, were used in food consumption (eating) and ritual activity (exchange, ceremony, accidental and deliberate breakage).

_____

7. An outstanding ethnographic example of ritual consumption of pottery is the ethnographic case reported by Reeve (1985) for the Canelos Quichua of eastern Ecuador. There, a month before the celebration of an annual *fiesta* called *jista* (whose purpose is to guarantee renewal of the tropical forest resources necessary for the survival of traditional culture and to renew inter-ethnic bonds), the women dedicate themselves to making *asua* (slightly fermented manioc or plantain gruel) and the pottery specifically needed for the *fiesta*. Each woman helper of the fiesta sponsor must make at least 7–10 *mucahuas*

8. Wobst's (1977) now classic article raises the question of how

Besides the provincial temples at Pachaca-mac, there were also pan-polity shrines at the site such as the pre-Inkaic Temple of Pacha-camac. As suggested above, certain units of Cahuachi in the central zone may have ful-filled such functions.

The overriding similarity I see between Pa-chacamac and Cahuachi is the presence of many similar mounds at both sites. It is this multiplicity I am trying to explain with the model of *ayllu* temple which is derived from Pachacamac's provincial temples.

How might that model have functioned on the ground, so to speak?

## THE POLITICAL CONCOMITANTS OF PILGRIMAGE: IMPLICATIONS OF ANDEAN KINSHIP AND ANDEAN CONCEPTS OF HIERARCHY

Studies of contemporary Andean kinship (Lambert 1977; Mayer 1974, 1977; Isbell 1974) strongly suggest that social groups such as the *ayllu* are organized as cognatic descent groups. Like unilineal descent groups which are generally considered to be corporate (i.e., persist over time), cognatic descent groups can also have characteristics of corporate descent groups but *only* if other criteria such as resi-dence, membership affiliation, or locality are added. This is because a cognatic descent group potentially traces all descendants (male

appropriate pottery would be as a marker of social identity, social boundaries, and in the process of information exchange. Because of the small size of most Nasca decorated pottery (save drums), the use of pottery as a manifestation of social affiliation presumes close physical proximity of a public. The very amount of fineware at Cahuachi may be explicable in terms of the fact that it is at Cahuachi where Nasca social identity is being af-firmed and the art style is a manifestation of participation in the unifying cult. Indeed, the regionalism of style in the Early In-termediate Period corresponds to Wobst's model of the role of stylistic behavior in forming and maintaining ethnic bound-aries.

Another issue which emerges from this discussion is the typ-ical equation, by archaeologists, of ceramic style with culture. As Lumbreras (1984) cogently points out, archaeologists typically consider the diffusion of the former to be the spread of the latter. Also, it remains to be determined whether all those who used Nasca pottery pertained to the same ethinic group or not. The conclusions of a recent study by Sue Grosboll (n.d. a, b) do not suggest that we can be overly optimistic about the utility of correlating style with ethnic groups, even when these are eth-nohistorically known.

and female), thereby creating overlapping, non-discrete groups. Potentiality arises be-cause *ego* has a choice of how to affiliate and the decision is not permanent; it can be changed to *ego's* advantage at the appropriate time.

By specifying any of the secondary criteria mentioned above, discrete groups of people can be generated that are organized either se-quentially or spatially or both. It is also possi-ble for all members of the descent group to be in one place at one same time. It is the nesting of component *ayllus* (or descent groups) that forms the larger social units that can range up to ethnic and macro-ethnic groups.

The question for us, in this section, is dual. Can contemporary Andean kinship patterns be traced back to the prehispanic era, and, if so, how do these manifest themselves in the archaeological record?

Zuidema (1977) has studied the Inka kin-ship system as this was recorded in early Span-ish colonial documents. He demonstrates that, with some modifications,[9] the cognatic princi-ple is operative in Inka kinship. Another im-portant point that emerges from Zuidema's study is the possibility of extending the degree of kinship relatedness (i.e., group member-ship) outward through the use of hierarchy (the categories of *collana, payan, cayao,* and *caru*) as well as through the use of first, sec-ond, third, and fourth marriages of, in this case, the Inka king. In this manner it was pos-sible to incorporate and place just about any person in the Inka Empire in some hierarchi-cal yet kinship-based relationship to the king. Zuidema's studies would therefore demon-strate the *elastic, flexible, expanding,* and *con-tracting* nature of Andean kinship-based social organizations as well as their inherent hierar-chical (i.e., internally differentiated) charac-ter.

It would be foolhardy to posit a direct, lin-

9. The modifications proposed by Zuidema are that descent of males is traced through males; descent of females is traced through females; and the basic cognatic descent group is one of four generations. There are certainly many among the kinship experts who would argue that these modifications are defini-tionally and structurally incongruous with what is held to be cognatic descent. I am aware of this problem.

eal, unchanged connection between Inka social organization in the highlands of southern Peru in the fifteenth and sixteenth centuries and Nasca social organization on the south coast more than a thousand years earlier. Nevertheless, there are certain patterns of culture that are pan-Andean and which have great temporal continuity. It is worthwhile, then, to examine those aspects of Andean social organization that could generate the spatial and material patterns that we have observed at Cahuachi. This exercise can be organized as a series of propositions against which the data from Cahuachi can be tested.

1. Under the principles of cognatic descent, there would be several discrete (yet perhaps overlapping) social groups using Cahuachi, each one with its own localized place of congregation. This would account for the repetitive spatial pattern of many mounds and plazas observed at Cahuachi. That this is so is supported by Dalton's (1977: 194) analysis of corporate descent groups as "a cohesive religious unit" with "common clan ancestors, heroic clan founders, special divine spirits and supernatural beings who mythically aided clan ancestors and founders" etc. as well as land-holding groups.

2. The short-term, transient, sequential gatherings of the social groups could be taken care of by a ritual calendar. For groups organized by cognatic descent, a well-organized ritual calendar to regulate and coordinate the operation of multiple, overlapping descent groups would help avoid social organizational chaos. It is this ritual calendar which regulates when the social groups come into physical existence by indicating who is to participate in what ritual. This harks back to the ephemeral qualities of Andean social organization discussed by both Zuidema and Urton.

At Cahuachi we do not have evidence of a large, permanent, domestic occupation but rather of the frequent, periodic use of the site as a pilgrimage center composed of many shrines and probably occupied by a relatively small cadre of priestly elite. The visits to the site and the shrines belonging to the different social groups were surely determined and pre-

scribed by a ritual calendar. It can be argued that the so-called Nazca lines, among their several functions, served as the physical representation of this ritual calendar (cf. Aveni 1986).

3. Each social group has its own developmental cycle; the groups are not evolving in unison. Some groups might be at their apogee while others are in decline. We know from Andean mythology (e.g., Zuidema 1973b) that cognatic descent groups typically trace their origin to specific ancestors emerging at known places (*pacarinas*). One could posit that the ritual use of a sacred place involves the long-term process of establishment of the shrine, periodic gathering, temple-building and temple-use, and expansion and contraction cycles according to the demographics of the social group. Also possible is the eventual, partial conversion of diachronically abandoned portions of the social group's temple into cemetery as members of the group die out and some are buried at the shrine, and finally the bringing of offerings, perhaps by remnants of the original social group that founded the shrine. This is the sequence of occupation in the Unit 19 mound (Silverman 1986: Chap. 7).

4. This cognatic model of social organization permits the existence of one all-embracing social group and would therefore prompt us to look for an appropriate locus of macro-group activity. Unit 2, which Strong labeled the "Great Temple" and which is significantly different from the other units and is centrally located at the site, with the Unit 16 plaza might have fulfilled such a function. There may be others as well. The various social groups each had their own *huacas* or shrines at Cahuachi but recognized the whole ceremonial center as the macro-Nasca religious center. Cahuachi thus fulfilled an *inclusive* role while permitting the expression of *exclusive* tendencies.

5. Cognatic descent groups operate according to context. The situational context in which the cognatic descent groups function can require the participation of small, medium or large, hierarchical or egalitarian

units. It is the context which determines the nature of activity involvement of social groups. A situation such as this would lead to the performance of conflict-expressing/conflict-resolving rituals such as those described by Turner (1967, 1974).

Villages in the Andes are and probably were composed of more than one social group (Rostworoski 1985). The *limpia acequia* (canal cleaning) ceremony of an irrigation canal running through the lands of a lower moiety would call into physical existence those groups forming the lower moiety. Membership in the lower moiety is claimed and affirmed by participation in this temporally limited activity. An entire village might mobilize itself for a boundary dispute against another village. Given that Andean villages are multi-componential (Rostworowski 1983), it is conceivable that certain Village A members would have to fight against their co-social group members in Village B.

The tensions inherent in the situation we are describing could have escalated over time to the point that ritual battles became necessary to express and resolve conflict. Cahuachi could have been the arena for such social drama as prescribed trophy-head taking in the post-apogee period (for which there is archaeological evidence in the Unit 19 excavations) and apogee period (e.g., some of Kroeber's graves on Unit A).

In this light it is interesting to note the iconographic and material evidence that Nasca people dressed up to go to Cahuachi rather than down (cf. Sawyer 1979: Figs. 13,14,15). This, as an aspect of pilgrimage to a shrine center, is in sharp contrast with the simple dress and homogenizing, egalitarian attributes of medieval, state-context, Christian pilgrimage that are emphasized by Turner (1979; Turner and Turner 1978).[10]

As Cieza de Leon (1551) noted throughout his chronicle, dress is a way of expressing ethnic identity. At Cahu   the otherwise dormant social groups must have regaled

themselves so as to recognize co-participant members of the group, express group identity in opposition to other groups, and compete for status with regard to these other social groups. At the same time, dress must have been part of the ritual symbolism of the pilgrimage which, with the iconography of early Nasca art, formed a cluster of ritual symbols, "a limited set of root metaphors or meta-ritual symbols" (Morinis and Crumrine ms.: 5; cf. also Wobst [1977] on the role of dress style). Cahuachi itself was the "aesthetic locus" of early Nasca society (cf. Maquet 1979, 1986).

6. From the above it follows that principles of hierarchy are expressed in pilgrimage. The sociology of the Qollur R'iti pilgrimage is particularly illustrative of this argument about the hierarchy inherent to Andean pilgrimage (Wagner 1978; Gow 1974):

> Pilgrimage in the Andes functions. . . . to affirm the internal, ultimately vertical (i.e., hierarchical) structuring of the social groups travelling to a pilgrimage shrine. Pilgrimage is an important means by which individuals attain prestige cargos within their community. As ritual representatives of their community, moreover, pilgrims identify throughout their journey with this local (hierarchized) group and not, as in some models of Christian pilgrimage [e.g. Turner and Turner 1978], with a larger, theoretically "undifferentiated" mass of pilgrims at a sanctuary [Sallnow 1981] (Poole n.d.: 32)

It is likely that the social groups which maintained the different mounds at Cahuachi constituted themselves en route to Cahuachi, on the pampas, and at the site itself (again the literature on Qollur R'iti exemplifies this point). Once their periodic celebrations at the ceremonial center were ended, the macrogroups would decompose into their smaller parts, these returning to their distinct home villages where other social group membership principles would exert their claims. The transient, marked social hierarchy would thus disaggregate into a less hierarchical, more permanent day-to-day social organization. I am not, however, suggesting the kind of egalitarian, sociopolitical context that would give rise

---

10. In comparing pre-Columbian pilgrimage to Catholic pilgrimage I realize that the social and political contexts of the two are literally worlds apart.

to Johnson's (1982, ms.) "sequential hierar-chy". Early Nasca society is complex society; the issue is how this complexity was infra-structurally organized. Recent settlement pat-tern data from the Pisco, Ica, and Acarí Valleys (Peters 1986; Massey 1986; Menzel and Riddell 1986) appear to support Rowe's (1963) original contention that Nasca was a short-lived, regional state on the south coast of Peru, but the appropriate socioeconomic differentiation of graves is absent (Carmi-chael 1988) as is, so far, a multi-level, de-cision-making, intersite hierarchy in the heartland for the period in question. On a smaller scale, Cahuachi's role as a pilgrimage center is comparable to that fulfilled by Pa-chacamac, the Ichimay pilgrimage center, and Batan Grande, the Middle Sican pilgrim-age center, each of which were the seats of political power as well as religious prestige of their respective polities.

7. Pilgrimage to a site, according to Turner (1967, 1974; Turner and Turner 1978) cre-ates *communitas*. Sallnow (1981), however, has shown that for modern Andean pilgrimage centers, manifestations of competition and conflict characterize this kind of multi-group encounter, the pilgrimage center then becom-ing the arena for the enactment of social drama (Turner 1974). This situation de-scribed by Sallnow fits the Nasca data better than Turner's model, especially in the later Nasca period when ritualized trophy-head taking becomes very important.

Sallnow (1981: 180; cf. also Poole cited above) also states that local identities are taken *along* on pilgrimage, seeing this as the cause of disharmony at the pilgrimage centers. I argue that these identities are enhanced *at* the cere-monial center and that it is precisely during the performance of rites, in the liminality of such a context, that hierarchical and structural changes in social organization can occur.

A shortcoming of Sallnow's work, however, is his lack of recognition of the significance of the final stage of social drama, that of reinte-gration or social recognition (Turner 1974: 37–42). This is when the changes in hierarchy that occurred at Cahuachi (and that could only oc-

cur there since during the rest of the time the component members of the larger social groups were in lesser contact with each other and dispersed over the landscape) became op-erational, at least until the next gathering and concomitant testing of the hierarchy estab-lished at the previous celebration.

Seen in this light, the enactment of social dramas at Cahuachi were political acts which, rather than solidifying a hierarchical social structure already in existence, may have served to inhibit its further institutionalization through the cyclical redistribution, if you will, of status. Comments by Poole on the role of dance in Andean pilgrimage and on the act of pilgrimage itself parallel our own political re-construction of early Nasca pilgrimage:

> . . .the religious and social transformation achieved through pilgrimage—a transformation itself closely related to *shifts in political ranking and prestige*—was specifically related to this jux-taposition of (a) movements along a straight line into a sacred precinct and (b) a spiral or circular movement around that center [Zuidema 1978] (Poole ms.: 28; my emphasis)

Through pilgrimage and ritual, early Nasca society was cyclically, periodically, and ephem-erally reordered. Each celebration at Cahua-chi provided the opportunity for the previous hierarchy to change. The crucial point to re-member is that there was hierarchy even if those occupying positions at the top of that hierarchy did not necessarily maintain their roles permanently. Personnel may have changed or deliberately rotated but a perma-nent hierarchy structure is posited to have ex-isted.

Morinis and Crumrine (ms.: 11) also em-phasize that the "artistic presentation of themes of pilgrimage in the context of pil-grimage performance serves to impress upon the audience of pilgrims the meaning of the activity in which they are participating . . ." (cf. also Maquet 1979: 30–31). The public perfor-mances at Cahuachi were not just religious but also political acts clothed in ritual and embody-ing Nasca ideology (cf. Webster 1976 and Silverman 1986: Part Three). Specifically insofar as ideology is concerned, recent Marxist archaeological literature has emphasized the role of ideology in the legitimization of relationships of social exploitation and domination, i.e., of the social order (cf. e.g., Braithwaite 1984; Tilley 1984; Patterson 1986 a, b). This public display of ideology and manipulation of ritual for demonstration of legitimacy is also a key point emphasized in Schele and Miller's (1986) pathbreaking interpretation of Maya culture. It is presumed to have operated similarly at Cahuachi.

8. From the above it follows that there could have been a hierarchy of architecture at Cahuachi based on the existence of differentially sized and endowed social groups. However, the difficulty of comparing large but lightly modified mounds to small but virtually solid adobe mounds has been mentioned. Furthermore, according to our model and the actual archaeological evidence encountered both by Strong and myself, various construction phases are represented in the distinct mounds at Cahuachi. To compare size of mounds as the criterion of hierarchy is to assume a synchrony which patently does not exist (cf. points 3, 10, 11, 12). The mounds grew over time and unevenly.

To these problems must be added the difficulty of assessing functional differences in the architecture of Cahuachi. I have noted (Silverman 1985a and above) a possibly significant aspect of architecture at Cahuachi which I call "compartmentalization" or roomed architecture. Most mounds at Cahuachi appear to have no surface subdivisions of space into activity areas (whatever their purpose might be) whereas other mounds evince the presence of rooms. Although most architecture at the site can be classified according to membership in one or the other group, the significance of such a distinction is not yet known.

Hence, it is not yet possible to talk of intra-site stratification at Cahuachi.

9. Related to points 7 and 8 is the question of political leadership and social hierarchy. Isbell (1977: 91), citing a native informant in Chuschi, defines *ayllu* as any group with a leader. The abilities of any particular *ayllu* leader would determine the fate of his group. A leader who could attract and hold many followers by manifesting great reciprocal generosity would be able to create a large social group and as a result he would dispose of the sufficient resources with which to build major constructions. But inasmuch as any individual person has overlapping group memberships, that leader could be abandoned by his group if he were not to perform adequately according to culturally defined standards. This is one possible political ramification of cognatic descent groups, particularly in the Andean context of a *señorio* (e.g., the political structure of the Chucuito polity in which reciprocal demands were made by the leader and the populace and in which the leader could be refused: cf. Garci Diez de San Miguel [1567] 1967).

10. Because new *ayllus* may be forming while old *ayllus* die out, and because these social groups change over time, agglutinative construction of a site and its component architecture rather than a single-phase master plan would be characteristic. The site would grow as new groups came into existence, and individual mounds would undergo accretionary growth and diachronic abandonment. The pervasive mound-and-plaza pattern at Cahuachi exists because the social groups are participating in the same tradition. The culturally prescribed spatial pattern is horizontally extended as new groups establish new foci at the site. Individual peculiarities of the distinct mounds reflect the lack of unitary control (religious or political) over these constructions (in contrast to the provincial temples of Pachacamac which, as indicated above, are totally replicative of a design) as well as naturally given differences at the commencement of building. Yet all mounds share certain features, not the least of which is their northward orientation, type of adobe construction, use of fills, frequent occurrence of patios, and a common association with plazas.

11. It is this diachronic accretion that accounts for the lack of precise site boundaries at Cahuachi. No physical markers indicate the

end of the site. Rather, the mound-and-plaza pattern simply peters out.

12. The two last points explain the filling-in of Cahuachi's surface areas as well as the increasing complexity of individual units of architecture over time (with new construction phases, abandoned portions of older buildings, etc.). Excavation at Unit 19 has permitted the delineation of the occupational history of one such particular mound. However, the brevity of Cahuachi's main occupation, its disturbed surface, and the secondary nature of construction fill material in the mounds defy, thus far, the chronologically precise elucidation of Cahuachi's overall occupational history and spatial pattern of growth despite the existence of a fine relative ceramic sequence for this period (Proulx 1968; Silverman 1977).

## CAHUACHI AND THE NAZCA LINES

Consideration of sacred space at and pilgrimage to Cahuachi cannot be divorced from the geoglyph-marked pampas north and south of the site and the traces of these on Cahuachi's own sacred ground (e.g., extending north from Unit GG). Examination of the geoglyphs is necessary to a proper understanding of Cahuachi. I argue that the pampas and Cahuachi together form a center of gravity and an irruption of the sacred for the near south coast (Ica, Río Grande drainage, Acarí) in the early Early Intermediate Period. Cahuachi was intimately and inextricably related to the pampas and was part of the same religious phenomenon.

In April 1985, architect José Pineda discovered, on the aerial photographs he was working with, a complex of geoglyphs immediately south of Cahuachi, on the Pampa de Atarco. He called my attention to these lines, indicating to me that some of them pointed directly at major mounds of Cahuachi (Fig. V.24). I had already observed (Silverman 1985a: 92) that the Camino de Leguia, the old Pan American Highway, is built over an

eleven-kilometer long Nazca line and points from Ingenio to Units VV-WW at Cahuachi (cf. also Williams 1980: 471; Fig. V.25; and cf. Chap. I, Fig. 1b; Chap. II, Fig. 1). In June 1985, so as to examine Pineda's discovery, I briefly foot surveyed the area behind Cahuachi with the help of José Pablo Baraybar and Sr. Armando Valdivia. I also flew over the pampa.

Access to the Pampa de Atarco, behind (south of) Cahuachi is gained by trekking up any of the gulleys (created by water erosion) that pockmark the site. One then walks past an irregular terrain of unmodified natural hills and quickly arrives on the flat pampa. The hills are separated from each other by little ravines. The hills vary from low ridges to high rises and are being eroded by the wind which decomposes the caliche outcrops into a soft, coarse sand covered by wind-blown gravel. From atop these hills behind the site, the view of the Pampa de Nazca on the north side of the Nazca River, opposite Cahuachi, is spectacular. Turning to the south, one can see Cerro Tunga, Cerro de Usaca and Cerro Uracangana where a marble mine operates. Local informants told me that with Cerro Blanco to the east, these are the sacred mountains of Nazca (cf. also Reinhard 1987).

Occasional single sherds and scarce concentrations of sherds from individual broken utilitarian vessels can be observed on some of the hills. The date of the utilitarian vessels could not be determined. The rare decorated pottery fragments that could be identified date to the late Middle Horizon and Late Intermediate Period.

At the base of one small ridge we observed a looted burial. It was superficial and had possibly been covered with the cobbles lying around the small looter's hole. The looter may not have excavated the whole burial; we did not continue the illicit excavation. The long bones, some ribs, and the pelvis are believed to belong to an adult male. The only material remains associated with this burial are a few scraps of discolored plainweave cotton cloth. This kind of unassociated, isolated, poor burial is reminiscent of three others (Burials 1,

11, 12) located at Cahuachi; they may be "bad deaths"[11] (cf., e.g., Uchendu 1965: 13).

The lines on the Pampa de Atarco are more easily seen from the air though many are visible from the surface. On the ground they show up as darker concentrations of small rocks on slight rises. These rises have been created by sweeping away the little rocks on the pampa surface to create the borders of the line. This is the same technique described by Maria Reiche (1968) for the geoglyphs on the main pampa. With the exception of one totally eroded Nasca sherd and three large, undiagnostic plainware sherds, there was no other ceramic material in the area surveyed. An interesting cultural feature, however, was a north-south alignment of five rock boulders on the east side of a curve of the great serpentine geoglyph seen on the plan. Seventy-two centimeters east of the southernmost boulder an obsidian flake was observed. As there are no other rocks of such size on this pampa, it is certain that the boulders have been deliberately carried in and set here, just on the west margin of a deep gulley running through the pampa at this point. Since obsidian is not native to Nazca (Burger and Asaro 1977), the flake was also either placed or dropped here.

As can be seen on the plan (Fig. V.24) and in the aerial photographs of this area, the lines cut across each other. There is the long, undulating line, narrow lines, small and large trapezoids, and trapezoids whose wide ends contain "garden beds." Garden beds are the piles of rocks within a cleared area and are the remains of geoglyphs that were not finished; Aveni (Chap. I) has observed that these rock piles are typically spaced an arm's length apart. A trapezoid can reach widths of 6 to 24 meters. Lines are much narrower. Interestingly, the lines go over slight rises on the otherwise flat surface of the plain. I believe these rises to be deliberate, man-made accumulations.

Clarkson (Chap. III, this volume) cogently argues that the Nazca *lines* are Middle Horizon and Late Intermediate Period in date while the *figures* of the main pampa pertain to the Early Intermediate Period; I independently and on other grounds reached the same conclusion (Silverman 1985b). I would now like to point out one possible major problem with both of our arguments: were the lines being kept ritually clean (cf. Urton, this volume), then earlier pottery would have been removed and only the most recent pottery would remain on the surface. Indeed, preliminary results of my 1988 survey in the Ingenio Valley suggest that the majority of lines, as well as figures, were made in Nasca (Early intermediate period) times. The presence of only Nasca pottery in association with the figures could mean that behavioral pattern was abandoned by the Middle Horizon whereas the lines (including lines, trapezoids, and ray centers) continued or began to be made. Hence, some lines are earlier than others and probably the intensity of line-making increased in the post-Nasca period. It is here argued that there is a connection of lines with Cahuachi, both during and after its apogee.

It is fairly simple to propose a model that would account for Nazca lines having some degree of relationship to an abandoned shrine. Although Cahuachi declined during Nasca 4 (in the sense of continued pace of monumental construction at the site), there is ceramic and other evidence for sporadic sub-

---

11. Bad deaths are those which do not conform to societally established and perceived norms. Such deaths might include early or untimely death and death by sorcery. Among the Igbo of southeast Nigeria such deceased individuals were not buried according to traditional custom but rather cast out (Uchendu 1965: 13). A sad contemporary Andean example of "bad death," harking back to pre-Columbian times, is the manner in which the eight Peruvian journalists massacred by Uchurrachay peasants were interred:

> The massacre had magical and religious overtones as well as political and social implications. The hideous wounds on the corpses were ritualistic. The eight bodies were buried in pairs, face down, the form of burial used for people the Iquichanos consider "devils"—people like the dancers of the *tijeras*, a folk dance, who are believed to make pacts with the Devil. They were buried outside the community limits to emphasize that they were strangers. (In the Andes, the Devil merges with the image of the stranger). The bodies were especially mutilated around the mouth and eyes, in the belief that the victim should be deprived of his sight, so he cannot recognize his killers, and of his tongue, so he cannot denounce them. Their ankles were broken, so they could not come back for revenge. The villagers had stripped the bodies; they washed the clothes and burned them in a purification ceremony known as *pichja*.). (Vargas Llosa 1983: 50)

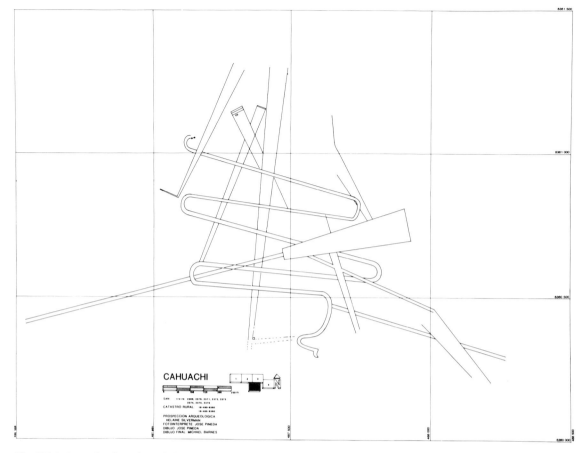

Fig. V.24. José Pineda's plan of the lines behind Cahuachi. This plan aligns with our Figures 3 and 4 as indicated in Pineda's key.

sequent use. A Nasca 4 vessel had been left as an offering along the north side of a wall at the base of Unit 19. In level 2 of the Unit 16 area excavations (a stratum postdating construction of the wall), various fragments of a fancy Nasca 5 vessel were discovered. A Nasca 5 sherd was in the fill underlying the cist in Room 1 of Unit 19 into which a trophy head had been placed. Strong's Burial Area 1 produced at least 30 vessels, ranging in style from Nasca 5 to early Nasca 6 (cf. Strong 1957: Fig. 14). The Room of the Posts on Unit 19 was ritually buried by Nasca 8 people and a Nasca 8 grave was also excavated by Doering (1958) at Cahuachi. Most of the cemeteries in the open areas at Cahuachi date to the Middle Horizon and Late Intermediate Period. Thus, even after Cahuachi no longer served as the principal early Nasca religious shrine, it still retained enough prestige to attract dedicatory offerings and serve as a sacred burial ground.

The lines in the Pampa de Nazca and Pampa de Atarco, therefore, do not have to date to Cahuachi's heyday. They can indicate continued, albeit intermittent and small-scale use of Cahuachi after its decline. Those lines

Fig. V.25. The Camino de Leguia was built over this long Nazca line between Cahuachi, in the Nazca Valley, and the Ingenio Valley. We are looking toward Ingenio.

which point at Cahuachi would indicate recognition of its continued sacredness.

I believe, however, that certain lines did function contemporaneously with Cahuachi. Not only are there lines which point at Cahuachi but from certain mounds at Cahuachi, especially Units 1 and 13, there is a superb view of the Pampa de Nazca opposite Cahuachi, the pampa on which the majority of the lines and figures are found and where Aveni's line centers tend to cluster (cf. Aveni, Chap. II, Fig. V.1, this volume). Furthermore, an association of lines with Cahuachi can be argued on the basis of the relationship of both with the act of prediction. Archaeologist Bernardino Ojeda, a native bilingual speaker of Spanish and Quechua, glosses Cahuachi as *qhawachi* meaning "make them see, make them observe, note, look." He interpets the word as indicating "an act which obliges someone to observe" (Ojeda, personal communication). Sergio Chavez, also a Peruvian bilingual archaeologist, likewise glosses Cahuachi as "when you go and make somebody look at something for you, to predict, to be able to see something" (Chavez, personal communication). Chavez also told me that "if you have bad luck you say you have *qhawachi*."

Zuidema (1982: 427), citing Guaman Poma (1980: 263, 264) has observed that the "health of the [Inka] king and his government was in direct correlation to his knowledge of *hucha* [sin] and to his ability to remove it from any part of his territory. . . ." To know *hucha* the Inka king, Tupa Yupanqui, consulted with twelve *huacas* to know or learn about the past and future. As we have seen, the glosses of Cahuachi also have a predictive or foretelling semantic connotation. This ability of the Inka king to know what a normal person cannot know is analogous to what occurs over the horizon. Here a comparison can be drawn between this invisible, temporally linear knowledge and *ceques* that can extend over the visible horizon. Zuidema (personal communication) suggests that this could tie in to shamans who, on their hallucinogenic journeys to get knowledge of distant places and times, go "over the horizon" and then return.

I suggest that there is a semantic and physical relationship between *ceque* and *cachahui* (both as used by Zuidema below) and Cahuachi. Of all the many functions ascribed to the lines (e.g., Reiche 1968; Kosok 1965; Mejía Xesspe 1940; Morrison 1978; Hawkins 1969; Reinhard 1985), theories which are not all mutally exclusive, perhaps the most satisfying is that which we can draw from Zuidema's (1964, 1973a, 1982) discussion of *ceques*.

Zuidema (1973a: 29) emphasizes the nature of *ceque* as "line." In the case of the *ceque* system of Cuzco, lines were not physically visible tracings but rather straight directions over which, in the latter case, a human sacrifice (*capac hucha*) would travel. From Molina's 1573 account, Zuidema (1982: 431) is able to discern three contexts of *ceques*:

> The first is composed of the offerings, *ceque* or *cachahui*, that are in direct visual contact to the *huaca* that is worshipped. The second context is that of the *ceque* system of Cuzco. Here the *ceques* are sightlines covering the whole valley, and because of their longer extension, various *huacas* as *cachahuis* are organized along each *ceque*. . . . In this case certain *ceques* went beyond the immediate horizon. . . . The third context is that of the *capac hucha*. Here the visual connection is expanded by the act of the *acclla* actually travelling as a *cachahui* ("messenger" or *ceque*) between two distant points . . . travelling in a straight line. . . .

Zuidema (ibid: 431) also mentions data of the seventeenth century chronicler, Murua, which indicate pilgrimages by priests who would, like the *capac hucha*, walk straight.

With the possibly unique exception of the long, curving line south of Cahuachi and, of course, the figures themselves, the Nazca lines are quintessentially straight. Furthermore, we have seen that some of the Nazca lines point right at Cahuachi, specifically Units 1 and 2 from the Pampa de Atarco (cf. Fig. V.24 which is south of and whose grid lines up with Fig. V.2) and Units VV-WW from the Pampa de Nazca (cf. Aveni 1986: 37 bottom figure). Other alignments could probably be found.

Aveni (1986), basing himself on Zuidema's research into the *ceques* and reviving Mejía

Xesspe's (1940) original notion of the lines as sacred roads, cogently argues that the Nazca lines functioned like the *ceque* system of Cuzco (Zuidema 1964). In other words, the Nazca lines were myriad religio-political phenomena: they were sacred roads across a sacred terrain (an end in itself) and to Cahuachi and functioned as routes of pilgrimage; they were the recording of an astronomical calendar which was used in ecological regulation as well as to order the performance of ritual; they were a "highly ordered hierarchical cosmographical map, a mnemonic scheme that incorporated virtually all important matters connected with the [Nazca] world view" (Aveni 1986: 37); they were *chhiuta* and *mit'a* (cf. Urton 1984) with a particular Nazca line possibly pertaining to a certain social group (Aveni [1986: 39] suggests that a particular line could have been assigned to its walkers); they are related to water sources (Reinhard 1985); and, finally, the ray centers as places of convergence may have been important places of worship or sacrifice.

If we accept the *ceque* nature of the Nazca lines, then a connection with Cahuachi becomes even more likely. It can be suggested that Cahuachi was the locus, among other things, for ceremonial activities involving prediction. The priests, as is suggested by Nasca iconography, probably had a shamanic-divining character. It would not be unreasonable to suggest that their foretelling activities were largely (but not exclusively) concerned with agricultural fertility, particularly the regularity and sufficiency of water with which to irrigate this desert zone. The regular periodicity of rain had to have been of great concern to the entire Nazca region and rituals designed to predict and ensure adequate water supply must have involved the situational participation of the largest group of people possible in contrast to rites of a more specific nature. I have argued that Nasca society was organized into cognatic descent groups. In the situational context of rites of agricultural fertility which affected the entire social group, it is highly likely that the entire social entity participated or was represented. Thus, it is of in-

terest to note the harvest festival scene textiles illustrated and described by Alan Sawyer (1979) in which the participation of hundreds of farmers is shown.

Prediction surely involved the observation of natural phenomena: the skies, the movement of heavenly bodies, animals, plants. Some lines have an astronomical orientation (Phyllis Pitluga, personal communication; cf. Kosok 1965: Chap. 6). It can be suggested that the Nasca priest-scientists observed the natural and supernatural world from Cahuachi and from the pampa. The pampa, with its lines, and Cahuachi, with its mounds, are part of a unitary religious complex in which observation for the purpose of prediction was a principal activity. Indeed, Reinhard (1985) proposes a direct relationship between the Nazca lines, mountain deities, rainfall, water supply and agricultural fertility. His theory is completely congruent with the views expressed here.

The coordination and scheduling of religious activities performed by the social groups comprising Nasca society could have been by means of a ritual calendar. This ritual calendar (a *ceque* system) is reflected on the pampa. It can be suggested that each line (*chhiuta*: cf. Urton 1984) was made at its proper moment of time (*mit'a* in the sense of fulfilling a ritual obligation) by a distinct social group (*ayllu*). This is analogous to Zuidema's (1982: 428) observation that the *huacas* of the *ceque* system and *huacas* in general represented the distinct sociopolitical units that worshipped there (cf. also Lathrap 1985: 252). Each *ayllu* or social group was responsible for its *huaca* and was, concomitantly, related to a *ceque*. If, following Lathrap (ibid.), each *huaca* is, at the same time, an *ushnu*, then each Nazca line is *ushnu*/opening, *huaca*/temple, temporal social group signifier, and ritual organizer.

Kosok (1965: Chap. 6) referred to the Pampa de Nazca as the "world's largest astronomy book." The analogy with *book* is a proper one for, indeed, in order to predict, knowledge has to be accumulated through empirically repetitive experiences (experiments) and then stored. The knowledge involved with

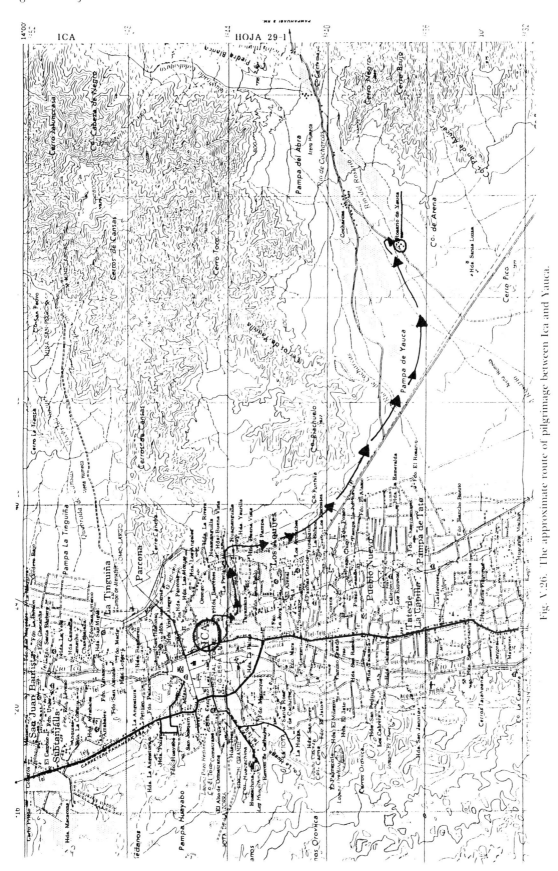

Fig. V.26. The approximate route of pilgrimage between Ica and Yauca.

prediction was being *written* (physically recorded) on the pampa. The pampa was a *text* that was *read*. The text was the product of many *words* (social groups), all of which were necessary to create the composite story. To read the *lines* (both senses of the word), the text had be *clearly* understandable. Phyllis Pitluga (personal communication) has observed that on the pampa some lines are more easily seen than others (they are brighter) and she attributes this to the practice of sweeping the lines by ancient peoples. Both Urton (this volume) and I agree that the lines were being kept ritually clean (cf. also Burger and Salazar-Burger 1985 on the sweeping or maintaining clean of ritual areas). Pitluga adds a pragmatic dimension to this sweeping. Not only was the sweeping of the Nazca lines a religious act involving distinct social groups but, at the same time, this sweeping aided the reading of the appropriate text by *highlighting* the relevant one so that one would not "read between the lines" (read extraneous matter no longer pertinent). The confusing proliferation of lines we see today is the result of the repetitive enactment of a ritual calendar based on astronomical prediction in which the lines were made to record the data (astronomical, social) necessary for such activity and at the same time serve as the loci for these activities.

With the decline of Cahuachi the locus of major ("big tradition," in a sense) religious activity shifted exclusively to the pampa. There

the pattern of cyclical use of the pampa for observation and recording as well as for the performance of other (related) sociopolitical-religious rites continued to evolve resulting in the confusing profusion of lines we see today.

These thoughts tie in very well with the idea, expressed earlier, that certain human behavior can transform the natural world into a cultural world. Just as I have argued that the two major walls of Cahuachi, Units 4 and 16, served to delineate one kind of space from another, so too it can be argued that the very act of making the lines served to transform the natural terrain into cultural terrain and, in this case, sacred terrain.

To draw a wall around an area is to bring it within one's sphere of control. At Cahuachi, where the artificial mounds are basically not much different from the unmodified natural hills around them, this "bringing within" was a necessary cultural act to create social space. Likewise, the tracing of the lines on the empty pampa surface brought this space within the human sphere, domesticated it so to speak. The pampa thus ceased to be a physical no-man's land (Eliade's vast expanse) and obstacle to be crossed so as to reach Cahuachi, but rather became an integral part of Nasca religion and the pilgrimage route. While crossing

Fig. V.27b. Low aerial view of Units K (left) and A (right). Unit K is one of the major truncated mounds of Cahuachi yet clearly its terraced north face was elaborated over the natural hill. Unit A is a largely unmodified, sprawling natural hill where Kroeber located a series of Nasca 3 graves in 1926. Note the adobe wall running along the east side of Unit A and turning left (to the east) toward Unit K.

Fig. V.27a. Looking east at Unit 2, Strong's Great Temple.

# FREQUENCY DISTRIBUTION OF EXCAVATED SHERDS
## (excluding those from Room of the Posts)

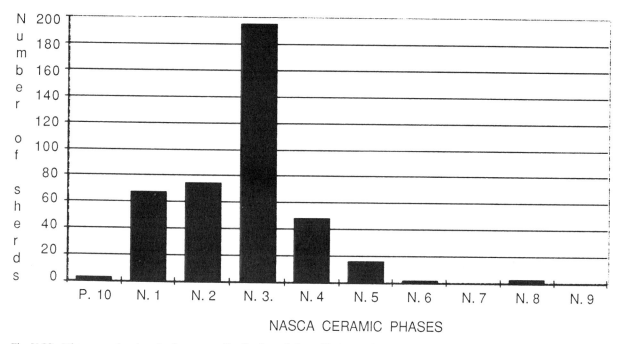

Fig. V.28. Histogram showing the frequency distribution of phaseable Nasca sherds recovered in excavations at Cahuachi. Clearly indicated is the Nasca 3 apogee of the site and subsequent dramatic decline in Nasca 4.

it, human beings entered the liminal phase that transformed them from the ordinary people they were to the ritual social beings they would become when they arrived at the sacred site of Cahuachi. It is quite likely that this transformation was achieved by dressing up, dancing, trancing, and masking, for which there is ample iconographic evidence as well as modern practice. Thus, in a comparison of the properties of Andean dance to the act of pilgrimage itself Poole (n.d.: 31) suggests that:

(a) the use and display of these hierarchical, spatial, and transformational principles in dance parallels and recursively reinforms the importance of these same abstract principles in the pilgrimage rituals which present the context for dance performance; and (b) that the ritualized movement of Andean pilgrimage derives much of its coherence and meaning as a religious, devotional act from these dances in which the formal characteristics of pilgrimage are presented in the entertaining, emotive, anonymous (masked) and artistic form of dance.

Morinis and Crumrine note (n.d.: 9) that "Patterns of human movement in pilgrimage are seen to take on cosmological significance, as journeys to shrines are identified with macrocosmic cycles of movement among the astral bodies." The Nasca and Nazca lines must be understood in the terms presented above.

Thus, we have a conjunction of factors that can explain why Cahuachi is where it is and, concomitantly, what it is. Cahuachi is a site of natural *huacas*. It is a place where water magically comes to the surface, even when the river is dry (as it is most of the year and sometimes year after year). And, it is connected to and on the edge of the pampas which played an integral role in early and later Nasca and Nazca religion as routes of communication with the valleys north and south of Cahuachi on which ceremonial pathways were traced. As such Cahuachi, with the adjacent pampas, forms an irruption of the sacred, an axis mundi, and a sacred conduit.

ACKNOWLEDGMENTS

The fieldwork on which this article is based was supported by generous grants from the National Science Foundation, Fulbright-Hays Act, Social Science Research Council, and the Institute of Latin American Studies at the University of Texas at Austin. The fieldwork in Peru was carried out under permit R.S. 165-84-ED in collaboration with the National Institute of Culture and the National Museum of Anthropology. All these institutions are warmly thanked for their help and coopera-tion. I am most especially grateful to my friend and colleague, Lic. Miguel Pazos Ri-vera, for his participation in the project. I also extend my thanks to Frances Hayashida, José Pablo Baraybar, Dennis Scott, Juan Antonio Murro, and José Pineda for their valuable as-sistance during different stages of the field-work. This article benefited from extended conversations with Tom Zuidema, Alma Gott-lieb, and Enrique Mayer. I, of course, am solely responsible for its final form and con-tent.

# VI. A Statistical Examination of the Radial Line Azimuths at Nazca

**Clive L.N. Ruggles**

## INTRODUCTION

The remarkable network of lines and interconnected line centers at Nazca is so extensive that we might hope to learn something of its purpose from a statistical study of the line azimuths. With this hope in mind Aveni supplied me with the available data on the azimuths and other characteristics of lines emanating from line centers (see Tables 2 & 3 in Chapter II of this volume). These data are of particular interest in view of the apparent importance of radial patterning in Andean cultures and of the possible links between the Nazca line centers and the later Inkaic *ceques* and *quipus*. In Chapter II Aveni has described the data in some detail and presented a first analysis in the light of hypotheses of possible relevance to the nature of Andean radial systems. In what follows I shall describe an attempt to take the analysis of the radial azimuth data somewhat further, drawing upon experience gained from statistical studies of the orientations of British prehistoric sites, work in which I have been involved for some years. Since the cultural context and many of the relevant hypotheses are described elsewhere in this volume, I shall concentrate more in this chapter upon the methods of analysis and the results obtained.

In the following section some general remarks are made about the strengths and limitations of the statistical approach, and about the lessons which can be drawn from studying British megalithic astronomy. I then proceed to a general description of the data at my disposal, followed by various analyses of these data. The conclusions are summarized in the final section.

## BACKGROUND

*Strengths and Limitations of the Statistical Approach*

The basic strength of the statistical approach is that it can help us isolate important trends among large quantities of data. Its basic weakness, when applied to the activities of human beings (rather than, for example, the physical properties of the universe), is that human behavior follows no hard-and-fast rules. Even the most widely accepted practices will be subject to the idiosyncracies of some individuals, the sheer perversity of others, conflicts with co-existing practices and attempts to compromise, and change with time. A statistical approach can hope to do no more than elicit general overall trends—if they exist.

The application of statistical techniques to archaeological problems is fraught with difficulties, and can arouse controversy and suspicion. The naive use of standard statistical tests is often misguided: they have been designed to cope with particular commonly arising situations, but most archaeological applications are far more complex. In order to do anything meaningful we must certainly probe more deeply.

One of the major problems is that few statistical approaches can take into account the wider and rather intangible background evidence which is essential to the final interpretation of a set of archaeological data in their cultural context. Can—and indeed should—statistical inference about a particular set of data take account of "prior information" accumulated from (subjective) experience not directly related to the data in hand? Different attitudes to this problem underlie a fundamental division amongst professional statisticians today (Barnett 1982).

The "classical" school, on the one hand, is concerned with estimation, tests of significance, and hypothesis testing. In classical inference we test a working (basic, null) hypothesis in order to decide whether to accept or reject it. The classical approach dictates that a concept of probability can only be adequately defined, and a statistical theory developed, for information obtained in a repetitive situation (potentially at least, if not practically)—i.e., observed outcomes from what are assumed to be independent repetitions of a situation under identical circumstances. It provides no statistical procedures capable of processing prior information accumulated from past (or external) experience.

The "Bayesian" school, on the other hand, maintains that inferences are made by combining an assessment of the state of knowledge and the practical situation. The state of knowledge is expressed in terms of the probability distribution of the parameters of a model "prior" to the current situation being taken into account, which is then modified by sample data arising from the current situation. The inferences are expressed (solely) by the posterior distribution of those same parameters.[1]

In previous work on British material (Ruggles 1984a), I have adopted a classical approach to the analysis of azimuth data, while attempting to pinpoint the most serious shortcomings. Perhaps the trickiest of these is that we may end up in effect testing a number of different hypotheses on the same data, thus rendering significance levels quite misleading—at least if they are interpreted literally.[2] More recently I have argued (Ruggles 1986d) that the Bayesian approach appears to have considerable conceptual advantages over the classical approach in many archaeological applications. It remains, however, to demonstrate that the Bayesian approach does have practical potential within archaeology. Thus here a classical approach, similar to that applied to the British material, has been followed. An attempt will be made in a further publication to apply a practical Bayesian ap-

proach to both the British and the Nazca azimuth data (Ruggles and Hills, in preparation).

As Barnett (1982) points out: "We can never expect any universal agreement on what constitutes a proper and correct approach to statistical inference. Subjective and personal elements must always remain." One fact, however, is not in dispute: it is that if a statistical analysis is to have any meaning at all *the data to be analyzed must be collected in a manner (demonstrably) free of any form of subjective bias* which would influence the result of the subsequent analysis. In practice, the selection of data often (and rightly) generates far more discussion than details of the method of analysis of those data.

In general terms, any statistical approach to archaeological data should perhaps be seen as complementary to other approaches, including "deduction by inspection." Its emphasis on rigor of selection and objective analysis may serve to dampen one's enthusiasm for too rampant speculation; on the other hand, when we are dealing with the complex, unpredictable, and often perverse activities of human beings, any attempt to restrict conclusions to those rigorously deducible on statistical grounds will be bound to miss evidence which could be picked up by subjective deductions in the light of cultural background knowledge. In this, we disagree with Hawkins (1969), who felt that "no matter what hypothesis is finally adopted, we must expect an almost total explanation for the lines," and strongly support the multidisciplinary approach favored by the other contributors to this volume. At the same time, we feel that attempts at rigorous analyses are important, and that their conclusions should color the wider-based and more subjective assessments of the evidence at hand.

*Analyzing Azimuths: Lessons from Studies of Megalithic Astronomy*

The idea of analyzing the orientations of prehistoric structures is well known from studies of the freestanding megalithic sites—stone rings, alignments, and single standing

---

1. Supporters of the Bayesian approach maintain that classical inference is inappropriate because (among other things) its view of probability is subjective, the choice of significance levels (which determine the results of hypothesis tests) are arbitrary, and it takes no account of prior knowledge; its opponents, on the other hand, draw attention to the intangibility of prior information and hence the difficulty in specifying prior probabilities; they also point out that practical demonstrations of the Bayesian method are few and far between.
2. A method that I have used (e.g., Ruggles 1984a) is actually to perform multiple testing, calculating the significance levels as if for each test in isolation, but then reducing the apparent significance level at which we are prepared to reject the null hypothesis in favor of any one of them. It must be understood, however, that there is no theoretical justification for this procedure and no reliable estimate for the extent to which the apparent significance levels need to be reduced, although Freeman and Elmore (1979) have given some guidelines. All it really enables one to do is to draw attention to the lowest significance levels obtained, and hence to the "most likely" astronomical hypotheses. The machinery to cope adequately with this problem within a classical framework is basically lacking.

stones—found in the British Isles. The main motivation for most of this work is the idea that many of these monuments might have had an astronomical significance. While the "megalithic astronomy" debate has until recently largely comprised arguments about the interpretation of a few individual sites, most notably Stonehenge (for a balanced account, see Heggie 1981), the most valuable evidence has come from the extensive work of Alexander Thom (see Thom 1967, 1971; and Thom and Thom 1978). In a series of analyses of putative horizon indications from a number of sites taken together, Thom accumulated evidence of deliberate astronomical alignments of ever greater precision. Many sites were, he claims, solar and lunar "observatories" using distant, natural horizon foresights such as notches, indicated by structures on the ground, to mark the complex motions of the sun and moon to a precision as great as a mere minute or two of arc.

A detailed reassessment of Thom's conclusions (Ruggles 1981, 1982b, 1983) has focused attention upon the selection of data. Freestanding megalithic sites come in a variety of forms, some complex, and one must decide at each site what constitutes an orientation worthy of consideration. It is of paramount importance to avoid making a series of individual decisions in the field, decisions which might vary from site to site and be influenced by one's own particular predilections and prejudices about the possible astronomical significance of the sites. The reassessment has drawn attention to many hidden selection effects in Thom's data and cast severe doubts on the idea that the sites were associated with high-precision solar and lunar observations. Independently, other authors such as Ellegård (1981) have drawn attention to the extreme practical difficulties in making some of the high-precision observations claimed, particularly in the case of the moon. Yet others have argued against "scientific" astronomy in ancient Britain by pointing out the dangers of ethnocentrism—that is, of unwittingly projecting our own motives and goals onto an alien culture, by seeking out what is of particular

interest to us and tending to ignore other, perhaps more mundane, cultural evidence: thus the astronomer sees ancient astronomers, the engineer sees ancient engineers, and so on.

In recent years the emphasis in prehistoric Britain has changed considerably. A number of investigations have now been undertaken in which astronomy is considered as merely one of a number of possible factors influencing site placement and orientation. At the same time statistical investigations have continued, but with an emphasis on the fair selection of data and on producing reliable evidence which can be fed into the wider archaeological equation. Thus in a study of some 300 western Scottish sites, based on fieldwork undertaken over eight years (Ruggles 1984a), rigorous criteria were established and adhered to in selecting sites and structures for consideration.

Recent work has produced a good deal of evidence that astronomical considerations *were* indeed a factor in laying out some of the prehistoric burial and ceremonial sites in Britain, though at a much cruder level than was envisaged by Thom. Astronomical observations, it is now generally felt, would have formed part of ritual and ceremonial practices, rather than having a "scientific" significance for the megalith builders. This is probably the light in which we should view the established facts that the sun's rays around the winter solstice would have penetrated to the center of the large chambered tombs at Newgrange in Ireland (Patrick 1974) and Maes Howe in Orkney (Burl 1981), and possibly explains the general axial orientation of Stonehenge towards sunrise around the summer solstice.

The study of 300 western Scottish sites mentioned above, corroborated by more detailed work in mid-Argyll and the island of Mull (Ruggles 1985), as well as by an investigation of the fifty "Recumbent Stone Circles" (RSCs) of eastern Scotland (Ruggles 1984b; Ruggles and Burl 1985) lends considerable support to the idea that astronomical, and particularly lunar, orientations were incorporated in a variety of megalithic ceremonial sites. But there is no simple, all-embracing explanation for any particular group of sites, even where their designs are superficially similar. At the RSCs, for example, there seems to be evidence of conflicting concerns such as lunar orientation, orientation upon conspicuous hilltops, and a desire for the large recumbent stone to face due south. We should also bear in mind the other factors that would inevitably have influenced the siting of a ceremonial center: the territory available to a particular set of builders, the desire to avoid prime agricultural land and so on.

The main lessons from prehistoric Britain, then, might be summarized as follows:

(1)  statistical investigations have an important place in more general cultural enquiries;

(2)  the selection of data is of paramount importance; and

(3)  it is dangerous to consider a single factor (such as astronomy) in isolation.

A fuller description of the British developments during the last five years is given in a recent review article (Ruggles 1984c).

## THE NATURE OF THE NAZCA DATA AND THEIR SELECTION

The data available on Nazca for analysis comprised information on a total of 516 lines radiating from 43 of the 62 documented line centers. The information for each line consisted of

(1)  the azimuth;

(2)  the quality of measurement (and hence the accuracy) of the quoted azimuth (Quality 1 or 2);

(3)  the width category (Wide or Narrow); and

(4)  whether it is a connector (Yes, No, or Possibly).

For connectors and possible connectors we were also given

(5)  the line center it (possibly) connects with;

and for connectors we were given

(6)  the straightness (Straight or Non-Straight).

See Aveni (Chap. II, Table 3, Note 1) for a discussion of the quality categories of these data (Quality 3 data are excluded).

The process by which these data were acquired has been described in detail elsewhere in this volume (Chapter II). This process is important, for while subjective decisions are inevitable, it is important to document them as fully as possible and to demonstrate that they have not resulted in the data being biased in favor of any particular hypothesis. In general terms, the boundaries of the mapped area were expanded by walking lines, pacing, and taking magnetic compass readings. When new line centers were discovered, a survey team was sent in to obtain more accurate theodolite measurements, including the azimuths of the radial lines. The mapping was undertaken as thoroughly and accurately as possible. The overall aim was to obtain, where possible, a comprehensive survey of the line centers. Thus whether a given line center was selected for accurate survey, and hence whether quality measurements are available, is unrelated to any particular hypothesis concerning the radial azimuths. The choice of width categories, the classification of lines as connectors, possible connectors or non-connectors, and the identification of lines as straight or otherwise, are all justifiable in a similar manner.

## PATTERNING IN THE NAZCA DATA

Many of the statistical procedures to be employed during the analyses that follow have been applied in the study of 300 western Scottish sites (see Ruggles 1984a: Chap. 12 for details). There are, however, two major factors which allow a considerable simplification when we consider the Nazca as opposed to the British material.

(1) There are far fewer problems in demonstrating the fair selection of data, since at Nazca we are dealing with *all* lines radiating from readily identifiable line centers. There are some problems, which will be discussed in the following section, but they are minor compared with the British case.

(2) When we compare astronomical and other, geographical and environmental, explanations for particular orientations, the astronomical ones need to take into account not only the azimuth of the structure in question but also the altitude of the horizon. At high latitudes, as in Britain, this effect is crucial (see, e.g., Ruggles 1982a: 96–99), but in the tropics the heavenly bodies rise and set almost vertically, so that the horizon altitude has relatively little effect and we can compare astronomical and other explanations directly on the basis of the azimuths alone.

## *The Overall Distribution of Radial Line Azimuths at Nazca*

A pure "classical" approach to the statistical analysis might maintain that we should take no account of subjective evidence external to the data in hand, and so it is of some interest to examine at the outset where such an approach would lead us. Basically, it has us trying to see whether we can spot any significant patterns *per se* among the data in hand.

We wish to check whether there is overall evidence of a non-random pattern in the radial azimuths. A number of statistical tests are available, but a particularly useful one is that of Neave and Selkirk (1983). This considers a set of points distributed on a circle (or, equivalently, a set of azimuths) and tests the hypothesis that they are randomly distributed against the alternative hypothesis of clustering or over-regularity. If the null (random) hypothesis is rejected, the test tells us whether

this is because of clustering or over-regularity, although it does not give any further details about the nature of either. The "test statistic" used ($t$) is the sum of the differences between each azimuth and its nearest neighbor, divided by 360 if the angles are measured in degrees. The expected value of $t$ under the random hypothesis is 0.5, but it may take any value between 0 and 1. Small values indicate clustering, whereas large values indicate an unnatural degree of regularity.

The resulting value of $t$ for the Nazca radial azimuth data as a whole (516 data points) is 0.484, insufficiently low to provide significant evidence of clustering, even at the 10 percent level. We have also performed separate analyses with connectors only, connectors and possible connectors only, and non-connectors only. The results are listed at the top of Table 1.[3]

## *Individual Line Centers*

When we consider individual line centers, however, then some results of apparent significance are obtained. The Neave-Selkirk test was applied to each line center for which azimuth data were available, and the results are listed in the remainder of Table 1. In the column marked '% pt' we note the corresponding percentage point of the standard normal distribution, a figure which is reliable when the number of azimuths $n$ is 30 or more, but which only provides an increasingly crude ap-

---

3. There is a slight problem here, since the Neave-Selkirk test assumes that each azimuth value is independent of all the rest, whereas lines which connect two line centers will actually generate two values exactly 180° apart (if they are straight) or generally near to 180° apart (otherwise). When a data set consists *entirely* of opposite pairs of azimuths, as would be the case with straight connectors, it is possible to take account of the fact by simply halving the assumed number of data points when we assess the significance of $t$ (Ruggles 1984a: Appendix II). The "near-opposite" pairs are a more serious problem. Thus in the case of connectors only, and of connectors and possible connectors only, we have run the test twice, once assuming single independent azimuths and once assuming opposite pairs. The true result should fall between the two obtained in this way, and since neither shows any evidence of clustering, we can safely conclude that there *is* no significant evidence of clustering amongst these data.

TABLE 1
Neave-Selkirk statistics for Nazca raw azimuth data.

| Subset | $n$ | $t$ | % pt | SL(clus) | SL(reg) |
|---|---|---|---|---|---|
| All data | 516 | 0.484 | −0.87 | — | — |
| Connectors only | 68 | 0.455 | −0.92 | — | — |
| Connectors only (PAIRS) | 34 | 0.422 | −1.13 | — | — |
| Connectors and possible connectors only | 113 | 0.473 | −0.71 | — | — |
| Connectors and possible connectors only (PAIRS) | 56 | 0.499 | −0.02 | — | — |
| Non-connectors only | 403 | 0.483 | −0.81 | — | — |
| Line center 4 | 7 | 0.385 | (−0.80) | — | — |
| Line center 11 | 9 | 0.466 | (−0.26) | — | — |
| Line center 12 | 13 | 0.236 | (−2.42) | 1% | — |
| Line center 16 | 10 | 0.484 | (−0.13) | — | — |
| Line center 17 | 17 | 0.448 | (−0.55) | — | — |
| Line center 19 | 9 | 0.151 | (−2.71) | 0.5% | — |
| Line center 20 | 7 | 0.480 | (−0.14) | — | — |
| Line center 21 | 10 | 0.455 | (−0.37) | — | — |
| Line center 22 | 6 | 0.536 | (+0.24) | — | — |
| Line center 23 | 6 | 0.461 | (−0.25) | — | — |
| Line center 24 | 2 | 0.115 | (−1.64) | — | — |
| Line center 25 | 4 | 0.098 | (−2.20) | 2.5% | — |
| Line center 26 | 9 | 0.378 | (−0.94) | — | — |
| Line center 27 | 3 | 0.333 | (−0.82) | — | — |
| Line center 30 | 10 | 0.480 | (−0.16) | — | — |
| Line center 31 | 8 | 0.560 | (+0.44) | — | — |
| Line center 33 | 11 | 0.282 | (−1.85) | 5% | — |
| Line center 34 | 9 | 0.305 | (−1.51) | 10% | — |
| Line center 35 | 35 | 0.497 | −0.04 | — | — |
| Line center 36 | 9 | 0.104 | (−3.07) | 0.5% | — |
| Line center 37 | 10 | 0.438 | (−0.50) | — | — |
| Line center 38 | 10 | 0.381 | (−0.97) | — | — |
| Line center 40 | 10 | 0.384 | (−0.94) | — | — |
| Line center 41 | 8 | 0.482 | (−0.14) | — | — |
| Line center 42 | 10 | 0.260 | (−1.95) | 5% | — |
| Line center 43 | 8 | 0.260 | (−1.77) | 5% | — |
| Line center 44 | 50 | 0.434 | −1.15 | — | — |
| Line center 45 | 19 | 0.518 | (+0.20) | — | — |
| Line center 46 | 20 | 0.301 | (−2.23) | 2.5% | — |
| Line center 47 | 18 | 0.207 | (−3.13) | 0.5% | — |
| Line center 48 | 12 | 0.199 | (−2.66) | 0.5% | — |
| Line center 50 | 20 | 0.367 | (−1.49) | 10% | — |
| Line center 51 | 3 | 0.684 | (+0.90) | — | — |
| Line center 53 | 11 | 0.137 | (−3.08) | 0.5% | — |
| Line center 54 | 9 | 0.515 | (+0.11) | — | — |
| Line center 55 | 13 | 0.190 | (−2.84) | 0.5% | — |
| Line center 56 | 20 | 0.626 | (+1.42) | — | 10% |
| Line center 57 | 8 | 0.262 | (−1.75) | 5% | — |
| Line center 58 | 17 | 0.787 | (+2.99) | — | 0.5% |
| Line center 59 | 3 | 0.625 | (+0.61) | — | — |
| Line center 60 | 9 | 0.603 | (+0.80) | — | — |
| Line center 61 | 26 | 0.797 | (+3.78) | — | 0.5% |
| Line center 62 | 8 | 0.524 | (+0.18) | — | — |

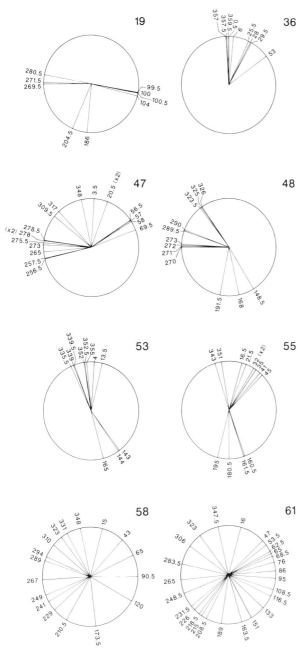

Fig. VI.1. Distribution of Azimuths of Lines in Selected Line Centers.

line centers[4] and evidence of over-regularity is obtained at three.[5]

It is particularly interesting that we obtain strong evidence of over-regularity at two line centers, Nos. 58 and 61. The distribution of the radial line azimuths at these line centers is shown schematically in Fig. VI.1. The over-regularity seems to imply that each of these centers and their radial lines were deliberately constructed according to a single plan which involved the line directions being spread fairly uniformly around the compass. If radial lines had been added in a more random manner, then any such pattern would soon have been upset. Furthermore, any selection effects due to our inability to retrieve all the original data—i.e., if we have missed any lines—would be highly unlikely to preserve the regular pattern. Thus we can be reasonably sure that we have spotted all the original lines.

It is also intriguing that such evidence seems to be confined to a single corner of the pampa. The line centers involved, Nos. 58 and 61—together with the one yielding weak evidence of over-regularity, No. 56—are all located in the northwestern part of the pampa toward its northern edge by the Ingenio Valley. A closer inspection of the results in Table 1 shows that the three line centers somewhat farther to the south, Nos. 59, 60 and 62, also yield *t* values above 0.5, deviating in the direction of over-regularity from the mean value which we would expect if lines had been set out without regard for their orientation. This property of the line centers in the northwestern part of the pampa seems to single them out from the remainder found elsewhere, which tend to exhibit clustering rather than over-regularity. (Contrast, for example, the behavior of the group in the northeastern extremity of the pampa, Nos. 42, 43, 44, 46 and 47.)

proximation for smaller *n*. If there is significant evidence of clustering or over-regularity at the 10%, 5%, 2.5%, 1% or 0.5% level, then the lowest of these is quoted in the relevant column. Significance levels were determined using Neave and Selkirk's own table (1983: Table 1) where *n* < 30, and from tables of the standard normal distribution otherwise.

Evidence of clustering is obtained at several

4. Evidence of clustering is particularly strong at line centers 19 (9 lines), 36 (9 lines), 47 (18 lines), 48 (12 lines), 53 (11 lines) and 55 (13 lines); somewhat less strong at line center 12 (13 lines); less strong again at line centers 25 (4 lines) and 46 (20 lines); marginal at line centers 33 (11 lines), 42 (10 lines), 43 (8 lines) and 57 (8 lines); and weak at line centers 34 (9 lines) and 50 (20 lines).
5. Particularly strong evidence of over-regularity is obtained at line centers 58 (17 lines) and 61 (26 lines); there is also weak evidence of over-regularity at line center 56 (20 lines).

The clustering evidence is more problematical, since the Neave-Selkirk test supplies us with no information about its nature. Schematic diagrams of the radial azimuth data at the six line centers showing the strongest evidence of clustering (see Fig. VI.1) begin to reveal the variety of factors which might be responsible. Two factors are particularly evident. One is that at many centers the radial lines are restricted to a small sector of the compass: thus at No. 36 all nine lines are restricted to a mere 60° of horizon centered on NNE, and in several other cases over half the horizon is avoided. In other cases much of the clustering appears to be due to close groupings of azimuths around certain values. At line center No. 48, for example, four of the twelve line azimuths fall in a close group around 271°, two fall around 290°, and three around 325°.

The first of these two factors suggests that the clustering of radial line azimuths at certain line centers may be due in part to their geographical situation. We must distinguish two effects that might be operating.

(1)  The local geography hindered or precluded the construction of radial lines in certain directions.
(2)  The local geography has resulted in the partial or total destruction of radial lines in certain directions.

At line center No. 4, for example, six out of seven lines for which data are available have azimuths between 340° and 354°, an effect which appears due to its largely being surrounded by the foothills of Cerro Portachuelo. Line center No. 36, however, is situated on the southern edge of the pampa overlooking the Nazca Valley. There would, it seems, have been few physical constraints preventing lines being constructed to the south; however it might have been far less important or convenient to construct lines off the pampa across valleys—especially if the valleys, then as now, were extensively cultivated. On the other hand, such lines might have existed but been obliterated by cultivation during the intervening centuries. The discovery elsewhere of lines

which do extend into the Nazca Valley (see Chap. II) suggests that both factors must be taken into account.

The highly clustered distribution of radial azimuths at line center No. 36, and similar effects at some other line centers, could thus be accounted for by the constraints of their situation. Conversely, it could be argued that if a uniform distribution of radial lines had been important here, as at the centers in the northwest, then different situations, e.g., slightly farther from the pampa edge, might have been chosen. It is noteworthy that the other line center showing a particularly strong overall grouping of lines, No. 47, has all its 18 lines falling within 180° centered on WNW, *toward* the pampa edge 500 m to the north, and apparently avoiding the open pampa to the south.

Some of the clustering observed at certain line centers may be due to the inclusion of twin or multiple lines, which were actually related parts of the same feature, as independent entities. For example, lines 10–13 at line center No. 47, with azimuths between 273°.5 and 278°, form two linked pairs, while lines 4–10 at line center No. 46, all seven of which have azimuths within a degree of 164°, form a parallel, zigzag pattern. In an attempt to assess the magnitude of this effect we replaced certain apparent instances of double or multiple lines with a single, mean value and reran the Neave-Selkirk test. The amended results are shown in Table 2.

The list of multiple lines is not claimed to be exhaustive or even totally objective: it merely serves to illustrate the effect of uncertainties about possibly related lines and how they should be treated. Indeed, this is a typical situation where the results of a statistical analysis rest implicitly upon a subjective judgment, in this case whether two or more nearby lines are unrelated (in which case the presence of both or all of them is judged to reflect the special importance of the azimuth concerned, which is weighted accordingly) or related (in which case a double or multiple line is judged to be a variation in the design of a single line, and to be intrinsically of no greater importance than

| Line center | Lines combined | n | t | %pt | SdL(clus) |
|---|---|---|---|---|---|
| | TABLE 2 | | | | |
| | Amended Neave-Selkirk statistics after certain instances of double or multiple lines have been combined. | | | | |
| 19 | 6a, 6b & 6d | 7 | 0.160 | (−2.36) | 1% |
| 30 | 9 & 10 | 9 | 0.614 | (+0.88) | — |
| 37 | 9 & 10 | 9 | 0.549 | (+0.38) | — |
| 43 | 3 & 4 | 7 | 0.262 | (−1.65) | 10% |
| 44 | 30 & 31 | 49 | 0.438 | −1.08 | — |
| 46 | 4–10 | 14 | 0.343 | (−1.49) | 10% |
| 47 | 2a & 2b; 3—5; 7 & 8; 10 & 11; 12 & 13 | 12 | 0.302 | (−1.75) | 5% |
| 50 | 17a & 17b | 19 | 0.372 | (−1.41) | 10% |

a wide line or any other type of line). In my view this sort of subjective decision is inevitable, should be acknowledged, and should be made on the basis of as thorough a background knowledge as possible. For this reason I am happy to accept the decisions inherent in the data provided as being the best available. An obvious instance is that the "linked" lines 10 and 11, and 12 and 13, at line center No. 47 are listed separately, whereas line 12 at line center No. 46 is listed as a "double line returning on itself" and entered as a single value. In more methodological terms, this illustrates the implicit dependence of even a "classical" statistical approach on subjective decisions based on "background knowledge" about the data.

Returning to the line centers exhibiting the strongest evidence of clustering, it is clear that many of the clustering patterns observed cannot simply be explained either by geographical constraints or by the presence of large numbers of "related" lines with similar azimuths. At line center No. 55, for instance, we find a general grouping of lines extending onto the pampa to the north, a small number running south toward the Nazca Valley, but none to the east or west. At line center No. 48, on the other hand, we find two general groupings of lines which appear to contour across the pampa to the NW and SSE, but no lines going up to the NE or down to the SW.

As a first attempt to investigate this patterning we shall look more closely at whether particular azimuths seem to be preferred or avoided. This information is unavailable from the Neave-Selkirk test.

*Azimuths Preferred or Avoided*

We have investigated preferred or avoided declinations by considering a selection of "target" azimuth ranges with various mean azimuths and widths. It is straightforward to compute the number of "hits" on any particular target scored by our observed data, the expected number of hits if our data were distributed randomly, and to calculate the probabilities that we would get as at least as many, or at most as few, hits as observed purely by chance. If one of these probability values is very small then we have evidence of preference or avoidance of the azimuth range concerned.

Before proceeding further, however, some words of warning must be given against accepting these probabilities at face value. Each time we pick a target range and perform our probability test, we are effectively testing the null (random) hypothesis for the Nazca data against a particular alternative. If a single such test were performed in isolation, then we would reject the random hypothesis with some confidence if a probability of less than 0.05 (1 in 20) were obtained. However, we could only repeat this process if a fresh set of Nazca lines were available on which to test each different target range. By being forced to reuse the same data we fall foul of the problem mentioned above: we are using the same data to test a random hypothesis against several interrelated alternatives.[6]

---

6. An everyday example may be helpful in illustrating this point. It is a fairly well-known, though on the face of it very surprising, result that if one collects together 23 people at ran-

We began our analysis by taking the data as a whole, and comparing the observed number of azimuths falling within given "target" azimuth windows with that expected if azimuths were distributed randomly. A full range of mean azimuths and window widths was considered. The former were taken at half-degree intervals and the latter varied from 50° down to 1°. Finer precision was considered unjustified (at least at this stage) in view of the inclusion of Quality 2 data accurate to only about 1°. For each target window we computed the nominal probability of getting by chance at least as many, and at most as few, hits as were actually observed. Where one of these values was less than 0.05, it was noted and marked on a table of all the target windows.

The complete table is too extensive to reproduce here (similar tables appear in Ruggles 1984a: Chap. 12), but we have summarized the most significant results in Part 1 of Table 3. The azimuths listed there are the mean azimuths of the intervals yielding the lowest nominal probability levels found locally in the complete table. Interval widths are given in brackets. The extent of the clustering or avoidance at each azimuth isolated in this way is determined by the nominal probability level $p$, and in order to simplify matters we have classified these as major if $p < 0.0005$, medium if $p < 0.005$ and minor if $p < 0.05$.

In addition to considering the data as a whole, we repeated the entire analysis for connectors only, connectors and possible connectors only, and wide lines only. The corresponding results are given in Parts 2–4 of Table 3.

Two major large-scale trends are evident amongst the data as a whole: there is a preference for azimuths around north and an avoidance of azimuths around east (as evidenced by the two intervals of width 50°). There are also minor clusterings on the medium scale, within about 10° of azimuth 50° and within about 5° of azimuth 220°. On the small scale, there are build-ups of radial line azimuths within a degree or so of the following values: 164°.5 and 349°, where the concentration is strong; 16°, 43°, and 204°, where the concentration is moderate; and 6°, 56°.5, 100°, 133°.5, 148°.5, 168°, 215°.5, 239°, 265°.5, 272°.5, 280°.5, 310°.5, and 354°, where the concentration is weak.

When we restrict our attention to connectors and possible connectors the large- and medium-scale trends disappear apart from the concentration around azimuth 220°. Several new medium-scale avoidances appear, but these are minor and seem merely to represent intervals where no small-scale clusterings are evident. The azimuths with strong or moderate small-scale concentrations are now 100.5°, 133°.5, 168°, 216°, 262°, 280°, 311°, and 348°; there are a further twelve minor small-scale concentrations.

When we further restrict our attention to firmly established connectors, the number of moderate concentrations at the small scale reduces to just six—at 100°, 133°.5, 168°, 280°, 312°, and 348°—there are now insufficient data for strong clusterings to be evident.

The picture is rather different when we restrict our attention to wide lines. On the large-scale there is a strong preference for azimuths

---

dom, the chances are virtually even that two of them will have the same birthday (assuming that the population's birthdays are evenly distributed through the year and ignoring leap years). The probability that two of them will both have a birthday on a *particular* date, however, is much smaller—about 0.0018 or under 1 chance in 500. Suppose, then, that we do collect 23 people together and that two of them have a birthday on June 2, a result of no significance whatsoever. If we proceed to test in turn the 365 hypotheses that there are more birthdays than would be expected by chance on each day of the year, the "June 2" hypothesis will appear, quite misleadingly, to be highly significant.

One way to view this problem is that as we examine each target range we are building up more and more knowledge about the data, knowledge which ought to be taken into account when we assess the significance of the number of "hits" on any particular target. Within a "classical" statistical framework it is possible to deal with this sort of multiple testing by calculating the probabilities as if for each test in isolation, but then reducing the apparent significance level at which we are prepared to reject the null hypothesis in favor of any one of them. The only difficulty is that no reliable estimate has yet been produced for how much we should reduce the significance level, although Freeman and Elmore (1979), for example, have given some guidelines. Thus, following Ruggles (1984a: Chap. 12), we shall merely look for the lowest overall probability values, note them, and claim that if any preference/avoidance phenomena are significant, then it is those isolated in this manner. We shall refer to probabilities calculated as if each test were performed in isolation as "nominal probabilities" as a reminder to the reader that they must not be taken literally.

TABLE 3
Summary of concentrations and avoidances found amongst the Nazca radial azimuth data.*

| Concentrations | | | Avoidances | | |
|---|---|---|---|---|---|
| Major | Medium | Minor | Minor | Medium | Major |
| | | **(1) ALL DATA, MEASURED AZIMUTHS** | | | |
| | | 6.0 ( 1) | | | |
| | 16.0 ( 1) | | | | |
| | | | | 37.0 ( 4) | |
| | 43.0 ( 1) | | | | |
| | | 49.0 (20) | | | |
| | | 56.5 ( 3) | | | |
| | | 100.0 ( 1) | | | |
| | | | | | 106.5 (50) |
| | | 133.5 ( 1) | | | |
| | | 148.5 ( 1) | | | |
| 164.5 ( 2) | | 168.0 ( 1) | | | |
| | 204.0 ( 1) | | | | |
| | | 215.5 ( 2) | | | |
| | | 220.0 (10) | | | |
| | | 239.0 ( 1) | | | |
| | | | | 253.0 ( 4) | |
| | | 265.5 ( 2) | | | |
| | | 272.5 ( 2) | | | |
| | | 280.5 ( 1) | | | |
| | | | | 286.0 ( 4) | |
| | | | 308.0 ( 3) | | |
| | | 310.5 ( 2) | | | |
| 349.0 ( 4) | | 354.0 ( 3) | | | |
| 356.5 (50) | | | | | |
| | | **(2) CONNECTORS ONLY, MEASURED AZIMUTHS** | | | |
| | | | 10.0 (20) | | |
| | | 21.0 ( 1) | | | |
| | | 40.0 ( 1) | | | |
| | 100.0 ( 1) | | | | |
| | | | 117.0 (30) | | |
| | 133.5 ( 1) | | | | |
| | | | 149.5 (30) | | |
| | 168.0 ( 1) | | | | |
| | 177.0 (20) | | | | |
| | | 222.0 ( 1) | | | |
| | 280.0 ( 1) | | | | |
| | 312.0 ( 3) | | | | |
| | | | 333.0 (20) | | |
| | 348.0 ( 1) | | | | |
| | | **(3) CONNECTORS AND POSSIBLE CONNECTORS ONLY, MEASURED AZIMUTHS** | | | |
| | | 0.0 ( 1) | | | |
| | | 15.5 ( 2) | | | |
| | | 21.0 ( 1) | | | |
| | | 34.5 ( 1) | | | |
| | | 40.5 ( 3) | | | |
| | | 45.0 ( 1) | | | |
| | | 60.0 ( 1) | | | |
| | | 71.0 ( 1) | | | |
| | | | 77.0 (10) | | |
| | | 84.5 ( 1) | | | |
| | 100.5 ( 1) | | | | |
| | | | 125.0 (15) | | |
| | 133.5 ( 1) | | | | |
| | | 149.0 ( 1) | | | |
| | 168.0 ( 1) | | | | |

(Continued)

| | Concentrations | | | Avoidances | |
|---|---|---|---|---|---|
| Major | Medium | Minor | Minor | Medium | Major |
| **TABLE 3 (Continued)** | | | | | |
| (3) CONNECTORS AND POSSIBLE CONNECTORS ONLY, MEASURED AZIMUTHS (Continued) | | | | | |
| | | 178.5 ( 1) | | | |
| | | | 193.0 (10) | | |
| | 216.0 ( 1) | | | | |
| | 220.0 (10) | | | | |
| | | 249.5 ( 1) | | | |
| | | | 256.0 (10) | | |
| | 262.0 ( 1) | | | | |
| | 280.0 ( 1) | | | | |
| | | | | 295.5 (30) | |
| 311.0 ( 1) | | | | | |
| | 348.0 ( 1) | | | | |
| (4) WIDE LINES ONLY, MEASURED AZIMUTHS | | | | | |
| | | 15.0 ( 2) | | | |
| 33.0 ( 3) | | | | | |
| 35.0 (50) | | | | | |
| | 41.5 ( 4) | | | | |
| 44.5 (50) | | | | | |
| | 52.0 (10) | | | | |
| | | 84.5 ( 1) | | | |
| | | | 94.0 (12) | | |
| | | | 148.0 (50) | | |
| | | 178.5 ( 1) | | | |
| | | 204.0 ( 1) | | | |
| | | 208.5 ( 4) | | | |
| | | | | 239.0 (40) | |
| | | 216.0 ( 1) | | | |
| | | 280.5 ( 1) | | | |
| | | | 293.0 (20) | | |
| | 352.5 ( 6) | | | | |
| (5) ALL LINES, AZIMUTHS RELATIVE TO THE DIRECTION OF CERRO BLANCO | | | | | |
| | | | | | 20 (30) |
| | | | 60 (30) | | |
| | 105 (30) | | | | |
| | | 155 (10) | | | |
| | | | 235 (10) | | |
| | 250 (20) | | | | |
| 290 (10) | | | | | |
| | | | 330 (30) | | |
| (6) ALL LINES, AZIMUTHS RELATIVE TO THE DIRECTION OF CERRO PORTACHUELO | | | | | |
| | | | | | 0 (50) |
| | | 30 (10) | | | |
| | | | 60 (50) | | |
| 100 (20) | | | | | |
| | | | 200 (10) | | |
| | | 240 (20) | | | |
| 280 (10) | | | | | |
| (7) ALL LINES, AZIMUTHS RELATIVE TO THE LOCAL DIRECTION OF WATER FLOW | | | | | |
| | 30 (50) | | | | |
| | 90 (20) | | | | |
| | | | 110 (20) | | |
| | | | 150 (10) | | |
| | | 180 (10) | | | |
| | | | 250 (50) | | |
| | | | 310 (20) | | |

(Continued)

| Concentrations | | | Avoidances | | |
|---|---|---|---|---|---|
| Major | Medium | Minor | Minor | Medium | Major |

TABLE 3 (Continued)

(8) CONNECTORS ONLY, AZIMUTHS RELATIVE TO THE LOCAL DIRECTION OF WATER FLOW

| Concentrations | | | Avoidances | | |
|---|---|---|---|---|---|
| | 290 (20) | | | | |
| | | | 310 (20) | | |

(9) CONNECTORS AND POSSIBLE CONNECTORS ONLY, AZIMUTHS RELATIVE TO THE LOCAL DIRECTION OF WATER FLOW

| Concentrations | | | Avoidances | | |
|---|---|---|---|---|---|
| | 180 (40) | | | | |
| | 290 (10) | | | | |
| | | | 320 (40) | | |

(10) WIDE LINES ONLY, AZIMUTHS RELATIVE TO THE LOCAL DIRECTION OF WATER FLOW

| Concentrations | | | Avoidances | | |
|---|---|---|---|---|---|
| | | | 30 (20) | | |
| 180 (40) | | | | | |
| | | | 310 (20) | | |

*Figures represent the mean azimuth of the interval in question, its width being given in brackets. Concentrations or avoidances classified as "Major" have nominal probability levels less than 0.0005 (1 in 2000), "Medium" ones have nominal probability levels less than 0.005 (1 in 200) and "Minor" ones have nominal probability levels less than 0.05 (1 in 20).

around NE and some avoidance of azimuths around SE and SW. On the small-scale we find concentrations around azimuths of 33° (major), 41°.5 and 352°.5 (moderate), and 15°, 84°.5, 178°.5, 204°, 208°.5, 216°, and 280°.5 (minor).

Possible factors which might have given rise to these trends are discussed in the next section.

## RADIAL AZIMUTH TRENDS AND CULTURAL HYPOTHESES

### Large-scale Trends

We can summarize the large-scale trends as follows. When the radial azimuth data are taken as a whole, there is a marked preference for directions around north and a similar avoidance of directions around east, but little difference in the south and west from the number of lines one might expect if radial line directions were completely random. No evidence remains of large-scale patterning in the data when we restrict our attention to connectors and possible connectors, or just to connectors. When, however, we look at wide lines

in isolation a rather different trend emerges. There is now a marked preference for directions around NE, and some avoidance of directions around SW and SE.

There are strong cultural reasons for supposing that these trends may be explicable—at least in part—not in terms of absolute azimuths but in terms of factors which vary from line center to line center. In particular, there are two important possibilities, discussed in Chap. II, that we should consider:

(1) orientation upon prominent landmarks such as hill summits; and
(2) orientation with respect to the local direction of water flow.

In order to investigate these possibilities we adapted our program so that it would analyze not absolute azimuths, but azimuths relative to a particular (reference) value, which might vary from line center to line center. In the case of (1) the reference value would be the azimuth of a given hill summit from that line center; and in the case of (2) it would be the local direction of water flow.

For these analyses a restricted range of target intervals was considered, with widths from 50° down to 10° and mean azimuths at five degree intervals. Smaller interval widths are pointless in the case of azimuths relative to the water flow direction, owing to the imprecision of the latter. In the case of hill summits, smaller interval widths were considered in directions roughly towards or away from the summit.

Let us look first at the azimuths relative to hill summits. The hill summits considered, which were admittedly identified from maps rather than because of their prominence from the Line Centers, were Cerro Blanco (grid reference of summit 182567 (see map, Chap. II, Fig. 1a); altitude 2070 m) and Cerro Portachuelo (083558; 1247 m) to the SE of Nazca and the line centers; Punton de los Chivatos (034687; 925 m) and Cerro del Fraile (925751; 953 m) in the foothills immediately to the NE of the pampa; Loma Jarhuapampa (992956; 1919 m) to the north, Cerros Coyungo (553761; 1005 m) to the NW and Cerros Tunga (732432; 1806 m) to the SW.

The results are given in Parts 5 and 6 of Table 3 for the two southeastern summits. Cerro Blanco is of particular interest since it is the highest peak and is referred to in ethnographic myths (see Chap. IV). Cerro Portachuelo is farther to the west along the same ridge.

There is no evidence of preferential orientation toward the peaks. The only major concentration of azimuths measured relative to Cerro Blanco is at 290° and there is no concentration at all around 0° (i.e., in the direction of the hill), either on the large or the small scale. In the case of Cerro Portachuelo there are major concentrations at relative azimuths of 100° and 280°, i.e., roughly at right angles to the direction of the hill, and a major *avoidance* of the direction of the hill itself.

We must seek an explanation of these trends. One is that there was actually a tendency to avoid orienting lines upon prominent landmarks, and perhaps a preference for setting them out roughly at right angles to the

direction of such features. However, we are not necessarily forced to such a conclusion. Both Cerro Blanco and Cerro Portachuelo are at a sufficient distance from the bulk of the Line Centers in our sample that their direction differs little from site to site, by no more than about 45°; thus we may be picking up an effect or combination of effects with rather different causes. An inspection of the lines involved reveals an apparently representative selection from the entire data sample, which tends to back up this conclusion. The results for the other hill summits were equally uninspiring. Only Loma Jarhuapampa showed some evidence of clustering in its direction— that is, to the north.

Next we consider azimuths relative to the local direction of water flow. This was estimated for each relevant line center to the nearest 10°, using the Instituto Geográfico Militar 1:50000 maps of the area. The values obtained are listed in Table 4. At line centers Nos. 12, 24, and 25 it was found impossible to estimate a water-flow direction; hence, lines radiating from these centers were omitted from this analysis.

The results of the analysis for the remainder of the lines are given in Part 7 of Table 3. The azimuths relative to the local water-flow direction do not manifest any particularly strong trends. The analysis was repeated using connectors and possible connectors only, connectors only, and wide lines only. The results are given in the remaining three parts of Table 3. The first two yield nothing of interest, but the last gave a single, very strong concentration within about 20° of 180°, i.e., in the opposite direction to the local water flow. This is so interesting that the entire data set has been reproduced in Table 5.[7]

---

7. It will be seen in Table 5 that 25 out of 99 wide lines give relative azimuths (rounded to the nearest 10°) between 170° and 200°, compared with the eleven that would have been expected by chance. The line centers represented are Nos. 4, 20, 22, 27, 30, 31, 35, 38, 44, 50, 54, 55, 60, and 62, a fairly representative selection. In addition, the following line centers have at least one wide line oriented "upstream," i.e., with an azimuth relative to the water-flow direction between 90° and 270°: Nos. 11, 16, 17, 21, 23, 33, 36, 40, 45, 48, 53, 57, and 59. This leaves only three where we have wide lines but none pointing upstream: Nos. 19, 37, and 51. Line centers Nos. 19 and 37 are amongst the small group bordering the pampa along the base of the

TABLE 4
Estimated directions of local water flow at the line centers for which we have radial azimuth data.

| Line center | Estimated direction of local water flow | Line center | Estimated direction of local water flow | Line center | Estimated direction of local water flow |
|---|---|---|---|---|---|
| 4 | 310 | 31 | 220 | 47 | 220 |
| 11 | 240 | 33 | 280 | 48 | 240 |
| 12 | ? | 34 | 230 | 50 | 210 |
| 16 | 180 | 35 | 220 | 51 | 240 |
| 17 | 190 | 36 | 270 | 53 | 250 |
| 19 | 180 | 37 | 200 | 54 | 190 |
| 20 | 220 | 38 | 210 | 55 | 210 |
| 21 | 280 | 40 | 250 | 56 | 240 |
| 22 | 280 | 41 | 250 | 57 | 220 |
| 23 | 280 | 42 | 220 | 58 | 240 |
| 24 | ? | 43 | 230 | 59 | 230 |
| 25 | ? | 44 | 270 | 60 | 230 |
| 26 | 200 | 45 | 220 | 61 | 250 |
| 27 | 210 | 46 | 230 | 62 | 230 |
| 30 | 220 | | | | |

There is strong general evidence of an interest in the upstream-downstream axis manifested in the directions of wide lines relative to the local water-flow direction. All but three line centers for which we have relevant information have at least one wide line oriented in the upstream half of the compass, and most have one oriented very near to (i.e., within about 20° of) the local upstream direction. One of the exceptions is the center of a labyrinthine figure and may have been misinterpreted as a line center; and the other two are amongst the group of line centers located along the northeast side of the pampa at the base of the Andes. All but one of this group have at least one wide line oriented very close to the downstream direction.

SMALL-SCALE TRENDS: INTRODUCTION

Having investigated some environmental factors which might have influenced line orientations, we shall look in this section at the small-scale concentrations in the light of various astronomical hypotheses which might have some cultural relevance.

Information on horizon altitudes was not available to us for this analysis. However, at a latitude of −15° the heavenly bodies rise and set sufficiently near to vertically that we can frame the analysis in terms of azimuths rather than declinations (see, e.g., Aveni 1980b: Chap. 3). In what follows we shall assume a mean horizon altitude of 3° (a safe approximation—see Aveni, this volume, p. 88, note 22). Tables giving the rising and setting azimuths of various astronomical bodies at latitude 15°S and horizon altitude 3° have been provided for us by Aveni (see Aveni 1972). For horizon altitudes between 0° and 6° the maximum error in an azimuth estimated in this way is about 0°.9 for directions near to east and west, but may be as great as about 5° very near to north and south.

___

Andes. At No. 19 there are two wide lines oriented at 100° and 204°, whereas the local water-flow direction appears to be south or slightly east of south. At No. 37 there are two wide lines oriented at 173° and 209°, flanking the *downstream* direction which is somewhat west of south. It is interesting that at the remaining line centers along the base of the Andes for which we have wide line information, Nos. 11, 30, and 44, only No. 11 fails to have a wide line oriented very close to the downstream direction.

Line center 51 appears to be an exception to the general trend. This is a curious example anyway, which I visited and surveyed during the fieldwork of 1984. It consists of a mound with just three radial lines, two narrow and one wide. The wide line was found to constitute the first straight stretch of a labyrinthine pathway centered upon this mound. This zigzagging pathway—narrowing to a uniform 1 m in width after the first corner—was traced for over 3.5 km before it terminated in a small spiral a few meters away from the start. The two other lines radiating from the central mound are much narrower and cut right across the labyrinth: taken in isolation they could be interpreted as a single line bending at this point.

TABLE 5
Wide lines sorted in order of their azimuth relative to the local water-flow direction.
The relative azimuths are quoted to the nearest 10°.

| Center | Line | Azimuth relative to the direction of local water flow | Connector? | Other end |
|--------|------|------------------------------------------------------|------------|-----------|
| 17 | 05 | 10 | ? | 25 |
| 37 | 02 | 10 | n | |
| 44 | 07 | 10 | n | |
| 62 | 06 | 10 | n | |
| 35 | 16 | 20 | n | |
| 19 | 02 | 20 | y | 27 |
| 4 | 07 | 40 | n | |
| 30 | 08 | 40 | y | 35 |
| 50 | 13a | 50 | n | |
| 45 | 12 | 50 | n | |
| 45 | 16 | 60 | n | |
| 35 | 17 | 60 | y | 45 |
| 62 | 08 | 60 | n | |
| 23 | 04 | 80 | ? | 21 |
| 51 | 01 | 80 | ? | 57 |
| 33 | 14 | 80 | n | |
| 48 | 11 | 80 | n | |
| 53 | 01 | 90 | n | |
| 54 | 05 | 90 | n | |
| 21 | 12 | 90 | n | |
| 33 | 13 | 100 | n | |
| 45 | 10 | 100 | n | |
| 53 | 03 | 100 | n | |
| 53 | 02 | 100 | n | |
| 53 | 04 | 110 | y | 51 |
| 16 | 05 | 120 | n | |
| 16 | 06 | 130 | n | |
| 55 | 01 | 130 | y | 53 |
| 40 | 05 | 140 | n | |
| 50 | 17a | 140 | n | |
| 55 | 02 | 140 | n | |
| 36 | 07 | 140 | y | 30 |
| 59 | 03 | 150 | n | |
| 23 | 06 | 160 | n | |
| 11 | 06 | 160 | n | |
| 22 | 05 | 170 | y | 21 |
| 62 | 01 | 170 | y | 61 |
| 4 | 08 | 170 | n | |
| 60 | 01 | 170 | y | 56 |
| 35 | 01 | 170 | n | |
| 20 | 06 | 170 | n | |
| 50 | 22 | 170 | n | |
| 60 | 02 | 180 | n | |
| 55 | 12 | 180 | n | |
| 55 | 03 | 180 | n | |
| 50 | 23a | 180 | y | 45 |
| 55 | 04 | 180 | ? | 45 |
| 35 | 05 | 190 | n | |
| 54 | 08 | 190 | n | |
| 31 | 03 | 190 | n | |
| 35 | 05a | 190 | n | |
| 55 | 05 | 190 | ? | 49 |
| 27 | 02 | 190 | n | |

(Continued)

| | | TABLE 5 (Continued) | | |
|---|---|---|---|---|
| Center | Line | Azimuth relative to the direction of local water flow | Connector? | Other end |
| 20 | 07 | 200 | y | 14 |
| 35 | 06 | 200 | n | |
| 30 | 01 | 200 | n | |
| 62 | 02 | 200 | ? | 58 |
| 44 | 36 | 200 | n | |
| 38 | 09 | 200 | n | |
| 54 | 01 | 200 | n | |
| 17 | 01 | 210 | n | |
| 35 | 10 | 220 | y | 30 |
| 27 | 03 | 230 | y | 17 |
| 60 | 03 | 240 | n | |
| 62 | 03 | 240 | ? | 60 |
| 17 | 03 | 240 | n | |
| 33 | 04 | 240 | n | |
| 57 | 03 | 240 | n | |
| 50 | 25 | 250 | n | |
| 54 | 02 | 250 | ? | 45 |
| 23 | 01 | 260 | y | 24 |
| 21 | 01 | 260 | y | 24 |
| 21 | 02 | 270 | y | 23 |
| 48 | 01 | 270 | ? | 45 |
| 27 | 04 | 270 | n | |
| 20 | 01 | 280 | n | |
| 19 | 06a | 280 | y | 11 |
| 60 | 04 | 290 | n | |
| 40 | 09 | 290 | y | 38 |
| 23 | 03 | 300 | n | |
| 16 | 01 | 300 | n | |
| 35 | 14 | 320 | y | 36 |
| 16 | 02 | 330 | n | |
| 37 | 01 | 330 | y | 35 |
| 45 | 15 | 340 | n | |
| 31 | 08 | 350 | n | |
| 35 | 15 | 350 | n | |
| 45 | 07 | 0 | y | 50 |
| 59 | 01 | 0 | n | |

*Small-scale Trends: The Rising or Setting Sun*

There is no clear large-scale preference for azimuths within the solar arc, that is, azimuths where the sun rises or sets at some time during the year. However solstitial and equinoctial orientations are of great interest, both in the light of Kosok and Reiche's claims (Kosok and Reiche 1947: 203; Reiche 1968b: 74–75) and Hawkins's refutations (Hawkins 1969) and because some *ceque* lines are solstitial (Zuidema 1981; Aveni 1981b). Most of Kosok and Reiche's astronomical claims in fact relate to features other than radial lines emanating from line centers; these claims are discussed elsewhere in this book (Chap. I). However, Reiche (1968b: 74) does refer to two long lines oriented upon sunset at the December solstice, and shows photographs (though the lines are not readily identifiable). One of them appears to be line no. 28 at line center 44, where I was taken during 1984 by Reiche's helpers to view sunset at the June solstice. (As we shall often be referring in this section to individual lines, we hereinafter adopt the notation "44–28" to mean "line center 44, line 28".)

The azimuths of solstitial sunrise and sunset (center of the solar disc) in the vicinity of Nazca, taken from Aveni's tables, are as follows:

|                          | AD 0   | AD 500 | AD 1000 |
|--------------------------|--------|--------|---------|
|                          | °      | °      | °       |
| June solstice, rise      | 64.5   | 64.6   | 64.7    |
| December solstice, rise  | 113.8  | 113.7  | 113.6   |
| December solstice, set   | 246.2  | 246.3  | 246.4   |
| June solstice, set       | 295.5  | 295.4  | 295.3   |

There are no accumulations of radial line azimuths around any of these values, either amongst the data taken as a whole or amongst any of the subsets such as connectors or wide lines. Lines oriented accurately upon solstitial sunrise are particularly scarce,[8] and only two

lines (44–3 and 37–6) are oriented within 2° of December solstitial sunset.[9] The azimuths of equinoctial sunrise and sunset are 89°.2 and 270°.8. There is a minor accumulation of azimuths between about 270° and 274°, and there are eleven lines within 2°.5 of the equinoctial sunset.[10]

Another culturally important hypothesis is orientation upon sunrise or sunset on the day of the sun's passage through the zenith or antizenith. We have calculated the relevant azimuths to be 104°.5 and 255°.5 (zenith passage) and 74°.0 and 286°.0 (antizenith passage). Again there are no overall accumulations of line azimuths near to these values: indeed, amongst the data taken as a whole there is a moderate avoidance of azimuths within 2° of 253° and 286°. This is reflected in the fact that no measured line has an azimuth between 250°.8 (44–4) and 255° (56–15) or between 283°.8 (44–8) and 289°.0 (44–16).[11] It is intriguing that line center No. 44 crops up yet again: in addition to its solstitial and equinoctial setting lines it has one line oriented within 5° of sunset on the day of zenith passage and two more oriented within 3° of sunset on the day of antizenith passage, the latter being the closest-oriented lines both to the left and right of antizenith sunset found on the entire pampa.

Finally, in relation to the rising and setting sun we shall consider a calendrical hypothesis. Both Urton (1982) in studying ethnographic material in the coastal zone and Zuidema (1982b) in work on Inkaic Cuzco refer to the importance of the calendrical dates associated

---

8. The only four lines oriented within 2° of the June solstitial sunrise are 41–5, 58–3, 61–4, and 61–5, and there are no lines at all with azimuths between 111°.2 (17–4) and 116°.5 (61–11). However, it is interesting that lines are oriented within 3° of both solstitial sunrises at line center No. 61.

9. Since line center No. 44 was known to Reiche, and its azimuth (245°.5) is somewhat to the left of the present-day solstitial sunset, it seems likely that 44–3 is one of the lines referred to by her (Reiche 1968: 74). The identity of the other remains a mystery. There are, however, six lines oriented within 2° of the June solstitial sunset: 42–6, 42–7, 44–28, 56–19, 58–13, and 62–8. Line center 44 has a line oriented upon each solstitial sunset, but it can hardly be claimed that this is a representative phenomenon.

10. These include 44–6, so that line center No. 44 has a line oriented within 2° of the equinoctial sunset as well as the two solstitial ones. Only a single line, 58–4, is oriented within 2° of equinoctial sunrise, although line 9 at line center No. 61, where there are two lines oriented roughly upon solstitial sunrise, has an azimuth of 95°.

11. There are, however, six lines oriented within 2° of sunset at zenith passage: 11–1, 16–10, 37–7, 47–7, 47–8, and 56–15.

with the various heliacal phenomena of the Pleiades. At present the heliacal rise of the Pleiades occurs around 3 June, the last rise at dusk and first set at dawn occur around the middle of November, and heliacal set occurs around 19 April. At the time of construction of the Nazca lines these events would have occurred somewhat earlier in the year.

The approximate dates on which the Pleiades events would have occurred between AD 0 and AD 1000, together with the azimuths of sunrise and sunset on those dates, are as follows:[12]

| | | | |
|---|---|---|---|
| Heliacal set | 18 Mar–3 Apr | 90.7–84.0 | 269.3–276.0 |
| Heliacal rise | 2 May–18 May | 73.1–68.7 | 286.9–291.3 |
| Last rise at dusk/first set at dawn | 17 Oct–2 Nov | 100.1–105.6 | 260.0–254.4 |

On the other hand the accumulations observed amongst the data, and the approximate calendar dates to which they correspond, are:

| | | | |
|---|---|---|---|
| 84.5 | Wide lines | 9 Sep | 2 Apr |
| 100.0 | All | 17 Oct | 23 Feb |
| 262.0 | Connectors | 12 Oct | 28 Feb |
| 265.5 | All | 3 Oct | 9 Mar |
| 272.5 | All | 16 Sep | 26 Mar |
| 280.5 | All | 28 Aug | 14 Apr |

It is possible that the accumulations around 100° and 262° could reflect orientations upon sunrise and sunset on the days of Pleiades events around AD 0; that the accumulation at 272°.5 could reflect orientations upon sunset on the day of Pleiades heliacal set around AD 500; or that the accumulation of wide lines around 84°.5 could reflect orientation upon sunrise on the day of Pleiades heliacal set around AD 1000. In the absence of data on horizon altitudes, and without considering independent evidence on the dating of the lines, it is difficult to say more.

To conclude our investigation of possible orientations upon solar rising and setting po-

sitions, we drew up a list of the sunrise and sunset azimuths on the following calendar dates of possible cultural importance: the solstices, the equinoxes, the dates of zenith passage and antizenith passage, and the dates of the Pleiades events described above. We then computed for each individual line center whether there were significantly more (or fewer) radial lines oriented upon these azimuths to within a given tolerance than would be expected by chance. The computations were repeated nine times, with three different assumed dates—AD 0, 500, and 1000—and three different tolerances—1°, 2°, and 3°. (Results are summarized below.)[13]

13. For a date of AD 0 we found a single highly significant result—six out of nine lines at line center No. 19 were within 1° in azimuth of one of the solar targets. The nominal probability of this occurring by chance is less than 1 in 20000. The associations are

| Line no. | Rise/set | Event |
|---|---|---|
| 3 | Set | Equinox |
| 4 | Set | Pleiades heliacal set |
| 6a, 6b, 6d | Rise | Pleiades, last dusk rise/ first dawn set |
| 6c | Rise | Zenith passage |

It is notable that two of the remaining three lines at this center, nos. 2 and 5, are connectors and so have a readily explicable independent purpose. We also found two marginally significant results at a tolerance of 2°: four out of ten lines at line center No. 42, and six out of 19 at line center No. 45, score "hits" upon the solar targets we have considered.

For a date of AD 500 we found one reasonably significant result. Five out of 12 lines at line center No. 48 were within 1° in azimuth of one of the solar targets. The nominal probability of this occurring by chance is about 1 in 500. The associations are

| Line no. | Rise/Set | Event |
|---|---|---|
| 4,5 | Set | Equinox |
| 6,7 | Set | Pleiades, last dusk rise/first dawn set |
| 8 | Set | Pleiades, heliacal rise |

We also found one marginally significant result at a tolerance of 2°—line center No. 42 as above. No other line centers showed up as significant for a date of AD 1000.

We should mention finally that the presence of several lines of possible solar significance at line center No. 44, as noted above, does not show up as significant in the present analysis because of the large total number of other radial lines at this center.

12. No attempt has been made to separate the two different events occurring in November since, in the absence of horizon altitude information, we are unlikely to distinguish them.

*Small-scale Trends: Stellar Risings and Settings*

The other major astronomical hypothesis we shall consider is that certain lines might have been oriented upon the rising and setting positions of certain stars. Aveni (1972) has tabulated the relevant azimuths for 24 bright stars and we have used his data for latitude 15°S, horizon altitude 3°, and dates of AD 0, 500, and 1000.

None of the major or moderate azimuth concentrations observed amongst the data as a whole corresponds to a particular star listed by Aveni, with the single exception of 204°, which corresponds to Achernar at about AD 900.[14] We can, however, extend the analysis of the previous section by adding to the azimuths of possible solar significance those which have a possible stellar significance. We can then see whether any particular line centers have significantly more radial alignments upon the rising and setting positions of the sun and stars than would be expected by chance. As before we repeated the computation nine times, with three different assumed dates—AD 0, 500, and 1000—and three different tolerances—1°, 2°, and 3°. Significant results are listed in Table 6.[15]

One line center—No. 45—certainly stands out from this analysis and may provide some important clues about astronomical influences on radial line azimuths. With an assumed date of AD 1000, all but one of its 19 radial lines fall within 3° of a solar or stellar rising or setting

position of interest. In fact, 15 of the 19 lines fall within 2° of a "target" azimuth and 12 fall within 1°, both results still yielding nominal probability levels below 0.003. With an assumed date of AD 500 we still obtain 17 out of 19 hits at 3° tolerance, but far fewer hits at lower tolerances. The number of hits falls off quite sharply before this date.

The details of line center No. 45 are given in Table 7. Each radial line is listed together with the closest astronomical target. The table should not necessarily be taken at its face value: even if many of the lines *were* astronomically aligned, many others which happen to fall near astronomical targets might not have been so intended; even astronomical lines might not have been aligned on the targets we have identified; changes in the assumed date would change the details; and so on. However, the data from line center No. 45 do indicate that at a few line centers astronomical considerations may have been an important, or even a prime, motivation in setting out the radial lines. This possibility clearly merits further, and careful, study.

## CONCLUSIONS AND DISCUSSION

As we stated at the outset, we feel that attempts at rigorous analysis are important, and that their conclusions should serve to color the wider-based and more subjective assessments of the evidence at hand that are necessary in any attempt to interpret the products of human endeavor. It has been the limited aim of this chapter to provide some conclusions which might, it is hoped, serve this purpose in the case of the radial line azimuths at Nazca.

The principal conclusions of the various analyses presented above may be summarized as follows.

(1) The distribution of radial line azimuths at the three large line centers in the northwestern part of the pampa, Nos. 56, 58, and 61, show strong evidence of over-regularity. This seems to imply that each of these centers and their radial lines were deliberately constructed

14. Some of the minor concentrations do correspond to the rising or setting of stars: these are 100° (Rigel at about AD 600); 148°.5 (α Crucis around AD 800); 215°.5 (α Crucis around AD 100 or α Centauri around AD 400); 265°.5 (Spica around AD 900) and 310°.5 (Vega toward AD 1000). However, in view of the fact that there are 24 stars on our list, each of whose azimuths changes by up to several degrees over the time span being considered, it is perhaps unwise to tread further on the basis of this evidence alone.

15. When interpreting these results it should be borne in mind that for tolerances of 2° and 3° approximately half the horizon is within the allowed tolerance of a solar or stellar "target." Since these targets are themselves clustered around the eastern and western parts of the horizon, and avoid directions around due north and south, low nominal probabilities at tolerances of 2° and 3° may simply reflect other factors to do with the overall azimuth trends at particular line centers. This is almost certainly the explanation of the several line centers where surprisingly few hits are observed upon solar and stellar targets, and may explain most of the instances where surprisingly many hits are observed.

TABLE 6
Line centers where significantly many or few "hits" were obtained upon selected solar and stellar targets.
Three different dates and three different tolerances were considered;
only the most significant result is listed for any individual line center.

| Line center | Date | Tolerance | Total no. of lines | No. of "hits" | Nominal probability |
|---|---|---|---|---|---|
| 45 | AD 1000 | 3° | 19 | 18 | 0.0001 (this many) |
| 19 | AD 0 | 1° | 9 | 7 | 0.003 |
| 47 | AD 500 | 2° | 18 | 13 | 0.016 |
| 42 | AD 500 | 3° | 10 | 9 | 0.017 |
| 56 | AD 0 | 3° | 20 | 15 | 0.037 |
| 57 | AD 0 | 3° | 8 | 7 | 0.049 (this many) |
| 25 | AD 1000 | 3° | 4 | 0 | 0.045 (this few) |
| 40 | AD 0 | 1° | 10 | 1 | 0.026 |
| 35 | AD 0 | 3° | 35 | 12 | 0.021 |
| 53 | AD 1000 | 3° | 11 | 2 | 0.018 |
| 33 | AD 0 | 2° | 11 | 1 | 0.016 |
| 36 | AD 1000 | 3° | 9 | 1 | 0.011 |
| 55 | AD 1000 | 3° | 13 | 2 | 0.005 |
| 4 | AD 1000 | 3° | 7 | 0 | 0.004 |
| 43 | AD 0 | 3° | 8 | 0 | 0.002 |
| 12 | AD 0 | 3° | 13 | 1 | 0.001 |
| 50 | AD 500 | 2° | 20 | 2 | 0.001 (this few) |

TABLE 7
Radial azimuths at line center No. 45 and their possible interpretation in terms of solar
and stellar rising and setting positions.

| Line no. | Azimuth | Rise/set | Stellar/solar event | Tolerance | Wide line? | Connector? |
|---|---|---|---|---|---|---|
| 7 | 216.1 | Set | Canopus | 0.0 | Yes | Yes—to 50 |
| 4a | 105.7 | Rise | { Sun at l.d.r./f.d.s. of Pleiades <br> Sirius | 0.1 <br> 0.1 } | No | No |
| 16 | 275.9 | Set | Sun at heliacal set of Pleiades | 0.1 | Yes | No |
| 1e | 74.2 | Rise | Antizenith sun | 0.2 | No | No |
| 10 | 317.6 | Set | Capella | 0.2 | Yes | No |
| 1a | 73.7 | Rise | Antizenith sun | 0.3 | No | No |
| 1b | 75.2 | Rise | Aldebaran | 0.4 | No | No |
| 5 | 148.6 | Rise | α Centauri | 0.4 | No | No |
| 8 | 215.7 | Set | Canopus | 0.4 | No | ?—to 55 |
| 2 | 84.8 | Rise | Sun at heliacal set of Pleiades | 0.8 | No | No |
| 3 | 100.3 | Rise | Rigel | 0.8 | No | Yes—to 35 |
| 9a | 265.8 | Set | Spica | 1.0 | No | ?—to 54 |
| 15 | 204.0 | Set | Achernar | 1.0 | Yes | No |
| 9b | 261.8 | Set | Rigel | 1.3 | No | ?—to 54 |
| 2a | 97.8 | Rise | Rigel | 1.7 | No | No |
| 12 | 273.1 | Set | Equinoctial sun | 2.3 | Yes | No |
| 4b | 108.4 | Rise | { Sun at l.d.r./f.d.s. of Pleiades <br> Sirius | 2.8 <br> 2.8 } | No | No |
| 14 | 39.7 | Rise | Capella | 2.9 | No | Yes—to 37 |
| 13 | 349.8 | Set | — | — | No | No |

according to a single plan which involved the line directions being spread fairly uniformly around the compass. This observation may be of some relevance in the light of Andean radial systems in general.

(2) There is a general preference for azimuths around north and an avoidance of azimuths around east, but little difference in the south and west from the number of lines one might expect if radial line directions were completely

random. No evidence remains of large-scale patterning in the data when we restrict our attention to connectors and possible connectors, or just to connectors. Wide lines, however, show a marked preference for directions around NE, and some avoidance of directions around SW and SE.

(3) There is strong general evidence of an interest in the upstream-downstream axis manifested in the directions of wide lines relative to the local water-flow direction. All but three line centers for which we have relevant information have at least one wide line oriented in the upstream half of the compass, and most have one oriented very near to (i.e., within about 20° of) the local upstream direction. On the other hand all but one of the line centers located along the northeastern side of the pampa at the base of the Andes seem to have at least one wide line oriented very close to the downstream direction.

(4) There is no general evidence of an interest in orienting lines upon hill summits. Indeed, analyzing azimuths relative to the direction of certain prominent hills actually uncovered apparent evidence that lines were preferentially set out approximately at right angles to the direction of landmarks such as Cerro Blanco and Cerro Portachuelo, and avoided lining up upon them.

(5) There is no clear large-scale preference for azimuths within the solar arc, and no evidence of an overall clustering of line azimuths in the vicinity of solstitial or equinoctial sunrise or sunset. However, certain individual line centers are of interest with regard to solar events. Line center No. 44 contains lines oriented within 2° of the equinoctial and both solstitial sunsets, one oriented within 5° of sunset on the day of zenith passage and two within 3° of sunset on the day of antizenith passage. Six out of nine lines at line center No. 19 are oriented within 1° of sunrise or sunset either on the day of a solar event or on that of a heliacal event of the Pleiades around AD 0.

(6) Most of the major small-scale concentrations amongst the data as a whole fall outside the solar range and well away from the most obvious stellar rising or setting targets. How-

ever, some minor concentrations may be interpretable in terms of the Pleiades, Achernar, Rigel, α Crucis, α Centauri, and Vega. There are indications that at a few individual line centers astronomical considerations may have been a very important factor in setting out the radial lines. Line center No. 45 appears to be a prime candidate, with all but one of its 19 radial lines falling within 3° of a solar or stellar rising or setting position of interest (and most doing so at rather smaller tolerances) at dates between AD 500 and AD 1000.

The statistical analysis of the Nazca radial azimuth data, let alone of azimuthal data from other geoglyphs at Nazca, need not stop here. As was mentioned above, exploration of an alternative approach to analyzing the data, along Bayesian lines, is one area where work is currently in progress. The most obvious other areas for future work are perhaps those following.

Further cultural hypotheses need to be identified and tested. For example, Urton (1981b) has noted the importance amongst a contemporary Andean culture both of the overall motions of the Milky Way and of dark- and light-cloud "constellations" within it: there is also evidence of dark-cloud constellations being identified amongst coastal cultures (Urton 1982).

If horizon altitudes can be obtained for many of the lines, then astronomical hypotheses can be explored further. For example at line center No. 45 it would be interesting to obtain horizon altitude data, to determine which date would fit the various astronomical possibilities best, and to see if this correlates with dates suggested by other evidence. We might also investigate whether any lines are aligned upon the solar rising or setting position on the dates of the heliacal events of some of the stars whose rising or setting positions are aligned upon.

The results of this analysis certainly seem to have raised more questions than they have answered. However, perhaps this is only to be expected when we dealing with the complex activities of human beings.

## ACKNOWLEDGMENTS

I am most grateful to Anthony Aveni, Gary Urton, and the Earthwatch group for allowing me to join them in their final period of fieldwork in 1984, and to the Science and Engineering Research Council who provided financial support. The analysis of the Nazca data has been possible thanks to the facilities available in the Computing Studies Department at the University of Leicester.

# VII. Aerial Photography of the Nazca Lines

Gerald W. Johnson, Douglas E. Meisner, and William L. Johnson

## INTRODUCTION

The Nazca lines should be comprehended in their totality before any assessment of their nature is attempted. One way to do this is to see them from the air; however, this is easier said than done. People fly over the lines and figures every day of the year, and during these flights hundreds of photographs are taken. The result of all this photography is many individual photographs, but no comprehensive picture of the magnitude and extent of this unique archaeological feature.

The required photographic coverage of the entire line system can be obtained in two ways: one or two high altitude photographs could cover the pampa, or a series of photographs taken from a lower altitude could be assembled together in a mosaic to cover the area. In the first case, an extraordinarily high altitude would be needed, requiring a plane such as the NASA U-2. Satellites, on the other hand, can easily provide such wide coverage. Fig. VII.1 shows two examples of satellite images of the pampa.

Figure VII.1a is from an electronic sensor called the Multi-Spectral Scanner (MSS) used in the Landsat satellites. These images are electronically transmitted to the ground, similar to television pictures, and then converted into photographs (Lillesand and Kiefer 1987). This example has also been computer-en-

Fig. VII.1a. Satellite images of the Nazca area.
1a. Landsat satellite image, taken by an electronic camera from an altitude of 900 km. This image was computer enhanced by the Environmental Research Institute of Michigan as part of a natural resource survey project. The prominent features shown are of modern origin (roads and a power line right of way). Photograph courtesy of the Environmental Research Institute of Michigan

Fig. VII.1b. Space Shuttle photograph, taken by a large format camera from an altitude of 220 km. The use of film provides considerably greater detail than Landsat's electronic camera, permitting a few prominent geoglyphs to be seen.

hanced to accentuate the spatial detail. The Landsat MSS has a resolution of about 80 meters (260 feet). Smaller features can be seen if they contrast greatly with their surroundings (such as the Pan American Highway or other roads), but this image shows only the most prominent of the geoglyphs. Figure VII.1b is a portion of a photograph taken from the Space Shuttle with the newly developed Large Format Camera (Doyle 1985). Using film rather than an electronic sensor, this camera provides considerably greater detail than Landsat, yet it is still insufficient to study the smaller features on the pampa.

A detailed analysis requires a closer view. The trade-off is that when the camera is closer to the ground less area is covered in each shot. To cover the whole area, therefore, multiple

photographs must be assembled in a mosaic (see Photo Appendix in jacket pocket). To produce a photomosaic, the camera axis must be within a few degrees of vertical at the time of exposure; otherwise scale variations within the photograph are too large to permit matching it with the adjacent photographs. The ideal equipment for such photography is the large format aerial mapping camera, which provides high resolution photographs on very large pieces of film (each negative measures $9 \times 9$ inches), thus allowing considerable enlargement. Unfortunately, the cameras are extremely expensive (one to two hundred thousand dollars); they are bulky and heavy to transport and require specially modified aircraft. This places use of such equipment well out of the reach of most archaeological mis-sions. As a result, use of mapping-quality photography is generally limited to situations where it is available from previous projects, such as government development programs, etc. However, availability of such photography to foreigners is frequently restricted, and even when the photos are available the flying height or other conditions may not be optimum for archaeological research. At Nazca, for example, government photography is available from an agricultural inventory, but the photographs were taken near noon and the camera exposure was set for the vegetated valley floors. As a result, the photos covering the pampa have minimal shadows and are overexposed, making the lines very difficult to discern. In addition, the photos had been taken at an altitude too high to allow clear identification of the lines.

If sufficient funds are available, of course, large format photography can be taken specifically for an archaeological application. Vertical photographs were taken of the Nazca lines in 1968 using a mapping camera, and were used to make highly accurate maps of the lines and figures (Hawkins 1974). This survey, however, covered only a small portion (about four square kilometers) of the pampa.

The question is, how can the archaeologist on a limited budget arrange for custom aerial photographic coverage, taken under optimum conditions for the study at hand? There are several possibilities.

One approach that has provided successful aerial photography of numerous archaeological sites is the use of a small format camera and an unmanned tethered balloon. It has two advantages: cost and transportability. Its low cost makes it affordable to many archaeological investigators, and the camera equipment and deflated balloon can be transported even to remote areas.

A second means of obtaining custom aerial photography is to use a light aircraft (a Cessna 172, for example) and a small format camera. Light aircraft are available in many parts of the world, and while not as inexpensive as a balloon, their cost is still relatively modest. The biggest limitation has been the difficulty

in obtaining vertical photography from them. In order to take a vertical photograph from the window of a small plane, the pilot must tilt the plane by steeply banking. One or two good photographs might result from several passes over the site, but it is not practical to obtain a long series of overlapping photographs in this way. This problem has limited the use of light aircraft for extensive vertical aerial photography in archaeological applications.

Other aerial platforms have been used for archaeological photography. One of these is the helicopter. The cost of chartering a helicopter puts it beyond the budget of most archaeological projects, unless there happens to be one based within a few minutes flying time of the site. A second drawback in some helicopters is vibration, which causes blur in the photographs. This requires either a handheld camera or use of a special mount. In spite of such limitations, the helicopter has provided useful photography. Deuel (1969) notes that the whale figure in Nazca was discovered by Maria Reiche while taking photographs from a helicopter. A most cost-effective aerial platform that is beginning to be used for archaeological photography is the ultra-light aircraft (Walker 1985). The flight characteristics of this type of aircraft, particularly its slow flying speed, make it useful in many situations. However, it is not yet widely available for projects outside the United States, and is limited to flying in moderate winds.

Given the importance of obtaining vertical aerial photography of the Nazca lines and the possible problems involved in such an undertaking, it was decided to consider two possibilities. First, low altitude, large-scale photography of several of the ray centers would be obtained using a tethered balloon. Second, smaller-scale photographs covering the entire pampa would be taken with a light aircraft using a special camera mounting system.

## BALLOON PHOTOGRAPHY

The first aerial photographs were taken by Gaspard Tournachon in 1858 from a manned balloon over Paris (Newhall 1969). By World

Fig. VII.2. The tethered balloon and camera used to photograph line centers in Nazca. The hydrogen-filled balloon measures approximately 3 m in diameter by 15 m long. The 70 mm Hasselblad camera is shown in the gimbal mount (which keeps the camera pointed down) and the antenna for the remote shutter release is visible. The camera has a motor drive to advance the film and cock the shutter between photographs.

kilograms or so, making its size an order of magnitude less than a manned balloon. This means that the camera equipment and balloon can be packed into a pair of duffle bags and carried to virtually any location.

The balloon must be inflated using a lighter-than-air gas, either helium or hydrogen. Despite a sometimes poor reputation, hydrogen is generally the preferred gas. Although helium is non-combustible, it does not have as much lift as hydrogen, it is more expensive, and most importantly, it is not readily available outside the United States. Hydrogen is usually available in major industrial cities, but when produced as a by-product the possibility of impurities may limit its lift capability. It is combustible, but a few precautions and a little common sense make it quite safe for tethered balloon flights.

The biggest problem in the everyday operation of the balloon is the wind. Early balloon models used in archaeology were spherical in shape, or sometimes cylindrical with spherical ends. In either case they could not be flown in winds greater than nine or ten kilometers per hour. The problem is that at these velocities the wind creates an additional downward force that, in combination with the weight of the balloon, camera, and tether line, can exceed the balloon's lift capacity. Later balloons have been built in the shape of a small dirigible, and the aerodynamic attributes of these balloons give them better flight characteristics. Typically they can be flown in winds up to 30 kilometers per hour.

The camera/gimbal is attached to the tether line 10 m below the balloon. This separation tends to dampen oscillations resulting from irregular balloon movements. When properly balanced in the gimbal, the optical axis of the camera stays within a few degrees of vertical. The camera must be motor driven, and it is triggered by a signal from a radio transmitter on the ground to a receiver mounted with the camera on the gimbal. Fig. VII.2 shows the balloon and camera used in the Nazca project.

The entire airborne assembly (balloon and camera/gimbal) is controlled from the ground by a person holding the tether line. The line,

War I the airplane had supplanted the balloon as the primary platform. The 1960s once again saw the balloon become a practical means for obtaining aerial photography. Much of the early work of developing a balloon/camera system for archaeological photography was done by Julian Whittlesey (Whittlesey 1970, 1975). Over the past twenty years hundreds of archaeological sites have been photographed from the air using balloon/camera systems developed from his early work (Johnson and Kase 1977; Myers and Myers 1980, 1985; Hyslop 1985).

The Whittlesey system combines an unmanned, hydrogen filled balloon supporting a small format camera mounted in a gimbal below the balloon. Manned hot air balloons are not generally practical for archaeological applications because they are too big, even when deflated, to be easily transportable. An unmanned balloon needs a net lift of only ten

mounted on a reel, is marked at specified intervals along its length so that the altitude of the camera can be determined by noting how much of the line is out. The tether line is moved to position the camera over the center of the site to be photographed. If there is no wind, the camera will be directly above the tether, making accurate positioning easy. If there is a wind, allowance must be made for the angle of the line, and it is necessary to have at least two observers at some distance from the center of the site to estimate visually when the camera is correctly located. At very low altitudes (tens of meters), the camera can be positioned more accurately by attaching additional lines to the gimbal. At higher elevations these additional lines are impractical since they tend to become tangled.

The effective altitude range of the balloon is approximately 10 m to 1000 m. Using 2-¼ by 2-¼ inch format film (120, 220, or 70 mm film size) and a 50 mm focal length lens, the ground covered on each photograph will be slightly larger than the altitude above ground, ranging from about 11 by 11 m (at 10 m altitude) to 1100 by 1100 m (at 1000 m altitude). Below 10 m bipod photography would be more effective (Whittlesey 1966). Above 500 m some discretion is advisable. In the case of problems, such as a sudden increase in the wind's velocity, it is difficult to recover 1000 m of line in a short period of time. In addition, at the higher altitudes it becomes increasingly difficult to position the camera accurately if a series of overlapping photographs is required.

A balloon/camera system, such as that developed by Whittlesey, is most effective for photographing limited areas. For sites ranging from tens to hundreds of meters in extent it results in high quality vertical photography. Even for sites up to several thousands of meters in size it provides excellent coverage.

## LIGHT AIRCRAFT PHOTOGRAPHY

As stated earlier, it has been difficult to obtain vertical aerial photography from a standard airplane. A similar problem in the re-source management field (forestry, crop monitoring, water quality, etc.) has led to a solution that can be directly applied to archaeology as well. Resource managers have found that aerial photography can be obtained quickly, efficiently, and inexpensively using small format photography taken from a light aircraft. To meet the requirement for vertical photography, many airplanes in the U.S. have been modified by adding a small floor hole to mount a camera vertically. Alternatively, specialized camera mounts have been developed that do not require modification of the aircraft.

One of these mounts that has proved particularly effective was developed by Merle Meyer of the Remote Sensing Laboratory at the University of Minnesota (Meyer and Grumstrup 1978). With the window open or removed it can be mounted on the left door of most high wing aircraft. This "side mount" holds the camera in a vertical orientation outside the plane and also permits the camera to be brought inside for film reloading (Fig. VII.3). When disassembled, the mount can be easily carried. Thus, wherever a suitable aircraft is available, vertical aerial photography can be obtained. This makes vertical photography practical in a great many more places in the world.

Several factors determine how low the plane can be flown and hence determine the scale of the resulting photography. The lower the flying height the greater the air turbulence. Too much turbulence makes it difficult to keep the camera vertical and hold the plane on a straight course along a desired flight line. Another problem with low altitude flights is image blurring. These factors limit the minimum altitude at which photography should be flown. Experience has shown that 300 m above terrain is a minimum altitude, and 450 m is a desirable minimum. Using a camera with a 2-¼ by 2-¼ inch format size and an 80 mm focal length lens, the 450 m flying height gives photo coverage of approximately 300 by 300 m.

Thus, the two forms of aerial photography are complementary. Large scale, highly de-

Fig. VII.3. Meyer side mount. This bracket fits onto the door of the airplane, enabling vertical photography to be taken. The camera is shown beneath the curved windscreen, and can be slid along the horizontal bar into the airplane for film reloading. The airplane is flown with the window opened, and the photographer (wearing goggles) leans out the window to confirm the exact alignment of the aircraft with the flight line. The camera is triggered at set intervals determined by the altitude and speed of the aircraft.

tailed photographs of small sites covering tens of hundreds of meters can be most effectively obtained using the tethered balloon; coverage of large sites covering thousands of meters can best be done using a light aircraft to take a series of photographs.

## PHOTOGRAPHING THE NAZCA LINES

The initial objective at Nazca was to photograph as many of the line centers as possible using the balloon and to obtain photography for a mosaic using the side mount on one of the small aircraft available at the Nazca airport.

The first requirement for the balloon photography was to locate a source of hydrogen. The only hydrogen available in Lima was not a commercial product but was a by-product of fertilizer manufacture, and this gas had to be used.

Two events limited the results of the balloon flights. First, after inflation it was found that the balloon did not have enough lift to reach the desired altitude above the terrain. As mentioned earlier this was almost certainly due to impure hydrogen. This meant that, besides lack of required flying height, the balloon had

unsatisfactory flight characteristics. In spite of this, line center No. 27 near the edge of the pampa was successfully photographed, and the balloon was then moved along the edge of the pampa toward the next ray center several kilometers away. The second event occurred during this move. A sudden wind with gusts up to 70 km per hour developed, and it became necessary to retrieve the balloon rapidly. There was no place to moor the balloon safely in the open pampa, and therefore it had to be deflated. The poor quality of the hydrogen argued against reinflating, and it was decided to forego any additional flights. Fig. VII.4 shows the balloon photograph taken over line center no. 27.[1]

The mosaic photography (see Photo Appendix) for overall coverage of the pampa (Fig. II.1a), including lines and centers, was obtained by using the side mount camera system on a locally chartered light aircraft. The area covered by the lines is approximately 16 km by 18 km. When obtaining full coverage of a large area, additional consideration must be given to flying height. While the minimum altitudes discussed previously would give more detailed results, each photo would cover only a small area on the ground. Hence, many more flight lines and rolls of film would be required, making the cost prohibitive. The flying height is therefore a compromise between obtaining a manageable number of photographs, calling for higher altitude, and obtaining a good usable scale, calling for lower altitude. For the Nazca project, it was decided that approximately 200 photographs obtained from a flying height of 1920 m would provide sufficient resolution and still be a practical number of photos to work with.[2] In addition, the coverage was limited to the southern three-quarters of the pampa, since the northern edge had been covered in detail by past surveys (e.g., Hawkins 1974b).

1. At 350 m, the 50 mm focal length lens provided a scale of 1:7,000 on the 2-¼ inch film. The photograph covers approximately 385 m on a side.
2. An 80 mm focal length lens was used on the camera, providing a contact scale of 1:24,000 on the 70 mm film. Each photograph covers 1320 m on a side.

Thirteen parallel flight lines were laid out in an east-west direction. The flight lines were spaced at one kilometer. Normally a flight plan such as this would be flown in an alternating pattern: west-east-west, etc. The pilot keeps the plane on line by picking out a prominent feature in line with the proposed flight path and beyond the far edge of the area, and flying directly toward this feature. However, in the Nazca area, there are few recognizable features, particularly on the pampa beyond the western edge of the lines. On the eastern edge, the Pan American Highway provides a border, and it was decided that an automobile would be positioned at successive points on the shoulder of the highway so as to indicate the start of each flight line. The odometer was used to measure the spacing between flight

Fig. VII.4. Sample balloon photograph taken over line center No. 27. This photograph, taken at an altitude of 350 m, shows a variety of lines and trapezoids, as well as two spiral figures which had not previously been detected (one is above the lower left corner, and another is only partially shown in the upper left corner).

lines along the highway. The pilot would pass over the car at the start of each flight line, and would fly the line by following a westerly heading on the aircraft compass. This is not as satisfactory as flying toward a fixed object because the plane can slowly drift off the desired flight path without the pilot or cameraman being aware of it. The width of coverage of each photograph was 1320 m, providing 15 percent overlap between the flight lines. Due to the inaccuracies of the navigation method, this was not sufficient to avoid some small gaps in coverage.

Since the auto was the only usable reference mark, all the photography had to be exposed using east to west flight strips, meaning that the flying time was essentially doubled. Total flying time for the project was 2.5 hours.

Certain areas of the pampa were flown with over 50 percent overlap from one successive photograph to the next. The overlap allows these areas to be viewed stereoscopically, since each feature is covered on two different photographs taken from different vantage points. Using a stereoscope to view the two images of the feature, the observer sees a three dimensional view of the area. The other areas were photographed with about 10 percent overlap, which does not allow for stereoscopic viewing. Figure VII.5 shows a sample frame of the aircraft photography.

In both the balloon and aircraft photography, black and white panchromatic film was used because of its high resolution. In many archaeological applications, black and white infrared or color infrared films are highly useful. In Nazca, the surficial nature of the lines and the lack of soil moisture and vegetation argued against employing infrared film. Two types of black and white film were used. Twelve exposure rolls of 120 size Kodak Plus-X Pan Professional Film were used to conserve weight in the balloon setup, while 70 exposure rolls of 70 mm Kodak Panatomic-X Aerographic II Film 2412 (Estar Base) were used to minimize reloading in the aircraft. The camera was a Hasselblad Model 500EL/M.

The photos could be taken either early or late in the day in order to maximize the shadows to enhance the lines. The balloon photographs were taken at approximately 9:00 a.m., and the aircraft photography was taken between 2:30 and 5:00 p.m. The advantage of low sun angle was emphasized by experience on the ground: while viewing the lines from the centers, one sees more of them early and late in the day than at high noon. This is not surprising, since the color difference between the exposed and undisturbed soil is very slight, as is the relief found on the edges of the lines due to stone piling.

The aircraft photographs have been used to produce a photomosaic, or photomap, of the Nazca lines. The photomap is assembled by taking one photograph near the center of the area and securing it to a mounting board with special adhesive. Then each of the surrounding photographs is cut to a best fit or match and secured to the mounting board, and the process continues until the entire area has been covered.

There are basic differences between a conventional topographic or planimetric map and a photomap (Photo-Appendix Fig. 2). Conventional maps are characterized by a constant scale, whereas scale in an aerial photograph will vary with ground elevation. The only vertical photograph with constant scale will be that taken of a flat area. Any reference to the scale of a photograph or photomap should be considered as an average scale only. Scale variations make it impossible to get a perfect match of features between adjacent photographs. There always will be slight discrepancies due to scale variation or relief displacement. Similarly, the finished photomap will show features only in their correct relative location, with some discrepancies in absolute location.

Despite these limitations, however, the photomap has several advantages over conventionally produced maps. Generally, it can be produced much faster and less expensively. It shows more detail than a standard map, since all features which show on the photography are on the map. For most the photomap is easier to comprehend and use because it pre-

Fig. VII.5. Sample aircraft photograph taken over the southeastern end of the pampa. The hill shown in the upper center of this photograph contains line center No. 27. To the north of this hill, the whale figure can just barely be seen (bisected by the kinked line to the right of the kink).

sents an actual view of the area, not just a stylized representation.

## SUMMARY

A complete picture was desirable to aid in the archaeological evaluation of the Nazca lines. This chapter has presented several possible methods for obtaining aerial photography and has concentrated on the requirements of the Nazca Project and the two methods chosen for it. The tethered balloon method and the light aircraft method were described in detail with their advantages and disadvantages enumerated.

Figs. VII.4 & 6 compare the level of detail

Fig. VII.6a. Comparison of photographs taken at different scales.
  6a. Aircraft photograph, taken at an altitude of 2000 m. This photograph has been enlarged and cropped to show the same area as Fig. 4.

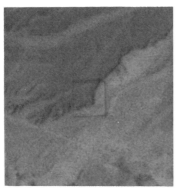

Fig. VII.6b. Space Shuttle photograph, taken at an altitude of 220 km. The marked area is the same as that in Figs. 4 & 6a.

shown at the balloon altitude (350 m), the aircraft altitude (2000 m), and the Space Shuttle altitude (220 km). The aircraft and shuttle photographs have been enlarged and cropped to show the same area covered by the full balloon photograph. The shuttle photograph only provides sufficient resolution to see the major features of the pampa.

This figure illustrates the advantage of detail provided by the balloon photography. Included in the balloon image are two spiral features (upper left and lower left corner of Fig. VII.4a) which had not previously been observed on the ground, even though one was within 100 m of the heavily studied line center. It is expected that similar features could be discovered if balloon coverage is taken of other ray centers.

The aircraft photographs offer the advantage of detail nearly equal to the balloon photo, plus sufficient coverage to allow construction of a photomosaic covering most of the pampa. Their primary utility is in showing the full extent of the long lines and the relative positions of the features across the pampa.

Each form of photography has a complementary role to play in aiding the investigations of the archaeologist. The aerial photography obtained at Nazca has made a contribution toward solving the mystery of this ancient archaeological feature.

*EPILOGUE*

There is a parallel between ancient Nazca and the remains of Nilotic peoples of ancient Egypt, who labored hard to exploit the delicate environment of that narrow fertile ribbon which threads its way through an otherwise vast wasteland. Like the Egyptians, ancient Nasqueños climbed up onto the dry desert to express themselves in ritual. Whatever else the Nazca lines were about, everyone seems to agree they had something to do with the enactment of social or religious rites.

Once you fly over the lines, you will be forever convinced that they were made to be seen from above. Many times I have heard visitors to the Nazca pampa utter that statement resolutely. But I might say with equal conviction that having walked a Nazca line on the ground, I was persuaded that the lines were meant to be trod upon; i.e., that they really were dead-straight pathways crossing over the pampa. Still others declare they are impressed by seeing a moonrise or sunset along a line. Scenes like the one depicted in Chapter I, Fig. 8, especially when viewed in the actual setting of the pampa, can go a long way toward convincing one of the validity of the astronomical theory.

Let us think for a moment about the significance of such subjective reactions. Actually, how we experience the lines ought not influence the determination of how the lines were experienced by them, the builders, for our perception has no arguable connection with that of the people who lived in ancient Nazca. The culture-based data help us to realize just how different ancient and modern societies are, in general. We simply have no need to assume the Nazca lines were constructed by primitive intellectuals —"cardboard" ancestors of twentieth century people or descendants of alien beings who mated with terrestrials, as those more intent on book-selling than human understanding have suggested.

Two significant elements serve to separate this text from most of its predecessors. First, there is culture. Not a single one of our hypotheses concerning the construction and use of the lines has been developed and presented outside the context of what we know about Andean culture. Indeed, where we have examined those explanations that lack a cultural basis, we have found them wanting. Second, the investigations reported in this text are based upon large, relatively complete masses of empirical data. For the first time the entire surface of the Nazca pampa has been surveyed, not only for lines (Chapter II), but also for other artifacts (Chapter III). That no one has bothered to make such a complete survey before us is alarming, for it implies that many investigators have not related the need to know the full extent of the information they are dealing with to the framing of an explanation. That completeness and rigor had not emerged as underlying criteria for proposing explanations came as a surprise to us.

Given these basic differences in the approach of our interdisciplinary team of researchers, what, then, emerges as new and different from this collection of essays?

Primarily, by resorting to a taxonomy based upon form and location of features, we have managed to separate out the straight linear features as being distinctly different from the figural drawings. Clarkson's survey transects of the pampa for all forms of remains reveal significant differences between the distribution of Early Intermediate Period and Late Intermediate Period ceramics. Trends in the data tend to place the figural drawings in the Middle Horizon and the Late Intermediate periods, while the straight lines seem to fall into the Late Intermediate Period. Of course, there is no way to prove that the ceramics Clarkson picked up were laid down well after the time the features were made. Nevertheless, until detailed excavations on the pampa are undertaken, the Clarkson survey suggests it would be safer to believe that line making and figure drawing were two chronologically separate, unrelated activities. If we had been approached with evidence that separate, unrelated activities had occurred years apart in the Roman Forum, or on the Athenian Acropolis, we would not have been at all surprised. In fact, given the long and sinuous nature of the history of the Classical world, we might have expected it. Why then, for all these years, have we been naive enough to adopt the guiding assumption that a single enigma confronted us on the pampa? We should have realized that New World cultures developed over time as did those of the Classical Western world.

Our second major conclusion is that once the straight features are considered separately, there appears a pattern, a connectedness to their arrangement that probably constitutes a meaningful and well-thought out system. Of the several hundred lines we surveyed criss-crossing the pampa, nearly all are connected via several dozen radial centers.

The problem of the centers and their constituent lines is addressed in one way or another by each author represented in the text, with the result that several ideas about both process and product relating to the Nazca lines begin to converge. These ideas, which overlap one another considerably, are at least four in number: ritual walking, irrigation, the radial principles of organization and the division of territory into cleared rectangular strips. All four notions contribute to an overall explanation.

Let me mention radiality first because it is one spatial socio-political principle of organization in a pre-Columbian Andean population center on which we have some reliable data. The *ceque* system of Cuzco, which was likely part of a network of radiating territorial/kinship divisions marked out on the physical environment, is but one manifestation of the concept of hierarchical dividing, splitting or bifurcating that we see reflected in Andean languages, in kinship, even in the organization of the *quipu*. In Cuzco, the radial *ceques* constituted both a prescription and a framework for worship, ritual, and kinship, as well as for the quadripartite division of time. On the pampa radial patterns are visible in a different way (at least to us) from that which one sees in Cuzco, where a ceque can be traced only by sighting along its component huacas. The medium is different (a sandy, flat desert covered with dark rock fragments, rather than a valley encapsulated by rocky hillsides), but the message may well be the same. What emerges

from these studies is that the empire of Cuzco is geometrically divided and subdivided in a way that is reminiscent of the division of the pampa of Nazca. But one must focus on the organizing principle—the manner in which the topography is carved up—rather than the way it looks to a modern observer.

Urton's studies at Pacariqtambo and elsewhere, while based on ethnographic analogy, reveal another manifestation of territorial division and organization that brings us even closer to what we see in the physical remains on the pampa. Urton defines *chhiutas* as rectangular territorial strips of land employed by contemporary highland people as representative social spaces. Each *chhiuta* is the product of the activity of an *ayllu*, or group of people defined on the basis of land-holding, kinship and labor and ceremonial obligations—the same unit that was central to social life in ancient Cuzco. He demonstrates that when representatives of a given *ayllu* show up in the center of Pacariqtambo on the day of a festival to sweep clean their specially designated strip of the plaza, they may be performing an act similar to that which took place on the pampa a millennium before their time. Urton hypothesizes that both *chhiutas* and Nazca lines can be viewed as mechanisms by which the social groups that made up two societies in different times and places and under different circumstances interacted with each other by dividing up among themselves their public spaces, moving over them, sweeping them and preserving them, thereby mapping out the division of responsibilities of parts of the collective whole. And so, while there is no direct evidence the elongated strips on the Nazca pampa were used in this manner, we do know that in some Andean communities today, long strips of territory are produced in the enactment of rituals by kin/labor groups.

At Quebrada de la Vaca, just south of Nazca, we see the divided plaza in a context that bridges archaeology with contemporary ethnography. Urton's study of early Colonial documents builds yet another bridge between ethnography and ethnohistory.

From the Visita de Acari (Appx III) we

learn that the division of labor and other tributary obligations similar to the social organization of contemporary Pacariqtambo, also may have existed in the Nazca valley. The Nazca pampa emerges as the dividing place between two sets of moieties. Moreover, it is reasonable to suppose that the river valleys were partitioned in such a complex manner that the organization of agricultural activities relating to the construction, use, and maintenance of irrigation facilities was coordinated symbolically via the division of spaces on the pampa in-between the two vital watershed areas. Indeed, the shared labor or *mit'a* concept applied to irrigation canals and roads in Peru is well documented, both at the present time and at the time of European contact.

These considerations lead us further into the subject of water and irrigation. The ecology of the Nazca region is very delicate, a transition zone between two extremes: the highlands to the east, the Pacific coast on the west. It scarcely ever rains on the pampa. All the water that flows in the canals is the result of rain that falls in the mountains east of the pampa. Long ago, both Kosok and Reiche had referred to the vital import of the control and use of water in the area. If there is one dominant commodity that correlates with the data collected on the line centers, it is water. All 62 line centers are located along the major river banks, on or near tributaries, or at the base of the last hill in a chain that descends out onto the pampa. The line directions match with stream orientations. The correlation is far too consistent to be coincidental. It is worth keeping in mind that irrigation also lies at the core of the *ceque* system of Cuzco.

It is precisely at this juncture where we might anticipate that astronomy would fit into the cultural picture. Ruggles' statistical analysis of radial line azimuths is a model of the rigorous approach not often followed in orientation studies. Though he and I disagree over the details, each of us has concluded that a small portion of the lines (just as a small portion of the *ceque* lines of Cuzco) are astronomically oriented. He, too, verifies the correlation with water evident in my own analysis.

It now seems unreasonable on cultural grounds to hypothesize that the whole of the pampa would constitute a calendar. I have tried to single out one of the most reasonable astronomical constructs: the slight excess of lines pointing in the direction of sunrise and sunset on the days of passage of the sun across the zenith. Not only is the observation of these events well attested to in the Hispanic Andean culture, but also it could have served as a practical means of formally anticipating the time when water would first appear in the canals— still today, the single-most important event in the local agricultural cycle.

I stated at the outset that one could almost intuit that people must have walked on the Nazca lines. Referring to Appendix II, a walk across the pampa, one is hard-pressed not to be persuaded that the lines were laid out to guide one on a journey across the pampa. As we cut across the dry stream beds on our way from Line Center 16, just north of the Nazca drainage basin, toward Line Center 27, high on the west bank of the Quebrada de Socos, we straddle a long, thin, perfectly straight pathway that precisely divides in half the two-meter wide straight feature. Rising up out of the last quebrada, about 300 meters from Center 27, we abruptly confront a large trapezoid, its entryway clearly marked, like so many others, by a pair of cairns, the same tell-tale rock piles that demarcate each line center, thus rendering it visible from very far away. Entering this huge trapezoid, one has the sense of being conducted into an area of assembly while at the same time moving toward a focal point.

But as I stated earlier, all this is pure speculation and taken by itself it means nothing. Aside from this, there remains a strong likelihood from what we know about the social organization of the Nazca and Ingenio Valleys at the time of the Conquest, that people would have had sound reasons to cross the pampa from one valley to the other, both to engage in the *mit'a* system of shared labor and to participate in the ritual activity of clearing the lines as a way of representing their group obligation. There appear be too many straight-line paths within the wide Nazca lines to deny that they were walked.

The chronicler Molina tells us that in Cuzco, the *capac hucha* walked the straight line ceques from all regions of the empire to bring sacrifices to the capital and to re-evaluate periodically the *ceques* and their *huacas*. And on their way back home, they did not follow the roads but pursued the straight line paths instead.

The collective, ritual movement of people also is a central element in Silverman's conclusion that Cahuachi, the largest ceremonial center found in the area, may have functioned as a pilgrimage center in the Late Intermediate Period. For Silverman, Cahuachi emerges as an abandoned shrine, later used as a place of assembly, a focus for ceremonial activities involving prediction relating to agricultural fertility as well as to the regularity and sufficiency of the flow of water.

Silverman argues that the social organization involved in the ritual maintenance of Cahuachi's archaeological features is based on principles similar to those that Urton finds in contemporary Pacariqtambo. She links the lines to the ceremonial center by pointing to the high degree of concentration of lines in the area along the north bank of the Nazca River immediately opposite Cahuachi's largest pyramid.

Water, walking, astronomy, kinship, division of labor and ceremonial responsibility, sweeping, radiality—what a strange set of explanatory bedfellows! Our interdisciplinary studies suggest we must find a place for all of these actions and concepts in the story of the Nazca lines. But, whatever the mosaic of explanations may be, everything must make sense in the context of what we know about Andean culture in general and Nasca culture in particular. We can no longer view the Nazca lines simply as the "largest astronomy book in the world." We have demonstrated that they are not the product of a massive work effort, all undertaken as a single-minded grand project. The builders required neither advanced technology nor a sophisticated knowledge of mathematics and geometry. And, it is extremely unlikely that they had any need of maps or blueprints in order to produce them. There is no necessity for any of these modern Western mental trappings to enter into any reasonable explanations about the lines. Oddly enough, we conclude by casting the people who built the lines in a more foreign light than most previous investigators. But by viewing the ancient people of Nazca and their work as different from ourselves and our own work, perhaps we the contributors to this volume have succeeded in making the Nazca lines a more interesting enigma—one to be approached in Andean terms, and on a human scale.

A. F. Aveni
Hamilton, NY
1 Dec 1989

# REFERENCES CITED AND PARTIAL BIBLIOGRAPHY ON NAZCA AND THE GROUND DRAWINGS

Adams, R., 1975, *Energy and Structure: A Theory of Social Power.* Austin: University of Texas Press.

Adams, R., 1978, "Man, Energy, and Anthropology: I Can Feel the Heat, But Where's the Light?" *American Anthropologist* 80(2): 297–309.

Albó, J., 1972, "Dinámica en la Estructura Inter-Comunitária de Jesus de Machaca," *America Indígena* 32(3): 773–816.

Allen, P., 1981, "The Evolutionary Paradigm of Dissipative Structures", in *The Evolutionary Vision,* ed. E. Jantsch, pp. 25–72. American Association for the Advancement of Science Selected Symposium 6.

Anonymous, 1953, "Kawachi: Ciudad Precolombina del Depart. de Ica; Descripción de las Ruinas-Estudios Estratigraficos Efectuados por Misión Norteamericana" (newspaper clipping dating to 1953; on internal evidence—source unknown).

Ascher, M. and R. Ascher, 1981, *Code of the Quipu.* Ann Arbor: University of Michigan Press.

"Autos que siguió don Garcia Nanasca, Cacique del Valle de la Nazca . . .", 1635, *Archivo General de la Nación* (AGN), *Derecho Indígena* (Lima), Legajo 5, cuaderno 91, folios 9.

Aveni, A., 1972, "Astronomical Tables Intended for Use in Astro-Archaeological Studies", *American Antiquity* 37: 531–540.

Aveni, A., 1980a, "Comment on Nazca: A Pre-Columbian Olympic Site?", *Interciencia* 5: 269.

Aveni, A., 1980b, *Skywatchers of Ancient Mexico.* Austin: University of Texas Press.

Aveni, A., 1981a, "Archaeoastronomy", in *Advances in Archaeological Method and Theory,* 4, ed. M. Schiffer, pp. 1–77, New York: Academic Press.

Aveni, A., 1981b, "Horizon Astronomy in Incaic Cuzco", in *Archaeoastronomy in the Americas,* ed. R. Williamson, pp. 305–318. Los Altos: Ballena Press and University of Maryland Center for Archaeoastronomy.

Aveni, A., 1981c, "Tropical Archaeoastronomy", *Science* 213: 161–171.

Aveni, A., 1986, "The Nazca Lines: Patterns in the Desert", *Archaeology* 39(4): 32–39.

Aveni, A., 1987a, "Archaeoastronomy in the U.S. Southwest: A Neighbor's Eye View", in *Astronomy and Ceremony in the American Southwest,* ed. J. Carlson and J. Judge. Papers of the Maxwell Museum of Anthro. No. 2, pp. 9–23. Albuquerque: Maxwell Museum of Anthropology.

Aveni, A., 1987b, "Review of *Lines to the Mountain Gods: Nazca & the Mysteries of Peru,* by E. Hadingham", *Antiquity* 61: 497–499.

Aveni, A., 1987c "Back to the Drawing Board: Review of *Lines to the Mountain Gods: Nazca & the Mysteries of Peru,*" by E. Hadingham, & *The Mystery of the Nazca Lines,* by Tony Morrison", *Nature* 330: 278–279.

Aveni, A., n.d., "A Preliminary Investigation of Geometric and Astronomical Order in the Nazca Lines". Grant proposal to the National Science Foundation, mimeo.

Aveni, A. and G. Urton, n.d., "A Preliminary Investigation of Geometric and Astronomic Order in the Nazca Lines". Research proposal to the National Geographic Society and National Science Foundation, 1980.

Avila F. de, 1966 [1608] *Dioses y Hombres de Huarochirí.* Lima.

Barnett, V., 1982, *Comparative Statistical Inference.* Chichester and New York: Wiley.

Barriga, V., 1939, *Documentos para la Historia de Arequipa, 1534–1558.* Arequipa: Editorial la Colmena, S.A.

Becker, M., 1979, "Priests, Peasants, and Ceremonial Centers: The Intellectual History of a Model", in *Maya Archaeology and Ethnohistory,* ed. N. Hammond and G. Willey, pp. 3–20. Austin: University of Texas Press.

Bennett, W., 1953, "Excavations at Wari, Ayacucho, Peru", *Yale University Publications in Anthropology,* no. 49. New Haven: Yale University Press.

Blasco B., C. and L. Ramos, 1980, *Ceramica Nasca.* Seminario Americanistas de la Universidad de Valladolid. Valladolid, Spain: Serio Americanista, vol. 13.

Bourdieu, P., 1979, *Outline of a Theory of Practice.* Cambridge: Cambridge Studies in Social Anthropology.

Braithwaite, M., 1984, "Ritual and Prestige in the Prehistory of Wessex, c. 2200–1400 B.C.: A New Dimension to the Archaeological Evidence", in

*Ideology, Power and Prehistory,* ed. D. Miller and C. Tilley, pp. 93–110. Cambridge: Cambridge University Press.

Breunig, G. von, 1980, "Nasca: A Pre-Columbian Olympic Site?" *Interciencia* 5: 209–219.

Bridges, M., 1986, *Markings: Aerial Views of Sacred Places.* New York: Aperture.

Burger, R., 1981, "The Radio Carbon Evidence for the Temporal Priority of Chavín de Huantar", *American Antiquity* 46(3): 592–602.

Burger, R. and F. Asaro, 1977, "Trace Element Analysis of Obsidian Artifacts from the Andes: New Perspectives on Pre-Hispanic Economic Interaction in Peru and Bolivia". Berkeley: Lawrence Berkeley Laboratory Report 6343.

Burger, R. and L. Burger, 1985, "The Early Ceremonial Center of Huaricoto", in *Early Ceremonial Architecture in the Andes,* ed. C. Donnan, pp. 111–138. Washington, D.C.: Dumbarton Oaks Research Library and Collection.

Burl, A., 1981, *Rites of the Gods.* London: Dent.

Caillavet, C., 1985, "La Adaptación de la Dominación Incaica a las Sociedades Autóctonas de la Frontera Septentrional del Imperio: (Territorio Otavalo-Ecuador)", *Revista Andina* 3(2): 403–424.

Callapiña, S., 1974 [1542] *Relación de la Descendencia, Gobierno y Conquista de los Incas.* Lima: Ediciones de la Biblioteca Universitaria.

Cané, R., 1978, "Algunas Ideas Sobre los Dibujos Gigantes y Grupos de Lineas Principalmente de la Zona de Palpa-Nasca en el Perú". *Actas del VII Congreso Arqueologia de Chile,* Vol. II (Santiago): 561–573.

Cané, R., 1985, "La Adoración de Montaña y la Interpretación de Algunos Geoglifos y Petroglifos de Quebrada Aroma, Chile y Pampa Nazca, Perú". *Estudios en Arte Rupestre* (Museo Chileño de Arte Precolumbino, Santiago) (unnumbered volume), pp. 233–241.

Carmichael, P., n.d. "Nasca Mortuary Customs: Death and Ancient Society on the South Coast of Peru." Ph.D. Diss., Dept. of Archaeology, Univ. of Calgary, Canada (1988).

Carpenter, E., 1973, *Eskimo Realities.* New York: Holt.

Castro, C. and D. Morejon, 1968 [1558], *Relación de Chincha,* in *Biblioteca Peruana,* Primera serie, 3, pp. 367–389. Lima: Editores Tecnicas Asociados.

Chavez van Dorne, R., 1973, *Esculturas Pre-Olmecas.* Guatemala: Ministro de Educación, Editorial J. de Pineda I.

Cieza de Leon, P., 1962 [1553], *El Señorio de Los Incas.* Lima: Colleción Autores Peruanas.

Cieza de Leon, P., 1973 [1551], *La Cronica del Perú.* Lima: Biblioteca Peruana.

Clarkson, P., 1985, "Archaeoethnography: Classic Maya Representations as Ethnographic Documents", in *Status, Structure, and Stratification,* ed. M. Thompson, M. Garcia, and F. Kense, pp. 307–319. Calgary: Proceedings of the Sixteenth Annual Chacmool Conference.

Clarkson, P., n.d. a. "Preliminary Report on the 1982 Field Season in Nasca". mimeo (1982).

Clarkson, P., n.d. b. "The Archaeology and Geoglyphs of Nasca, Peru". Ph.D. dissertation in Archaeology, University of Calgary, Canada (1985).

Cobo, B., 1956 [1653], *Historia del Nuevo Mundo,* Madrid: Biblioteca de Autores Españoles, Vol. 91–2.

Conkey, M., 1980, "Context, Structure and Efficacy in Paleolithic Art and Design", in *Symbol as Sense,* ed. M. Foster and S. Brandes, pp. 225–248. New York: Academic Press.

Conklin, W., 1982, "The Information System of Middle Horizon Quipus", in *Ethnoastronomy and Archaeoastronomy in the American Tropics,* ed. A. Aveni and G. Urton, pp. 261–281. New York: *Annals of the New York Academy of Sciences,* 385.

Conrad, G., 1981, "Reply to Paulsen and Isbell", *American Antiquity* 46(1): 38–42.

Cook, A., n.d., "Ritual Tribute as an Expression of Huari Political Organization", paper presented at the Roundtable on Huari Political Organization, Dumbarton Oaks, 16–17 May, 1985.

Craig, A., 1968, "Marine Desert Ecology of Southern Peru: Final "Report". Boca Raton: Florida Atlantic University.

Craig, A. and N. Psuty, 1968, "The Paracas Papers: Studies in Marine Desert Ecology", Reconnaissance report, vol. 1, no. 2, *Occasional Publication No. 1 of the Dept. of Geography.* Boca Raton: Florida Atlantic University.

"Cuaderno que contiene los títulos de la viña e Ingenio de San José de la Nazca.." 1644 *Archivo General de la Nación* (AGN) *Títulos de Propiedad* (Lima), Legajo 4, cuaderno 82, folios 244.

Cusihuamán, C.A., 1976, *Diccionario Quechua Cusco-Collao.* Lima: I.E.P.

Dalton, G., 1977, "Aboriginal Economics in Stateless Societies", in *Exchange Systems in Prehistory,* ed. T. Earle and J. Ericson, pp. 191–212. New York: Academic Press.

Damp, J., 1982, "Ceramic Art and Symbolism in

the Early Valdívia Community", *Journal of Latin American Lore* 8(2): 155–178.

Daniken, E. von, 1971, *Chariots of the Gods*. New York: Bantam.

Davis, E., 1981, "Shamanism and Ikonography [sic] of Paleoindians: The Exciting Story of the Deserts [sic] Stone Mythology", *Great Basin Foundation Newsletter.*

Deuel, L., 1969, *Flights into Yesterday: The Story of Aerial Archaeology*. New York: St. Martin's Press.

Diez de San Miguel, G., 1964 [1567], *Visita Hecha a la Provincia de Chucuito por Garci Diez de San Miguel en el año 1567*. Versión Paleográfica de la Visita y una Biografía del Visitador por Waldemar Espinoza Soriano. Documentos Regionales para la Etnología y Etnohistoria Andinas, Tomo I. Lima: Ediciones de la Casa de la Cultura del Perú.

Doering, H., 1958, "Bericht über archäologische Feldarbeiten in Peru", *Ethnos* 23(2–4): 67–99.

Dorn, R., 1989, "Cation: A Geographical Perspective," Progress in Physical Geography 13.

Dorn, R., D. Bamforth, T. Cahill, C. Dohrenwend, B. Turrin, D. Donahue, A. Jull, A. Long, M. Macko, E. Weil, D. Whitley, and T. Zabel, 1986, "Cation-ratio and Accelerator Radiocarbon Dating of Rock Varnish on Mojave Artifacts and Landforms", *Science* 231: 830–833.

Dorn, R.I., A.J.T. Jull, D.J. Donahue, T.W. Linnick, and L.J. Toolin, 1989, "Accelerator radiocarbon dating of rock varnish". *Geological Society of America Bulletin* 101: 1363–1372.

Dorn, R. and T. Oberlander, 1981a, "Microbial Origin of Desert Varnish", *Science* 213: 1245–1247.

Dorn, R. and T. Oberlander, 1981b, "Rock Varnish Origin, Characteristics, and Usage", *Zeitschift für Geomorphologie* 25: 420–436.

Dorn R. and D. Whitley, 1984, "Chronometric and Relative Age Determination of Petroglyphs in the Western United States", *Annals of the Association of American Geographers* 74(2): 308–322.

Douglas, M., 1966, *Purity and Danger*. Baltimore: Penguin Books.

Doyle, F., 1985, "The Large Format Camera on Shuttle Mission 41-G", in *Photogrammetric Engineering and Remote Sensing*, vol. 51(2), pp. 200–206, February 1985.

Duviols, P., 1967 [1592], "Un inédit de Cristóbal de Albornóz: La instrucción para descubrir todas las guacas del Pirú y sus camayos y haziendas", *Journal de Société des Américanistes* 56(1): 7–40.

Dwyer, J., n.d., "Chronology and Iconography of Late Paracas and Early Nasca Textile Designs", Ph.D. dissertation in Anthropology, University of California at Berkeley (1971).

Dwyer, J., 1979, "The Chronology and Iconography of Paracas-style Textiles", in *The Junius B. Bird Pre-Columbian Textile Conference*, ed. A. Rowe, E. Benson, and A. Schaffer, pp. 105–127. Washington, D.C.: The Textile Museum and Dumbarton Oaks.

Eckhardt, R., 1985, "Reinterpretation of a Nazca Desert Figure: From Las Manos to Resting Bat", *Current Anthropology* 26(4): 516–517.

"El maestro de campo Don Nicolas devalos y Rivera alcalde hordinario desta ciudad de los Reyes . . ." 1677, *Archivo General de la Nación* (AGN) *Real Hacienda* (Lima), Legajo 6, cuaderno 58, folios 23.

Eliade, M., 1959, *The Sacred and the Profane*. New York: Harcourt, Brace, and World.

Ellegård, A., 1981, "Stone Age Science in Britain?" *Current Anthropology* 22: 99–125.

Engel, F., 1973, "New Facts about Pre-Columbian Life in the Andean Lomas", *Current Anthropology* 14: 271–280.

Engel, F. (ed.), 1980, *Prehistoric Andean Ecology* (2 vols.). New York: Humanities Press, CUNY Hunter College.

Engel, F., 1981, *Prehistoric Andean Ecology. The Deep South*. New York: Humanities Press, CUNY Hunter College.

Erickson, J., D. Read, and C. Burke, 1972, "Research Design: The Relationship Between the Primary Functions and the Physical Properties of Ceramic Vessels and their Implications for Ceramic Distributions on an Archaeological Site", Berkeley: *University of California Publications in Anthropology* 3(2): 84–95.

Espinoza S., W., 1981, "El Trabajo de los *Yanayacos* en las Tierras del Inca", in *Los Modos de Producción en el Imperio de los Incas*, ed. W. E. Soriano, pp. 299–328. Lima: Amaru Editores S.A.

Fairchild, A., n.d., "Rakiy: The Ritual Expression of Discontinuities in a Quecha Community" (ms., Cornell University Anthropology Department, 1979).

Fajardo Osco, H., 1984, "Maria Reiche", *La Region* 28: 6–11.

Freeman, P. and W. Elmore, 1979, "A Test for the Significance of Astronomical Alignments", *Archaeoastronomy* (supplement to *Journal for the History of Astronomy*), no. 1: S86–96.

*Fundación del Convento Hospital de Yca*, 1774 [1549–

1744], *Archivo General de la Nación* (AGN), *Archivo de la Beneticencia, 1 ca, #44.*

Fung Piñeda, R., 1969, "Las Haldas: Dedalo", *Revista del Arte y Arqueologia,* V (Sao Paolo).

Gade, D. and M. Escobar, 1982, "Village Settlement and the Colonial Legacy in Southern Peru", *Geographical Review* 72(4): 430–449.

Galdos, R.G., 1977, "Visita a Atico y Caravelí (1549)", *Revista del Archivo General de la Nación* (Lima) no. 4–5.

Garcia Payón, J., 1958, *Malinalco—Official Guide.* Mexico: I.N.A.H.

Garcilasco de la Vega, (El Inca) 1966 [1609], *Royal Commentaries of the Inca* (2 vols.), H. Livermore (trans.). Austin: University of Texas Press.

Gasparini, G. and L. Margolies, 1980, *Inca Architecture.* Bloomington: Indiana University Press.

Gayton, A. and A. Kroeber, 1927, "The Uhle Pottery Collections from Nazca." *University of California Publications in American Archaeology and Ethnology* 1: 1–46.

Gelles, P., n.d., "Agua, Faenas y Organización Comunal en los Andes: El caso de San Pedro de Casta". Pontificia Universidad Católica del Perú (Lima), M.A. thesis (1984).

Glick, T., 1970, *Irrigation and Society in Medieval Valencia.* Harvard: Belknap.

González Holguín, D., 1952 [1608] *Vocabulario de la Lengua General de todo el Perú Llamada Qquechua o del Inca (1608).* Instituto de Historia, Universidad Nacional Mayor de San Marcos (Lima).

González, G., 1978 [1935], "Los Acueductos Incaicos de Nazca", in *Tecnología Andina,* ed. R. Ravines, pp. 129–156. Lima: Instituto de Investigación Technologica y de Normas Tecnicas.

González de San Segundo, M., 1982, "El Doctor Gregorio González de Cuenca, Oidor de la Audiencia de Lima, y sus Ordenanzas Sobre Caciques e Indios Principales (1566)", *Revista de Indias* 42(169–170): 643–667.

Goris, R., 1969, "Pura Besakih, Bali's State Temple", in *Bali: Further Studies in Life, Thought, and Ritual,* pp. 75–88. The Hague: W. van Hoeve.

Gow, D., 1974, "Taytacha Qoyllur R'iti", *Allpanchis Phuturinqa* 7: 49–100.

Grosboll, S. n.d., a, "Domestic Architecture as an Artifact: Survey Data from Huánuco, Peru" (ms.).

Grosboll, S. n.d., b, "Ethnic Boundaries within the Inca Empire: Evidence from Huánuco, Peru" (ms.).

Guaman Poma de Ayala, F., 1980 [1584–1614] *El Primer Nueva Corónica y Buen Gobierno por Felipe Guaman Poma de Ayala.* Edición critica de John V. Murra y Rolena Adorno, Mexico: Siglo Veintiuno.

Gutiérrez de Santa Clara, 1963 [1599?], "Quinquenarios o Historia de las Guerras Civiles del Perú". Madrid: Bibliotheca de Autores Españoles, Vol. 165–167.

Hadingham, E., 1987, *Lines to the Mountain Gods: Nazca and the Mysteries of Peru.* New York: Random House.

von Hagen, V., 1955, *Highway of the Sun.* New York: Duell, Sloan and Pearce.

von Hagen, V. (ed.), 1959, *The Incas of Pedro Cieza de Leon,* tr. H. de Onis. Norman: University of Oklahoma Press.

Hally, D., 1986, "The Identification of Vessel Function: A Case Study from Northwest Georgia", *American Antiquity* 51(2): 267–295.

Hammond, N., 1984, "Place of Pilgrimage", *Quarterly Review of Archaeology* 5(4): 1.

Hawkes, J., 1967, "God in the Machine", *Antiquity* 41: 174–180.

Hawkins, G., 1963, "Stonehenge Decoded", *Nature* 200: 306–308.

Hawkins, G., 1966, "Astro-archaeology", Cambridge: *Smithsonian Institution Astrophysical Observatory Special Report* No. 226.

Hawkins, G., 1969, "Ancient Lines in the Peruvian Desert—Final Scientific Report for the National Geographic Society", Cambridge: *Smithsonian Institution Astrophysical Observatory Special Report* No. 906–4.

Hawkins, G., 1973, *Beyond Stonehenge.* New York: Harper & Row.

Hawkins, G., 1974a, "Astronomical Alignments in Britain, Egypt and Peru", *Transactions of the Royal Society* (London) Series A, 276: 157–167.

Hawkins, G., 1974b, "Prehistoric Desert Markings in Peru", *National Geographic Research Reports for 1967:* 117–144.

Hawkins, G., 1975, "Astroarchaeology: The Unwritten Evidence", in *Archaeoastronomy in Pre-Columbian America,* ed. A. Aveni, pp. 131–162. Austin: University of Texas Press.

Heggie, D., 1981, *Megalithic Science.* London: Thames and Hudson.

Herrán, E., 1985, *The Nazca Lines: New Designs, New Enigmas.* Lima: Friba Publishers.

Horkheimer, H., 1947, "Las Plazoletas, Rayas y Figuras Prehispánicas en las Pampas, y Crestas de la Hoya del Río Grande", *Revista de Universidad Nacional de Trujillo* (Epoca II) (No. 1): 47–63.

Hyslop, J., 1984, *The Inka Road System*. New York: Academic Press.

Hyslop, J., 1985, "Astronomical Alignments and Mapping at Inkawasi", Appendix 3, in *Inkawasi, the New Cuzco*, pp. 129–136. Oxford: British Archaeological Reports (International Series) 234.

Hyslop, J. and J. Urrutía, 1980, "Un Camino Prehistórico en la Costa Norte", *Boletín de Lima* 6: 14–20.

Iensen, E., 1971, "Exploración y Reconocimientos Aereos para la Arqueología en la Zona Norte de Chile", *Revista Geografica de Chile* (Santiago), no. 2: 189–192.

Illescas Cook, G., 1952, *Astronomos en el Antiguo Perú*. Lima: Editores Kosmos.

Iribarren, J., 1968, "Dispersión de las Figuras Rupestres en el Norte de Chile", *Actas y Memorías del XXXVII Congreso Internacional de Americanistas*, Vol. II (Buenos Aires), pp. 391–418.

Isbell, B.J., 1974, "Parentesco Andino y Reciprocidad. Kuyaq: Los que Nos Aman", in *Reciprocidad e Intercambio en Los Andes Peruanos*, ed. G. Alberti and E. Mayer, pp. 110–152. Lima: Instituto de Estudios Peruanos.

Isbell, B.J., 1977, "Those Who Love Me: An Analysis of Andean Kinship and Reciprocity Within a Ritual Context", in *Andean Kinship and Marriage*, ed. R. Bolton and E. Mayer, pp. 81–105. Special Publication of the American Anthropological Association, number 7.

Isbell, B.J., 1978, *To Defend Ourselves*. Austin: University of Texas Press.

Isbell, B.J. and A. Fairchild (n.d.), "Moiety Systems and the Integration of Socioeconomic Space in the Andes" (ms.).

Isbell, W., 1977, "The Rural Foundation for Urbanism", *Illinois Studies in Anthropology*, no. 10. Urbana: University of Illinois Press.

Isbell, W., 1978, "The Prehistoric Ground Drawings of Peru", *Scientific American* 239(4): 140–153. Reprinted in *Pre-Columbian Archaeology*, ed. G. Willey and J. Sabloff. San Francisco: W.H. Freeman), pp. 189–196.

Isbell, W., 1979a, Review of Reiche: *Geheimnis der Wüste (Mystery on the Desert)*, *Archaeoastronomy Bulletin* 2(4): 34–36.

Isbell, W., 1979b, "Review of G. Hawkins: 'Final Scientific Report to the National Geographic Society'", *Archaeoastronomy Bulletin* 2(4): 38–40.

Isbell, W. and K. Schreiber, 1978, "Was Huari a State?" *American Antiquity* 43(3): 372–389.

Izumi, S., 1971, Selected Works of Seiichi Izumi 4, Ancient Civilization of the Andes—Title in Japanese. Tokyo: Yomiuri Shinbunsha.

Jiménez, B., A and A. Bueno M., 1970, "Breves Notas Acerca de Pachacamac", *Arqueología y Sociedad* 4: 13–25.

Johnson, G., 1982, "Organizational Structure and Scalar Stress", in *Theory and Explanation in Archaeology*, ed. C. Renfrew, M. Rowlands, and B. Segraves, pp. 389–422. New York: Academic Press.

Johnson, G. n.d., "Dynamics of Southwestern Prehistory: Far Outside-Looking In", in *Dynamics of Southwestern Prehistory*, ed. D. Schwartz, a volume in the School of American Research Advanced Seminar Series (in press).

Johnson, G. and E. Kase, 1977, "Mapping an Ancient Trade Route with Balloon Photography", *Photogrammetric Engineering and Remote Sensing* 43(12): 1489–1493.

Julien, C., 1974, Report in "Current Research", *American Antiquity* 39(2): 384.

Kauffmann, Doig, F., 1969, *Manual de Arqueología Peruana*. Lima: Iberia, S.A.

Kelley, D. and D. Bonavía, 1963, "New Evidence for Preceramic Maize on the Coast of Peru", *Ñawpa Pacha* 1: 39–41.

Kern, H. and M. Reiche, 1974, *Peruanische Erdzeichen/Peruvian Ground Drawings*. Munich: Kunstraum München E.V.

Kolata, A., 1980, "Chanchan: Crecimiento de una ciudad Antigua", in *Chanchan: Metropolí Chimu*, ed. R. Ravines, pp. 130–154. Lima: Instituto de Estudios Peruanos.

Kosok, P., 1940, "The Role of Irrigation in Ancient Peru", *Proceedings of the 8th American Scientific Congress* 2: 169–178.

Kosok, P., 1947a, "Pre-Inca Markings in Peru", *Life* 23: (28 July): 75–76.

Kosok, P., 1947b, "Desert Puzzle of Peru", *Science Illustrated* 2(9): 60–61, 92.

Kosok, P., 1959, "Astronomy, the Priesthood, and the State: New Aspects of Ancient Nasca", *Zeitschrift für Ethnologie* 84: 5–18.

Kosok, P., 1965, *Life, Land and Water in Ancient Peru*. Brooklyn: Long Island University Press.

Kosok, P. and M. Reiche, 1947, "The Mysterious Markings of Nazca", *Natural History* 56: 200–207, 237–238.

Kosok, P. and M. Reiche, 1949, "Ancient Drawings on the Desert of Peru", *Archaeology* 2(4): 206–215.

Kroeber, A., 1942, "Peruvian Archaeology in

1942", Viking Fund Publications in Anthropology, no. 4.

Kroeber, A., 1956, "Toward a Definition of the Nazca Style", Berkeley: *University of California Publications in American Archaeology and Ethnology* 43(4) (Mimeographed sheets dated 1982).

Kroeber, A., n.d., Untitled manuscript in the Kroeber collections at the Field Museum of Natural History, Chicago.

Lambert, B., 1977, *Peru Before the Incas.* Englewood Cliffs: Prentice-Hall.

Lancho, J., n.d., Untitled mimeograph sheet on Nazca lines in vicinity of Cantalloc.

Lanning, E., 1967, *Peru Before the Incas.* New York: Prentice-Hall.

Lapiner, A., 1976, *Precolumbian Art of South America.* New York: Abrams.

Larco Hoyle, R., 1948, *Cronología Arqueologica del Norte del Perú.* Buenos Aires: Sociedad Geografica Americana.

Lathrap, D., 1974, "The Moist Tropics, the Arid Lands, and the Appearance of Great Art Styles in the New World", in *Art and Environment in Native America,* ed. M. King and I. Traylor, Jr., Lubbock: Museum of Texas Tech University, Special Publication No. 7.

Lathrap, D., 1985, "Jaws: The Control of Power in the Early Nuclear American Ceremonial Center", in *Early Ceremonial Architecture in the Andes,* ed. C. Donnan, pp. 241–268. Washington, D.C.: Dumbarton Oaks Research Library and Collection.

Lehmann-Nitsche, R., 1928, "Coricancha", *Revista del Museo de la Plata* (Argentina) 31: 1–260.

Liefrinck, F., 1969, "Rice Cultivation in Northern Bali", in *Bali: Further Studies in Life, Thought, and Ritual,* pp. 1–74. The Hague: W. van Hoeve.

Lillesand, T. and R. Kiefer, 1987, "Remote Sensing and Image Interpretation (Edition 2)", in ? New York: Wiley, pp. 533–561.

Lothrop, S. and J. Mahler, 1957, "Late Nazca Burials in Chaviña, Peru", Cambridge: *Papers of the Peabody Museum of Archaeology and Ethnography* 50(2).

Lumbreras, L., 1960, "La Cultura de Wari, Ayacucho", *Etnología y Arqueología,* 1: 130–226 Lima: Universidad Nacional Mayor de San Marcos.

Lumbreras, L., 1974, *People and Cultures of Ancient Peru,* (tr. B. Meggers). Washington: Smithsonian Institution Press.

Lumbreras, L., 1981, *Arqueología de la America Andina.* Lima: Editorial Milla Batres.

Lumbreras, L., 1984, "Le Ceramica como Indica-

dor de Culturas", *Gaceta Arqueologica Andina* 12:3.

Lyon, P., 1968, "A Redefinition of the Pinilla Style", *Ñawpa Pacha* 6: 7–14.

Lyon, P., 1966, "Innovation through Archaism: The Origins of the Ica Pottery Style", *Ñawpa Pacha* 4: 31–47, 51–61.

Maquet, J., 1979, *Introduction to Aesthetic Anthropology,* (2nd ed.). Malibu: Undena Publications.

Maquet, J., 1986, *The Aesthetic Experience: An Anthropologist Looks at the Visual Arts.* New Haven: Yale University Press.

Mariscotti, A., 1978, "Los Curi y el Rayo", *Actes du XLII Congress International des Americanistes* (1976), Vol. 4 (Paris): 365–376.

Marquina, I., 1951, *Arquitectura Prehispanica.* Mexico: I.N.A.H.

Mason, J., 1926, "Dr. Farabee's Last Journey", *Museum Journal* (Philadelphia: The University Museum) XVII (2): 128–165.

Massey, S., n.d., "Sociopolitical Change in the Upper Ica Valley BC 400 to 400 AD: Regional States on the South Coast of Peru". Ph.D. Dissertation, Dept. of Anthropology, UCLA.

Masson, D., 1976, "Those Nazca Lines", *Lima Times,* July: 7–11.

Matienzo, J. de, 1967 [1567], *Gobierno de Perú,* Edition et Etude Préliminaire par G. Lohman Villena. Paris-Lima: Institut Français d'Etudes Andines.

Matos, R., 1980, "Las Culturas Regionales Tempranas", in *Historia del Perú,* ed. J. Mejia B., Vol. 1, pp. 353–524. Lima.

Maurtua, V., 1906, "Discurso de la Sucesión y Gobierno de los Yngas (Manuscrito anonimo sin fecha)", *Juicio de Límites entre el Perú y Bolivia,* Prueba Peruana, Vol. 8, pp. 149–165. Chunchos.

Mayer, E., 1974, "Las Reglas del Juego en la Reciprocidad Andina", in *Reciprocidad e Intercambio en los Andes Peruanos,* ed. G. Alberti and E. Mayer, pp. 37–64. Lima: IEP.

Mayer, E., 1977, "Beyond the Nuclear Family", in *Andean Kinship and Marriage,* ed. R. Bolton and E. Mayer, pp. 60–80. Special Publication of the American Anthropological Association, number 7.

Mayer, E., n.d., "Production Zones". Paper presented in "An Interdisciplinary Perspective on Andean Ecological Complementary", Wenner-Gren Foundation Symposium, Florida (1983).

McCluskey, S., n.d., "Science, Society, Objectivity and the Astronomies of the Southwest", (ms.).

McIntyre, L., 1975, "Mystery of the Ancient Nazca Lines", *National Geographic* 147(5): 716–728.

Mejía Xesspe, T., 1927, "Acueductos y Caminos Antiguos de la Hoya del Rió Grande de Nasca", Lima: Museo de Antropología.

Mejía Xesspe, T., 1940 [1927], "Acueductos y Caminos Antiguos de la Hoya del Rio Grande de Nasca", *Actas y Trabajos Científicos.* XXVII Congreso Internacional de Americanistas, Lima (1939), Tomo I: 559–569.

"Memoria y apuntos por donde se vera el derecho que el Collegio de la Compañía de Jesús tiene a las tierras y viña de la hazienda nombrada San Joseph . . .", 1648, *Archivo General de la Nación* (AGN) *Derecho Indigena* (Lima) Legajo 7, cuaderno 146.

Menzel, D., 1959, "The Inca Occupation of the South Coast of Peru", *Southwest Journal of Anthropology* 15(2): 125–142.

Menzel, D., 1964, "Style and Time in the Middle Horizon", *Ñawpa Pacha* 2: 1–106.

Menzel, D., 1966, "New Data on the Huari Empire in Middle Horizon Epoch 2A", *Ñawpa Pacha* 6: 47–114.

Menzel, D., 1971, "Estudios Arqueologicos en los Valles de Ica, Pisco, Chincha, Cañete", *Arqueología y Sociedad* 6 (Lima): Universidad Nacional Mayor de San Marcos).

Menzel, D., 1976, *Pottery Style and Society in Ancient Peru.* Berkeley: University of California Press.

Menzel, D., 1977, *The Archaeology of Ancient Peru and the Work of Max Uhle.* Berkeley: R.H. Lowie Museum, University of California.

Menzel, D. & F. Riddell, 1986, *Archaeological Investigations at Tambo Viejo, Acarí Valley, Peru, 1954.* Sacramento: California Institute for Peruvian Studies.

Menzel, D., J. Rowe, and L. Dawson, 1964, "The Paracas Pottery of Ica, a Study in Style and Time", Berkeley: *University of California Publications in American Archaeology and Ethnology,* 50.

Metraux, A., 1934, "L'Organisation Sociale et les Survivances Religieuses des Indiéns Uro-Čipaya de Carangas (Bolivie)", *XXV International Congrès des Américanistes* (La Plata, 1932) vol. 1: 191–213.

Meyer, M. and P. Grumstrup, 1978, "Operating Manual for the Montana 35mm Aerial Photography System". St. Paul: University of Minnesota, Remote Sensing Laboratory, Report 78-1.

Moller, H. and E. Aguilar, 1982, "El Enigma de Macahui", *Mexico Escondido*, no. 66: 4–7.

Monzón, L., 1881 [1586], "Descripción de la Tierra del Repartimiento de los Rucanas Antamarcas de la Corona Real, Jurisdicción de la Cd. Guamanga, 1586", in *Relaciones Geograficas de Indias,* ed. M. Jímenez de la Espada, Vol. I: 197–216. Madrid.

Morinis, E. and N. Crumrine, n.d., "La Peregrinación: The Pilgrimage in Latin America".

Morris, C. and D. Thompson, 1985, *An Inca City and its Hinterland.* London: Thames and Hudson.

Morris, R., 1975, "Aligned with Nazca", *Artforum* 14: 26–39.

Morrison, T., 1978, *Pathways to the Gods, the Mystery of the Andes Lines.* Lima: Andean Air Mail and Peruvian Times.

Morrison, T., 1987, *The Mystery of the Nazca Lines.* Suffolk: Nonesuch.

Moseley, M., 1983, "Central Andean Civilization", in *Ancient South Americans,* ed. J. Jennings, pp. 178–239. San Francisco: W.H. Freeman and Company.

Moseley, M., 1975, "Prehistoric Principles of Labor Organization in the Moche Valley, Peru", *American Antiquity* 40(2): 191–196.

Murphy, R., 1936, *Bird Islands of Peru; Oceanic Birds of South America.* New York: Macmillan.

Murra, J., 1980, *The Economic Organization of the Inka State.* Greenwich, Connecticut: JAI Press, Inc.

Myers, J. and E. Myers, 1980, "The Art of Flying: Balloon Archaeology", *Archaeology* 33(6): 33–40.

Myers, J. and E. Myers, 1985, "Aerial Atlas of Ancient Crete", *Archaeology* 38(5): 18–25.

Nabokov, P., 1981, *Indian Running.* Santa Barbara: Capra.

Neave, H. and K. Selkirk, 1983, "Nearest-neighbor Analysis of the Distribution of Points on a Circle", Nottingham: University of Nottingham Research Report 05–83.

Netherly, P., 1984, "The Management of Late Andean Irrigation Systems on the North Coast of Peru", *American Antiquity* 49: 227–254.

Netherly, P., n.d., "Local Level Lords on the North Coast of Peru", Ph.D. dissertation in Anthropology, Cornell University, Ithaca, N.Y. (1977).

Newhall, B., 1969, *Airborne Camera: The World from the Air and Outer Space,* New York: Hastings House.

Niemeyer, H. and J. Montane, 1968, "El Arte Rupestre Indigena en la Zona Centro Sur de Chile", *Actas y Memorias del XXXVII Congreso Internacional de Americanistas,* vol. II (Buenos Aires), pp. 419–452.

Nuñez, L., 1976, "Geoglifos y Trafico de Caravanas en el Desierto Chileño", in *Homenaje al Dr. Gustavo LePaige, S.J.*, pp. 147–201. Antofagasta, Chile: Universidad del Norte.

ONERN (Oficina Nacional de Evaluación de Recursos Naturales) 1971, Inventario Evaluación, y Uso Racional de Los Recursos Naturales de las Costa Cuenca del Río Grande, Vols. 1 and 2, *Oficina Nacional de Evaluación de Recursos naturales,* Lima: Presidente de la Republica, Republica del Perú.

Ossio, J., 1981, "Expresiónes Simbólicas y Sociales de los Ayllus Andinos: El Caso de los Ayllus de la Comunidad de Cabaña y del Antiguo Repartimiento de los Rucanas-Antamarcas", *Etínohistoria y Antropología Andina,* ed. Amalia Castelli, y otros, pp. 189–214. Lima.

Pan American Union, 1965, "Annotated Index of Aerial Photograph Coverage and Mapping of Topography in Peru". Washington, D.C., Department of Economic Affairs.

Patrick, J., 1974, "Midwinter Sunrise at Newgrange", *Nature* 249: 517–519.

Patterson, T., 1966, "Pattern and Process in the Early Intermediate Period Pottery of the Central Coast of Peru", *University of California Publication in Anthropology* 3.

Patterson, T., 1986, "Ideology, Class Formation, and Resistance in the Inca State", *Critique of Anthropology* VI(1): 75–85.

Patterson, T., n.d., "Andean Cosmologies and the Inca State", paper presented at the Conference on Andean and Lowland South American Cosmological Systems, University of Chicago, 16–17 May 1986.

Paulsen, A., 1983, "Huaca del Loro Revisited: the Nasca-Huarpa Connection", in *Investigations of the Andean Past,* ed. D. Sandweiss, pp. 93–121. Cornell University, Ithaca: Papers from the First Annual Conference on Andean Archaeology and Ethnohistory.

Paulsen, A., n.d., a "Pottery from Huaca del Loro, South Coast of Peru" (ms.).

Peters, A., n.d., b "Pachinga: Habitation & Necropolis in the Lower Pisco Valley". Paper presented at the 51st Annual Meeting of the Society of American Archaeology, New Orleans, 1986.

Peterson, J., 1980, "Evolución y Desaparición de las Altas Culturas Paracas-Cahuachi (Nasca). Lima: Universidad Nacional Federico Villareal.

Pezzia, A., A., 1962, *La Cultura Nazca.* Lima.

Pezzia, A., A., 1968, *Arqueología de la Provincia de Ica.* Ica y el Perú Precolombino, vol. I, Ica, Perú: Ojeda S.A.

Pezzia, A., A., 1969, "Guia del Mapa Arqueologico Pictografico del Departamento de Ica", Lima: Editorial Italperu (reissued 1978).

Pezzia, A., A., 1979, "El Rayado Descomunal Nazquense", Ica, Perú: Instituto Nacional de la Cultura, Oficina Departmental.

Platt, T., 1982, "Estado Boliviano y Ayllu Andino", Lima: I.E.P. (Instituto de Estudios Peruanos).

Poole, D., n.d., "Rituals of Movement, Rites of Transformation: Pilgrimage and Dance in the Highlands of Cuzco, Peru" (ms.).

Proulx, D., 1966, Report in Current Research, *American Antiquity* 35(5): 775.

Proulx, D., 1968, *Local Differences and Time Differences in Nasca Pottery.* Berkeley: University of California Publications in Archaeology, vol. 5.

Proulx, D., 1970, *Nasca Gravelots in the Uhle Collection from the Ica Valley, Peru.* University of Massachusetts, Department of Anthropology, Amherst.

Proulx, D., 1983, "The Nasca Style", in *Art of the Andes: Pre-Columbian Sculptured and Painted Ceramics from the Arthur M. Sackler Collections,* ed. L. Katz, pp. 87–106. Washington, D.C.: Arthur M. Sackler Foundation.

Proulx, D., n.d., "A Thematic Approach to Nasca Mythical Iconography". Paper presented at the 51st Annual Meeting of the Society for American Archaeology, New Orleans, 1986.

Putnam, F.W., 1914, "The Davenport Collection of Nazca and Other Peruvian Pottery", *Proceedings of the Davenport Academy of Sciences* (Davenport, Iowa) 13: 17–46.

Ramos, L. and C. Blasco B., 1977, "Las Representaciónes de 'Aves Fantasticas' en Materiales Nazcas del Museo de America de Madrid", *Revista de Indias,* XXXVII, nums. 147–148, Madrid.

Ravines, R., 1968, "Un Deposito de Ofrendas del Horizonte Medio en la Sierra Cental del Perú", *Ñawpa Pacha* 6: 19–46.

Reeve, M., n.d., "Identity as Process: The Meaning of RUNAPURA for Quichua Speakers of the Curaray River, Eastern Ecuador". Ph.D. dissertation in Anthropology, University of Illinois at Urbana-Champaign (1985).

Regal, A., 1943, "Los Acueductos Precolumbinos de Nasca", *Revista Universidad Catolica del Perú* (Lima) 11(4–5): 210–213.

Reiche, M., 1949a, *Mystery on the Desert: A Study of the Ancient Figures and Strange Delineated Surfaces Seen from the Air Near Nazca, Peru.* Nazca, Peru.

Reiche, M., 1949b, "Los Dibujos Gigantescos en el Suelo de las Pampas de Nasca y Palpa", Lima.

Reiche, M., 1951, "Orientación y Medidas en los Dibujos Antiguos de las Pampas de Nasca", *Homenage al IV Centenario de la Fundación de la Universidad, Conferencia de Ciencias Antropologicas* pp. 219–227. Lima: Universidad Nacional Mayor de San Marcos.

Reiche, M., 1955, "Prehistoric Ground Drawings in Peru", *Photographie und Forschung* 6(4) (Stuttgart): 97–108.

Reiche, M., 1958, "Interpretación Astronomica de la Figura del Mono en la Pampa al Sur del Río Ingenio", *Centro de Estudios Historicos-Militares del Peru. Actas y Trabajos del II Cong. Nac. del Perú, Epoca Prehispanica*, Vol. I, pp. 285–286.

Reiche, M., 1968a, "Giant Ground Drawings on the Peruvian Desert", *XXVII International Congress of Americanists* (Stuttgart, 1968) vol. I: 379–384.

Reiche, M., 1968b, *Mystery on the Desert*. Stuttgart: Eigenverlag.

Reiche, M., 1969, "Ratselbilder in der Wüste", *Hobby* 9: 66–75.

Reiche, M., 1973, "How the Nasca Lines Were Made", *Peruvian Times* (Lima), 23 Apr.: 9–13.

Reiche, M., 1974, "Las Gigantescas Huellas de Nazca y Palpa", *Imagen*, no. 3, Lima.

Reiche, M., 1980, *Geheimnis der Wuste/Mystery on the Desert/Secreto de la Pampa*. Stuttgart: Heinrich Fink Gmbh and Co.

Reinhard, J., 1983a, "Las Lineas de Nazca, Montañas y Fertilidad", *Boletín de Lima* 2: 29–49.

Reinhard, J., 1983b, "Las Montañas Sagradas: Un Estudio Etnoarqueologico de Ruinas en las Altas Cumbres Andinas", *Cuadernos de Historia* 3: 27–62.

Reinhard, J., 1985a, "Sacred Mountains: An Ethno-archaeological Study of High Andean Ruins", *Mountain Research and Development* 5(4): 299–317.

Reinhard, J., 1985b, "Chavín and Tiahuanaco: A New Look at Two Andean Ceremonial Centers", *National Geographic Research* 1(3): 395–422.

Reinhard, J., 1987, "The Nazca Lines: A New Perspective on Their Origin and Meaning", Lima: Editorial Los Pinos (1st ed. 1985).

Reinhard, J. 1988, "The Nazca Lines, Water, and Mountains: An Ethno-archaeological Study", in Recent Studies in PreColumbian Archaeology, ed N.J. Saunders & O. de Montmollin, pp. 363–414. BAR International Series 421(ii).

"Repartimiento de las Aguas del Río Nazca", 1772. *Archivo General de la Nación* (AGN) *Juzgado de Agua* (Lima), 3.3.4.11. folios 9.

Richardson, J., 1978, "Early Man on the Peruvian North Coast, Early Maritime Exploitation, and the Pleistocene and Holocene Environment", in *Early Man in America from a Circum-Pacific Perspective*, ed. A. Bryan, pp. 274–289. London: Archaeological Researches International, Ltd.

Roark, R., 1965, "From Monumental to Proliferous in Nasca Pottery", *Ñawpa Pacha* 3: 1–92.

Robinson, D., n.d., "An Archaeological Survey of the Nasca Valley, Peru", M.A. Thesis in Archaeology, Stanford University (1957).

Rogers, M., 1966, *Ancient Hunters of the Far West*. San Diego: San Diego Museum of Man.

Rossel C., A., 1942, "Sistema de Irrigación Antigua de Río Grande de Nasca", *Revista del Museo Nacional* (Lima) 11(2): 196–202.

Rossel C., A., 1947, "Lineas Geometricas Prehispanicas del Río Grande de Nasca", *El Comercio* (Lima) (15 Jan. 1947): 8.

Rossel C., A., 1959, "Figuras Geometricas Prehistoricas de la Hoya de Río Grande de Nasca", *Actas y Trabajos del II Congreso Nacional de la Historia del Perú*, (Lima) vol. I: 351–359.

Rossel C., A., 1977, *Arqueología Sur del Perú*. Lima: Editorial Universo.

Rossello Truel, L., 1977, "Sistemas Astronomicas de Campos de Rayas", *III Congreso Peruano: El hombre y La Cultura Andina, Actas y Trabajos*, ed. R. Matos M., (Lima), Vol. 2: 521–534.

Rossello Truel, L., 1986, "Función y Significado de las Linas de Nasca". Lima, privately printed.

Rossello Truel, L., C. Huapaya and L. Mazzotti, 1985, "Rayas y Figuras en la Pampa Canto Grande", *Boletín de Lima* 39: 41–58.

Rostworowski, M., 1977, Etnía y Sociedad, Costa Peruana Prehispanica", Lima: I.E.P.

Rostworowski, M., 1978a, "Patronyms with the Consonant /f/ in the *Guarangas* of Cajamarca", in *Andean Ecology and Civilization*, ed. S. Masuda, I. Shimada, and C. Morris, pp. 401–422. Tokyo: University of Tokyo Press.

Rostworowski, M., 1978b, *Señoriós Indigenas de Lima y Canta*. Lima: I.E.P.

Rostworowski, M., 1981, *Recursos Naturales Renovables y Pesca, Siglos XVI y XVII*. Lima: I.E.P.

Rostworowski, M., 1983, "Estructuras Andinas del Poder", Lima: I.E.P.

Rowe, J., 1945, "Absolute Chronology in the Andean Area", *American Antiquity* 10(3): 265–284.

Rowe, J., 1946, "Inca Culture at the Time of the Spanish Conquest", *Bureau of American Ethnology Bulletin*, 143(2): 183–330.

Rowe, J., 1948, "The Kingdom of Chimor", *Acta Americana* 6: 26–59.

Rowe, J., 1954, "Max Uhle, 1856–1944. A Memoir of the Father of Peruvian Archaeology", Berkeley: University of California Publications in American Anthropology and Ethnology, 46.

Rowe, J., 1956, "Archaeological Explorations in Southern Peru, 1954–55", *American Antiquity* 22(2): 135–150.

Rowe, J., 1959, "Archaeological Dating and Cultural Process", *Southwestern Journal of Anthropology* 13(4): 317–324.

Rowe, J., 1960, "Nuevos Datos Relatívos a la Cronología del Estilo Nasca", *Antiguo Perú: Espacio y Tiempo*, pp. 29–46. Lima: Juan Majía Bac.

Rowe, J., 1961, "Stratigraphy and Seriation", *American Antiquity* 26(3): 324–330.

Rowe, J., 1962a, "Alfred Louis Kroeber 1876–1960", *American Antiquity* 27(3): 395–415.

Rowe, J., 1962b, "Stages and Periods in Archaeological Interpretation", *Southwestern Journal of Anthropology* 18(1): 40–54.

Rowe, J., 1963, "Urban Settlements in Ancient Peru", *Ñawpa Pacha* 1: 1–27.

Rowe, J., 1979a, "An Account of the Shrines of Ancient Cuzco", *Ñawpa Pacha* 17: 1–80.

Rowe, J., 1979b, "Archaeoastronomy in Mesoamerica and Peru", *Latin American Research Review* 14(2): 227–233.

Rowe, J. and D. Menzel (eds.), 1967, *Peruvian Archaeology, Selected Readings*, pp. 293–320. Palo Alto: Peek Publications.

Ruggles, C., 1981, "A Critical Examination of the Megalithic Lunar Observatories", in *Astronomy and Society in Britain During the Period 4000–1500 B.C.*, ed. C. Ruggles and A. Whittle, pp. 153–209. Oxford: British Archaeological Reports (International Series 88).

Ruggles, C., 1982a, "Megalithic Astronomical Sightlines: Current Reassessment and Future Directions", in *Archaeoastronomy in the Old World*, ed. D. Heggie, pp. 83–105. Cambridge, England: Cambridge University Press.

Ruggles, C., 1982b, "A Reassessment of the High Precision Megalithic Lunar Sightlines, 1: Backsights, Indicators and the Archaeological Status of the Sightlines", *Archaeoastronomy* (Supplement to *Journal for the History of Astronomy*) no. 4: S21–S40.

Ruggles, C., 1983, "A Reassessment of the High Precision Megalithic Lunar Sightlines, 2: Foresights and the Problem of Selection", *Archaeo-astronomy* (Supplement to *Journal for the History of Astronomy*) no. 5: S1–S36.

Ruggles, C., 1984a, *Megalithic Astronomy: A New Archaeological and Statistical Study of 300 Western Scottish Sites*. Oxford: British Archaeological Reports (British Series) 123.

Ruggles, C., 1984b, "A New Study of the Aberdeenshire Recumbent Stone Circles, 1: Site Data", *Archaeoastronomy* (Supplement to *Journal for the History of Astronomy*) no. 6: S55–S79.

Ruggles, C., 1984c, "Megalithic Astronomy: The Last Five Years", *Vistas in Astronomy* 27: 231–289.

Ruggles, C., 1985, "The Linear Settings of Argyll and Mull", *Archaeoastronomy* (Supplement to *Journal for the History of Astronomy*) no. 9: S105–132.

Ruggles, C., 1986, "'You Can't Have One Without the Other'? I.T. and Bayesian Statistics, and Their Possible Impact Within Archaeology", *Science and Archaeology* 28: 8–15.

Ruggles, C. and A. Burl, 1985, "A New Study of the Aberdeenshire Recumbent Stone Circles, 2: Interpretation", *Archaeoastronomy* (Supplement to *Journal for the History of Astronomy*) no. 8: S25–S60.

Sallnow, M., 1981, "Communitas Reconsidered: The Sociology of Andean Pilgrimage", *Man* (N.S.) 16: 163–182.

Sallnow, M., 1982, "A Trinity of Christs: Cultic Processes in Andean Catholicism", *American Ethnologist* 9(4): 730–749.

Salomon, F., n.d., "Ethnic Lords of Quito in the Age of the Incas: The Political Economy of North-Andean Chiefdoms", Ph.D. dissertation, Ithaca: Cornell University (1978).

Santo Tomás, F., 1951 [1560] *Lexicon*. Lima: Edición Facsimilar, Instituto de Historia, Universidad Nacional Mayor de San Marcos.

Sawyer, A., 1961, "Paracas and Nazca Iconography", in *Essays in Pre-Columbian Art & Archaeology*, ed. S. Lothrop et al., pp. 269–298. Cambridge: Harvard University Press.

Sawyer, A., 1966, "Ancient Peruvian Ceramics: The Nathan Cummings Collection", New York: New Museum of Art.

Sawyer, A., 1972, "The Feline in Paracas Art", in *The Cult of the Feline*, ed. E. Benson, pp. 91–116. Washington, D.C.: Dumbarton Oaks Research Library and Collections.

Sawyer, A., 1979, "Painted Nasca Textiles", in *The Junius B. Bird Pre-Columbian Textile Conference*, ed. A. Rowe, E. Benson, and A. Schaffer, pp.

129–150. Washington, D.C.: The Textile Museum and Dumbarton Oaks.

Schele, L. and M. Miller, 1986, *The Blood of Kings: Dynasty and Ritual in Maya Art.* Fort Worth: Kimbell Art Museum.

Scholten D'Ebneth, M., 1959, "Un Posible Sistema en la Antropo-Geografía del Perú Antiguo", *Actas y Trabajos del II Congreso Nacional de la Historia del Perú* (Lima), vol. I: 339–353.

Schreiber, K. and J. Lancho R. 1988, "Los Puguios de Nasca: Un Sistema de Galerías Filtrantes", *Boletín de Lima* 59: 51–62.

Schumacher, E., 1983, "One Woman at 80, Continuous Quest to Solve Puzzle in Peruvian Desert", *New York Times* (9 Aug.): C1–2.

Seler, E., 1923, "Das Buntbemalten Gefässe von Nazca", *Gesammelte Abhandlungen zur Amerikanischen Sprach- und Alterttumskunde* Vol. 4: pp. 160–438. Berlin: Verlag Gehrend U.

Shawcross, W., 1984, "Mystery on the Desert—the Nazca Lines", *Sky and Telescope* 67: 198–201.

Shepard, A., 1956, *Ceramics for the Archaeologist.* Washington: Carnegie Institute of Washington, Publication 609.

Sherbondy, J., n.d., "The Canal System of Hanan Cuzco", Ph.D. dissertation, University of Illinois, Urbana-Champaign (1982).

Shimada, I., 1982, "Horizontal Archipelago and Coast-Highland Interaction in North Peru: Archaeological Models", in *El Hombre y su Ambiente en los Andes Centrales*, ed. L. Millones y Tomoeda, *Senri Ethnological Studies* 10: 137–210.

Shipton, P., 1984, "Strips and Patches: A Demographic Dimension in Some African Land-Holding and Political Systems", *Man* 19: 613–634.

Silverman, H., 1977, "Estilo y Estados: El Problema de la Cultura Nasca", *Informaciónes Arqueologicas* (Lima) 1: 49–78.

Silverman, H., 1985a, "Cahuachi: Simplemente Monumental", *Boletín de Lima* 41: 85–95.

Silverman, H., 1985b, "Report on Proyecto Arqueologico Cahuachi", *Willay* 18: 11.

Silverman, H., 1985c, "Monumentos y Monumentalidad", *Anthropologica* 3: 249–259.

Silverman, H. 1988, "Cahuachi: Non-urban Cultural Complexity on the South Coast of Peru". *Journal of Field Archaeology* 15(4): 403–30.

Silverman, H., n.d., a, "La Investigación Arqueologica, el Uso de la Analogía Etnografica: El Caso de los Plazas y Espacios Abiertos de Cahuachi", *Revista Andina* (in press).

Silverman, H., n.d., b, "Informe Final del Estudio de Factibilidad Realizado en el valle de Nazca", final report presented to the Instituto Nacional de Cultura, Lima, Perú (1983).

Silverman, H., n.d., c, "Cahuachi: An Andean Ceremonial Center", Ph.D. dissertation in Anthropology, University of Texas at Austin (1986).

Silverman, H. and M. Pazos, n.d., "Asiento: un Asentamiento Nasca en la Frontera del Territorio Nasca". (ms.).

Spencer, M., 1983, "Bean Sprouts New Theory", *South American Explorer* 9: 3–8.

Stern, S., 1982, *Peru's Indian Peoples and the Challenge of Spanish Conquest: Huamanga to 1640.* Madison: University of Wisconsin Press.

Stierlin, H., 1983, *La Clé du Mystère.* Paris: Albin Michel.

Stierlin, H., 1985, *Nazca: La Solución de Un Enigma Arqueologico.* Barcelona: Editorial Planeta.

Strong, W., 1952, "La Expedicíon Ica-Ocucaje-Nazca", *Revista del Museo Regional de Ica* 4(5) (Ica, Peru): 7–11.

Strong, W., 1955, "The Origin of Nazca Culture", *Bulletin of the Philadelphia Anthropological Society* 8(2): 1–2.

Strong, W., 1957, "Paracas, Nazca and Tiahuanacoid Cultural Relationships in Southern Coastal Peru", *American Antiquity* 22(4, part 2): Society for American Archeology Memoir, 13.

Tello, J., 1917, "Los Antiguos Cementerios del Valle de Nazca", *Proceedings of the Second Pan American Scientific Congress* (Washington), Section 1, Anthropology, vol. 1, pp. 283–291.

Tello, J., 1940, "Vaso de Piedra de Nasca; Primeros Indicios de una Cultura Megalitica Semenjante a la de Chavín en la Regíon Central del Peru", *Chaski* 1(1): 27–48.

Tello, J., 1942, "Origen y Desarrollo de las Civilizaciónes Prehistoricas Andinas", *Actas y memorias del XXXVII Congreso Internacional de Americanistas* (Lima) vol. 1: 589–720.

Tello, J., and T. Mejía Xesspe, 1967, "Historia de los Museos Nacionales del Peru, 1822–1946", *Arqueologicas,* vol. 10, Lima.

"Testimonio de la escritura de compra-venta . . . del asiento y tierras de Usaca . . .", 1665. *Archivo General de la Nación* (AGN), *Títulos de Propiedad* (Lima), Legajo 6, cuaderno 185, folios 10.

"Testimonio de los autos que se siguieron por antes el Alcalde ordinario de la ciudad de los Reyes, don Francisco de Zárate, sobre la apertura del testamento que otorgó don Garcia Nazca . . . ," 1569. *Archivo General de la Nación*

(AGN), *Derecho Indígena* (Lima), Legajo 23, cuaderno 616, folios 18.

Thom, A., 1967, *Megalithic Sites in Britain.* Oxford: Clarendon Press.

Thom, A., 1971, *Megalithic Lunar Observatories.* Oxford: Oxford University Press.

Thom, A. and A. Thom, 1978, *Megalithic Remains in Britain and Brittany.* Oxford: Oxford University Press.

Thompson, J., 1954, *The Rise and Fall of Maya Civilization.* Norman: University of Oklahoma Press.

Tilley, C., 1984, "Ideology and the Legitimation of Power in the Middle Neolithic of Southern Sweden", in *Ideology, Power and Prehistory,* ed. D. Miller and C. Tilley, pp. 111–146. Cambridge: Cambridge University Press.

"Titulos de la Hacienda de San José de la Nazca, en el Valle del Ingenio . . . ," 1620. *Archivo General de la Nación* (AGN) *Títulos de Propiedad* (Lima), Legajo 8, cuaderno 165, folios 87.

Topic, T., 1982, "The Early Intermediate Period and Its Legacy", in *Chan Chan: Andean Desert City,* ed. M. Moseley and K. Day, pp. 255–284. Albuquerque: University of New Mexico Press.

Topic, T., n.d., "Excavations at Moche", Ph.D. dissertation in Anthropology, Harvard University (1977).

Townsend, R., 1985, "Deciphering the Nazca World: Ceramic Images from Ancient Peru", *Museum Studies* 11(2): 116–139.

Turner, V., 1967, *The Forest of Symbols.* Ithaca: Cornell University Press.

Turner, V., 1974, *Dramas, Fields, and Metaphors: Symbolic Action in Human Society.* Ithaca: Cornell University Press.

Turner, V., 1979, "Death and the Dead in the Pilgrimage Process", in *Process, Performance and Pilgrimage,* ed. V. Turner, pp. 121–142. New Delhi: Concept.

Turner, V. and E. Turner, 1978, *Image and Pilgrimage in Christian Culture, Anthropological Perspectives.* New York: Columbia University Press.

Uchendu, V., 1965, *The Igbo of Southeast Nigeria.* New York: Holt, Rinehart, and Winston.

Uhle, M., 1914, "The Nazca Pottery of Ancient Peru", *Proceedings of the Davenport Academy of Sciences* (Davenport, Iowa) 13: 1-16.

Uhle, M., 1920, "Los Principios de las Antiguas Civilizaciones Peruanas", *Boletín de la Sociedad Ecuatoriana de Estudios Historicos Americanos* (Quito) 4: 448–458.

Ulloa, L., 1909, "Documentos del Virrey Toledo: Visita General de los Yndios del Cuzco, Año del 1571, Provincia Condesuyo", *Revista Historica* (Lima) 2: 332–47.

Uphill, E., 1972, "The Concept of the Egyptian Palace as a 'Ruling Machine '", in *Man, Settlement and Urbanism,* ed. P. Ucko, R. Tringham, and G. Dimbleby, pp. 721–734. London: Gerald Duckworth and Co., Ltd.

Urton, G., 1979, "Review of T. Morrison, Pathways to the Gods", *Archaeoastronomy Bulletin* 2(4): 31–33.

Urton, G., 1981a, "Animals and Astronomy in the Quechua Universe", *Proceedings of the American Philosophical Society* 125(2): 110–127.

Urton, G., 1981b, *At the Crossroads of the Earth and the Sky.* Austin: University of Texas Press.

Urton, G., 1982, "Astronomy and Calendrics on the Coast of Peru", in *Ethnoastronomy and Archaeoastronomy in the American Tropics,* ed. A. Aveni and G. Urton, pp. 231–259. New York: Annals of the New York Academy of Sciences, Vol. 385.

Urton, G., 1984, "Chuta: el espacio de la Práctica Social en Pacariqtambo, Perú", *Revista Andina* 3: 7–43.

Urton, G., 1985, "Animal Metaphors and the Life Cycle in an Andean Community", in *Animal Myths and Metaphors in South America,* ed. G. Urton, pp. 251–284. Salt Lake City: University of Utah Press.

Urton, G., 1987, "Calendrical Cycles and Their Projections in Pacariqtambo, Peru", *Journal of Latin American Lore* 12(1): 45–64.

Urton, G., n.d., a. "Communal Cash-Cropping and Social Cohesion in Pacariqtambo", in *Through an Andean Kaleidoscope,* ed. B. J. Isbell (in press).

Urton, G., n.d., b. "The History and Geography of Origin Places in Pacariqtambo, Peru" (ms.).

Urton, G., n.d., c. Field Notes, Nazca (1981).

Urton, G., n.d., d. Report on Fieldwork in Nazca, Peru (1982).

Urton, G. and A. Aveni, 1983, "Archaeoastronomical Fieldwork on the Coast of Peru", in *Calendars in Mesoamerica and Peru; Native American Computations of Time,* ed. A. Aveni and G. Brotherston, pp. 221–234. Oxford: British Archaeological Reports, International Series 174.

Valcarcel, L.E., 1932, "El Gato de Agua", *Revista del Museo Nacional* (Lima), 1(2): 1–29.

Vargas Llosa, M., 1983, "Inquest in the Andes", *The New York Times Magazine* (31 July): 18–56.

Vescelius, G. and E. Lanning, 1963, "Some New Finds at San Nicolas", *Ñawpa Pacha* 1: 43–45.

Vitale, L., 1981, "El Imperio Incaico: una Sociedad de Transición", in *Los Modos de Producción en el*

*Imperio de los Incas,* ed. W. Soriano, pp. 231–246. Lima: Amaru Editores S.A.

Wachtel, N., 1976, "Le Système d'Irrigation des Chipayas", *Les Colloques de l'Institut National de la Santé et de la Recherche Médicale,* INSERM 63: 87–116.

Wachtel, N., 1982, "The *Mitimas* of the Cochabamba Valley: The Colonization Policy of Huayna Capac", in *The Inca and Aztec States, 1400–1800,* ed. G. Collier, R. Rosaldo, and J. Wirth, pp. 199–264. New York: Academic Press.

Wagner, C., n.d., a, "The Feathered Killer Whale Motif in Nazca Pottery: A Preliminary Investigation" (ms.).

Wagner, C., n.d., b, "The Nazca Creatures: Some Problems of Iconography" (ms.).

Wagner, C., n.d., c, "The Dialectic of Life and Death: The Role of Sexuality in Nazca Iconography" (ms.).

Wagner, C., n.d., d, "Coca, Chica, and Trago: Private and Communal Rituals in a Quechua Community", Ph.D. dissertation in Anthropology, University of Illinois at Urbana-Champaign (1978).

Wagner, E., 1979, "Danikenitis y el Enigma de las Figuras de Nazca", (Separato de La Revista), LINEAS (Mexico City).

Waisbard, S., 1977, *Les Pistes de Nazca.* Paris: Editions R. Laffont. (Reissued 1980, *Las Pistas de Nazca,* Barcelona: Plaza y Janes).

Waisbard, S., 1981, "Enigmatic Messages of the Nazcas", in *The World's Last Mysteries,* pp. 281–287. Pleasantville: Reader's Digest Association.

Walker, J., 1985, "Ultra-light Reconnaissance, Another Tool", *Technical Papers, 51st Annual Meeting, American Society for Photogrammetry* (Washington, D.C.), vol. 1: 371–380.

Wallace, D., 1971, "Sitios Arqueologicos del Perú Segunda Entrega J. Valles de Chincha y de Pisco" (tr. L. Watanabe). *Arqueologicas* (Lima: Museo Nacional de Antropología y Arqueología) Vol. 13.

Wallace, D., n.d., a, "Ceremonial Roads in Chincha: Symbolic Political Implications", paper presented at the 42nd Annual Meeting of the Society of American Archaeology, New Orleans (1977).

Wallace, D., n.d., b. "Symbolic and Socio-Economic Locational Segmentation: The Chincha Roads", paper read at NE Andean Archaeological meeting, Cornell, Ithaca, Nov. 1982.

Webster, D., 1976, "On Theocracies", *American Anthropologist* 78: 812–828.

Wegner, S., n.d., "A Stylistic Seriation of Nasca 6" (ms.).

Wheatley, P., 1971, *The Pivot of the Four Quarters.* Chicago: Aldine Press.

Whitten, D. and N. Whitten, 1978, "Ceramics of the Canelos Quichua", *Natural History* 87(8): 90–99.

Whitten, N., 1985, *Sicuanga Runa. The Other Side of Development in Amazonian Ecuador.* Urbana and Chicago: University of Illinois Press.

Whittlesey, J., 1966, "Bipod Camera Support", *Photogrammatic Engineering* 32(11): 1005–1010.

Whittlesey, J., 1970, "Tethered Balloon for Archaeological Photos", *Photogrammetric Engineering* 36(2): 181–186.

Whittlesey, J., 1975, "Elevated and Airborne Photogrammetry and Stereo Photography", in *Photography in Archaeological Research,* ed. E. Harp, Jr., pp. 223–258. Albuquerque: University of New Mexico Press.

Williams, L. C., 1980, "Arquitectura y Urbanismo en el Antiguo Perú", in *Historia del Peru,* Vol. 8, ed. J. Baca, pp. 369–585. Lima: Editorial Juan Mejía Baca.

Williams, L. C., and M. Pazos, 1974, "Inventario, Catastro y Delimitación del Património Arqueología del Valle de Ica", Lima: Instituto Nacional de Cultura.

Wilson, D., 1988, "Deseort Ground Drawings in the Lower Santa Valleys, North Coast of Peru", *American Antiquity* 53(4): 794–804.

Wobst, M., 1977, "Stylistic Behavior and Information Exchange", in *Papers for the Director: Research Essays in Honor of James B. Griffin,* ed. C. Cleland, pp. 317–342. Ann Arbor: Anthropological Papers of University of Michigan Museum of Anthropology.

Wolfe, E., 1981, "The Spotted Cat and the Horrible Bird: Stylistic Change in Nasca 1–5 Ceramica Decoration", *Ñawpa Pacha* 19: 1–62.

Woodman, J., 1977, *Nazca, Journey to the Sun.* New York: Simon and Schuster Pocket Books.

Yacovleff, E., 1931, "El Vencejo (cypselus) en el Arte Decorativo de Nasca", *Wira Kocha, Revista de Estudios Antropologicos* (Lima) 1(1): 25–35.

Yacovleff, E., 1932a, "Las Falcónides en el Arte y en las Creencias de los Antiguos Peruanos", *Revista del Museo Nacional* (Lima) 1(1): 35–111.

Yacovleff, E., 1932b, "Arte Antiguo Peruano, La Deidad Primitivo de las Nasca", *Revista del Museo Nacional* (Lima) 1(2): 103–160.

Yacovleff, E., 1933, "La Jíquima, Raíz Comestible

Extinguida en el Perú", *Revista del Museo Nacional* (Lima) 4(1): 31–102.

Yung, S., n.d., "Relation of Nazca Figure Drawings to Nazca Geometrical Drawings" (ms., Colgate University, 1981).

Zeilik, M., 1985, "The Ethnoastronomy of the Historic Pueblos. I. Calendrical Sun Watching", *Archaeoastronomy* (Supplement to the *Journal for the History of Astronomy*) Vol. 13: S1–26.

Zelko, Z., 1982, *A Kosivatag Titka*. Budapest: Magveto Kíado.

Zuidema, R., 1964, *The Ceque System of Cuzco: The Social Organization of the Capital of the Inca*. Leiden: Brill.

Zuidema, R.T., 1965, "American Social Systems and Their Mutual Similarity", *Bijdragen Tot de Taal-, Land- en Volkenkunde*, 12(1): 103–109.

Zuidema, R.T., 1972, "Meaning in Nazca Art, Iconographic Relationships Between Inca, Huari and Nazca Cultures in Southern Peru," *Arstryck 1971* (Göteborg: Etnografiska Mus.): 35–54.

Zuidema, R.T., 1973a, "Kinship and Ancestor Cult in Three Peruvian Communities", *Boletín del Instituto Frances de Estudios Andinos* 2(1): 16–33.

Zuidema, R.T., 1973b, "The Origin of the Inca Empire", in *Les Grandes Empires*, pp. 733–757. Brussels: Société Jean Bodin.

Zuidema, R.T., 1977a, "The Inca Calendar", in *Native American Astronomy*, ed. A. Aveni, pp. 219–259. Austin: University of Texas Press.

Zuidema, R.T., 1977b, "The Inca Kinship System: A New Theoretical View", in *Andean Kinship and Marriage*, ed. R. Bolton and E. Mayer, pp. 240–281. Washington, D.C.: Special Publication of the American Anthropological Association, no. 7.

Zuidema, R.T., 1978, "Shafttombs of the Inca Empire", *Journal of the Steward Anthropological Society* 9(1–2): 133–178.

Zuidema, R.T., 1981a, "Comment", *Latin American Research Review* 16(3): 167–170.

Zuidema, R.T., 1981b, "Inca Observations of the Solar and Lunar Passages through the Zenith and Anti-Zenith at Cuzco", in *Archaeoastronomy in the Americas*, ed. R. Williamson, pp. 319–342. Los Altos: Ballena Press and University of Maryland Center of Archaeoastronomy.

Zuidema, R.T., 1982a, "Bureaucracy and Systematic Knowledge in Andean Civilization", in *The Inca and Aztec States, 1400–1800*, ed. G. Collier, R. Rosaldo, and J. Wirth, pp. 419–458. New York: Academic Press.

Zuidema, R.T., 1982b, "Catachillay: The Role of the Pleiades and of the Southern Cross and Alpha and Beta Centauri in the Calendar of the Incas", in *Ethnoastronomy and Archaeoastronomy in the American Tropics*, ed. A. Aveni and G. Urton, pp. 203–230. New York: Annals of the New York Academy of Sciences, 385.

Zuidema, R.T., 1982c, "Myth and History in Ancient Peru", in *The Logic of Culture: Advances in Structural Theory and Methods*, ed. I. Rossi, pp. 150–175. J.F. Bergin Publishers, Inc.

Zuidema, R.T., n.d., a. "Llama Sacrifices and Computation: Roots of the Inca Calendar in Huari, Tihuanaco Culture" (ms.).

*APPENDICES*

## Appendix I: An Analysis of the Cantalloc Spiral

The Cantalloc spiral (Chap. I, Fig. 6) is part of a large figure located on a sheltered strip of land in between two tributaries of the Nazca River about 5 km SE of the city of Nazca adjacent to the Hacienda Cantalloc. We sought to obtain as precise a map as possible of the spiral portion of the figure and to determine its mode of construction.

The spiral lies at the N end of a long, thin triangle (apex angle 1°45′), the axis of which points toward azimuth 161°44′ according to our transit measurements of 27 July 1981. The length of the figure is 900 m and it appears to point 2° left (E) of a prominent mountain of elevation 3° at about 10 km distance. A line emanates from the point of the triangle to a distance of 200 meters before making the first of sixteen abrupt turns that carry it in a saw-tooth or zigzag pattern back and forth over the triangle on an uneven course. This form of figure-triangle and zigzag is duplicated in a number of other figures on the pampa, e.g., adjacent to the monkey figure one finds another triangle with an arrangement of zigzag lines crossing it (cf. Chap. I, Fig. 4e). Even the number of zigzag crossings is the same—sixteen. Moreover, both of these figures comprise not only a long geometrical figure and a zigzag pattern, but also a spiral. It may be significant that, leaving the wide end of the trapezoid, one must make sixteen more turns before entering the monkey figure. The labyrinthine spiral, which in the Cantalloc figure is wrapped around the base end of the trapezoid, appears off to one side and one must enter the monkey to pass through it. Both trapezoids point east of south and both spirals exhibit nine turns.

On the Cantalloc figure, a small rubble cairn averaging 1 m in width and 0.5 meter in height accompanies the inside of each turn. In each instance the angular bend of the path is different (it averages about 10°) and penetrates to the edge of the pampa on opposite sides of the triangle to a different distance (the average path length before each bend is about 110 meters). After the last crossing, 600 m down the ever-widening axis of the triangle, the line, still continuous and not having crossed itself, takes a final bend. This time it runs parallel to the axis, but then it begins to close in a counter-clockwise direction upon itself, thus forming a labyrinthine spiral; the spiral cuts across the triangle fifteen more times.

We found the geometric center of the spiral to be a point 18 meters from the center of the axis of the triangle or 17.5 meters along a perpendicular from the near (eastern) edge of the triangle, on the same side from which the pathway emanates from the apex of the triangle. The loaf-shaped edging of the figure, which results from an accumulation of the rubble that had been removed from the area comprising the triangle, averages 50 cm in width and 20 cm in height.

We determined the center of the spiral by two different methods: (a) we bisected the line between a pair of rubble cairns (A and B) at the innermost bends of the spiral (call the midpoint $X_1$ in Fig. 1a). (b) Using a metal tape, we laid out a line tangent to the inner edges of the path, marking the position where the line met the middle of the path (call it $X_2$). The center was defined as the averaged position of $X_1$ and $X_2$ (labeled X). The distance $X_1X_2$ was approximately 30 cm.

To make an accurate map of the spiral we placed the transit at X, leveled it, and took a sun shot (Aveni 1980b: 128–132). Normalizing the azimuth of the transit to read 0° at true north, we then drove a spike at one end of a metal tape into the ground at a point where the plumb bob of the transit met the ground and we took readings of the distance to the midpoint of each line comprising the spiral from point X at 10°-intervals of azimuth. We accomplished this task rather expeditiously by placing workers on each of the nine visible arms of the spiral to read the tape, while a tenth worker recorded the data under the direction of yet another person who moved the viewing instrument in azimuth by 10° intervals and also aligned the tape. The map of the spi-

Appendix I. Fig. 1. The Cantalloc Spiral. (a) Determining the center of the spiral

Appendix I. Fig. 1b. Map of spiral

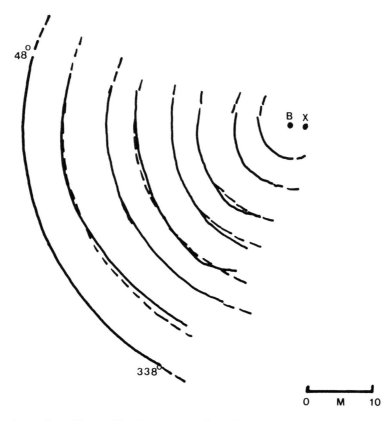

Appendix I. Fig. 1c. Circular segments of spiral

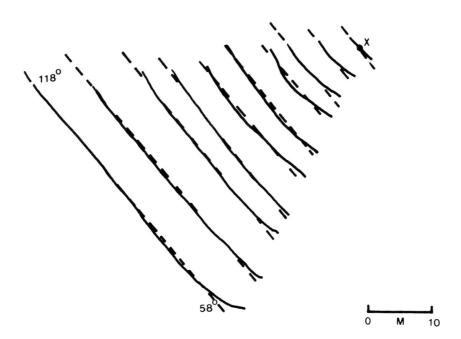

Appendix I. Fig. 1d. Straight line segments of spiral

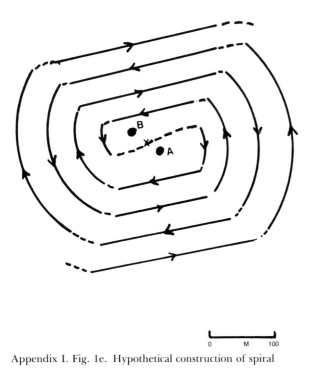

```
        L_____L_____L
        0        M        100
```

Appendix I. Fig. 1e. Hypothetical construction of spiral

the eastern edge of the triangle (point Y in Fig. 1b).

Let us see what detailed conclusions can be drawn from each of these observations:

Observation (a). The location of every bend in the zigzag portion of the figure occurs within a few meters of the place where the edge of the pampa falls off into either of the dry *quebradas* that surround the east and west sides of the figure. In fact, the whole completed figure barely fits into the space it occupies. Examine the bends and turns in the aerial photograph of Chap. I, Fig. 6. This fact suggests that the immediate topography likely served as the strictest determinant of the size and shape of the figure. These observations contradict the notion that the dimensions and proportions of the figure were conceived prior to construction, then executed on the pampa. The spiral appears to be squeezed into an oval shape, the long axis of which follows the direction of both the immediate landscape and the axis of the triangle. Maximum compression of the spiral occurs on the eastern side of the triangle, precisely where the edge of the pampa approaches closest to the center of the spiral. This compression could not have been an afterthought incorporated into the figure once several turns of the spiral had been built, for the flattening of the figure along the axial direction can be perceived along every arm of the spiral all the way to its center; this figural compression is not visible in the Kern and Reiche map of the spiral (Kern and Reiche 1974: fig. 26). On the west side of the intersecting triangle there is barely enough room to continue two arms of the spiral. Hardly twenty meters of distance remains between the western edge of the triangle and the precipitous drop-off into the *quebrada* on that side of the narrow spit of land upon which the figure is constructed. These considerations prove unequivocally that the spiral was constructed *after* riverine erosion produced the plateau.

Observation (b). What technique might the builders have employed if they were confronted with the prospect of having to squeeze

ral resulting from this procedure is shown in Fig. 1b.

At first glance, the spiral appears to be rather crude in its construction and it is difficult to imagine that the builders paid very much attention to principles of symmetry or to the use of precise units of measurement. Still, we are as much concerned with the problem of how it was constructed as with the issue of whether it appears to be as precise as we would make it if we were assigned the task. With these concerns in mind, we offer three potentially useful observations pertaining to the construction of this particular spiral:

(a) The whole arrangement and shape of the figure seems to be dictated by the natural contour of the relatively flat pampa on which the figure is constructed.

(b) The spiral seems to be a composite of relatively straight and circular segments, an observation which is likely related to (a).

(c) The continuous line, over 3600 m in length, that departs from the apex of the thin triangle, nearly loses itself in the many crossing points of the triangle; it seems to terminate at an intersection of an arm of the spiral with

the spiral into the space nature allowed for it? Given the evidence, we believe the simplest method would have consisted of piecing together circles and straight lines. We tried, with some success, to approximate the actual shape of the figure by linking together straight lines and arcs of circles. Thus, in Fig. 1c we note that for the 60° arc segment between azimuths 338° and 48° (and again between 138° and 168°) nearly all arms of the spiral can be fitted quite well to circular segments. On the other hand, between 58° and 118° the spiral arms, particularly the outer ones, are more or less straight lines that run parallel to the eastern edge of the plateau (Fig. 1d). Note also that even the arm passing through the center of the spiral lines up parallel to the axial direction of the figure. And, the 9th (outer) arm continues as a straight line that moves away from the spiral until it takes a sharp westward bend where it is transformed into a zigzag.

But how did they construct the figure? One clue lies in the position of Cairn B, which could have served as an excellent center of curvature from which to mark out with cords each of the circular segments between azimuth 338° and 48°. Hypothesizing that Cairn B was so used in the construction, we ruled the circular segments centered upon it that are shown as dotted lines in Fig. 1c. In the figure, these arc segments deviate by no more than 50 cm from the middle of any of the actual lines (i.e., by not more than the average width of the line). It is likely that Cairn A, on the opposite side, served a similar function, but the data on the shorter circular segment between azimuth 138° and 168° are insufficient for us to judge whether this was the case. Moreover, the triangular portion of the figure obstructs the path of the spiral in this region.

In Fig. 1d we separate out the line segments in the azimuth zone 58°–118°. Notice the remarkable difference between the shape of these lengthy segments and those of the same arc length in Fig. 1c; the comparison is enhanced when the sectors are plotted separately. Again, our straight line approximations are shown as dotted lines. The deviation of each segment from a straight line, admit-

tedly less for the middle arms, is nonetheless never more than 50 cm. Distances between successive circular arcs average 4 meters (about 2 paces), the same as the distance between Cairns A and B, but the arcs lying on the southern side of the figure seem to be staggered at distances averaging 160 cm greater from Cairn A than those lying on the north side are situated from Cairn B. Between azimuths 48° and 68°, and especially between azimuths 118° and 148°, the spirals make very sharp turns, thus supporting the notion that the constructors were attempting to tie together roughly the linear and circular segments they employed to make up the figure.

Having analyzed these data, we suggest the spiral could have been constructed quite easily as follows (Fig. 1e):

(1) A pair of points, A and B, about 2 paces apart, were selected and posts or stakes were driven there.

(2) Circular arcs about 60° long and also roughly 2 paces apart were ruled by attaching ropes to the posts and suitable markers to the ends of the ropes. One set of such arcs centered about B was marked out to the north and another set centered about A was ruled to the south. Those in the southerly direction were begun at about 1 ½ times the distance of the first set.

(3) Straight line segments, some up to 60 meters long, paralleling the bisector of the triangle (or, better, paralleling the edge of the plateau), were laid out either by eye or perhaps by pacing, guided by ropes pulled taut.

(4) The circle and line segments, the ends of which never were more than 15 meters apart, were connected in free-form style, by approximation (dotted lines, Fig. 1e). The staggering of the circular segments made it a simpler task to join circles and lines into a labyrinthine spiral figure.

(5) Finally, the line between points A and B was halved and the "center" of the spiral so determined. Incidentally, this is the same as one of the methods we devised to determine where to place our transit in order to make the measurements. By following this plan exactly, we were able to produce the sketch of the ide-

alized labyrinthine spiral shown in Fig. 1e, which may be compared with Fig. 1b.

Though it is dangerous to speculate further, it is also possible to suggest that the builders had intended to construct the double spiral by joining together two sets of circular segments employing staggered radii. They may have begun by building the two aforementioned sequences of 60° circular arc segments and simply run out of room. Then they chose to approximate the eastern side of the spiral by straight line segments rather than by moving to another location and starting over.

Observation (c). If the spiral served as a labyrinthine pathway, we might inquire: Where would one have entered and left it? Here we suspect some deliberate trickery, for all our workers found it impossible to follow the processional direction directly simply by looking at the figure on the map or walking on the ground. In Fig. 1b, we depict by arrows one possible unicursal walking sequence. Walking the feature on the ground, we nearly always lost our way when we tried to pass over the triangle that bisects it at a point halfway along its short radial axis. To make matters worse, the remnant of the path on the west side of the triangle is quite obliterated (only two fragments of the path still can be viewed today). Could the triangle represent a later figure that overlies the spiral? If that is the case, we might not expect to find its apex angle connected to the sinuous pathway that ultimately leads one into and through the spiral. Our best guess for the end point of the path is position Y in Fig. 1b where the spiral, winding outward on its eighth and last turn about the center, empties the walker onto the large triangle at its eastern edge.

## Appendix II: A Walk Across the Pampa

In this section, we have selected for detailed consideration some of the more prominent centers among the 62 that we catalogued in Chapter II. We begin our description of representative line centers with one among a relatively large number that lies at the base of the Andean foothills. Then we visit a second center from the rarer sample located in the middle of the pampa, and finally, a third from among those located on the riverbanks. All three of these centers are adjoined by connectors (cf. Chap. II, Fig. 1b). Later, we describe other centers at the SE end of the pampa near the present location of the modern town of Nazca. With the use of a magnifying lens, one may be able to sight a number of the connectors on the photomosaics (in the jacket pocket).

### LINE CENTER NO. 30 (See Fig. 1)

Line center No. 30 (Chap. II, Fig. 3 (30)) consists of a prominent oval hill of natural origin with dimensions 100 × 75 m; it is located 900 m west of KM 433.1 on the Pan American Highway (Fig. 1a). The axis of this hill is aligned roughly NW to SE and it is elevated about 15 m above the pampa. It is the southwesternmost of a series of topographic features that descend from the Cerro Putón de los Chivatos range onto the pampa. Ten lines converge on the hill, seven from the side opening to the pampa and in the general direction of the Nazca River drainage (southwest). The broadest feature, line no. 1, is a trapezoid 430 m long that measures 48 m at the base and narrows to 25 m at the top of the hill, to the eastern side of which it attaches before it merges with the other lines. This trapezoid is well cleared, the detritus that once constituted its 16,000 sq. m of surface having been neatly piled to form a hummock-shaped border that measures about 1 m wide by ½ m high; this border, clearly discernible in Fig.

1b, is noticeably darker than the cleared region.

Line no. 2 (Fig. 1c), the narrowest feature, also is the most difficult to follow. It keeps a constant width of about ¼ meter along the 2 ¾ km course over which we could follow it. According to Reiche's (1968:30) map, the feature ends at the apex of a large triangle. Though we could not follow the line all the way to the geometrical figure because the area was badly eroded, nevertheless, we were able to reach this general area by pursuing the same direction from the center. Line no. 8 extended 4.3 km, at which point it joined line center No. 35 (Chap. II, Fig. 3 (35)), see also Fig. 2b, connector line). The line began at the top of the hill on center No. 30, where it resembled a broad sort of avenue 17 m wide. The east side of it connected to the trapezoid (feature no. 1), while the south side merged with the northern side of line 6, as the map of Fig. 3 (30) and the photo in Fig. 1a shows. At the base of the hill, line 8 narrowed to 12 m and at range 200 m from the base of the hill its width was 5.9 m. The line then maintained a nearly constant width of 5 m ± ½ m all the way to center No. 35 (where we designate it 35–10; Fig. 3 (35)). Like the other two long lines, it possessed a clearly delineated footpath of undetermined age along the middle of its course—in some places, two footpaths. We temporarily lost the line in traversing three dry washes along its course. There is little doubt that streams had flowed in these channels since the connecting line was constructed, though one cannot be sure whether the streams washed away the lines or the lines were never built there because of stream activity. As one departed farther from center No. 30 along the course, the stark white hill in the middle of the pampa that forms center No. 35 loomed ever more prominently on the horizon, having been visible to us for most of the distance.

We followed line no. 6, the middle of the three long ones in Fig. 1c, for 6 ½ km. Along the way, we encountered a well and irrigation

Appendix II. Fig. 1a. Line center No. 30: aerial view from the west. (P. Clarkson)

Appendix II. Fig. 1b. Line center No. 30 from the ground; view from the center of the hill looking NE along the broad feature labeled no. 1 in the previous figure.

Appendix II. Fig. 1c. Line center No. 30 from the top of the hill looking southward, showing the abbreviated features 4, 5, 7 and the long lines 2, 6, and 8. Note that 5 and 7 terminate in a dry *quebrada*.

canals on the south (river) side of the dunes not far from the Nazca drainage. This line was one of the most clearly marked features we walked, the borders being well defined with stones; it extended up and over several low hills as one approached its southern extremity and it keeps a constant width of approximately 3 m all the way. A narrow footpath was visible down the middle of the entire course of this line. It terminated in a sand dune (line center No. 36; Fig. 3–36) just as one arrived at the first overlook of the main Nazca drainage.

Unlike lines no. 2, 6, and 8, which continue all the way across the pampa, lines 3, 4, 5, and

7 leave the base of the hill and extend 30–50 m before terminating abruptly. The sudden termination of two of these lines might be related to the presence of a small dry wash (cf. lines 5 & 7; Fig. 1c. See also Fig. 4 for another example). Another short line, no. 11, is situated on the top of the hill, while lines no. 9 and 10, a nearly parallel pair of connector features, can be traced on the photographs, though only vaguely, to center No. 37, 7 km to the NW.

Do lines actually converge at a specific point on the hill that constitutes a line center? i.e., were they all constructed from a single point location? To answer this question, we took the

Appendix II. Fig. 2a. Construction details of line center No. 36: Grooves or pathways along broad feature 36-6. The Nazca valley lies beyond the dune-like hill (arrow) from which the lines of this particular center emanate.

Appendix II. Fig. 2b. Similar parallel lines near center No. 23.

Appendix II. Fig. 2c. Neat piles of unremoved detritus about an arm's length apart may suggest a method of cleaning.

Appendix II. Fig. 2d. Aerial view of same.

## LINE CENTER NO. 36 (SEE FIG. 2)

This line center (Chap. II. Fig. 3 (36)) was discovered on the ground after we followed line 30–6 (= 36–7) to its conclusion. Center No. 36 is typical of a host of centers that are situated along the banks of the major river valleys and from which one has a relatively expansive view of both the pampa and the drainage area. It is constituted of a pair of 100 m long dunes about 10 m high, that adjoin each other. These are among the large number of such natural features that form the high bluffs along the northern bank of the Nazca River, about one-third km from the present water source. Nine lines radiate northward out onto the pampa from the two focal points, where we also found some decorated sherds (see discussion in Clarkson,

long lines, no. 2, 6, and 8 (all perfectly straight features), and carefully bisected them with the aid of the surveyor's transit. We laid out string along the middle of each line and followed it across the top of the hill from which the lines seemed to emanate. Extrapolated backward, the three lines were found to fall within a rather large triangle of dimensions 12 × 16 × 24 m on the NE downslope of the hill. Therefore, at least in this instance, point convergence is only approximate. But, as we shall see below, we encounter quite a different situation when we explore the meeting of lines at center No. 35.

Appendix II. Fig. 2e. Occasionally on areas of the pampa impoverished in rock fragments, only a line of stones serves to define the border of a feature (Clarkson).

Chap. III). Lines 1 and 2, both narrow features, lead the walker to centers No. 37 (nearly 9 km away) and 35 (at 3 km), respectively, while line no. 7, a wide feature much of the way, leads to center No. 30. All three of these lines are cross-cut many times along their courses by more recent stream flow and in many instances the route is difficult to follow. This is particularly true in the case of line 1, which actually disappears as one approaches the heavily eroded region south of center No. 37. It is also the case that some of the lines bend considerably while others are perfectly straight. Note, for example, in Chap. II, Table 3, that line no. 2 departs center No. 36 at 359°44′ but arrives at center No. 35 (line 35–14) at an azimuth of 4°24′. On the other hand, the direction of 36–7 differs by only 4 minutes of arc from 30–6, its counterpart.

Line no. 6 (Fig. 2a) is one of the most interesting and unusual features on the pampa. It begins as a narrow feature that widens about 200 m out from the center into a rectangular feature about 100 m long. We followed the narrow line bisecting this feature a bit further and discovered that, typical of most wide features on the pampa, a few hundred meters out

it widened again into another broad feature of about the same dimensions as the first. This second feature is unusual in that the detritus has been gathered into a dozen or more hummock-like lineations that run the entire length of the interior of the rectangle (see Fig. 2a,b). In some places the angled pieces were gathered into small piles separated by an extended arm's reach of a person situated among them. Figs. 2c,d call attention to this sort of arrangement. There is a resemblance between what we see here and the piles the local farmers still make in the Nazca valley when they gather together stones and pebbles to clear their fields for planting. Therefore, it is possible that these curious features were lines in the process of being constructed.

LINE CENTER NO. 35 (SEE FIG. 3)

This is one of the largest line centers, both in its lateral extent and in the number of lines that appear to converge there; but quite atypically, it is located in the open pampa away from both the Nazca and Ingenio Rivers and far from the Andean foothills (Fig. 3a,b,c,e

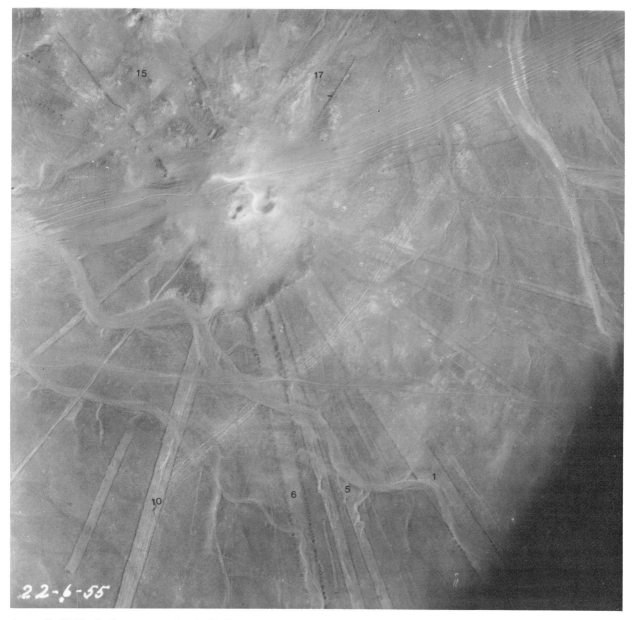

Appendix II. Fig. 3. Features associated with line centers No. 35, 11, 60, and 58 compared with other centers: a. Aerial view of line center No. 35. The holes at the top of the hill are looters' pits. Feature no. 15 is the large trapezoid opening on the upper left. (SAN Photo 0-17156)

Appendix II. Fig. 3b. Line center No. 35 looking eastward in the general direction of center 30 (arrow), to which it is connected by line 35-10.

Appendix II. Fig. 3c. Line center No. 35, close up (see Chap. II, Fig. 3 (35)).

Appendix II. Fig. 3d. Panoramic photo of horizon and departing lines as viewed from center No. 11 (see next page). The individual line numbers are labeled (see Chap. II, Fig. 3(11)). Photo above shows the small peak from which the lines radiate.

and Chap. II. Fig. 3(35) ). We mapped 32 lines converging on a natural double mound 70 m long by 50 m wide, lying barely 5 m above the pampa. Eight more lines were mapped on a smaller, lower mound located about 100 m to the SE—the general direction of the axis of

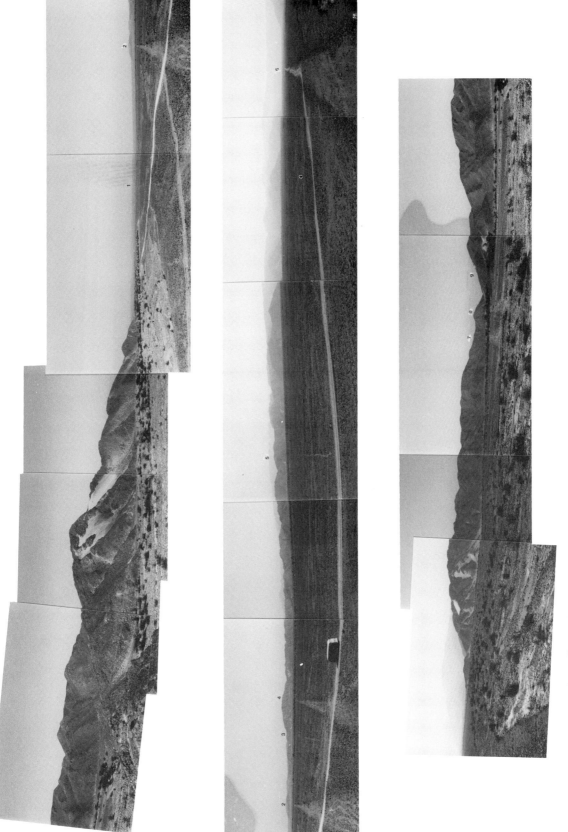

Appendix II. Fig. 3d (continued). Panoramic photos of horizon and departing lines as viewed from center No. 11. The individual line numbers are labeled (see Chap. II, Fig. 3(11).

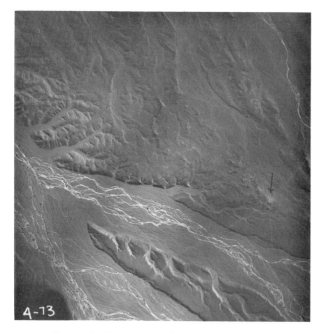

Appendix II. Fig. 3e. A more elevated view of center No. 35 reveals that, like No. 11, it overlooks a broad tributary of the Nazca River. (University of Minnesota Remote Sensing Lab)

Appendix II. Fig. 3f. Aerial view of line center No. 60. (University of Minnesota Remote Sensing Lab)-

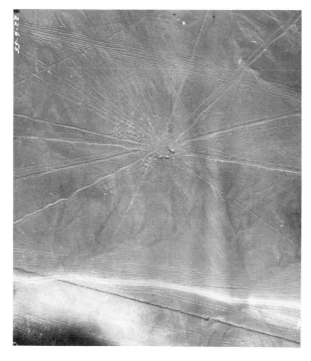

Appendix II. Fig. 3g. Aerial view of line center No. 58. (University of Minnesota Remote Sensing Lab)-

the larger mound. Several smaller mounds are situated immediately to the SE and a large fossil wash passes a few hundred meters to the SE.

Except for two *huaquero* pits at the top of the

double mound and a modern well drilled some 100 m SW of the center, the only visible signs of human construction on or near the line center consist of a few hundred fist-sized boulders that once may have comprised cairns that we find commonly associated with many line centers. A badly deteriorated reed construction alongside the well, together with modern artifacts such as tin cans, suggests that the facility has been used in modern times, so we cannot be sure of its antiquity.

Of the lines we were able to sight with the transit, nearly half can be classified as broad features. We established four definite connectors to other centers by walking and from the photographs and transit measurements we may have discovered one more. Line 1, of 13 m width near the mound, changes its form from rectangular to trapezoidal at exactly the place where it encounters a bend in the wash. The southeastern edge of the trapezoid neatly borders the bank of the wash, which then proceeds to run along its entire length of nearly 350 m. It is as if the dry wash were intended to define the border and to lend a general shape to the figure. This is one of a number of examples of Nazca features that give the appearance of being tailored specifically to the con-

Appendix II. Fig. 4. One of a number of geometrical features that seem to have been designed to fit the landscape; note that the wide base of the trapezoid (upper right) borders a *quebrada* and that two cairns are located at the opposite end. (P. Clarkson); cf. Chap. II, Fig. 13.

tours of the landscape. The spiral feature on the pampa Cantalloc, discussed in Appendix I, offers another example.

Other lines that depart center No. 35 and widen into trapezoids at distances on the order of 1 km from the center include nos. 6, 23, 24, and 25. In each instance, the trapezoid is several hundred meters in length and its shape appears to fit the surface of the pampa, which has been intricately sculpted by the water that has flowed over it for eons. In every case, the narrow end of the trapezoid points toward the line center.

Line no. 15 is an immense trapezoid (0.9 km long and 90 m wide at the base) that departs the center in the general direction of the Nazca River (SSE). As we have seen in this appendix, many trapezoids align in a more-or-less perpendicular direction to the major river valleys, usually with their broad bases toward the river. Other examples include the pair of large trapezoids found at the ends of long lines emanating from centers No. 14 and 19, and a series of more than a dozen such features along the south bank of the Rio Inge-

nio (see Chap. II, Fig. 13). Trapezoid 35–15 terminates in a line of stones at just about the point where the line center becomes invisible over the sloping horizon. A footpath departs the western edge of the trapezoid and continues onto an otherwise featureless hill still 2 km from the Nazca River.

Line no. 16 is an even broader feature, the border of which is marked not by a continuous hummock of cleared debris, but rather by stone piles one-quarter meter high, approximately 0.5 m wide and 3 m apart. These may have served to better delineate the edge of the feature, which otherwise could not be marked clearly owing to a low density of coarse material in this area (cf. Fig. 2e).

Line no. 18 passes northward 3.5 km to line center No. 37, a hill elevated about 30 m above the pampa that marks the westernmost projection point of the Andean foothills out onto the pampa. These two centers are easily visible one from one other. Walked from the latter (see Chap. II, Fig. 3(37) line no. 1), the line emerges from a long triangle, the base of which is centered on No. 37 and which points

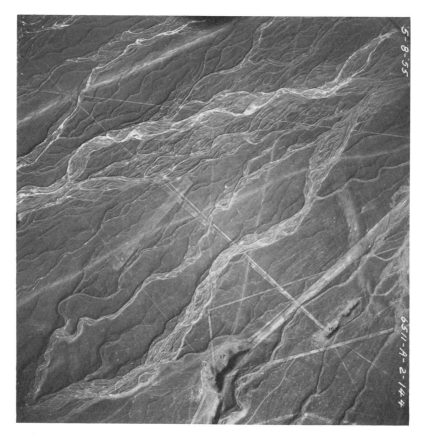

Appendix II. Fig. 5. Aerial view of centers No. 16 and 17 (large numbers). The small
numbers denote some of the more prominent lines. (SAN. Photo 6511-A-2-144)

directly to center No. 35. A narrow footpath covers the entire length from the apex of the triangle. The line borders are clearly marked and the whole feature keeps a constant width (about 1 ½ m) along its entire course.

Line 17 begins as a 12 m wide avenue and it, too, becomes intermittently lost and recovered as one walks its course westward; apparently it also was affected by superposition due to later stream flow. The line ends at center No. 45, nearly 5 km away, the central mound of which is visible quite prominently as one approaches it.

Finally, lines 10 and 14 give access to two other centers we have already described, namely No's. 30 and 36, respectively.

Standing on a line center and turning-through 360 °, one acquires a strange visual impression (see Fig. 3c or d). Lines of various width fly off toward the horizon in a seemingly random radial pattern, yet one has the feeling that these lines were constructed very

precisely so that they would converge at a point (Fig. 3e,f,g). While we found strict convergence not to be the case with the relatively small number of lines comprising center No. 30, the result of bisecting the lines of No. 35 with a string and extending them across the mound offered a quite different result. Twenty of the 26 lines fell within a circle of 5 m radius centered on the mound (see inset to Chap. II, Fig. 3–(35) & Fig. 3b). This result clearly demonstrates that whoever erected the lines, whether employing ropes and strings and/or any sort of preconceived plan, undertook the task with considerable care and precision at least on this occasion.

LINE CENTERS NO. 16 AND 17 (SEE FIGS. 5–6)

Line centers No. 16 and 17 consist of 26 lines centered on a pair of natural hills, the

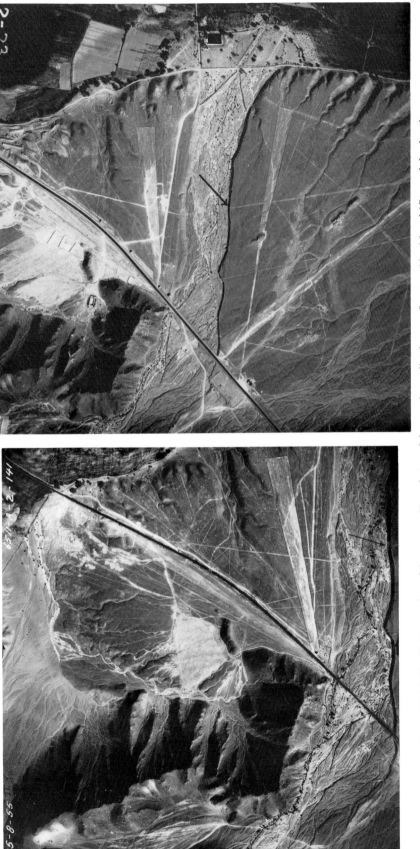

Appendix II. Fig. 6. Destruction of the pampa. Two photos of the area immediately east of centers No. 16 and 17 reveal the drastic change that has resulted from human occupation. Arrow indicates the broad feature that crosses the river and continues on the other side. Photo a (S.A.N) was taken in the mid-1950's, photo b (University of Minnesota Remote Sensing Lab) in the mid-1980's.

last of a series that descend from the mountains located to the east of the pampa (Fig. 5). These centers lie about 200 m apart and they line up with the direction of the flow of water across the SE end of the pampa near Nazca. Their proximity to the Pan American Highway, which lies only 800 m to the east, makes them readily accessible to modern passers-by; consequently, the destruction that has been wrought in the area by four decades of motor traffic and land modification is all too apparent. For example, in Figure 6 we compare a selected 1955 SAN photo with one of the same area taken in 1984 by the Minnesota group. In particular, note the erasure of figures close to and on the western side of the highway.

The western mound Chap. II, Fig. 3 (16/17), the larger of the two, has some 40 stone piles at its southern base, each about 1 ½ meter in diameter. This hill (center No. 17) seems to be the focal point of 20 of these lines, six of which fit our "broad" classification. Two of these, nos. 1 and 5, are giant trapezoids that open outward from the center and extend several hundred meters. Two of the narrow lines (nos. 10 and 12) are connectors which can be walked quite easily, 3 ⅓ km to center No. 27 and 4 km to center No. 26, respectively. The first walk, beginning on a rather faint and narrow line, takes one immediately across the dry *quebrada* that borders center No. 17 on the west. Its course can be traced quite easily on the photomosaic. Dropping into the *quebrada* and moving ahead, one is in danger of losing the line unless he fixes his eyes at a point on the distant bank or upon the horizon behind it in the direction indicated. Emerging from a second section of the *quebrada* about 500 meters out from center No. 17, one finds that the narrow line has suddenly broadened into a trapezoid that begins to widen even further (from 40 to 45 meters) as one moves along the next kilometer of the traverse toward center No. 27, which becomes even more distinctly visible as a very high dune on the west bank of the Rio Socos. Could the builders have intended to complete this feature and make it a trapezoid all the way along the course? The major portion of the Rio Socos basin obliter-

ates portions of this line for much of the rest of its length but at precisely the halfway mark (to within 10 meters as measured on the photographs), one finds a pair of large cairns (5 meters wide and 2 meters high) evenly spaced from the edges of the trapezoid (Fig. 7). The cairns lie at the western edge of a steep bank of a *quebrada* into which one must descend in order to follow the trapezoidal path. But for the presence of these cairns, one cannot really fix one's eyes on any prominent point on the western bank of the *quebrada* as one descends below the east bank into the fossil wash 360 meters away. We suspect that these stone piles, like those which one so frequently sees dotting the hilltops of the centers themselves, were intended as visual markers to keep the walker on course as he proceeded across the hazy, horizonless pampa. The last segment of the walk between centers No. 17 and 27 is completed on a clearly delineated 45 meter wide segment of line 17–10 (also 27–3) that leads up to the location of center No. 27 on its 10 meter high bluff overlooking the intersection of the Nazca River and its tributary, the Rio Socos.

Line no. 12 from center No. 17 is even easier to follow; it passes unchanging in its dimensions (40–50 cm) across the grain of the pampa from the SE to the NW, cutting through various strands of the Rio Socos until it terminates on the relatively high summit of center No. 26 (Fig. 8). A third connector, line no. 1, is a very short one that joins center No. 16 where it becomes line 16–4.

Most of the lines associated with this pair of centers terminate either in the Nazca basin to the south and west or where they reach various tributaries of the Rio Socos, but there are some very interesting exceptions—lines that bend sharply and go off in non-radial directions, sometimes returning to their point of origin. For example, consider broad line no. 15 Chap. II, Fig. 3 (16/17) (width 13 ½ meters); it strikes the near bank of the neighboring *quebrada* 120 m out and then, as if reflected off the *quebrada*, it immediately turns at a 105 ° angle to the north and proceeds for a distance of 950 m to center No. 14, which is

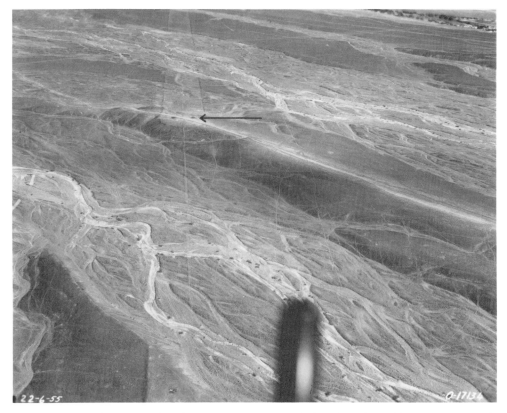

Appendix II. Fig. 7. Frequently, cairns (arrow) seem to mark the point where a line narrows just as it drops into a quebrada. (SAN Photo 0-17134).

Appendix II. Fig. 8. Atop line center No. 26 looking toward center No. 17 (arrow).

also the lowermost peak of a chain that descends from the mountains down to the pampa. This hill lies only 50 m north of the Pan American Highway (at km 438 ½) and consequently, the features around it are in very poor condition, though they can be traced on the photos if one moves the eye out a bit from the center, e.g., it can be seen on Fig. 6 at the narrow ends of the two large trapezoids.

The bent line, 17–15, also is noteworthy because it passes over the figure of a whale and an adjacent feature that may be identified tentatively as a bird's foot, both zoomorphs being rather rare at this end of the pampa. (They are visible on Fig. 5 near the bend in the line.) There is no question that the line *overlies* the animal. Here, we have offered this example along with a host of others to demonstrate quite consistently that the plant and animal geoglyphs must have been laid down before the lines, a result that is consistent with the archaeological work of Clarkson, reported elsewhere in this volume.

Broad line no. 16–6 exhibits a similar pattern of seeming deflection or reflection off a natural water course. In this case, the walker is first conducted across the two *quebradas* to a third, which is situated about 0.1 km from the point of departure. The path then turns sharply (also coincidentally at about 105 °, this time to the west; a stone cairn marks the inner angle of this turn. At this point, the line also narrows from about 10 m width to a meter or two. After continuing for about 150 m, the feature doubles back upon itself and takes the form of the familiar zigzag, a pattern which we were able to follow criss-crossing itself for more than a kilometer in length before we lost it. Line 16–6 and its companion feature, 16–5, which we also were able to trace over one kilometer straight across the pampa NW of center No. 16 before losing it, converge together into a single line on mound No. 16. But departing mound 16 in the opposite (SE) direction, this broad feature splits into two lines, 16–1 and 16–2. Here is another situation already familiar to us at other centers: the apparent fracturing of a single broad

feature into two or more narrower ones as one crosses over a mound. (See the discussion of center No. 30, above.)

LINE CENTER NO. 27 (SEE FIG. 9)

Our close examination of center No. 27 (Fig. 9) reveals why one must survey the pampa on the ground and not simply rely on aerial photography in order to pick up the wealth of detail present there. Fairly uninteresting on the aerial photographs, No. 27, which is crowned by a rock cairn (cf Fig. 10), offers a commanding view from its location on the top of a cape or bluff that juts out onto the Rio Socos basin; this bluff is the focal point of at least 17 narrow and 9 broad features. We have already described the 3.5 km walk from center No. 17 to 27 (along 17–10 = 27–3), which ends as one climbs out of the steep, westernmost channel of the Socos basin up onto the pampa. We found that none of the rather broad triangular features that depart No. 27 in the direction of the open pampa seems to proceed very far.

We were able to follow broad feature no. 4 across the Rio Socos and we were fairly able to convince ourselves that it must have been intended to terminate there at the east bank. Broad feature no. 2 ends abruptly after it passes about 200 m to the tip of a smaller bluff, which turned out not to be a line center. The area between this feature and the edge of the Socos valley had been cultivated since the 1955 survey photos were taken. The other broad features are all triangles between 100–200 m in length with apex angles of 2 °–15 °, most of them having common bases at the focal point of center No. 27 on the tip of the bluff. The apexes of all these triangles touch the near bank of a small *quebrada* that passes about 200 m NW of the center on the surface of the pampa (Fig. 9, top left). Groups of piled stones, again about an arm's length apart, dot much of the area at the base ends of these triangles and may represent material that was awaiting clearing.

Several trapezoids of decametric dimen-

Appendix II. Fig. 9.   Aerial photo of center No. 27 taken from a thethered balloon (see Chap. VII for discussion). (University of Minnesota Remote Sensing Lab).

Appendix II. Fig. 10.   Cairns that are visible for a considerable distance often mark the line centers. This particular example is from center No. 53.

sions, bearing no apparent physical connection to these triangles, reside on the interior of the pampa immediately on the other side of the *quebrada* at which the triangles terminate. One of these trapezoids lies at the end of a line that emanates from center No. 14, 4 ½ km to the NE; the line bends sharply along its course. Technically, then, centers No. 14 and 27 are connected, but in order to proceed from the former to the latter, one must move along a line that bends sharply and feeds into a trapezoid. Walking to the base end of the trapezoid, one can enter the tip of one of the triangles which proceeds to center No. 27. In Chap. II, Fig. 16 we illustrate this course along with some other examples of connecting paths

that depict sharp angles. Thus, we begin to discover, as we saw in the case of 16–5, 16–6, and 17–5, that random-looking arrays of lines lying atop one another all across the pampa actually can be disentangled and resolved into a number of connecting patterns that join one line center to another.

Not visible in any of the aerial photographs and only barely discernible at ground level were at least a dozen very narrow straight lines that proceeded southwestward from center No. 27 toward the direction of the Nazca drainage. We tried to follow several of these, but only proceeded to lose them when they led us into the heavily cultivated area on the north side of the Nazca Valley.

## Appendix III: Partial Transcription of Archival Materials

### A. ARCHIVO GENERAL DE LA NACION, LIMA DERECHO INDIGENA, LEG. 7, CUAD. 146 (1648)

Mem.a y apuntam.tos por donde se vera el derecho que el colegio de la Compañia de Jesus tiene a las tierras y viña de la hazienda nombrada San Joseph del Valle de Yngenio de la Jurisdicion de la Nasca llamada el Valle del Collao de Lucanas [separado de] los Titulos que de ella tiene el dho Colegio del Cuzco, con las citas por sus folios, de los instrumentos, tiempos y escrivanos ante quien pasaron, medidas, composiciones y aprovaciones.[?] y confirmacion por su Magestad . . . Los Curacas de la Nasca Don Fran.co Ylimanga vendieron el valle del Collao (que oy se llama de Ingenio) todo el desde el nacimiento del agua hasta el Tambo viejo de Pedro Suarez el viejo por escripto en el Tambo de Yca ante Fran.co de Talavera escrivano R.l en 19 de Julio de 1546 [?] Pedro Suarez vendio y traspaso todo el dho Valle al veedor Garcia de Salcedo en la Ciudad de los Reyes en 15 de Marzo de 1549 ante Alonso Valencia, escrivano de su Mag.d publico y de.l[?] a[?] buelta—Don Garcia Nasca y Don Alonso Limanga Caciques, hijos de los de arriva ratificaron las dos ventas anteriores porssi y por sus Curadores en favor de Beatriz de Salazar Viuda del Veedor Garcia de Salcedo ante Juan de padilla escrivano publico y de l.n[?] en la Ciudad de los Reyes en primero de [?] de 1556 anos desde [?] hasta 59. y la aprovaron [?] 53 conprovada con escrivanos Rs [?] 59 buelta—El [?] Marques de Canete en nombre de su Mag.d confirmos este valle y todas sus ventas hechas assi por los Caciques como por los demas a Beatriz de Salazar Viuda del dicho Veedor atento a ser de los primeros Conquistadores de los Reynos, y el primer oficial R.l que su Mag.d tuvo y el primero que hizo edificio de Ing.o de Acucar, despacha esta confirmacion en la Iglesia de la Madalena por Fran.co de Carvajal en ll de Agosto de 1570—Consta de los titulos de [?] 22 buelta hasta [63?] y esta confirmacion se saco del libro de Confirmaciones de los [?] de Govierno por Alvaro Ruiz de Navamuel Secretario de Camara y de govierno a 21 de Junio de 1570 [?] 63. D.a Beatriz de Salazar vendio este valle todo al Capitan Diego Maldonado Vezino del Cuzco y a Pedro Gutierrez Vezino de la Nasca que lo tuvieron indiviso y por partir pero dividiose de esta manera . . .

### B. ARCHIVO GENERAL DE LA NACION DERECHO INDIGENA Y ENCOMIENDAS, LEG. 23, CUAD. 616, FF. 18, 1569–71

f. lr. . . .

En la ciudad de los rreyes Provincias destos rreynos del piru biernes quatro dias del mes de nobiembre año del nacimiento de nuestro salvador JesuXpo de mill e quinientos e sesenta e nuebe años ante el muy magnifico Dn. Francisco de Zarate alcalde ordinario en esta dha ciudad [de los Reyes] y su tierra e juridicion por su Magestad y en presencia de mi Juan Garcia de nogal escrivano publico del Numero dello

f. lv

Parecio presente alonso gutierrez Vezino desta ciudad e dixo que don garcia Nasca cacique principal del Valle y Repartimiento de la nasca y caxamarca es fallecido y muerto agora poco a e porque hizo e otorgo su testamento cerrado que es el que tiene el presente escrivano y el que se presento ante su merced e porque se sepa a donde se Manda enterrar y se entierre el cuerpo y se cunpla su anima Pidio a su merced Mande rrecibir ynformacion de como otorgo el dho testamento y el ffallecido e muerto e Pasado desta presente bida y mando abrir el dho testamento para que se publique e se cunpla a la voluntad del dho difunto y lo mande dar Por testimonio e ynterponga en ello su autoridad y decreto judicial y pidio justicia _____El señor alcalde mando que de ynformacion de lo contenido en su pedimiento y dado prober a juera ante

mi Juan garcia de nogal escrivano publico—
f. 5r. . . .

En el nombre de la santisima trinidad padre
y hijo y espiritu sancto tres personas y un solo
dios Verdadero que bive y rreyna Para siempre jamas y de la gloriosa su madre siempre
Virgen sancta Maria con todos los sanctos y
sanctas de la corte celestial sepan quantos esta
carta de testamento Vieren como yo don garcia de nasca cacique
f. 5v

Principal de los . . . Valles de la nasca y
caxamarca estando en esta ciudad de los
rreyes al presente enfermo del cuerpo y sano
de la boluntad y en mi buen ? juizio y enten-
dimiento y cunplida memoria temiendome de
la Muerte que es cosa natural y deseando
poner mi anima en carrera de salbacion cre-
yendo como ffirme y Berdaderamente creo en
la sancta ffe catolica y en la santisima trinidad
y todo aquello que bueno fiel y catolico
cristiano deve tener y creer tomando por mi
abogado e yntersesoria al gloriosisima siempre
Virgen Nuestra senora sancta Maria a quien
suplico que quiera rrogar a su muy Precioso
hijo Ntro. Sr. y Redentor JesuXpo que por los
meritos ve su santisima pacion quera perdo-
nar Mi anima y llevar la a su santisimo rreyno
para donde fue criada otorgo y conosco que
hago y ordeno Este mi testemento y Ultima
Boluntad y las mandas legato Pias causas en el
contenidos en la forma y orden siguiente——
Yten mando que despues de pagadas todas
mis deudas E mandas y obras pias e causas y
legatos se haga tres partes de la viña grande y
las dos dellas se ay mando que queden para los
dhos mis yndios para que dellos se paguen los
dhos dozientos pessos y todo aquello que mas
rrentare de los dhos dozientos pesos arriba declarados. Las dichas dos partes de la dcha viña
y heredad mando le ayan *los dhas mis yndios de
mi parcialidad* y que la una parte de la dha viña
se de y es mi boluntad la goze y aya mi capilla
de san pablo donde perpetuamente se digan

misas por mi anima y la de mis padres y de-
cendientes con que primeramente y ante todas
cossas Mando que se de lo que sobrare de las
dhas dos partes de rrenta de la viña sacados
los dozientos pessos se saquen quinientos Pesos corrientes para *los pobres de las tres parcialidades de yndios que es la de cantad y poromas y
collao* y si a mis albaceas les pareciere que el
mejor para ayuda de tributos de las dhas tres
parcialidades Mando se paga y luego sacados
los dhos quinientos pesos dexo libremente las
dhas dos partes de la dha viña y lo procedido
dellas a los dhos mis yndios y que las rrepartan
los arriba declarados con condicion que *ordi-
nariamente los yndios de la dha mi parcialidad den
doze [yndios?]*
f. 6v

*por sus mitas Para el beneficio de la dha viña* Pa-
gandoles por su travajo El salario acostum-
brado que se susten pagar a los dhos yndios y
con estas condiciones se lo dexxo Por Restitu-
cion por quanto la hizieron y labraron Los
dhos mis yndios————————
f. 7r. . . .

Yten declaro Por mi hijo ligitimo a don garcia y heredero de todos mis bienes con que no
se lo den hasta que sea de hedad para gover-
nar e tan entre tanto dexo Por governador de
los yndios a mi hermano don pedro Vilcupu-
ma—Yten mando que sean mis albaceas el se-
nor arcobispo y El padre polaneo como mi
confesor e juan ffernandez gutierrez para que
pagan bien por mi anima y cunplan todo fe
[lo?] contenido y declarado en este mi testamento y a diego jertex[?] de cordova Mer-
cader desta ciudad a los quales les encargo la
consencia Para que pagan bien
f. 7v

por mi anima y asi como ellos lo hizieren
con ella lo . . . [?] . . . dios con ellos que fue
fecha e acabada en quatro de nobiembre de
mill e quinientos y sesentae nuebe anos don
garcia nanasca yo juan garcia de nogal escrivano de su Magestad Pubilco. . . .

# Index

Page numbers in italics indicate illustrations; *t* following a page number indicates a table

hypotheses on, 136–137
in Inka roads, 29–30, *32*, 107–108
in line centers, 136, 326, *327*
in Nazca pampa archaeology, 136–137, *138*
on Cantalloc Spiral, 307, 311
size of, 136
Calendar(s)
coastal, 58, 88
in Cahuachi, 232, 240
in Nazca line hypothesis, 15–21, 112
in Nazca radial line azimuth statistics,
264–265
Inka, 52, 52*n*–54*n*, 54–58, *54*
*Callao*
as *ceque* type, 51
Camera(s)
in aerial photography, 274–280, *278*
Camino de Leguia
near Cahuachi, 236, *238*
*Camino religioso*
Nazca lines as, 30–31
Canopus
alignment of, 98
Cantalloc
ceramics at, 168
Cantalloc spiral
analysis of, 307, *308–310*, 310–312
as pathway, 312
competitive running on, 36
contruction hypotheses on, 310–312
in geometrical hypothesis, 23–25, *24*
location of, 307
map of, *308–309*
topographic features of, *13*, 38, *38*
*Capac hucha*
defined, 239
ritual walking during festival of, 170
Capella
heliacal rising of, 91*n*
Carahuarazo Valley
ceremonial water channels in, 168–169
Caravelí
*visita* to, 187, 189–190
Carrizal ceramic(s), 126, *141*, 144–146,
*152–154*
motifs in, 144
Celestial llama
defined, 56
Cemetery(ies). *See* Burial site(s)
Census taking
in Spanish bureaucracy, 187–190, *188*
α and β Centauri
alignment of, 98
in celestial llama, 56
*Ceque(s)*
administration of, 31
as mnemonic devices, 50
astronomy and, 19–20, 52, 54–57
Cahuachi and, 239–240
*chhiutas* and, 193
classification of, 51
competitive running on, 36
defined, 31
doubled, 59
forms of, 34
in irrigation, 201
in Nazca line hypothesis, 110–112
line centers as similar to, 44, 58–59, 71
linking together of, 59
Quebrada de la Vaca plazas and, 193

radiality in
Nazca lines and, 288–289
system of, 50–52, *53–55*, 54–59, 71
Ceramic(s)
at Quebrada de la Vaca, 184
at Quebrada Honda, 184
chronology of
problems in determining, 159
ethnic homogeneity and, 230*n*–231*n*
functions of, 151, 159
possible funerary, 166
in archaeological survey, 140, *141–143*, 144, *145–150*,
151, *152–154*, *156–158*
Carrizal, *141*, 144–146, *152–154*
Early Intermediate, 140, *141–143*, *145–147*
Late Horizon, *141*, 144–147, *156–158*
Late Intermediate, 140, *141*, 144–146, *152–154*,
156–157
Middle Horizon, 140, *141*, *148–150*
Nasca, 140, *141–143*, *145–147*
Poroma, *141*, 144–146, *156–157*
in Cahuachi, 230, 230*n*, 237–238, *243*
in prehistoric period classifications, 123–124
motifs in, 140, 144–146
Nasca, 124–125, 140, *141–143*, *145–147*. *See also* Nasca
ceramic(s)
near stone circles, 136, *137*
near stone structures, 137
on Pampa de Atarco, 236–237
ornamentation of, 124–126, *145–147*, 150, 154, *156–158*
ritual smashing of
*See* Ritual ceramics smashing
Ceremonial site(s). *See also* Religion
astronomical orientation of, 57
Cahuachi as, 209, 215–216
Nazca lines and, 290
in Nazca pampa, 179
radiality in, 203
Cerro Blanco
as legendary water source, 25
Cahuachi and, 221
ceremonial importance of, 87
geographical features of, 117, *118*
in Nazca radial line azimuth statistics, 260, 268
line orientation and, 87
Cerro Picchu
pillars of, 55
Cerro Portachuelo
in Nazca radial line azimuth statistics, 260, 268
Cerro Utua
stone structures on, *128*, 137
trapezoids on, 128, *128*
Chala
*visita* to, 187–188
Chavín de Huantar
archaeological site at, 124
Chaviña
Nasca ceramics at, 167
Chert lithic(s)
in archaeological survey, 151, *160*
*Chhiuta(s)*
boundary divisions in, *180*, 181, *182*, 183
defined, 33, 34*n*, 180
in Cahuachi, 225–227
in Pacariqtambo, 180–181, *180*, *182*, 183, 225–227
flexibility of, 191
Quebrada de la Vaca plazas versus, 190–191
in Quebrada de la Vaca, 186
Nazca lines and
overview of, 288

Space shuttle photograph of the south coast of Peru. The Paracas peninsula is visible to the northwest of the true north indicator. The area of the Nazca pampa enlarged in the photomosaic (jacket pocket) is outlined in black (see also Chap. I Frontispiece, Chap. II, Figs. 1 and Chap. VII Fig. 1b.)